THE JEWS OF WINDSOR
1790–1990

THE JEWS OF WINDSOR

1790–1990

~ A Historical Chronicle ~

Jonathan V. Plaut

With a Foreword by Dr. Larry Kulisek

DUNDURN PRESS
TORONTO

Editor: Andrea Knight
Designer: Jennifer Scott
Printer: Thistle Printing Ltd.

Library and Archives Canada Cataloguing in Publication

Plaut, Jonathan V.

    The Jews of Windsor, 1790-1990 : a historical chronicle / Jonathan Plaut.

Includes bibliographical references and index.

ISBN 978-1-55002-706-8

    1. Jews--Ontario--Windsor--History. 2. Jews--Ontario--Windsor--Biography.
3. Windsor (Ont.)--Biography. I. Title.

FC3099.W56Z7 2007   971.3'32004924   C2007-900085-1

1 2 3 4 5   11 10 09 08 07

We acknowledge the support of the **Canada Council for the Arts** and the **Ontario Arts Council** for our publishing program. We also acknowledge the financial support of the **Government of Canada** through the **Book Publishing Industry Development Program** and **The Association for the Export of Canadian Books**, and the **Government of Ontario** through the **Ontario Book Publishers Tax Credit** program and the **Ontario Media Development Corporation**.

Care has been taken to trace the ownership of copyright material used in this book. The author and the publisher welcome any information enabling them to rectify any references or credits in subsequent editions.

J. Kirk Howard, President

Printed and bound in Canada
www.dundurn.com

Dundurn Press
3 Church Street, Suite 500
Toronto, Ontario, Canada
M5E 1M2

Gazelle Book Services Limited
White Cross Mills
High Town, Lancaster, England
LA1 4XS

Dundurn Press
2250 Military Road
Tonawanda, NY
U.S.A. 14150

This book is dedicated to

my grandparents
Jonas and Selma Plaut
Harry and Therese Strauss

my parents
Rabbi W. Gunther and Elizabeth S. Plaut

my wife
Carol Plaut

my children
Daniel and Amy Plaut
Deborah and David Elias

and my grandsons
Steven Andrew Elias and Jeffrey Benjamin Elias

Table of Contents

Preface and Acknowledgments

My thirty-seven year journey to publish this book began in 1970 after I had assumed my first rabbinical position in Windsor, Ontario. At that time, I had also decided to study for my doctorate and was looking for a suitable topic on which to base my dissertation. Apart from my love of history, what ultimately prompted me to decide to research the background of the Windsor Jewish community was a meeting with Arthur B. Weingarden, then the president of my congregation, which included a visit to the grave of Moses David, the founding father of Windsor's Jewish community. A whole new world opened up for me when Mr. Weingarden told me that he had in his files some interesting background material on this man and that he was willing to share it with me.

It was during my tenure as spiritual leader of Congregation Beth El that I began writing the early history of Windsor's Jewish community for my doctorate, which was awarded in 1977. In the early 1980s, a publisher not only suggested that the manuscript be rewritten in a style more suitable for publication, but also encouraged me to further update the manuscript since my research ended in 1940. Within a few years, however, I had embarked on a new rabbinical assignment in California, forcing the project to be put on hold, at least for the time being.

The incentive to complete this project was renewed in 1993, when my family and I came back to the Detroit-Windsor area. I now had easy access to local libraries and other research facilities. Research into some fifty years was required and I was fortunate that my new professional responsibilities allowed me enough spare time to truly focus on this venture. I tackled it with renewed energy and much enthusiasm.

Several histories broadly describing Canada's Jewish scene had been written and published in the past, but very few had dealt with specific Jewish communities such as Windsor. Despite its comparatively small size, I do believe that its members played an important role in the development of southwestern Ontario.

This book is a two-hundred-year chronicle of the events that took place in Windsor. While writing it, every effort was made to accurately reconstruct the events based on available information provided from a variety of sources and any errors are totally unintentional. In particular, although every effort has been made to trace all the

Jews who settled in the Windsor area, either shortly before or soon after the turn of the century, we regret that we were unable to establish the identities of everyone. Every effort has been made with available records and recollections to properly list the names of these early settlers, but errors do occur. Some of the people in question may have changed their names and/or religion, and the descendants of others may not have been aware of our search. I deeply regret any errors I may have made and apologize in advance for any omissions or inaccuracies in regard to family relationships.

I was fortunate to have access to ample data documenting the life and times of pioneer settler, Moses David, and his relationship with Detroit and Montreal. However, I found only scant primary material about others who inhabited the Windsor area at that time. Having chosen to cover the period between 1790 and 1940 for my doctoral dissertation, I perused all available newspaper accounts and existing archives of that era. To chronicle the years from 1940 until the end of the century, I had at my disposal the minutes of board meetings of several organizations — the Windsor Jewish Community Council, the I. L. Peretz Shule, Congregation Beth El, and some pertaining to Shaar Hashomayim Synagogue. I am indebted to Harvey Kessler and Donna Petoran of the Windsor Jewish Federation; to Anna Mae Gumprich, Lorraine Victor, Katerina Stecko, and Connie Cullen of Congregation Shaar Hashomayim; and to Rabbi Jeffrey Ableser, Carol McDowell, and Mary Zaltz of Congregation Beth El for making these records available to me. I would like to take this opportunity to thank Miriam Beckerman for translating the I. L. Peretz Shule minutes from Yiddish into English. Regarding the activities of congregations Tifereth Israel and Shaarey Zedek, I had to rely on oral testimonies from members of these institutions. I wish to express my thanks to them all. I want to extend my appreciation to the *Windsor Star* for permitting me to use their photos, the Windsor Community Museum, the Shaar Hashomayim Synagogue, the Jewish National Fund, Michael Sumner, and Sara Kirzner. I also thank Martin Gervais for permission to liberally use material from Alan Abram's book

Why Windsor? An Anecdotal History of the Town of Windsor and Essex County (Wilson and Black Moss Press, 1981).

Several individuals were instrumental in making the entire project become a reality. I owe a debt of gratitude to Arthur B. Weingarden for his constant encouragement and support.

Many oral histories were recorded and transcribed for my doctoral dissertation on the early years of Windsor's Jewish community. I would like to express my thanks to all those who granted me interviews or so willingly responded to my many questions. I would like to thank Ruth Booth, Elaine Cohen, Judy Frank, and George and Donna Lane for their research assistance.

While chronicling the last sixty years, I was greatly assisted by the following men and women who generously supplied me with new material or filled in obvious gaps in my story:

Rabbi Jeffrey Ableser, Pam Albert, Senator David Croll, Rhonda Ellis, Rabbi Edward Feigelman, Gerald Freed, David Glaser, the Honourable Herb Gray, Larry Greene, Rabbi Ira Samuel Grussgott, Diana Giunta, William Hurwitz, Rabbi Miriam Jerris, Dr. Marilyn Miller Kronmal, Sandi Malowitz, the Honourable Mr. Justice Saul Nosanchuk, Burt Pazner, Richard Rosenthal, Rabbi Yosie Rosenzweig, Amy Shafron, Isaac (Izzy) Sigal, Kurt Weinberg, Arthur B. Weingarden, Rabbi Sherwin Wine, Anne Winograd, and Shalamas Zimmerman.

I also wish to commend librarians Maggie Bacon, Ann Swaney, Charla Kramer, and Rochelle Hammontree at the Helen and Mark Osterlin Library at Northwestern Michigan College for their efforts on my behalf, as well as for so hospitably offering me the use of their computers during my frequent visits to Traverse City.

This manuscript has gone through many rewritings over the years. Some years ago, Lesley Wyle became my editor and did an outstanding job with the initial reworking of the manuscript. Throughout the editorial process, she offered me valuable suggestions and ideas with regard to content and style and brought conflicting textual information to my attention.

I appreciate the services provided by a select group of readers I consulted on this project. They include Rabbi Jeffrey Ableser, Belle Adler, Arthur Barat, Herb Brudner, Joseph Burk, Carl Cohen, Jackie Eisenberg, Larry Greene, Nancy (Klein) Helm, Fred Katzman, Harvey Kessler, Jack Shanfield, Isaac (Izzy) Sigal, Rabbi Dr. Samuel Stollman, Paula and Harold Taub, Arthur B. Weingarden, Milton Whiteman, and the Honourable Mr. Justice Carl Zalev. Thanks to their familiarity with Windsor's history between 1940 and 2000, they not only were able to verify several facts, but also provided me with a great deal of new information about that period.

I extend sincere thanks to Christine Bonhomme for the superb job she did arranging appointments for me, doing extensive fact-checking, transcribing interviews, transferring corrections, and painstakingly co-ordinating all footnotes and checking them for accuracy.

I am also especially grateful to Dr. Larry Kulisek, Professor Emeritus of History at the University of Windsor, for agreeing to write the Foreword for this book. He suggested new ways that this manuscript should be arranged, provided valuable information on how best to connect Windsor communal life in general to the events of the Jewish community. He truly helped my story come to life by reorganizing the wealth of material gathered from so many different sources. Without his patience, diligence, and commitment, this project never could have been brought to fruition.

My thanks to Kirk Howard, president of Dundurn Press, for agreeing to publish this manuscript and for his efforts in bringing it into book form. From my initial discussion with Malcolm Lester, he was an invaluable resource that helped steer this process step-by-step and stood by me until its conclusion. He introduced me to Andrea Knight, who did the final editing. I want to thank her for her many hours of work in adjusting the text and footnotes to conform to the same style and ensure the fewest possible errors. As a historian herself, I am much indebted to her for her valuable work.

I would like to make particular mention, with my sincere thanks, of the most generous support I received from the Morris and Beverly Baker Foundation. These funds helped cover some of the expenses incurred in connection with this project.

Last but not least, I wish to thank my dear wife, Carol, for the love and encouragement she showed me during the very long time it took to research, write, and complete this book. I also commend her for her patience, having had to put up with countless boxes of reference material and other files used in this study that cluttered our various homes for a considerable length of time. She now can reclaim all that space and bring our house back to normal!

Farmington Hills, Michigan
J.V.P.

Foreword
Dr. Larry Kulisek

This book is a chronicle of the Jews of Windsor, Ontario, recounting their origins, aspirations, experiences, and achievements. It is not a text nor is it a comparative study of Jewish experience elsewhere in North America. Rabbi Plaut's focus is on the Jewish community who made Windsor their home. Living in a Canadian border community in the heart of North America, just a stone's throw from Metropolitan Detroit, and even closer in mind and spirit to world Jewry and Israel has made Windsor's Jews citizens of the world.

The author has scoured decades of newspapers, tracked down obscure archival sources, sought to integrate informing literature, and built up an impressive archive of personal accounts, interviews, and oral histories. He allows the participants to tell their own stories, some of which are important for their entertainment value while others — from rabbis, Jewish Community Council executives, and influential laymen — provide the insights and analysis from those most responsible for leading the community.

At times numbering a single soul, as in Moses David's day, or a handful of pioneer founders in the 1880s, and never more than 3,000 at its zenith, Windsor's big little Jewish community settled, survived, and prospered. As they ventured out of the familiar East European shtetls they had created to maintain their ancient history, customs, and traditions to live "in the world," these newcomers struggled with the dilemma of putting down roots in a new country — how to remain Jewish while becoming Canadians.

For over two hundred years, Jews have had a vital presence in Windsor. They established their synagogues, schools, and institutions, occasionally quarrelled; and regularly united as a community to demand their rights and protect their heritage. They grew alongside the wider community and today form a significant part of it. This book honours their journey.

Dr. Larry Kulisek
Professor Emeritus, University of Windsor

PART I

Introduction

While several works have been published that provide a broad canvas of the Canadian Jewish scene, there are only a few communal Jewish histories. Windsor is not one of Canada's premier cities such as Toronto, Montreal, or Vancouver, nor is its Jewish community comparable in size, but the important role that Windsor Jews played in the development of the Ontario Southland is a story deserving to be told.

The story begins in the eighteenth century when Jewish merchants and military provisioners accompanying the victorious British forces into Montreal in 1760 surveyed the economic opportunities opened up by their victory over the French. With the existing French economic system leaderless, a functioning fur trade composed of a series of forts and routes, native alliances and technical expertise, and a continent to exploit — the lure to Anglo entrepreneurs was irresistible. Jews made up a major part of the Montreal merchant community during this transition and many of them participated in the far-flung fur trade itself. A Jewish consortium of five, including Ezekiel Solomon and Chapman Abraham at Michilimackinac and Detroit, respectively, were among the first Anglos to the Great Lakes, the stepping stones to the Northwest and the Rockies. These Jewish fur traders worked throughout the Great Lakes region, peddling their wares to the Indians and coming into contact with the leading military, economic, and social figures in the region. Although many of these Jews had permanent associations with the Montreal community, they made this Great Lakes area their centre of operations for a westward-expanding fur trade and gradually made this part of the continent their home.

Windsor's place in the story begins with the activities of another one of these Montreal families — the Davids — a remarkable family closely associated with the city's developing Jewish community. This family of practising Jews was intimately connected with the founding of the first synagogue in 1768. Moses David, the third son, was posted to Detroit, extending the family's business to the Great Lakes just as large scale Loyalist migrations and settlement resulting from the American Revolution forced the creation of Upper Canada. When the community of Sandwich was established across the Detroit River in 1797 to accommodate residents who wished to remain under British rule, he became the first Jewish settler in what is now Windsor, and married Charlotte

Hart, daughter of the first Jewish settler in Canada. Moses David's experiences in establishing a home, business, family, and community life begins a two-hundred-year chronicle of the Jewish experience in Windsor, Ontario.

It would be over half a century following Moses David's death before the other founding pioneer families of Windsor arrived to re-establish their Eastern European shtetl in a North American environment. United by common origins, many from the same villages or regions, and family connections leading to chain migrations, the Jews of Windsor were not immune to disagreements, bickering, and petty quarrels among themselves. Yet in spite of divergent religious, political, and economic interests, they established synagogues, schools, and an organized communal structure. This book is a memoir of that community and those who led, inspired, and laboured on behalf of its success.

The Windsor Jewish community tended to be far more traditional in all respects than its Detroit counterpart. The earliest settlers in Detroit, coming after the 1848 revolutions, were of German Jewish origin and by the end of the century had merged themselves with the wider community. Economically successful, they established Conservative and Reform synagogues and a number of secular institutions. Indeed, this established group of Jewish pioneers in Detroit found little in common with the masses of the Great Migrations (from the 1880s to the 1920s) who were arriving from Eastern Europe with their Old World ways intact and determined to recreate their experience in the New World. Windsor's pioneer families were among these Eastern European immigrants, mainly Poland and Russia, and did not arrive in Canada to establish a permanent settlement until after the pogroms of 1881.

Many of the basic patterns of Windsor's settlement are sufficiently reminiscent of Detroit to warrant comment, but the Windsor Jewish community compares most closely to its smaller counterparts in Canada and the United States. While there are some clear similarities in that the early settlers were peddlers and small shopkeepers, from the outset Jews in Windsor burst the bonds of the ghetto and were represented on City Council, actively involved in commu-

nal organizations, and appointed to judicial posts. By 1930 Windsor had a Jewish mayor. A tradition of public service beginning with Moses David allowed Windsor's Jewish community to produce a number of outstanding individuals whose careers and contributions could not be contained in the local context. Windsor can boast of Canada's first Jewish cabinet members, provincially and federally, in David Croll and Herb Gray.

While Shaarey Zedek, the first congregation in Windsor, was founded in 1893 near the firehouse within the emerging Jewish ghetto, over time the Jews moved out of the downtown core. Early on, it was thought that Ford City, which was emerging around its namesake's Canadian automotive complex, attracting workers with its moving assembly lines and $5-a-day wages, would be the ultimate centre of the community. For those residents who lived in East Windsor, religious services were held at Congregation Tifereth Israel, the second area synagogue. As the Jews settled and became merchants and active citizens of the community, the leadership turned to building a prominent house of worship to show their non-Jewish compatriots the glory and pride of their ancient tradition. In some comparative communities, Jews remained fearful of demonstrating their success too openly, thereby inviting Old World pogroms and anti-Semitism. This was not so in Windsor. An expanded Shaarey Zedek served the more traditional members, but community leaders demanded a new edifice, the Shaar Hashomayim Synagogue, that would highlight their new affluence and status.

Although Orthodox congregational leadership was the norm, by the 1920s, Windsor's Jewish community had grown large enough to foster alternative visions and institutions. The Talmud Torah, with its Hebrew language and Zionist ideology, and the I. L. Peretz Schule, where Yiddish and Jewish culture were the main focus, challenged the synagogues for support and student enrolment. In the mid-1930s, a volunteer community structure emerged that led to a fully operating and professionally directed community centre in the early 1940s. While these two traditions — religious and secular — clashed or co-operated, Windsor remained immune to challenges to Orthodox Judaism. Disputes over Old World traditions, synagogue seating, and the role of women and youth were contained within the Orthodox family. It would be the 1960s before the Reform challenge emerged.

Windsor's Jewish community supported World War I without active military participation, but contributed to community efforts to aid the troops and the war effort. They were particularly animated by the Balfour Declaration of 1917, which pledged British support for a Jewish homeland in Palestine. Zionism had always been popular among many in Windsor's Jewish community and they cheered three of their sons who volunteered to fight for the establishment of the British Mandate over the area. In the 1930s, when Canada's leaders refused to take in desperate European refugees fleeing from racist regimes, Windsor's community rallied on behalf of saving Jews in other lands. In World War II, Windsor's Jews actively supported the soldiers and the war effort. Jewish families sent their sons to war and several of them paid the ultimate price. When Israel became a state, Jews again were most generous in their total commitment to the new nation. When the Windsor Jewish community needed to rally, all differences ended in the name of *k'lal Yisrael* — the community of Israel.

In the post-war period, modernity and the growing influences of Zionism and Conservative/Reform Judaism challenged the Orthodox, traditional, and leftist leanings of the community's founders. With the establishment of Congregation Beth El and the introduction of Reform Judaism in 1959, many young families with children joined, gradually forcing consolidation within the other institutions as Reform became a dominant influence in the communal landscape. By the end of the 1970s, the Peretz Schule and Congregation Tifereth Israel had both closed, several attempts at forming Hebrew day schools had fallen short, and Beth El's student enrolment had surpassed that of Shaar Hashomayim.

The Windsor Jewish Community Council became the recognized umbrella organization that unified the many divergent views. Empowered to be the only organization to raise money for Israel and support local needs, the board of the Jewish Community Centre included representation from all the many organizations within the Jewish community. While this book reveals the arguments that ensued from time to time, the Jews of Windsor were united in supporting Israel and fighting anti-Semitism, as well as in confronting other challenges common to all of its community members.

The Jewish population continued to decline as the new millennium approached. When the young moved away to attend college, most did not return. Instead the young men and women moved to Toronto or to other cities in the United States, causing a continuing diminution of the Jewish population. The religious schools of Congregation Beth El and Congregation Shaar Hashomayim joined together as the enrolment of both institutions did not warrant remaining separate. Shaarey Zedek continued to serve their small membership, but the aging of the community in general threatens further consolidation to maintain viability. In the twentieth century, the declining Jewish community of Windsor forced the leadership to grapple with how best to restructure in order to meet current realities. Since the first settler, Moses David, made Windsor his home two hundred years ago, Windsor's Jewish community has met each new challenge. This is its lasting legacy.

Chapter 1
Moses David:
Windsor's First Jewish Settler

According to documented evidence, Moses David was the first Jew to settle in the community that is now Windsor. Recognizing the opportunities the interior of the country offered, he extended the reach of his family's Montreal-based fur trading business to this new frontier. In the process, he would become an equal rights champion for Jews in Upper Canada, establishing an impressive list of "firsts." Whether in land grants from the Crown, militia appointments, or civil government posts, Moses David set precedents and proved himself unwilling to accept discrimination for being a Jew. The third son of a well-known family of Canadian Jewish pioneers, he never relinquished his ties with them nor with Shearith Israel in Montreal, Canada's first Jewish congregation and his spiritual home.

Lazarus David and his remarkable progeny were one of the founding families of Montreal's Jewish community. They were intimately tied to the fur trade, Montreal's first synagogue and burial ground, and the growing achievements of the Jewish community as they became a part of the Canadian national experience.[1] Lazarus began the process of transformation from supplying military provisions to meeting the needs of the fur trade and settlers, while his sons, especially

David, would preside over the modernization of Montreal's economy into banking, canals, and industrialization.[2] Second son Samuel joined David as his Montreal partner, while third son Moses — the subject of this chapter — carried the family's fortunes to Detroit and the new frontier of Upper Canada.

The David Family

Lazarus David was born in Swansea in 1734 and started a fur trading business in Montreal soon after his arrival from Wales in the early 1760s.[3] Like other English-speaking merchants, he became involved in the city's bustling economic life as a contractor and supplier to the British occupational army. In 1761,[4] he married Phoebe Samuel in New York, where their first child, Abigail — "Branny" — was born on May 13,1762.[5] Returning to Montreal, three sons followed in regular fashion, David (1764), Samuel (1766), and Moses (1768) before a fifth child, a second daughter, Frances, completed the family in 1770.[6] The daughters, first and last of the David children, played the role assigned to them by the customs of the day and entered into appropriate marriages that contributed to the family's success and reinforced the small Jewish community and the economic connections with the fur trade.

Abigail married Andrew Hayes, a New York City merchant and silversmith of Dutch origin who had moved to Montreal around 1763. He rapidly established himself as a successful merchant and a prominent member of the nascent Jewish community centred around the Shearith Israel synagogue.[7] The marriage took place in 1778 and the first of their seven children was born the following year. Their most prominent son, Moses Judah Hayes, and other Hayes grandchildren would carry on the family tradition in Montreal's Jewish community and take a leading part in the revival of the synagogue and restoration of Shearith Israel in the 1830s and 1840s.[8] In 1777, as a token of esteem for her father, Lazarus David, Andrew and Abigail Hayes had some copper coins minted bearing his name. Deposited in the cornerstone of the first synagogue, these mementos were then moved to the Chenneville Street building when it opened in 1828, and from there, in 1890, to the Stanley Street Synagogue. They still are housed in the present Lemieux Street building that was completed in 1947.[9]

The youngest daughter, Frances (Franny) David, was born in 1770.[10] She married Myer Michaels who was trading furs at Michilimackinac as early as 1778.[11] The marriage in 1793 united the families in two ways as Michaels was joined in formal partnership with David David's company from 1793 to 1795 and informally thereafter. Perhaps Moses David's growing stature in Detroit and the Great Lakes trade made the partnership redundant, or Michael's closer ties with the emerging North West Company drew his attention beyond the Great Lakes to the far west. Michaels, according to Samuel's diary, had teamed up with Mackenzie, the McGillevrays, and other fur traders from the North West Company when, in 1787, that alliance produced the larger organization, which eventually took over control of the entire St. Lawrence fur-trading territory. Michaels was already a member of the prestigious Beaver Club in 1793, while David David and brother Samuel remained more independent and diversified in their interests and did not become members until 1808 and 1811 respectively — at a time when contacts and financial investment, rather than actual participation in the northwest trade was most important for Club membership. While the North West Company consortium increasingly controlled the fur trade, the Davids became most closely associated with the process of diversification and modernization of the economy. The Davids' fur-trading business was ultimately sold to the North West Company, but upon David David's death, the company still owed him a substantial sum.[12] Frances shared her family's dedication to Montreal's Jewish community and her large contribution of £575 to the Spanish and Portuguese congregation's building fund served an impetus for others during its 1838 reorganization. Their donations made possible the acquisition of a new piece of land on Chenneville Street, near Lagauchetiere Street, on which the new synagogue, Shearith Israel, could finally be built.[13]

"The David Family had joined the Harts and the Josephs as the acknowledged leaders of Montreal Jewry during these years. In contrast to many of Lower Canada's early Jewish families, the children of Lazarus and Phoebe David all married Jews, save for the eldest, David David, who remained 'single.'"[14] And as soon as some economic stability had been achieved, Lazarus David began to dream of a synagogue for the nascent community. Settlement had not been easy for the Jews of Montreal. Faced with a hostile environment, they had used their innate survival skills to overcome the rigors and hardships of this awakening frontier. By utilizing their collective strength, they eventually succeeded as merchants, fur traders, and peddlers, and in service-oriented pursuits that not only helped them gain some degree of acceptance within Montreal's greater community, but also gave them the courage to build Canada's first synagogue — only the sixth on the North American continent.[15]

Shearith Israel held its first public worship in rented quarters on St. James Street.[16] Even though many of its members were Ashkenazi Jews, it had adopted the Sephardic rites, mainly because its founders, who had come from the American colonies and from Great Britain, still had close ties with the Spanish-Portuguese synagogues of New York and London.[17] In 1775, Lazarus David purchased a lot on St. Janvier Street, near Dominion Square in Montreal, in order "to serve in perpetuity as a cemetery for individuals of the Jewish faith." [18] Lazarus David died on October 22, 1776, one year before the first synagogue was erected at the corner of Notre Dame and Little St. James streets on land he had bequeathed to his son David, who had in turn donated it to the congregation. Even though Lazarus David had not lived long enough to see the building completed, he had the unique distinction of being the first Jew in Canada to be interred in the cemetery.[19]

Fortunately, the widow Phoebe David was made of stern stuff. While raising five children, she took over the family assets, managed the mercantile business, and carried out her late husband's wishes. As she reported to Governor General Frederick Haldimand in 1780, it was a struggle to maintain five children "out of the profits of a small shop, her only support." Shortly before her death, a visiting British merchant took tea with her and was charmed by "a very sensible clever old woman" who was "very entertaining in her conversation." Shown the synagogue by one of her sons, the visitor reported that it was "a very neat one for so small a congregation."[20] Phoebe David died on October 10, 1786.[21] David became the head of the family business with brother Samuel as a partner. Moses was in charge of buying furs from the Indians. That he proved his skills many times over was borne out by the fact that he had established a reputation for his ability to procure and select the finest pelts at the best possible prices for the entire Montreal market.

Moses David:
Pioneer Loyalist, Merchant, and Equal Rights Advocate

Moses was acting as the family's representative in the Detroit area as early as 1790.[22] In 1793, an early Detroit trader, Thomas Dugan, complained to Colonel Alex McKee, the British Indian Agent,[23] that Moses David, "another cheap shop adventurer, the same that was here three years ago

[1790], is arrived with a Cargo, it appears that he and his competitor Mr. Pattison, are fully resolved to undersell all the other traders of this place."[24] The charge against Moses as a "cheap shop adventurer" suggests that he was not a permanent resident who was part of the community with established premises, and strengthens the notion that Moses was not yet committed to Detroit as a permanent location for his entrepreneurial activities. It is interesting to note that nothing further is heard of the complainant, while David and Pattison become major figures in the region.

By 1793–94, the region was about to undergo a fundamental transformation.[25] For years after the 1783 Treaty of Paris that ended the American Revolution, the British remained in the border posts in United States territory, using the excuse of unresolved debts and obligations to their native allies. Another outcome of the Revolution was the Loyalist migrations to Quebec fostering settlement and growth and the decision in 1791 to divide British North America into provinces of Upper and Lower Canada. Loyalist settlers required provisions and services, which stimulated demand for merchant expertise in the Niagara and Detroit regions. With the Americans developing a military capable of enforcing their boundary pretensions and preoccupied with Revolutionary France on the Continent, Britain in 1794 decided to regularize relations with the new republic.

Jay's Treaty and the establishment of the international boundary committed British subjects and military forces to relocating to the Canadian side of the boundary. In preparation for handing over Detroit to the Americans in 1796, the Settlement of L'Assomption (later Sandwich) was chosen as the temporary seat of government for the Western District of Upper Canada and land opposite the Island of Bois Blanc (later Amherstburg), because of its strategic position commanding the entrance to the river, was selected as the place where the military post and naval station would be established. The Indian Department also set up its headquarters there. It was assumed that Amherstburg would become the dominant urban centre on this Upper Canadian frontier.[26]

Since the end of the Revolutionary War, a number of British adherents living in the town of Detroit crossed over and settled on what is now the Canadian side of the river. This was mostly in the Township of Malden near the fort, in the section of Petite Côte north of La Rivière aux Dindes where the original French settlement had started in 1749 or in the New Settlement on Lake Erie. Earlier French settlement, later reinforced by Loyalist grants, resulted in most of the riverfront from the mouth of the river to Lake St. Clair being occupied. British residents who stayed in Detroit in 1796 were given one year to make a declaration of their intention to remain British subjects living in American Territory, or they would be considered American citizens. A number of British subjects made the declaration — enough to alarm the new American officials in Detroit — but many others moved across the river, preferring to live under the British flag. This group included merchants and government officials who contributed much to the development of the business, social, and cultural life of the area.[27]

Moses David may have anticipated this move as early as 1793–94. The Godfreys suggest that Moses David had already chosen the Canadian side of the boundary when he accompanied the militia force that stopped the American forces under General Wayne at Fort Miami near Detroit. They place him as a merchant in Sandwich as early as 1794 and credit him with having built one of its first residences.[28] Whether Moses had already made up his mind to locate his enterprise on the Canadian side of the river, he was an active trader in the Detroit area and volunteered for Lieutenant Governor Simcoe's Upper Canadian militia during the 1796 war scare.

Sandwich

Merchants still closely tied to Detroit found the military settlement at Amherstburg too far from the centre of economic activity in the area. For the convenience of these citizens, in the summer of 1797, the Honourable Peter Russell, president of the Executive Council of Upper Canada, bought the reserve at the Huron Church containing 1,078 acres on the Canadian side of the Detroit River. It was a barren sandy plain, a gore, that stretched along the river from Rivière à Gervais to the Huron Church. An area of sixty-one acres along the river near the church was reserved for the use of the Huron Indians. The grant also included improved lands of Wm. Hands and Thomas Pajot that had already been alienated from the Indians through private deals.[29] June 1797 was the deadline for British subjects to declare whether they would remain British or become Americans. The British could lose them to the American side if there was not an equally convenient place for business provided on the British side of the river. Part of the purchase was divided into one-acre lots for settlement; three streets were laid out parallel to the river — Peter, Russell, and Bedford — and cross streets were established from Detroit Street to South Street — Mill, Huron (Brock), and Chippewa. At the corner of Bedford and Huron (Brock), the four corner lots were reserved for public use.[30] Eventually, a military barracks, a courthouse, and St. John's Anglican Church and burial ground graced this community centre.

A drawing of lots in Sandwich was held July 7, 1797. To encourage building in the new town, Russell directed that those settlers who built the first houses should be given park lots of twenty-four acres to the rear of the town site. The first four to receive this bounty were John McGregor, Robert Innis, Wm. Park, and Richard Pattison, Moses David's old competitor, who had built houses.[31] Russell rather over-optimistically reported to Lieutenant Governor Simcoe that several houses had already built there and expressed hope that, "it promises to become soon the most beautiful town in the province."[32] Moses David had not applied for a town lot in Sandwich in the first instance, probably because he was not yet perceived as a permanent resident of the area. He did not fit the Governor General's categories of "former inhabitants of Detroit" nor "Merchants who seated themselves with the Fort at Amherstburg on the first evacuation of Detroit."[33] Moses did have, however, sufficient presence and military experience and merit to apply for a two-hundred-acre crown grant in 1797. Surprisingly, he was refused on the cause that he was tied to the Lower Province and not sufficiently rooted in Upper Canada to be awarded land. A deeper and more insidious explanation emerged in the aftermath of his rejection when Chief Justice Elmsley issued his opinion that Jews could not be granted Crown lands in Upper Canada. Apparently, Moses David took Elmsley's decision seriously because he travelled to Lower Canada and in March 1799 applied for a 2,000-acre grant on the basis of his military service. David was refused a second time in December 1799, his application denied as "too late under present instructions."[34]

Moses David had been turned down for government land grants in both provinces, not ostensibly for his Jewishness but for technical reasons. However, Elmsley, as Chief Justice and chairman of the Land Board of York, had proclaimed in early 1798 that "Jews cannot hold land in this province."[35] "For Jews who wanted a place where citizenship was not defined in such a way as to exclude them and where land would be granted equally to Jews and where there would be equality of opportunity," Elmsley's decision was potentially devastating.[36] Undeterred, Moses returned to Sandwich determined to achieve social justice.

Upon his return, Moses David found that Sandwich had been designated as the Western District capital and, in a further attempt to promote its successful growth, government officials had built a courthouse and jail to uphold the law and provide a proper setting for building houses and businesses.[37] And recognizing the need for a Protestant place of worship to uphold British morality and loyalty, officials decided to place a "discreet clergyman" in Sandwich and give him a church there "as an antidote to American contagion." They chose Richard Pollard, a merchant colleague of Moses David turned minister, to lead St. John's, the mother parish of the Protestant Episcopal Church of the Western District and State of Michigan.[38]

Neither the erection of government buildings nor inducements for private housing produced the anticipated building boom. A report received by the Executive Council at York from the Grand Jury of the Western District asserted that a great number of town lots in Sandwich granted in 1797 still remained unimproved, although the times stipulated for such improvements had expired.

Grand Jury Report, Sandwich 8 July, 1800 to Council Chambers at York [Summary]:

Great number of lots still unimproved, 3 years time limit gone; settlement of town impeded, long indulgence, bounty abused, no intentions of improving them sold to others, who could not originally obtain and many have deeds to lots without requirement of improvements.

It has been represented to us by many individuals as a particular hardship, that they cannot obtain a grant of a Lot, although there are only seven or eight houses in the whole town, but that some of them (all British subjects) have been obliged to purchase, and others cannot obtain Lots upon any terms in a suitable situation for their Commerce.

Recommend — to forfeit all the vacant or unimproved Lots in the town of Sandwich, and to grant them to the first applicants, under a restriction and build thereon in a certain limited time; by which means the County Town would soon be settled and add not a little to the wealth of the District.

Brush cut and streets opened in said town immediately and require statute labour from Lot holders whether improved or not.[39]

Settlement of the town had been greatly impeded, streets were not yet opened and only seven or eight houses had been built. Many of the men who had been granted lots resided elsewhere and were holding these lots for speculation. Moses David was a perfect example of the individuals referred to in the Grand Jury report as suffering from the consequences of the government's reluctance to enforce their own policies. Unwilling to await the recommended forfeiture process and blocked temporarily by Elmsley's interpretation, Moses purchased a town lot from one of the original grantees — Jean Baptiste Barthe, a brother-in-law of John Askin. Moses purchased Lot 3 on the east side of Bedford Street and began making improvements. One of his improvements was the purchase of a house on an adjoining piece of property on August 6, 1801, from the innkeeper John Hembrow and one Robert Jonas for £14. (140 Designated as part of Lot No. 4, it contained "6 feet in front upon the said street by 50 in depth, making 300 square statute feet."[40] John Askin sheds some light on the purchase of the Barthe property in a business letter dated September 8, 1801. It appears that Moses had an agreement with the Barthes, probably backed by a mortgage or some sort of payment scheme, but they no longer held the deed as they had borrowed from Askin using the deed as collateral. Askin informed Moses David that if he did not take the goods that were charged, "It's your fault, not mine and as a consequence there can be no deductions made on the account."[41] Another letter written two-and-a-half months later by Askin, is significant. The letter states:

Sir,

Having your payments to make at this present time, I will thank you for the balance due me. My son John, I believe, mentioned that I had advanced in cash last year 77 pounds, 1 shilling New York Currency for the deed of the lot on which you have built. I need hardly tell you that if anything was to happen, Mr. Barthe, that if Mrs. Barthe and her son I thought proper to take advantage, I had the deed now in my possession you would lose the whole of your improvements.[42]

In his veiled threat to David, Askin was just applying some pressure on his fellow merchant about the outstanding account mentioned earlier. David contested the account and may have been withholding payment as a matter of principle or while awaiting legal advice. In any case, Moses completed his Lot 3 transactions with the Barthes in February and March 1803:

Memorial of bargain and sale of Lot #3 on the eastside of Bedford Street in the Town of Sandwich in the county aforesaid containing 1 square acre of land and same more or less with all and singular the appurtenance and [to] have and to hold unto the said Moses David, his heirs and assigns forever, for and (in) consideration the sum of 16 pounds of the currency of this province, a receipt whereof the said Jean Batiste [sic] Barthe and Genevieve, his wife have acknowledged and which deed of bargain and sale is witnessed by Lewis...James Fields, and Thomas Smith, and is hereby required to be registered pursuant to the said act, by me the said Moses David the grantee named in the said Deed of bargain and sale.

Witness my hand and seal at Sandwich aforesaid on this eighth day of March in the year of our Lord, one thousand eight hundred and three.
[signed] Moses David[43]

As Moses pursued a private strategy, Sandwich real estate was in flux after the 1800 Grand Jury complaints. Although Moses purchased Lot 3 from the original grantees, he was ready to try and leverage that property and his improvements to claim a park lot for his improvements and building a residence on the property. As soon as Moses had struck a bargain with the original grantee, Barthe, he began his improvements and made application for a government granted park lot. In April 1801, David again applied for land in Upper Canada, this time requesting a park lot in Sandwich and forwarding a certificate from the churchwardens of Sandwich verifying that his building was already completed. When his petition received no answer, Moses reapplied on January 8, 1803. By this time, Moses must have been exasperated. He had complied with all of the requirements, was a resident of area, was committed, and, perhaps more importantly, he had a tradition of Jewish rights from Lower Canada. In demanding an answer, the Godfreys suggest that "his family's long-time success in the colony and his position as a natural-born subject gave him the confidence to push for his rights."[44]

In any case, on March 9, 1803, he went over Elmsley's head directly to Lieutenant Governor Hunter. He recited his contributions to the growth and development of this frontier and challenged Elmsley directly by asking whether his petition had been rejected "under the idea that his religion precludes him from any grant in His Majesty's Colonies."[45]

The Lieutenant Governor referred David's petition to the Executive Council headed by Henry Alcock, Elmsley's successor. David's application was approved and David was finally given letters patent to twenty-seven acres of land in the township of Sandwich on February 20, 1804.[46]

Moses David's equal rights challenge went beyond Upper Canada or even British North America; he was demanding recognition of religious rights throughout the British Colonies. And his victory seemed applicable to other aspects of the colony's life such as military positions and civil or government posts.

Military and Government Posts

Moses David had been participating in militia activities in one capacity or another since the early 1790s, and he had been appointed an ensign in the Essex militia sometime before 1803. In that year, he was promoted to lieutenant. According to the Godfreys, Moses "was the first professing Jew to be appointed a commissioned officer in the militia. And he may have been the first Jew to be appointed a com-

missioned officer in the whole empire…."[47] How Moses David managed to obtain his commission without swearing the state oath and complying with the Test Act is unclear, but the practice was repeated when he was made a captain in 1807.[48]

In 1808, Moses David was offered the position of coroner of the Western District by Lieutenant Governor Francis Gore. Again according to the Godfreys, this was the first instance of a Jew "being appointed by commission to a government office" in Upper Canada. "It showed how far the government of Upper Canada was willing to go in adopting innovative solutions to allow a person of the Jewish faith to participate in society, without swearing state oaths." The innovative solution in this case was the posting of a bond as security for the performance of duties in lieu of the state oaths with their Christian/Anglican declarations. As in Moses' struggle for land rights, the solution of posting bonds in place of taking the state oaths opened the way for other religious minorities seeking equal rights. "Never again was there to be any doubt as to the rights of Jews to obtain grants of land from the crown in Upper Canada or to receive and hold at least some civil and military positions."[49]

Trading, Forwarding, Money Lending, and Banking

As were many of his contemporaries, Moses David was a full-service merchant. He dealt with a number of local individuals and companies representative of the whole spectrum of humanity in the area. As a fur trader, Moses had developed close contacts with a number of native groups; as early as April 1794 he was purchasing furs from Antoine Badichon,[50] and other French Canadians from Detroit. And from his brother David's rather large consignment of fur packs to Gabriel Godfroy on credit[51] just before the Detroit fire of 1805, one can assume that he relied upon Moses to protect the family's interests here.

From September 26, 1800, to August 1807, Moses David's name appears in William Hands' ledger book. Hands was a merchant of Sandwich and a neighbour of Moses on the next-door property, which he had acquired from the Indians before the laying out of Sandwich. He crossed over from Detroit in 1799 and took up residence at about the same time Moses David began his improvements on the neighbouring property. Hands was a one-man civil service of the Western District, holding a number of posts that included sheriff, treasurer, postmaster, and registrar of the Surrogate Court.[52] Moses furnished Hands with a diverse list of items — loadstones, wood, sand, bricks, boards, shingles, cabbages, a lamb, a spelling book, paper, a comb, tea, nails, pipes, and even a bottle of peppermint.[53] A close connection with Hands was invaluable in business and legal matters.

Moses also participated in banking and lending although these transactions were usually associated with property, at least as collateral. In 1800 Moses loaned John Boyle, a tailor from Malden £41 4s,[54] probably with property as collateral, and on May 18, 1800, witnessed a land sale of property owned by Jonathan Schieffelin, Indian agent and territorial legislator, and Thomas Smith, merchant and surveyor of both Detroit and Sandwich. Of special interest is the fact that Schieffelin was employed in the 1760s in Detroit by the openly avowed Jewish merchant Chapman Abraham. Schieffelin may have been a Jew, although not openly.[55] He was called a Jew by Francois Baby during a personal conflict between the two while both were Indian Department officials.

Moses also involved himself in the forwarding business — to Mackinac, the Upper Lakes, and beyond. On May 29, 1800, he wrote to Jacob Franks, a Jewish merchant in Mackinac and Green Bay:

> Your boat[s] arrived late last eve. I have provisioned them from this day, for twenty days, should they arrive in a shorter time they will have to account to you. With respect to Duties, which may be laid on at Mackinac, you will no doubt get every information there. I shall write you by the next Boats.
>
> Your humble servant[56]

Legal Business

Although he was not trained as a lawyer, Moses had a good education for his day. He was certainly literate, his activities suggest a fine legal mind and he was aware of the legal requirements of the business of his day. Court records, in which Moses David was involved either as plaintiff, defendant, or solicitor for clients are numerous. Among them is a suit he filed against the partners in the firm of Forsythe, Smith and Company for non-payment for merchandise. Although the document pertaining to the action is almost illegible, it does show that the hearing judge, Elijah Brush, (a trustee of Detroit and treasurer of the Michigan Territory in 1806) had declared in favour of Moses David:

> On the first day of December in the year of our Lord 1802, at Sandwich in the presence of Upper Canada, twice at Detroit and in said county of Wayne, and within the transaction of this court was indebted to the said Moses in the sum of three hundred and fifty dollars lawful money of the United States for goods, monies and merchandise by the said Moses, before that time sold and delivered to the said Forsythe Smith and Company and at this special instance and neglect and so indebted they, the said Forsythe Smith and Company in consideration then and these undertook and faithfully promised the said Moses to pay him the said sort mentioned sum of money.[57]

In another court action, Jacques Peltier and Jacques and Francoise Lavelle accused Moses David of "picking out all the good skins to be sent to Canada but keeping the bad ones to pay your debts here."[58] The plaintiffs probably were justified in making that claim, since Moses, as his family's trusted representative in the field, likely made sure that all the best merchandise went to Montreal.

In view of the diversity of his business ventures, Moses David came in contact with many prominent people, for some of whom he did favours on various occasions. One of them was Francis Badgley, who practiced law in Montreal with his brother James. In a letter to Solomon Sibley, written on April 28, 1804, he mentions Moses' name.[59] Solomon Sibley was a Detroit lawyer who was elected to the first legislature of the Northwest Territory in 1799, and was named the delegate to Congress from the territory of Michigan between 1820-1823. He subsequently served as a judge of Michigan's Supreme Court. Sibley acted as Badgley's attorney, when he, as the last surviving partner of Francis Badgley and Company, sued a Mr. Joseph Campeau for money owed to the firm. The following excerpts, from that letter, show Moses' involvement in the case:

Sir,

I duly received your favour of the first of December, last, Mr. D. will no doubt have advised you, so this paper as I conceive it was very sufficient. I wrote to Mr. D. that if he made out his objections so stated to his satisfaction what he might allow that amount to be deducted from the account as it then stood and, in order to close the business until I have done with (the gentleman), either in money or good pelts at the current cash prices. Certainly nothing can be more fair on my part. I now repeat with respect to the interest for two years past, I am willing to have it to Mr. David's discretion, although I shall never think otherwise than that is my just due. The demand Campeau made of 10% more on his furs than the market price is an abominable advantage he wishes to take of me and which no man could admit for a moment in the discharge of a debt long due. At the time there might have been

some reason for such an idea, had payment been closed 12 months before the payment was due, but certainly not in the present case. You mentioned that you should write me again with a statement of what proof was necessary. Not having received any further advice from you or Mr. David on the subject, I can say nothing further on the business but that in a few days I shall send you a detailed account of every particular with the book of origin entry which my brother kept in Detroit. In the meantime, please communicate this to Mr. David. In hopes of soon hearing that the matter is settled,

I remain, your obedient servant,
[signed] Francis Badgley[60]

In a subsequent letter of August 25, 1804,[61] Badgley advises Sibley that Moses David had informed him of the judgment the lawyer had obtained in Detroit against Joseph Campeau that "serves to request that you will pay the amount of the claim into the hands of my attorney, Mr. Moses David, whose receipt will exonerate you therefrom."[62]

On the back of that letter, Moses had inserted the total sum of the judgment, less court costs. The following notation made at the bottom of the letter, appears to refer to the interest charges Moses had added to the original judgment:

Received Sandwich, September 25, 1804 of Solomon Sibley, attorney at Law the above sum of 1380.50, being the amount of the judgment above S. Sibley 3 percent commission for collection per the written order received by me.[63]

The Detroit Fire of 1805

The Detroit Fire of 1805 was a major disaster and damaged the area's economy even across the river in Sandwich, so integral were the communities. The following correspondence demonstrates that David did not always succeed in collecting his debts. James May, the first chief justice of the Court of Common Pleas in 1796 and a prominent Detroit merchant, was a personal friend of Moses David. Although he had owned a shop and had kept slaves, by 1806 he appeared to have fallen on hard times. The following excerpts from a letter he wrote to Moses David in August of that year sheds some light on prevailing general economic conditions, but specifically on May's personal plight:

Dear Sir:

I have this moment received your letter and am very sorry to inform (you) at this present juncture, it is totally out of my power to assist you with cash. My situation is pretty much the same with your own. I have experienced nothing but a series of disappointments from all quarters. I should have answered your letter enclosing my account, but was in every expectation of seeing you over on this side in order to make some remarks on your account current relative to the deficiency which you have charged my account with. Also the vinegar for Badgley's estate and the astonishing amount of the box of toys, but more of it when we meet. Suffice my good friend that I am to the trouble to apologize for asking for your own is what I have no right to expect. I am in hopes that something will turn up before long that will give a little circulation of cash. If not, the Lord only knows what will become of the country and the people in it. I never saw anything equal to the great scarcity of money as at present. I remain, dear sir, with sentiments of respect.

Yours truly,

[signed] James May [64]

Moses also was well acquainted with James Henry, another Detroit merchant. Active in politics, he also was the judge of the Court of Quarter Sessions, serving it as commissioner as well. Moses wrote to him on January 30, 1809, requesting help in settling the aforementioned James May's account, which he agreed to do.[65] Again on June 25, 1812, Moses wrote to Henry, this time asking him to remit the payment he had promised to make on an overdue draft issued in Philadelphia. Enclosed with that letter was the ledger page of Henry's account with Moses, which clearly showed the diversity of his business dealings. Covering the period between November 1809 and June 24, 1812, Moses apparently had supplied Henry with such items as a "tea kettle, maid's hose, table cloths, book, calfskin, flour, drawing knife, and nails."[66]

Even though Moses David continued to engage in business with prominent Americans, businessmen as well as political figures, he remained loyal to Great Britain. Anxious to come to her aid, should he be required to do so, he became a captain in the Northeast Regiment, Essex County Militia on May 22, 1807.[67] The company under his command included one lieutenant, an ensign, a sergeant, twenty-two privates, twenty-two arms, and sixty-six rounds of ammunition. On June 4, 1807, his name appeared together with those of other officers, in the papers of his former business associate John Askin, who meanwhile had become a colonel.[68]

Moses David was influential in breaking down barriers in Upper Canada that threatened to limit Jewish opportunity and equal rights concerning land ownership and military and political participation.

In reversing this practice, Moses David, a natural-born British subject resident in Essex, played an important part. The change, however, was de facto rather than de jure. In 1803 the Executive Council granted his prayer for relief and he received the patent, in his own right, for land in Sandwich on 20 February 1804. He did so without swearing the oath of adjuration in its Christian form. He seems to have avoided this when he was commissioned a militia officer prior to 1803 although the state oaths were a formal requirement. When appointed coroner of the Western District in 1808, he again escaped taking the oaths by posting a performance bond, an innovative practice designed to meet the requirement of the oath of adjuration.[69]

The Land Speculator

There is no doubt that Moses David was well respected. He was even favoured by the exclusive Family Compact, a group that had emerged when John Graves Simcoe became Upper Canada's first lieutenant governor and attempted to create a local aristocracy. Not only had he appointed his Loyalist friends to powerful government positions, he had also granted them enormous tracts of Crown reserves. These were usually kept unproductive and dormant, even though the lands were badly needed for new settlements. This system remained intact until popular discontent forced reform. Under these conditions, Moses David was able to acquire a number of prized tracts of Crown land in the Western District.

In John Clark's magisterial work, *Land, Power and Economics on the Frontier of Upper Canada*, Moses David is presented as a major player among the land speculators on this western frontier:

An interesting facet of commerce was that over time the nature of the speculators changed with the economy. In the earlier period, many of the land speculators or mortgage investors were directly involved in the fur trade and Indian trade or at least in supplying the fur trade. Askin and McGill are the most obvious examples, but the list also includes...others among the 144 speculators who were recognizably merchants but who had less obvious connections to the fur trade. These included... Moses David, William McCormick, George Meldrum, William Munger, Charles Askin, and Francis Baby.[70]

Moses David apparently adopted one of the common strategies of land speculators, that of buying tax delinquent lands much less than he would have paid the Crown or private land companies. Price was one advantage and another was the fact that lands purchased in that fashion could be held for eight years without paying any tax, allowing the speculators to better employ their capital in more profitable ways.[71] A sample of Moses David's land purchases and sales demonstrate his knowledge of local development trends.

Aside from his urban real estate in Sandwich town, Moses had properties in the village of Amherstburg, the site of Fort Malden, the major British stronghold on the frontier. The community grew and became more influential than Sandwich. On September 27, 1805, Moses paid George Ermatinger ten shillings for a property that included a house and auxiliary buildings,[72] and on September 11, 1806, at a price of £68 1s 8p, he bought one hundred of the two hundred acres Thomas Smith had received from the Crown free of charge two years earlier. Located in Sandwich East, that parcel of land was no more than a swamp at the time. However, since it bordered on Lake St. Clair, it offered good possibilities for future development as a prime waterfront property.[73] This area was a favourite of John Askin, who put together a parcel of lots along Lake St. Clair and the rivers draining into the lake. Accessibility by water remained a crucial component of value in an area still largely devoid of roads. On November 20, 1807, Smith sold the remaining one hundred acres to Moses David,[74] who resold them to a Joseph Mayoux on January 16, 1808 — just a few months later.[75]

Moses also became owner of additional lands; some in the Township of Sandwich,[76] as well as 114 acres in the Township of Colchester,[77] properties that had cost him ten shillings each. Moses apparently later sold this property to Alexander Mackenzie and his partner Frederick William Ermatinger. And in a quirk of fate, six years after Moses' death, on September 6, 1820, McKenzie resold the property to David David, with F. W. Ermatinger releasing all claims to the property.[78]

Eventually David David inherited all the properties from the estate of his late brother, in particular, the 114 acres in Colchester. Some eight years after David David's own death on October 9, 1832,[79] his executors sold the land to Henry Hoffman for £250. However, during David David's lifetime, as early as 1805, he must have been quite active in the border city area. Records reveal a correspondence he had with a Gabriel Godfroy[80] of Detroit to whom he had shipped a consignment of fur packs, for which he had not received payment in the amount of £1,766 18s 11p.[81] Since David also allowed his brother to act as his agent in a variety of local land deals, there is no justification for the notion that Moses was not on good terms with his family. David not only visited his brother but also took an interest in his affairs.

Additional Family Connections

Taking on apprentices was common practice among many businessmen and David was instrumental in arranging a two-year apprenticeship in March 1805 for Jean Baptiste Dodlain,[82] for whom Moses had to provide all the necessities of life. David subsequently became involved on his brother's behalf with the drafting of another contract. This involved the apprenticeship of their nephew David Hayes in Sandwich. That agreement, reproduced here in part, is of even greater significance since it contains the first reference to Andrew and Abigail Hayes' son David, whose birth

had remained unrecorded until May 6, 1805, the date on which the following document was drawn up:

> Before the subscribing public notaries residing in the city of Montreal in the province of Lower Canada, personally came and appeared David Hayes, a minor son of Andrew Hayes of Montreal, aforesaid merchant being duly assisted by and with the consent and approbation of his said father testified by his present and as subscribing these presents. And declared the said David Hayes that he hath of his own free will and accord placed and bound himself apprentice to Moses David of Sandwich in Province of Upper Canada a merchant, his brother David David of Montreal merchant being present and accepting for him and in the name of Moses David, to be taught in the art of science and trade; to live, continue and serve him as an apprentice henceforth unto the full term of four years hence next ensuring and fully to be compleat and end.[83]

Listed as residing in Sandwich, the name of David Hayes subsequently appeared as a witness to several land transactions concluded by Moses David.[84]

Moses David, besides acquiring properties for himself, his brother David, and for others in trust, he also lent money to various people, including Jean Baptiste Parre, who borrowed £50 11s from him on June 21, 1806.[85] Among Moses' land purchases were two hundred acres known as South Gore for which he paid £200. The lands were located between lots No. 11 and No. 12, in the Second, Third, and Fourth Concessions of the Township of Colchester.[86] Other land transactions show that on April 6, 1807, he bought land in Gosfield from John Bell,[87] and purchased a lot in Elizabethtown on September 12, 1809, from Robert Livingston.[88] As well, he acquired property from James Heward, to whom he may have given a long-term mortgage, as he did not take possession of it until January 31, 1811.[89] Among the land Moses took as collateral for loans was Lot No. 42 in the Second Concession and another property against which he registered a mortgage on July 2, 1807, in the amount of 127 pounds, 13 shillings, 9 pence, and 3 farthings.[90]

Moses and Charlotte

Although a great deal of material has been uncovered about Moses David's business activities, the only somewhat oblique reference to his social life is contained in a March 12, 1805, letter written to him by his friend James May of Detroit. Inquiring about an illness Moses appears to have had, he expresses the hope that "it did not proceed from your frolic at Mr. Henry's — when you were imprudent enough to cross this river at midnight."[91] Moses' religious life, although interesting, also is enigmatic. We know that he owned a set of Hebrew prayer books, inscribed, "Sandwich, Upper Canada 1803,"[92] that he supported the synagogue in Montreal, and that he occasionally returned to that city on business and religious missions. But Moses was isolated in Sandwich/Detroit from fellow Jews and forced to choose between Assumption, the existing Roman Catholic church, and St. John's Anglican Church, both in Sandwich. St. John's was the only Protestant place of worship in the Sandwich area and it would seem natural for Moses to have chosen the Protestant church for social and business reasons, if no other. It is also quite traditional for Jews to support wider community needs with contributions — his family in Montreal, for example. In Quebec, it was also tradition to consider Jews as Protestant in terms of rights, being non-Catholic. Reverend Pollard of St. John's was a former fur trader and probably good company for Moses — and not overly sanctimonious given his merchant background.

Since his name appears at the end of a list of persons who attended a vestry meeting on March 23, 1807, his only interest in the gathering was likely the fact that the sale of various properties was one of the topics.[93] He was also a witness to the marriage of Joseph Eberts, merchant and Ann Baker, spinster," performed by Reverend Richard Pollard at St. John's Church on July 24, 1810.[94] Dr. Eberts was a fascinating character who left Montreal in the dead of night after performing an autopsy in violation of church and civil law. In Detroit in 1804, he suffered through a highly publicized divorce, which damaged his reputation further. It is possible that Moses was the only person in Sandwich willing to stand up for him.[95] Back in Montreal, his older brother Samuel also married in 1810, perhaps giving Moses pause to consider his own marital status.

Because of Moses David's position in the community, he had an association with that church and even held a pew seat there, as claimed by Windsor historian George F. Macdonald in his compilation of data about Moses' life,[96] but that he remained a Jew throughout his life is borne out by the fact that he was buried in the backyard of his Sandwich home, rather than in the cemetery adjoining St. John's Church.

Moreover, there were indications that Moses David occasionally visited his family in Montreal, since a journey he made in the summer of 1804 is mentioned in his brother Samuel's diary,[97] as well as in a letter to Moses from Francis Badgley.[98] On one of these trips he must have been introduced to Charlotte, daughter of Dorothea (née Judah) and Aaron Hart,[99] — Canada's first Jewish settler. Born on June 4, 1777,[100] in London, England, she became an astute and active businesswoman in her own right, a most unusual phenomenon in the nineteenth century. Using a portion of the money she had inherited from her father, on October 6, 1804, Charlotte registered a £500 mortgage against a property held by Robert Lester and Robert Marrogh.[101] It stipulated that the loan be repaid within three months and that if Charlotte married and/or in case of her death, her brothers would be entitled to the repayment.

Moses must have asked for Charlotte's hand in marriage some time before September 29, 1811, when he and his bride-to-be entered into a pre-nuptial agreement that stated, in part, that they shall and will have and take each other to be man and wife and that their marriage shall be celebrated without delay according to the rites and forms of Jewish laws and, further, that there shall not be any communacity or community property between them, the said Moses David and Charlotte Hart, either of the real and personal property, which now belongs to them or either of them, or shall or may be acquired by or come to them or either of them during their intended marriage in any manner or way whatsoever any have wage or custom to the contrary notwithstanding.[102]

In addition, Moses David had to give £1,000 to his prospective wife in lieu of dower — that part of a husband's property that his widow inherits for life after his death — allowing her to use it in any way she deemed proper. Even though the contract further stipulated that the marriage should take place "without delay," no exact date was given. According to a notebook kept by Harline David Ruben, the wedding did not take place until some time in 1812. One might wonder why this 44-year-old groom and his bride, who was close to her thirty-fourth birthday, would have delayed the wedding at all. It also is unclear why he would have gone to Montreal twice — first, in September 1811 to sign the marriage contract, and again several months later to attend his wedding. The only conclusive proof that the ceremony had been performed some time before October 2, 1812, is the fact that on that day Moses and Charlotte met at her mother's house on Gabriel Street in Montreal,[103] where they signed an addendum to their marriage contract as a married couple. It not only acknowledged their original agreement of September 29, 1811, but also reaffirmed the circumstances relating to the disposal of the monies Charlotte had inherited from her late father.[104] In addition, the addendum gave David David and Alexander Hart joint powers-of-attorney to purchase bills at interest.

Returning to Sandwich after the onset of cold weather when travel was far more difficult,[105] Moses would have brought his new wife to a house built on one of the lots he owned. It was likely the one he purchased on August 6, 1801, from John Hembrow and Robert Jonas for £14.[106] In 1813, a few months before Moses' death, he and Charlotte sold a piece of lots No. 3 and No. 4 on the east side of Bedford Street, where they resided, to Augustine Roy.[107]

Throughout her marriage to Moses, Charlotte remained in full control of all the properties she owned, as well as continuing to conduct her own business affairs. Indicative of her activities as a moneylender, is the following note in French:

> Le 2 September 1812, Charlotte Hart qui avait épousé Moses David, de Sandwich, Haut-Canada, transportait à sa mère une créance de deux cent cinquante livres à elle léguée par son père et due par Sir John Johnson.[108]

On March 18, 1813, Charlotte gave birth to a son named Moses Eleazer. Regrettably, his father died when the boy was only about 18 months old. He was subsequently "educated in Edinburgh and Paris, and lived almost half of his life abroad."[109] On November 25, 1846,[110] in Philadelphia, at the age of 33, Moses Eleazer David married Rosina, who was born on February 11, 1827,[111] the daughter of Jacob Levy Florance. She bore him two children,[112] Charlotte (Nina), born in London in December 1847, and Arthur Meredith, called Florance, born on October 5, 1849, in Montreal.[113] Rosina David died on December 8, 1850, in Teignmouth, England, and was buried in Philadelphia on February 9, 1851.[114] On December 8, 1853, her daughter Nina died in Montreal at the age of 6, and was buried next to her mother.[115]

On April 15, 1872, at the age of fifty-nine, Moses Eleazer David married a second time to Ada S. Abraham of Bristol, England.[116] We must conclude that he returned to Montreal with his new wife, since records show that he laid the cornerstone for the new synagogue building on Chenneville

Street.[117] Following in his family's footsteps, he was an active supporter of the Spanish-Portuguese congregation, as well as becoming involved in more mundane ventures. Keen on horse racing, he entered a horse in the first King's Plate race,[118] run at Trois Rivières on July 27, 1836. Records also show that he was a founder of the St. James Club,[119] served as a militia officer in 1837 and 1851,[120] and had an interest in the Grand Trunk Railway.[121] In 1891, he sold the land in Sandwich that his late father had originally received from the Crown.[122]

The End of the Moses David Family Line

Moses David died on September 26, 1814, the cause of death unknown. Although some have wondered why he was not buried at the same place as other members of his prominent family, the answer may lie in the fact that it would have been very difficult for his wife to travel to Montreal for the funeral with her infant son.

On January 14, 1811, Moses David had bought a piece of land from George Meldrum and William Park, for which he paid £10. According to the diagram attached to the memorial of bargain and sale, he may also have intended that narrow strip running the full depth of Lot No. 4 to be his gravesite. Its precise location is described in that document as follows:

> An indenture of Bargain and Sale dated the fourteenth day of January in the year of our Lord one thousand eight hundred and eleven, made between George Meldrum and William Park of Sandwich in the Western District Esquire of the one part and Moses David of Sandwich merchant of the other part. Whereby the said George Meldrum and William Park for and in consideration of the sum of ten pounds New York currency to them in hand paid, grantee, bargained, sold alien and confirming unto the said Moses David

and to his heirs and assigns for ever a certain piece of ground being the northern part of lot number four Bedford street with the appurtenances situated lying and being on the east side of Bedford street, aforesaid, in the town of Sandwich in the county of Essex, which said piece of ground is butted and bounded as follows, that is to say, beginning at a jog or offset at the Easterly end of a purchase made from John Hembrow, containing six feet in breadth and thence running the whole depth of the lot along the sideline of lot number three as described in the margin from A to B six feet thence in depth to C-D and all profits, commodities, and appurtenances whatsoever to the premises belonging or in any wise appertaining and the reversion and reversions remainder and remainders, rents, issues and profits of all and singulars the said premises, which saw indenture of bargain and sale is witnessed by the Reverend Richard Pollard of Sandwich, clerk and John McGregor of Sandwich, Esquire and is hereby required to be registered pursuant to the said act by the said Moses David.[123]

Although Moses David owned all of Lot No. 3, as well as a strip of Lot No. 4, there is no specific record of his intentions for a Jewish cemetery or his own burial. However, later documents reveal that his actual burial plot was on land acquired on October 22, 1913, by Adolphe S. Gignac from Jane Phyllis McKee, which included the

> Northerly fifty-feet in width lot number three on the east side of Bedford street by the full depth of the said lot, excepting therefrom the Jew Cemetery at the east corner thereof.[124]

The so-called "Jew Cemetery" had only one grave, that of Moses David.[125]

After returning to Quebec, Charlotte David continued to look after her own business interests, as well as those of her deceased husband. Attempting to wrap up his affairs, she wrote to tell Detroit lawyer Solomon Sibley in August 1819:

> Sir,
>
> Will thank you to inform me if Mr. George Meldrum has made you any payment in account of the bond due the estate of the late Mr. Moses David and what sum you have received from the estate of the late Mr. James Henry.
> I am sir, your obedient servant.
> [signed] Charlotte David[126]

By 1825, Charlotte was residing in Montreal with her young son. As part of her business activities that year, she lent £500 to the Church of Our Lady of Montreal[127] on July 15, against which she registered one mortgage on November 29, 1825,[128] and another one on December 17, 1825.[129] Four years later, when she was getting ready to travel in Europe, she appointed Alexander Hart and Moses J. Hayes to act as her attorneys during her absence.[130]

Charlotte David died one day after her sixty-seventh birthday, on January 5, 1844.[131] Reverend David Piza officiated at her funeral, which was recorded in his registry book as follows:

> Charlotte Hart, widow of the late Moses David, in his life-time of Sandwich, Canada West, died on the fifth day of January, one thousand eight hundred and forty four, and was buried by me on the twelfth day of January, one thousand eight hundred forty four, in the presence of Moses Samuel David of the city of Montreal, Advocate, and of Moses N. Binley of the same place, Advocate, and of G. Joseph of the same place, Advocate, aged sixty-seven years.
> [signed] David Piza, Minister."[132]

Moses Eleazer David, son of Charlotte and Moses and the last direct descendant of Moses David, died on October 1, 1892, at his residence at 704 Sherbrooke Street in Montreal.[133] The following is the death notice for Moses Eleazer as it appeared in the registry book of the Spanish and Portuguese Synagogue:

> Moses Eleazer David, of the city of Montreal died on the first day of October, one thousand eight hundred and ninety two, and was buried by me on the third day of October, one thousand eight hundred ninety two, in the presence of the undersigned witnesses J. L. Samuel, A. Hirschberg.
> [signed] D. Mendola de Sola, Minister.[134]

With Moses Eleazer's death, the Moses David family line came to an end.

An Epilogue for Windsor's First Jewish Citizen

On June 25, 1880, Moses David's tombstone became the subject of an article published in the *Amherstburg Echo*. Although the given date of his death is incorrect, the description of that particular memorial is of interest:

> Sandwich has an old relic in the shape of a tombstone which was erected to the memory of Moses David by his wife, Charlotte David. The stone fence is 6 feet wide by 5 1/2 feet long. On the tombstone are engraved the following words: "in memory

of Moses David, who departed this life August 21st, 1815 aged 46." Those wishing to see, can do so by asking Mr. Dentz, of the Dominion House, or James McKee.[135]

As a consequence of this study of Moses David's life, as well as an assessment of the contributions he had made to Windsor's Jewry, interest in him was regenerated and the question of desecration of his gravesite entered discussions. From the time he purchased parcels of land, which he may have designated as his burial ground, ownership had changed many times. Yet, in most of the pertinent documents the "Jew Cemetery" was excluded from each sale, such as in the transaction between Jane Phyllis McKee and Adolphe Gignac on October 22, 1913.[136] The specific clause was omitted, however, when Gignac transferred ownership of the property to his wife, Homeline, on November 20, 1923.[137] After her death, the property passed to her heirs, specifically, Marie Louise Gignac, who resided there until her own death.[138] In accordance with the terms of her will on May 12, 1977, the land was sold to Steve Riolo.[139] Since the law does not require a title search beyond a forty-year period, the new owner was free to use it in any way he wished. Word that a high-rise apartment building might be erected on the site not only rekindled interest in Moses David, but also in the sanctity of his burial plot.

Jewish law requires that burial grounds remain undisturbed and there were discussions in 1978 to consider the feasibility of disinterment and reburial of Moses David's remains. In response to my requests for action in this regard, Joseph Eisenberg, executive director of the Jewish Community Council of Windsor contacted archaeologist Leonard Kroon, a professor at the University of Windsor.[140] His offer of assistance was the first step in the process to uncover the gravesite, which had remained undisturbed for over 160 years.

To help survey the burial ground, Professor Kroon brought in Kirk Walstedt of Maidstone Township, another archaeologist. After locating the grave's surface in the southeast corner at the back of Miss Gignac's former home,

workers proceeded to remove, piece by piece, the large, covering mound of trash. Trowels and brushes were used to cautiously hand pick and sift their way through the rubble. While so doing, numerous items were revealed: handmade bricks, cut limestone blocks (forming the north, east, and west portions of the rectangular piece of land), broken pieces of ceramic and glass, all of late-nineteenth-century vintage, and even a newspaper fragment dating back to 1914. The search was rewarding for these determined explorers — it reached its pinnacle with the discovery of an extremely large memorial stone. Still entirely intact, and set upon a brick floor, it bore the following inscription:

> In Memory of Mr. Moses David
> Who Departed this life Sept 27, 1814
> Age 46 years
> This tomb was erected by His Affectionate Wife
> Charlotte David

That archaeological find was indeed the gravesite of Moses David! It revealed that what was believed to have been a southerly "brick wall" was the remnants of a pedestal, on which the memorial stone had once rested. After viewing the stone "in situ," it was removed to a safe place for further study. During the final stages of exploration, it became clear that the pedestal had a solid foundation, consisting of several thick and heavy slate slabs that had been set on the floor in a level position. When the rest of the "tomb" was later cleared, it provided evidence that the floor, pedestal and inner wall were composed of brick. Eleven geese, symbols normally used by Indians as part of their funeral rites, had been placed around the pedestal, and inner wall, including a padlock found on the floor of the tomb.

Five feet below ground, in a test pit area measuring five feet by five feet, the skeleton was finally uncovered. Dr. Samuel S. Stollman, who had been the rabbi of Shaar Hashomayim congregation for over a quarter century and then was its rabbi emeritus, was called upon to act as religious authority in the disinterment, which was performed in accordance with Jewish law. That law not only forbids the viewing of skeletal remains, so that the soul of the deceased may rest in peace, but also requires that the coffin be made completely of wood. Professor Kroon meticulously followed these religious stipulations. Without disturbing the consecrated earth surrounding the skeleton, he exposed, solely for verification purposes, only a small area of bone. He then removed the remains in situ, making sure that iron did not come into contact with them.

A special plywood casket was designed, equipped with wooden dowels and corner blocks, and held together with glue, with a separate bottom or palette that would fit into a cement vault. After using a back hoe to excavate a wide area around the burial site, an archeological team again trowelled and brushed its way to the shredded remnants of the original

rough box that then was pedestalled before setting the plywood framing over it and positioning the palette beside it.

On the day of disinterment, the complete unit was lifted up and out of the pit and set inside the cement vault resting on the bed of an open truck waiting nearby. After placing a cover over the vault, the earthly remains of Moses David were transported to Pillette Road, the site of Shaar Hashomayim cemetery. It was there that Windsor's illustrious first Jew was re-interred with all the Jewish religious rites due to him. Adorned with the original tombstone, this new grave is a fitting resting-place for the man who had established the first familial and cultural links between Montreal and Windsor — the new frontier. It is a monument to all those Jews who came after him to pioneer in this very challenging environment.[141]

PART II

Chapter 2
The Earliest Jews Who Choose Windsor

The Rise of Windsor

The end of the War of 1812 and the establishment of peaceful relations between Canada and the United States assured the separate futures of these two nations. As settlers poured in, the fur trade, which had been so important to the area's economy in Moses David's day, declined. The 1821 merger of the Montreal-based North West Company with the Hudson's Bay Company resulted in a shift in the trade and its requirements away from Detroit to the North, where furs were plentiful and transport by Hudson Bay more economical. Detroit would suffer little from this change as it was becoming a frontier metropolis — a centre of trade and shipping as well as the territorial capital. As "Michigan fever" attracted thousands of settlers, steamships appeared on the Great Lakes, the Erie Canal opened in 1825, giving direct access to New York City, and the Welland Canal in 1829 offered a similar connection to Montreal. By 1837 Michigan achieved statehood and began the evolution toward the urban industrial complex Detroit would become in the twentieth century.

In the 1820s the small ferry landing opposite Detroit began to emerge, soon surpassing its more historic neighbour, Sandwich, which continued to slumber under its status as capital of the Western District of Upper Canada. Its legal and administrative functions were not matched by entrepreneurial activities as downriver Amherstburg outgrew its fortress functions to become a major port and business centre and the Ferry — the future Windsor — blossomed as the major transportation centre and border crossing in the region. Roads, regular stage and ferry crossing schedules, and business activity that focused not only upon the local and immigrant trades but also on a steady stream of customers from Detroit and the US led to surveys, land subdivision, and the emergence of a municipality. In 1836 Windsor's citizens chose its name. A financial panic followed by the rebellions of 1837–38 ruined early railroad plans and retarded the economic growth of the area for a decade. By the 1850s, however, renewed railway construction provided a stimulus to immigrant workers and the arrival of the Great Western Railroad gave Windsor new importance as the premier rail crossing to the United States along the New York–Chicago corridor. Other railway lines reached Windsor in the 1880s, all seeking river outlets and ferry connections with the United States. In 1882, the Grand Trunk took over the Great Western; a year later the Canada Southern shifted its operations from Amherstburg to Windsor (Essex Cutoff) and the Canadian Pacific Railway, Canada's transcontinental line, arrived before the end of the decade. The municipality achieved city status in 1892 — the community had arrived and awaited the new century with anticipation and optimism. It could expect to garner its share of immigrants to the New World seeking opportunities and new lives. Three border communities with nearly contiguous boundaries — Sandwich, Windsor, and Walkerville — were soon to be joined by a fourth, Ford City. Together, the Border Cities constituted a formidable urban entity by the beginning of the twentieth century.

From earliest times, the region had hosted a diverse population. The first inhabitants were Native peoples, followed by pioneer French Canadians. Fur traders and merchants of many nationalities worked closely with the military contingents, French or British, who were established at Fort Detroit. In the wake of the American Revolution and the resulting political division of the continent in 1796, Loyalists from the South poured into the emerging colony of Upper Canada. After 1815, these pioneers were joined by a new wave of British immigrants, culminating in the massive Irish influx of the 1840s and 1850s. As a railway centre and international border crossing, Windsor received a significant volume of the immigrant traffic bound for the United States. Sick immigrants were often refused entry and turned back by Detroit customs officers, dumping responsibility for the problems of medical attention, isolation facilities and general care on the young border community.

The Fugitive Slave Act of 1850 produced new problems and opportunities for Windsor as an influx of black residents, often destitute, arrived seeking freedom and a new life in Canada. Henry Bibb's *Voice of the Fugitive*, published in Windsor/Sandwich during these years, served as a beacon of hope for the oppressed. Mounting Civil War pressures and border incidents provoked nationalist responses on both sides, and for a short time the imposition of a restrictive passport system, but the border usually remained open allowing easy access between the two countries.

The Windsor community consisted of a mix of people; it was a place where all sorts could make their way. By the time of the Great Migration of the 1880s, Windsor had developed sufficiently to be attractive to newcomers, offering a variety of opportunities enhanced by border location, proximity to Detroit, and a relatively porous border. The flat, but fertile agricultural lands of Essex County and improved communication with the completion of the Gravel Road (Howard Avenue) made Windsor the market centre of a growing agricultural economy.[1]

The First Jews

The Jews who came to Windsor from Russia seeking economic opportunity found the community a good place to earn a livelihood. They hoped that, after their initial struggle, other members of their families and friends could be brought over to the New World. Suited for work in a capitalist economy, the early Jewish settlers adapted to the border's relatively open and tolerant atmosphere, even though the language was foreign and the culture and customs were strange.

Windsor had always been a place where people came for a short time and, when possible, moved on to the United States. Some pioneering Jews found that the Canadian side of the Detroit River held great promise and although they had relatives in Detroit, traded there, and relied upon the larger community for services unavailable to them on this side of the border, they settled in Windsor. The evidence about this early period is sketchy — much information has been lost, and unfortunately, primary sources are scarce — but after careful research, a pattern of Jewish settlement does emerge from the scattered records.

Following the death of Moses David in 1814, we can safely assume that no other Jew settled in the Windsor area until the 1870s, since neither local newspaper accounts nor census figures show any signs of Jewish activities during that period.[2] The first viable Jewish presence in Windsor was established about 1878, when the first group of Eastern European immigrants arrived there. They were mostly from Suwalk and Shtabin, and other small Russian-Polish towns in Bialystok Province, close to the Lithuanian border, and the typical pattern of these immigrants was for a few key family members to secure a base in Canada before asking their relatives to join them there. Determined to succeed in the country that had given them the chance to make a fresh start, they and others who came after 1881 to escape the Russian pogroms were a courageous, industrious, and hard-working lot, well conditioned to withstand hardships in difficult times. They were eager to perpetuate the familiar lifestyle they had left behind, so that Jewish nucleus soon transformed Windsor into their own kind of shtetl, making it their fortress amid an initially hostile environment in which differences in language, customs, manners, and dress set them apart from the rest of the population. Most of them readily embraced the free-enterprise system, at first peddling for their livelihood before saving up enough money to bring over family members and friends. They, in turn, assisted expansion into more established businesses. Gradually gaining confidence and status, they ultimately took their proper places in Canadian society and, specifically, in Windsor's big little Jewish community.[3]

William Englander

Although the picture of Essex County's early Jewish settlement is incomplete, the records indicate that the first Jew to make Windsor his permanent home around 1876 was William Englander. Born in 1850,[4] he had left his native Hungary as a young man and, after living in China, Japan, and Australia, had made his way to the United States.[5] He landed in New York City in 1876, boarded a train for Cleveland, Ohio, where he had a first cousin and, after staying there for a while, moved on to Detroit.[6] We do not know

what motivated him to cross the Detroit River to the Canadian side, but by 1891, he was listed in Windsor's *City Directory* as a peddler living at 122 Windsor Avenue. Three years later, he opened a store on the same street and even though the sign above the shop read, "W. Englander Groceries and Meat, Butter, Eggs, and Poultry," he was likely a *shochet*, a Jewish butcher specializing in the ritualistic slaughter of animals.[7]

Since William Englander spoke several languages, including German, Russian, Bulgarian, Polish, Yiddish, and Bohemian, starting about 1895 he also acted as a court interpreter whenever his services were required.[8] Then, in December 1898, it was rumoured that he was planning to run in the upcoming municipal election as an alderman. On January 3, 1899, the *Evening Record* reported that, "In ward three, Mr. Englander, a new man, surprised his friends by heading the poll with a very substantial majority."[9]

William Englander.

Having become the first Jew to be elected to public office in Windsor, he celebrated his victory by attending a dinner that same night and, a few days later, a party at the home of Mayor John Davis.[10] Thanks to his earlier stint as a court interpreter, Englander was well prepared for his new job. In February 1899 he was appointed to the market and property committee, as well as to the light committee[11] and, likely in recognition of his newly attained position, he was also granted a Certificate of Naturalization.[12]

Englander's interest in city politics had probably been sparked long before he actually became an alderman. In the early years, when Windsor was a pioneering community, hawkers and peddlers had been able to walk the streets and roam the countryside undisturbed. Gradually, however, shop owners must have perceived these "outsiders" as a threat to their more established enterprises. A by-law passed three years earlier that required the "licensing and regulation of Hawkers and Petty Chapman and others,"[13] would have had a profound effect on William Englander's own business. Amended on May 3, 1886, it stipulated:

> That no person not a resident of the town of Windsor, and in the case of tea, dry goods, and jewelry, not having a shop, store or place of business within the said town in which to pursue his trade or calling, shall exercise the calling or occupation of a peddler, hawker or petty chapman within the units of the said town, nor go on foot or otherwise offering for sale (etc.)…without first having obtained a license so to do in the manner hereinafter provided.[14]

Englander the businessman should have welcomed the law regulating street vendors' activities. As an alderman, however, his objectivity on the subject was, at times, questionable. While insisting on strict observance by others, he himself appeared to sidestep any restrictions that interfered with the pursuit of his personal aims and objectives. For example, on June 26, 1899, the market and property committee received a complaint that "William Englander had been buying poultry during prohibited hours."[15]

Despite his reprehensible behaviour, coupled with his seemingly less than regular attendance of Council meetings, he was re-elected in 1900 and, during his second term in office, was again censured for contravening the by-law designed to keep "hucksters off the market until 10 a.m."[16] In that connection, the *Evening Record* of January 29, 1900, reported that,

> Mr. Englander was suppressed twice or thrice before but he does not stay suppressed. His latest scheme to evade the law is to make his bargains before 10 a.m. and have the goods delivered after that hour, hoping by this thin device to escape the penalty.
>
> Mr. Englander on a former occasion justified his action on the ground that the farmers were opposed to the 10 o'clock clause. Mr. Englander's error seems to lie in forgetting that the by-law is framed in the interest of the people who maintain the market."[17]

Fortunately, that particular complaint did not reach Council and, despite a motion passed on March 19, 1900, requesting the police commissioners to advise the chief constable and policemen to enforce the hawkers and peddlers regulations, William Englander remained undaunted. In fact, his prominence seemed to reach its peak on April 17, 1900, when the *Evening Record* reported that he had built "a handsome residence on the corner of Windsor Avenue and Wyandotte Street."[18] Still unable to accept "that clause of the market by-law which seeks to retain the market for the people until 9 o'clock by keeping hucksters off the grass up to that hour,"[19] William Englander again was taken to task on August 1, 1900, when the following item appeared in the *Evening Record*:

On a recent market day he approached a youth with a wagon during prohibited hours and offered to buy all the chicks he had. He had seven pairs. The youth demurred, saying it was against the law. "Oh," replied the alderman, "I make the laws for this town; anyway if there is any trouble you just say I contracted for those chickens last Thursday."

The fears of the farmer were allayed by the alderman into carrying away the fowls. Word of the transaction was carried to Market Clerk Lidell, who warned him to keep the law, but many such warnings do not seem to restrain the alderman."[20]

Although Englander himself was never punished for violating any of these laws, he not only joined Alderman B. G. Davis in September 1900 in laying a charge against Wolfgang Feller, a well-known hotel owner, for buying chickens during prohibited market hours but, a month later, even proposed the following resolution:

> Moved by Mr. Englander, seconded by Mr. Blackburn, that whereas the Hawkers & Peddlers By-law has been enforced in this city since the 1st day of June last and no conviction for an infraction thereof has yet been made in the police court, although it is a notorious fact that said by-laws continuously are openly violated by a large number of persons, the Council is of the opinion that the police constables whose salaries are paid by the City are severely remiss in their duty and deserve severe censure. Also that a copy of this resolution be furnished the police commissioners. Carried.[21]

Despite a fellow alderman's attempt, on November 26, 1900, to have the hawkers' by-law repealed altogether, it was amended on February 11, 1901, allowing those who had paid their license fees to receive a refund. By that time, however, William Englander's popularity had waned, obviously because of his double standard of justice. Defeated in the 1901 election, he lost his seat on Council.[22]

Between 1906 and 1907, the city directory again shows him as a retail grocer. However, likely in appreciation of his past public service, and because of his language skills, he was appointed immigration officer, some time after 1913. Probably stationed at the ferry docks at the foot of Ouellette Avenue, he held the post until 1924–1925, as well as continuing as a part-time court interpreter. In fact, some records described him as a gentleman who knew the "Provision Trade for he used to deal in butter and eggs before devoting himself entirely to immigration matters."[23]

William Englander had known Windsor as a small village and had enjoyed seeing it grow. Some people remembered him as a small, rotund, and soft-spoken man with a kind disposition, who apparently helped many people with their problems. Even though he was not wealthy, it was said that he liked to put money aside "for a rainy day." Not an Orthodox Jew, he nevertheless played an active role in the budding community's religious affairs.[24]

William was married to Wilhelmina, née Santer, a woman from Cleveland, Ohio to whom he likely had been introduced by her brother, a resident of Detroit. On December 19, 1906, the couple had adopted a daughter through the Jewish Infants Orphan Home in Cleveland. A native of St. Joseph, Missouri, they named her Rose. Wilhelmina Englander died at a young age and was buried in Detroit. In 1920, her father met Regina Stern of Detroit and after a year's courtship, they were married in her hometown.

On September 2, 1925, Rose Englander became the wife of Israel Milton (Slaw), son of Aaron Meretsky in a double wedding ceremony that took place at the Masonic Temple in Windsor. The other bride was Aaron Meretsky's daughter Lillian. She was marrying Harry, the son of Michael Meretsky, who was her first cousin — a phenomenon not uncommon for those days. On April 1, 1926, seven months after the wedding, Rose's stepmother, Regina Englander, died. Eight days later, on April 8, 1926, her father, William, passed away.[25]

Aaron Meretsky and his Family

Aaron Meretsky was the first Jewish immigrant to come to Windsor from Shtabin, Poland. Born there in 1854, he was the second son of a family of four boys and three girls. His mother and father were simple, hard-working people, who eked out a meagre existence in Russian Poland. That was in sharp contrast to the parents of Katherine Barowsky, the woman Aaron eventually married. Born in 1856, she came from a wealthy family who had owned a tannery in Poland. In 1880, either shortly before or soon after her husband's emigration, she gave birth on March 6, 1880, to their first child, Simon.[26]

Aaron Meretsky came to Windsor without his wife and child. Having brought with him enough money to get established, he did not have the financial hardships other immigrants had to endure. Although he had only a limited knowledge of English, he must have had some education as he could read and write Yiddish.[27] Trying to fit into his new surroundings, he soon decided to change his first name to Joe, sometimes using it in conjunction with his family name, but mostly calling himself Adelman, because he thought it was easier to pronounce and spell than Meretsky. He began to work on his own as a peddler, but also appeared to have been in business with William Englander for a while. He then moved to Wallaceburg, where he pursued two occupations — as a junk merchant in the summer and as a fur dealer during the winter. He also carried on business in Sarnia, briefly returning to Wallaceburg before permanently settling in Windsor.[28]

After being in Canada for seven years, Aaron sent for his wife, Catherine, and their young son.[29] She also must have brought a great deal of money with her,[30] since the couple soon was able to bring over her parents, her sisters, and one of her brothers, as well as Aaron's brothers, Abraham,

Aaron Meretsky.

Photo courtesy of Shaar Hashomayim Synagogue

Meretsky family home in Windsor, Ontario (n.d.).

43

The Jews of Windsor

Jacob, and Michael, and his three sisters — Annie, who later married Joseph Mintz; Gishe (Jessie), who eventually became the wife of Orke Williams; and Ete Rive (Rebecca), who came together with her husband, Max Bernstein.

Between 1894 and 1903, Katherine Meretsky gave birth in quick succession to five more children — Tibe, born in 1894; Harmon Cem, born in 1896; Libby, born in 1898; Edsel, born in 1900; and Israel (Slaw) born in 1903. Being an astute businesswoman in her own right, Catherine soon acquired properties in Windsor, including seven houses on Mercer Street; she and her family lived in one of them, while a second became the home of her parents.[31]

Aaron established a lucrative junk business in Windsor and became a wealthy man.[32] In his mid-fifties, he began to take an interest in municipal affairs. Having announced his intention to run as an alderman in the 1910 election, he conducted an active campaign and won a seat on Windsor's City Council.[33] Supported by Mayor Hanna, he was immediately appointed to the Board of Public Works, as well as to the fire and parks committees.[34] The *Evening Record* gave the following colourful account of the first session attended by Alderman Meretsky:

> The manner in which the business of the evening was dispatched, the newly elected Alderman will give the city a good and business-like administration. Mayor Hanna was in exceptionally good humour and radiated cheerfulness everywhere. Ald. Meretsky and the Mayor seemed to be getting along famously. The mayor asked Meretsky to fill the big leather-backed chair on the dais during part of the reading of a by-law. Meretsky was somewhat backward in coming. The 1911 City Council got fairly underway last night at its meeting in the City Hall chambers and, judging from the forward, and explained that he was "green at the business," but he finally took the throne, with Mayor Hanna nearby to coach him on

"council etiquette." Meretsky was loudly applauded when he took his seat in the mayoralty chair.[sic]

Alderman Aaron Meretsky is one of the leaders in Windsor's Jewish Colony, and is full of native shrewdness. He is said to own about 20 houses in the city, and gives his business as a real estate man.[35]

Described by the local newspaper as a man who spoke "at a rate of 300 words a minute,"[36] Aaron became known for his "joking" manner, despite the fact that he sometimes appeared dogmatic, strong-willed, and opinionated during Council meetings. Partly because of his charismatic personality, he subsequently received several other political appointments, including the chairmanship of the committee that selected the members for the Board of Health. Supporting among others, such amendments as making New Year's Day the official date for municipal election, and establishing six wards instead of four, he voted against withholding a billiard license to a local business, despite complaints from neighbours. Not afraid to tackle controversial issues, he took a strong position on a matter concerning payment of certain rental fees. That brought him into conflict with a Mr. Applebe whom he accused of driving thirty families out of Windsor by serving the needs of the Erie Tobacco Company. The ensuing violent argument between the two gentlemen received the following coverage in the June 20, 1911, issue of the *Evening Record*:

> After the county buildings question had been dealt with, Ald. Meretsky repaired to the lobby. Later, Mr. Applebe came out. He approached Mr. Meretsky and was about to reprimand him for incivility when a near fight seemed in order as discussion became snappy." I'm sorry, you're not a young man or I'd certainly trim you," said Mr. Applebe. "Alright, come ahead now.

Just drop that cane and I'll break every bone in your body. I'm right here with the goods and if ever I got my hand on your throat I would pity you," replied Meretsky. "You've got a few dollars, but what did you ever do for Windsor? How much did you ever give for charity?"

Meretsky finally went back and took his seat in the council chamber. He was welcomed by much laughter and apparently felt himself the hero of the hour.[37]

However, it was Aaron Meretsky's avid concern for local small businesses that prompted him to urge City Council to take more interest in street maintenance, including the construction of curbs on the south side of Pitt Street between Windsor Avenue to Market Lane. In July 1911, he presented five other petitions for street paving and sewers. A month later, while chastising a fellow council member for objecting to the payment of $35 to cover the travel expenses for someone who wanted to attend a convention, Meretsky quipped,

> That's all right...we all know you are an employee of the Railway and get passes whenever you want to travel. You have just returned from a trip to Toronto and your Railroad fare didn't cost you a cent. When the question of granting the Windsor and North Essex Agricultural Society a per grant of $3,000 with which to erect fair buildings came up, you were right there in supporting it.[38]

Stories were told about Aaron Meretsky falling asleep during Council sessions and, even though he missed quite a few around the 1911 High Holiday season, he was present and paying attention when the time came to announce his intentions to again run in the next election.[39] Once nominated, he appealed to his constituents to vote for a candidate who stood for the people's rights and was progressive enough to support certain worthwhile building projects.[40] Yet he was frugal enough to oppose expenditures he considered unnecessary, such as the $17,000 earmarked for some fire hall equipment.[41]

A Liberal Party supporter who had also sat on the dais at a Conservative Party convention, Aaron Meretsky handily won his City Council seat. Mayor Hanna, also re-elected by a big plurality, immediately appointed him to the fire and light committee, as well as making him chairman of the market and property committee.[42] Regrettably, the mayor died early in 1912, leaving a big gap in Windsor's political hierarchy.

Meretsky continued to make strides promoting Windsor as a good place for industry to grow by supporting motions such as granting bonuses to companies interested in locating there. In his attempt to improve the market, he proposed that a new building be erected. However, to make the project financially more viable, he suggested to the police commissioner that, while the market would be housed on the ground floor, the upper level could be used for a new police headquarters. In that connection, the *Evening Record* carried the following report on the front page of its July 20, 1912 edition:

> I am going to try and have a fine building put up, one that will be a credit to the city of Windsor," stated Ald. Meretsky. "I would like to see a market building here as good as they have in Chatham, or better. If I can get the council to back me up, I will arrange for a building with police cells in the basement and a police court room upstairs for the magistrate. The cells over at the city hall are in no condition for anybody. It is not right to ask our Police Department to remain in that place. The Chief and his men should have decent accommodation. As things are now, they are cramped for room and vermin play tag with them.
>
> Then, the magistrate is not satisfied with conditions in the police courtroom,

also in the basement. The air is damp and the ventilation is not as good as it might be. We ought to provide the right kind of accommodation for our officials.[43]

Although Meretsky's market concept was rejected, his civic pride emerged in a number of other ways. He requested that repairs be made to the City Hall, that more money be spent on paving and curbing streets, that the water main be extended, and that the city help finance projects such as Emancipation Day celebrations. On the other hand, he showed displeasure with aldermen who used municipal funds to finance out-of-town excursions that were not entirely in the public interest. He himself felt uncomfortable about charging his own trips to the public purse unless they led to the growth and development of his city.[44] At one point in his colourful career, he even introduced a motion for a by-law whereby a $100 license fee would be imposed on any theatre proprietor who refused admission to children under 15 years of age — an unusual proposal believed to have been the result of an argument Aaron had had with his son Simon who, by then, owned all the movie houses in the city.[45]

Meretsky lost the 1913 election but he regained his seat the following year.[46] Named to a committee specially set up to administer a $1,000 relief program for the unemployed and starving people of Marion Avenue, he also was reappointed to the public works, fire, and market committees.[47] Since a new market remained his favourite project, he promoted another by-law that would authorize expenditure of $75,000 for a new building, arguing that the ultimate profits and receipts from such a venture would cover all construction costs. Well received by the public, the proposal was temporarily pre-empted by other issues, and eventually dropped altogether in favour of a new City Hall.[48] Undaunted by the setback, Meretsky championed other projects that could help the local business community and improve conditions in the city. Opposing the early-closing law for shops and trying to enforce licensing of all wholesale meat dealers, he even attempted to stop the use of American-made baskets in the market.

In December 1914, Aaron Meretsky began to campaign for re-election. Despite attempts to publicize his achievements on a far more grandiose scale than before, he was defeated by Alderman William Weir.[49] Yet, his political career was far from over. Relying on his ability to stay on as parks commissioner, a position he continued to fill intermittently until one year before his death, he not only sponsored a plan for a municipal golf course, but also actively promoted other recreational facilities, as well as ways to beautify the town.

Those interests formed the major part of Aaron Meretsky's contributions to the City of Windsor. A highly visible and influential member of both the outer circle — city government — and of the Jewish community, Meretsky was a portly man, whose manners, apparently, were quite crude. Whatever he lacked in social graces, he made up with his willingness to help others. Apart from performing numerous charitable acts, he participated in the affairs of Windsor's first synagogue and, even before becoming its president, liked to share with its members the warm and familiar Sabbath and holiday observances they all had enjoyed in the old country. There is no doubt that he passed on to children his love for Jewish tradition as well as his social conscience, since they all became respected members of the Windsor community.

Abraham, Jacob, and Michael Meretsky

Abraham, Aaron Meretsky's older brother, stayed in Windsor only for a short while. He then moved to Detroit, where he worked as a tailor. Little is known about him, except that he arrived at Aaron's house every Friday afternoon to spend the Sabbath with him and his family. On those occasions, the two brothers, apparently often shared a bottle of whiskey.

According to some newspaper articles, Aaron's brother Jacob, who was five years older than he, had arrived in Windsor as early as 1875. However, it is more likely that he came later than Aaron.[50] He first ran a boarding house, maintaining a "bottle" yard at the same time, while his later business ventures seemed to have included the buying and selling of real estate.[51] In 1909, he also tried his luck in city politics, but failed in his bid to get elected.

Jacob and his wife, Shaney (Jenny), née Doniel, whom he had married in the old country, had eight children — Herman, Fanny, David, Bella, Libby, Clara, Peter, and another offspring who had died in early childhood. Herman, the eldest, born in 1878, eventually opened a furniture store on Pitt Street; he died in 1932. Fanny married Gilbert Weingarden in 1896, later divorcing him to become the wife of a man by the name of Komar. [52] David, the second son of Jacob Meretsky, was born in 1884, attended medical school but never completed his studies. He went into business in 1903 and later became president of Meretsky & Gitlin, a firm that had started as a small second-hand store.[53] David married Max Bernstein's daughter, Goldie, and they adopted two children[54] — Jerry, a son, about whom nothing is known, and Lillian, a daughter, who was married twice — first, to a Dr. J. R. Rogin and then to a Mr. Ouellette. Jacob and Jenny's daughter, Bella, married Isaac Weingarden. Libby became the wife of Joshua Gitlin, Clara that of a Mr. Gutenberg from Detroit and, their youngest son, Peter, born in 1880, became a peddler at the age of 16. Jacob Meretsky died in 1925.[55]

Aaron Meretsky's brother, Michael, born in Sztabin in 1873, came to Windsor in the 1890s. At first, he made his living as a peddler and then went into the scrap iron business. In the 1920s, he was made a county police constable. Having married Rachael Kahn of Bay City, Michigan in 1893, Michael and his wife became the parents of four daughters (Libby, Rhea, Rose, and Freda) and two sons (Harry and I. Bert). Rhea married Milton Simon, who died when he was 49 years old. Freda, born in 1909, became the wife of Edward Shonberg; she died at age 54. Rose was married to Cyrus Glass. I. Bert married Freda Cohen, and as noted earlier, brother Harry became the husband of Lillian, the daughter of his uncle Aaron.

Max Bernstein and His Family

Another early Jewish immigrant from Sztabin was Max Bernstein. He and his wife Ete Rive (Rebecca), Aaron Meretsky's sister, arrived in Windsor some time before 1894, together with their two children — 4-year-old Albert and 3-year-old Sarah. In Russian Poland, Max had been a Hebrew scholar. However, since he could not continue his rabbinical studies in Windsor, he became a junk dealer. Max's original family name had been Benstein. Soon after setting up residence at 24 Assumption Street, he added the "r" to it to avoid being confused with his first cousin Eli Herman Benstein, who often mistakenly received merchandise addressed to Max.[56] After a while, Max must have felt that business opportunities would be better south of the border. He moved his family to Detroit, only to come back to Canada some time later and, although we do not know the exact date of their return, it must have been before August 24, 1887, since on that day the birth of their daughter Goldie was recorded in Sandwich, Ontario — the second Jewish child to be born in the Windsor area after Moses Eleazer David.[57] Max and Rebecca had five more children. Peter, also born in Sandwich, arrived on August 22, 1888 and eventually became a dentist. A third son, Michael, died when he was just 4 years old and, another daughter, Libby, passed away on September 30, 1904, at the young age of 14; she was buried at the Beth Olam Cemetery in Detroit. Another son, Monte, later became a physician, and Belle, their youngest, eventually married Dr. Eli Levin.[58]

Max Bernstein's brothers Nathan, Shel, and Tevia and his sisters, Rifka and Chankie, also came to Windsor. Nothing is known about Shel and Tevia. However, Nathan's name appears in the city directory as early as 1894. Their sister Rifka, later married a Mr. Wiseman, and Chankie became the wife of Abraham Bernstein (no close relation of the family).[59]

Trying to fit into his new environment, Max Bernstein peddled his wares as judiciously as his brother-in-law, Aaron Meretsky. Although he failed to have the financial success some of his other brethren eventually reaped, he plodded along and, thanks to the strong identity he had gained as a Jew and as a respected member of his community, he apparently led a rewarding life.

Eli Herman Benstein

Eli Herman Benstein, Max Bernstein's cousin, did not come from Shtabin. Born in 1865 in the then-Polish town of Grodno, Russian Poland, he was the son of Itzchak Benstein and his wife, whose first name is unknown but whose maiden name was Teplitz. Neither they nor their son Edsel ever came to Canada. But their daughter Eva and Edsel's children (Vichna, Sarah, Mary, and Isaiah) joined Herman in Windsor, soon after his arrival in the early 1880s. Eva eventually married a peddler by the name of Philip Fisher. Living at 31 Mercer Street, in the heart of Windsor's Jewish ghetto, they had three sons — Milton, Herman, and Roy — and two daughters — Fanny and Rose. Fanny married Sam Schwartz, and Rose became the wife of Harry Freidgert.[60]

Unable to speak English, Herman Benstein started out as a peddler, trading eggs, produce, and other wares, most of which he would acquire in Detroit. Venturing into the countryside on Monday mornings, always taking along his own food supplies and carrying a pack on his back, he would return home at the end of the week in time for the Sabbath.[61]

Herman did well in business and, in 1891 or 1892, married his niece, Vichna, who was about six months older than he. Since no rabbi was available in Windsor to perform the ceremony, the wedding took place in Detroit. Vichna and Herman had four children. Mary, the eldest, was born in 1890. She eventually married Joseph Becker and they had one son, Edsel, and two daughters — Vivian, born November 10, 1914, who became the wife of Louis Berry, and Leah, born August 1, 1918, who married Albert Kaplan. The Benstein's second daughter, whose name and birth date are unknown, was crippled and lived in a home in Toronto; a third girl died of diphtheria at a very young age. In 1898, shortly after giving birth to her youngest and only son, Edsel, Vichna developed pneumonia and died a few months later.[62]

Two years after her death, Herman married Rebeccah (Rifka) Sarasohn. The couple's extended family included Herman's nieces — his late wife's sisters — who all were married by then: Sarah had become Mrs. Samuel Sumner and Mary the wife of Bernard Moskovitz (Moss). They had two daughters — Gert, who married a Mr. Moss and Ida, who became Mrs. Harris. Herman's nephew Isaiah, who had crafted furniture for the Czar before coming to Canada, married a woman named Jennie, whose maiden name is unknown.[63]

Herman was still listed as a peddler in 1902, although he had, by then, built Windsor's first apartment house. Located at the corner of Pitt and McDougall streets, across from the city market, it was adjacent to Windsor's first synagogue. In 1903, he opened a general store in the same building and, similar to other merchants, chose to live in the apartment above the shop. Since customers from his peddler days continued to buy from him, his business grew steadily. Besides taking care of the small children from his first marriage, Rebeccah also must have contributed to her husband's success, since she was known as a very good dressmaker, who also excelled in embroidery, crocheting, and other types of needlework. Between 1905 and 1906, the following advertisement appeared in the local newspaper as well as in the Windsor *City Directory*:

> Herman Benstein, the only general store in the city. Dry goods, clothing, gent's furnishings, boots, and shoes, groceries, crochet, and glassware, 56–58 Pitt Street East.[64]

Like many other Jewish shopkeepers, Herman was in a quandary when it came to working on the Sabbath. An observant Jew, but also anxious to improve his financial condition, he now had to choose between keeping the store open and transgressing the law. Transgressing the Sabbath raised the ire of co-religionists who insisted on the traditional observance of the Sabbath. They lost two days' income, since the town's Sunday closing regulations were strictly enforced.

Many years later, Herman's son, Edsel, ran the family store. He had married Ida Jalofsky in 1928 and they had two children — Eli Herman, born in August 1929, who eventually married Shulamith, the daughter of Rabbi Morris Adler, and Vicky Elaine, born February 28, 1935, who became the wife of an Avrum Greene of Toronto.

Following a lengthy illness, Herman Benstein died on December 26, 1928. Leaving behind a lasting legacy of loyalty and dedication to Windsor's budding Jewish community, he was survived by his children and his wife, Rebeccah. She and Simon Meretsky's wife, Nelly, died tragically in 1950, as a result of a train accident.

The Weingarden Family

Isaac Weingarden, who was born in Russia in 1872, came to North America in 1890 as a young man of 18. He spent some time in New York and Buffalo, but then decided to move on to Detroit. On his way there, he stopped over at the Bernsteins' house in Windsor, where he met his future wife, Bella, daughter of Jacob Meretsky. The idea of staying there must have appealed to him. He soon acquired a horse and wagon, and started to travel through the countryside, buying muskrat skins from farmers around LaSalle and selling them in Detroit.

In 1891, Isaac married Bella Meretsky and she bore him eleven children — three daughters and eight sons. Lillian, the eldest, born in 1892, was married twice — first to Joe Finkel and then to William Gottesman. Her sister, Anne, born in 1907, became the wife of Jack Greenberg (Greene) on October 17, 1926; her other sister, Florence married Larry Margolin. The Weingardens' eldest son, David, became a doctor; he also fought in World War I. He married twice; first, Rosena Lemle of Monroe, Louisiana, and then Ethel Bress. His brother Abner, born on October 9, 1895, married Esther Bennett. Her sister, Gertrude, born February 14, 1907, became the wife of Abner's younger brother Dan, born on January 1, 1901. Brother Harry was married to Lena Orechkin. Brother George became the husband of Molly Ghinason of Detroit; brother William also took a wife, but her name is unknown. Brother Max became the husband of Dorothy Talberg, and Arthur, born on May 17, 1912, married 20-year-old Millie Berenholz on March 24, 1935.[65]

Isaac Weingarden eventually established a second-hand store, which he later sold to his brother-in-law, David Meretsky who eventually ran it in partnership with his brother-in-law, Joshua Gitlin.

The Kovinsky Pioneers

Jacob, Joseph, and Samuel Kovinsky and their three sisters — Yenta, Lena, and Lottie — were born in Suwalk Guberna, Russian Poland. Although their parents, Frank and Molly, never immigrated to North America, every one of their children did. Joseph Kovinsky, born in 1875, must have learned about Windsor and the opportunities it had to offer from the Barowsky's — Aaron Meretsky's parents-in-law — at whose tannery he had worked in Poland. He arrived in New York in 1887. There he met and married Annie Subelsky. Their first-born son, Simon, died in New York as a small child; their second son, Abraham, also born in New York in 1894, later became a physician. He changed his last name to Kovan and was married three times. It is uncertain where Joseph and Annie's eldest daughter, Lottie, was born. It may still have been in New York or her birthplace may have been Windsor, since her parents had decided to move there in about 1894. She eventually married Ed Wolfe and they had four children — Roy, Morton, Stanley, and Charles.[66]

Despite the fact that the *City Directory* listed a number of Kovinskys, Kovenskys, Kovanskys, and Kowinskys between 1893 and 1894, Joseph likely was the only one to permanently settle there.[67] First working as a peddler, he later became a scrap iron dealer, while both his brothers eventually went into the junk business — Samuel in Chatham, Ontario and Jacob in Pontiac, Michigan. One or two of their sisters either took up residence on the Canadian or on the American side of the Detroit River.

While living in Windsor, Joseph and Annie Kovinsky had eight more children. Their second daughter, Sarah, was born in 1898; she eventually married Dr. Harry Lewin. Their third girl, Betty, arrived two years later; she became the wife of Morris Passman. Their fifth child was stillborn, but in 1901, Annie gave birth to twin boys — Benjamin and Charles. It is unknown who eventually became Benjamin's wife. However, since Charles was killed in an auto accident at the age of 21, it is unlikely that he ever married. Another son, Tonnie, was born in 1904. He married Irene LaPointe, who bore him two children — William and Anna. In 1909, Annie Kovinsky gave birth to Milton; he married Betty Salsky in 1929 and they had two children — Iris, born in 1932, and Henry, in 1940. The Kovinskys' youngest child was Minnie, who became the wife of Arthur Hirschman in June 1928.[68]

Joseph Kovinsky's brother-in-law, Louis Subelsky, also had come to Windsor, some time after 1897. Records indicate that he first worked as a peddler and he later acted as an agent for Stelo Washed Wipers, but also ran a scrap metal and waste paper business, which his son, Harold, took over on April 1, 1923.[69]

Joseph Kovinsky and all the members of his family became well-respected and prominent citizens of Windsor. Like the Meretskys and the others who had come from Suwalk and Shtabin, their transition from the old world to the new had been successful because they had consistently strengthened their family ties.

The Gellers

Not all the immigrants had come to Windsor through family connections. Samuel Geller, born in Kolaby-Brody, then Austria, in 1862, was a "lone pioneer." Having taken a circuitous route via New York, Halifax, and Toronto, he finally landed in this fledgling community, where he became a city peddler. He soon married Mary Borof, who bore him thirteen children: Max, Francis, Edward, Donna, Eileen, Helen, Jacob, William, Byron, Maurice, Milton, Dorothy, Milton, and Peter. Samuel Geller died on October 31, 1931.

Samuel's cousin, Jacob Joseph Geller, also had arrived in Windsor prior to 1900. However, he went back to his native Austria to find a wife, but never returned to Windsor. Another relative of the Geller family was Jacob Topkin. Listed as a Windsor peddler between 1891 and 1900, additional records indicate that he filed a lawsuit against the city in 1895, charging that he had received a short weight of coal. He won the case and, subsequently, was awarded damages in the amount of $60.[70]

Other Pioneer Settlers

Most of the Jewish immigrants arrived in Windsor during the late 1800s. However, little or nothing is known about those who stayed only for a comparatively short time and then left for Detroit or other cities in the United States. Among them was Joseph Mintz, who had been brought over by his brother-in-law, Aaron Meretsky. Working in Windsor as a junk dealer, he and his wife, Annie, lived at 116 Mercer Street. Ten years later, they moved to Detroit, where all their children were born. Their daughters now live in Cleveland, Ohio, while their son took up residence in Oak Park, Michigan.[71]

Joseph Labetsky was among those Jews who also moved to Detroit during the 1900s. However, he must have maintained his ties with Windsor's Jewish community, since some people remembered him as the very religious and knowledgeable gentleman who, occasionally, conducted their High Holiday services. He also must have regularly returned to the farm he owned in Belle River, since others recalled that he often brought strawberries from there to his Windsor friends.[72]

Typical for those Jews who remained in Windsor is the fact that the majority, at first, made peddling the mainstay of their existence. Michael Rosen, born in 1866, peddled scrap iron before going into business with one of the Meretskys.[73] The sign above their store read: "Meretsky and Rosen. Highest price for rags, scrap iron and copper, brass, rubber etc. phone 234." Shown in 1896 as a resident of 50

The sign here reads "Meretsky & Rosen, Richest Prices Fine Rags, Scrap Iron/Metals/Copper/Brass/Rubber." Pictured from the left are Michael Meretsky, Michael Rosen, Aaron Meretsky, and an unknown person, 1890.

Howard Street (Avenue), Rosen moved to 30 Assumption Street three years later.[74] He was married to the sister of Michael Meretsky's wife Rachel, née Kahn. Two of their children eventually settled in the United States — Samuel in Nashville, Tennessee, and Monte in Indiana; their daughter, Sadie, died at the age of 21. Michael Rosen passed away on January 17, 1944.[75]

Meyer (formerly Inegrove) Wine, whose name appeared in Windsor's *City Directory* as early 1891, was a resident of 91 Mercer Street.[76] After pursuing Hebrew stud-ies in his native Poland, he had planned to enter the rabbinate there. However, since it had been his fervent wish to come to Canada, he abandoned that idea, boarded a boat, and eventually settled in Windsor; the rest of his family followed some time later. He married Reva Leah Stolnitsky, who bore him six children: two boys — Harry and Louis — and four daughters. Sara later became Mrs. Blaustein, Mary married a Mr. Pregerson, Bessie became the wife of a Mr. Glick, and Julia that of a Mr. Rabin. For the first two or three years after coming to Windsor, Meyer Wine worked as a peddler. He then went into business with Berman Sarasohn, apparently a relative of Rebeccah, Herman Benstein's second wife. Since he had chosen to use his first name as his last, their clothing store became known as the Berman-Wine Company.[77]

Joseph and Elizabeth Stein, parents of one daughter, were first listed as Windsor residents in 1895. Joseph may have had a sister, Yetta, whose name appeared in the 1891 city directory as a clerk, working and boarding in Detroit. Abraham Stein, possibly a relative, apparently, entered the produce business in 1899. He and his wife, Lena, were the parents of one daughter.[78]

Possibly related to the Steins, were Benjamin and Nathan Kaplan. Although little is known about Benjamin, except that he was a resident of 127 Goyeau Street in 1897, Nathan, born in 1859, is remembered as a bearded gentleman, who served Windsor as a *shochet* for a time. He and his wife, whose first name is unknown, had four children — three sons and one daughter.[79]

Joseph Stone was related to Katherine Meretsky. However, around 1895, there may have been two Jewish men with that name in Windsor. Between 1905 and 1911, one apparently earned his living as a peddler and milkman, residing first on Mercer and then on Aylmer Street. The other Joseph Stone was also a peddler, but the records show that he died in Detroit's Harper Hospital in 1901.[80]

Jacob Brown may have come to Windsor because his wife's relative, Catherine Meretsky, already was living there.

The fact that his name was listed in the *City Directory* as a cattle dealer as early as 1875 again raises the question whether some Jewish pioneers hadn't actually arrived earlier than existing documents indicate. In 1897, Louis Brown, who may have been related to Jacob, was shown as a peddler living at 55 Mercer Street.[81]

Solomon and Sarah Glazer owned a second-hand store at 12 McDougall Street. The September 2, 1893, edition of the *Evening Record*, and the 1894–96 Windsor *City Directory* listed another second-hand dealer by the name of Isaac Jacobson. Benjamin Jacobson, who was working at the Malleable Iron Works, may have been Isaac's son or his brother, since the 1899 city directory showed them living at the same address.[82] Meyer Wartelsky's name appeared in the directory as early as 1900.[83] However, little else is known about him, except that he had a daughter who later lived in Detroit.

These Jewish immigrants were neither saints nor sinners but people with different customs and religious practices who erred at times like their Christian neighbours in their struggles to survive in a primitive community. The earliest pioneers made Windsor their home, established a viable Jewish community for their children and later generations, who still bear their names. Thus the seeds for future settlement were sown by a handful of Russian immigrants who remained either by choice or by stroke of luck. At this point, however, the future of the Jewish community in Windsor certainly seemed full of promise.

Chapter 3
A Community Takes Root

Windsor in the New Century

The first decade of the twentieth century saw active immigration to Canada, especially to the Prairie provinces, which needed more settlers to cultivate the vast agricultural lands. A similar growth also took place in Canadian cities, which were experiencing the twin dynamics of urbanization and industrialization. The establishment of Ford Motor Company of Canada in 1904 spawned a fourth Border City — Ford City — community, which grew rapidly to achieve town status and join the existing border municipalities. The automobile industry was sparked by the development of the internal combustion engine and moving assembly lines, which made mass production of low-priced automobiles possible. The application of these revolutionary manufacturing methods not only created thousands of jobs in the auto industry, but also stimulated the growth of numerous related businesses. Detroit had emerged as the world centre of this new economic bonanza and the Border Cities across the river were along for the ride.

Continuing to develop its position as a transportation centre and border gateway, Windsor's ferry service expanded its operations beyond passengers and railway cars and added both grander, more luxurious pleasure vessels and new automobile ferries. The first railway tunnel under the Detroit River was opened in 1910, and it carried passengers as well as freight. Mass transportation — the ferries, railways and streetcars — were not yet ready to surrender to the automobile age. The Sandwich, Windsor, and Amherstburg street railway (SWA) that connected the Border Cities was purchased by the Detroit United Railways and expanded into a true interurban electric railway by 1907, extending from Tecumseh in the east to downriver Amherstburg. The following year, the Windsor, Essex, and Lakeshore Railway brought Essex, Kingsville, Leamington, and other county centres into the Border Cities' sphere.

The industrial committee of City Council, supported by a progressive Board of Trade, actively sought industry and investment through bonuses and other incentives as well as through publicity and self-promotion. Municipally planned factory districts offered fully serviced properties in prime industrial areas. The Border Cities claimed to be the "Auto Capital of Canada," if not the British Empire, and boasted of its title as the "Branch Plant Capital of Canada," listing dozens of American firms that had taken advantage of favourable tariff regulations to expand their operations into Canada and the Empire.

Establishing a Permanent Community

At the same time that Windsor was growing and developing into a major industrial and economic centre, the fledgling Jewish community was also growing and developing — a process that was not always smooth.

Windsor's founding Jewish community established their first synagogue in the 1890s, but the apparent cohesiveness of the little Jewish community assumed by outsiders, proved to be less harmonious in practice. Differences leading to arguments and lawsuits led to a proliferation of groupings and institutions; with others to follow.[1]

Before 1895, Windsor's Jewish pioneers had relied on Detroit for most goods and services. However, as their community began to grow they wanted their own rabbi, Hebrew teachers for their children, kosher meat, an appro-

priate burial ground but most especially, a place where they could gather and worship together. Since the desire for such a place was very strong, a handful of determined people got together to establish the town's first synagogue.

Between 1888 and 1890, that nucleus of Windsor's Jewish community, which included the Meretskys, Bernsteins, Bensteins, and Kovinskys, opened their homes to provide the initial shelters for the observance of Sabbath services.[2] Two years later, a small house was found on Sandwich Street East (now Riverside Drive), where High Holidays services could be held.[3] Since only the basement was available, the space was soon too small to accommodate the ever-increasing number of worshippers.

The First Synagogue

Windsor's first synagogue was at 50 Pitt Street East.[4] It was in a store rented for $5 a month, from either Herman Benstein,[5] who then may have been the owner of the building, or from William Englander who, according to the *Evening Record* in 1895, was "said to own the synagogue."[6] Since it was next door to the fire hall, we might picture a

Firehouse with part of the 1893 synagogue shown on the side.

The beginnings of business in the Windsor area for the Meretsky family, with slight view of the synagogue in the 1890s.

group of pious gentlemen engaging in fervent prayer, oblivious to the clanging fire truck bells and other ambient street sounds piercing the atmosphere. The unavoidable co-existence with the noisy outside world must have added a light-hearted touch to an otherwise solemn situation.

To make services meaningful, the congregants acquired a Torah that was installed in a makeshift Ark on the upper floor of the building.[7] The only available seats were a few ice cream parlour chairs, which Jacob Geller well remembered carrying up the very narrow staircase when he was a young child. To perform such religious functions as weddings, itinerant rabbis usually were brought over from Detroit. The first of these ceremonies is described in the following newspaper account, dated July 15, 1895:

> A crowd of about 500 people were attracted into the little Hebrew church adjoining the fire department on Pitt Street last evening at 7 o'clock. It was the performing of the matrimonial functions that made Michael Brosen [sic, Rosen] of this city, and Lena Kalin [sic, Kahn, sister of Rachael Kahn Meretsky] of Bay City, Michigan, man and wife. A scene of this kind has not been witnessed in Windsor since three years, and as the little church boosts a flock of but twenty, Rabbi A.M. Ash-uskey [Ashinsky] of Detroit, united the contracting parties.[8]

A year later, the Pitt Street synagogue was already listed in the Windsor *City Directory*.[9] However, anxious to observe other Jewish customs and practices such as having matzah for the Passover feast, the growing congregation wanted it to be more than a place of worship. In that connection, the *Evening Record* of March 21, 1899, carried an item that dealt with the fact that Windsor's Jewish population had been

> made to pay duty on a wagonload of unleavened bread by the local custom authorities…. They claim that according to the Canadian Customs Regulations Articles [needed] in public worship should be admitted free, and they intended to apply to the government for a refund of the amount paid.[10]

Regular Sabbath observances were soon extended to include one Friday night service at six o'clock as well as two on Saturday; one at eight in the morning and a second one at four in the afternoon. By then we know that festivals such as Purim, Succot, Simchat Torah, and Passover were judiciously celebrated at the small Pitt Street synagogue, and even regularly reported in the local press.[11] We can only rely on oral recollections and preserved memorabilia for other information about Jewish life during 1890s. Indicative of the congregation's attempts to engage its own spiritual leader is the following item in the *Evening Record* of March 11, 1897: "Rabbi Weistfield is anxious to know if he can marry on this side, or he has been offered a job in his colony in the east end. Mr. Bartlet is looking up the law."[12]

The following newspaper story confirms that a religious leader had indeed been found by the end of the year 1900:

> Max Bernstein stepped down from the "pulpit" and explained the customs of the New Year. He said this was "Rosh Hashono." It was the year 5661 and the colony here was celebrating the occasion. Rev. J. Hirsch of St. Louis, Missouri, had charge of the services, which began last night. He was assisted by Max Bernstein, president and A. Moretsky [sic, Meretsky], trustee. The congregation consisted of Jewish residents in the city numbering about sixty, including the women and "children of the ghetto." They wore loose-flowing garments such as are pictured in biblical illustrations.[13]

Reverend Hirsch was listed in the Windsor *City Directory* by September 24, 1900, and he likely stayed with the congregation for a year or two. Although it is doubtful that he was an ordained rabbi, he probably served as both *baal Koreh* (reader of the Torah) and as *shochet.*

Other readers may have been brought in to perform such dual functions during the High Holidays. In 1902 for example, when the number of Jewish families on record was fifteen, the Belle River farmer, Isaac Labetsky, preached the sermons at the two Rosh Hashanah services.[14] Despite the fact that he was living in Detroit by the spring of 1903, he must have regarded it as a great honour to be asked to lead the Purim services as well as to officiate as *chazan* at Yom Kippur in the fall. Confirmation that he regularly returned to Windsor to attend to these functions is provided by the 1904 newspaper article, which referred to him as "the Rabbi in charge of the High Holiday services."[15] Other records, however, show that weddings were almost exclusively held in Detroit, with the exception of the few ceremonies performed in Windsor by ordained rabbis brought in from Detroit.[16]

In 1903, Samuel Geller became president of the synagogue[17] and a year later, during Aaron Meretsky's presidency,[18] Rabbi Morris Gitlin was brought over from Russian Poland, likely by the Meretsky family. Ordained in Pinsk, this stocky gentleman, no more than a few inches over five feet tall, became the synagogue's spiritual leader.[19] As well, he served as religious teacher and *shochet.*[20] Soon after taking office a conflict developed between him and his congregation. Despite the fact that its members all had the same Orthodox background, they were certainly not a homogeneous body. By then, some had become so assimilated that they saw Rabbi Gitlin's very strict rules as a hindrance to their efforts to earn a livelihood. They advocated new approaches to the way services were conducted. In view of the fact that this very pious traditionalist was obviously unwilling to implement any changes, there is reason to believe that some of the more intractable members even decided to attend the Reform services that had become available in Detroit.[21]

The discord between rabbi and congregation ultimately provoked internal squabbles that often degenerated into such severe differences that the police had to be called to restore order. Occasionally, these disagreements led to court actions, which were frequently reported in great detail in the local newspaper. In 1903, for example, Samuel Geller charged Jacob and Peter Meretsky with "disturbing the peace at a meeting in the Jewish Synagogue."[22] Fines of $5 and $10, plus court costs, were levied against both Meretskys.[23] At another time, Joseph Kovinsky accused Aaron Meretsky of using insulting language in the synagogue. The case was delayed, apparently to give Aaron more time to prepare his defence. However, during the trial, he turned the tables on the plaintiff, accusing Joseph of eating pork. A week later, the latter was fined $5 plus $7.25 in court costs.[24]

Another case, involving alleged infractions of dietary laws, led William Englander to bring charges against Barney Kaplan. Denouncing him for using insulting language in the synagogue, Kaplan countered by accusing Englander of eating pork.[25] Although Englander admitted his guilt, Kaplan's boisterous courtroom behaviour earned him a fine of $2.[26] Englander was embarrassed to find congregation members present to hear his confession in court. He felt his dignity somewhat restored, however, when he heard that Joel Gelber and Simon Meretsky (the synagogue president and vice president, respectively) had been caught buying potatoes and poultry at the market on a Saturday morning.[27] In the old country such disagreements would normally be settled by a *bet din* (Jewish court) or within the Jewish community and would never be resolved by a civil authority. Taking their disagreements to a civil court seemed an acceptable practice and indicated conformity to their new surroundings.

Not Strictly Kosher?

Just as Windsor's Jewish community had its ups and downs during the pre-1900 growth period, *shochetim* (Jewish butchers) also had a difficult time getting established. They had to find additional sources of income because many individuals either slaughtered animals in their own backyards, or they brought in kosher meat from Detroit.[28] The first was of course illegal and if discovered, resulted in fines.[29]

William Englander may have been the first to offer kosher meat to Windsor's Jewish residents at his butcher shop at the corner of Wyandotte and Windsor streets.[30] Subsequently, others acted as the *shochet* or set aside a portion of their shops for the sale of kosher meat. Since many of them also stocked non-kosher meat, disputes arose between the "real *shochet*" and the butcher storeowners. Not only were they accused of selling meat that was not really kosher, they were also berated by non-Jews who were astonished to be offered food that had been rejected by the Jews.[31] These and other controversies may have persuaded some Jewish women to continue buying their meat in Detroit, even though it was then available in Windsor at lower prices.[32] Nathan Cherniak was one of Windsor's first residents to become a *shochet* and *melamed* (teacher).[33] Having left his hometown of Shiletz in the Russian Province of Mohilev, he had followed Esther Rogin, the woman he loved, who emigrated, with her family in 1902, to New York. When Cherniak saw an advertisement for a *shochet* and *melamed* in a town called Windsor in Canada, he applied for the job and got it. After his beloved had joined him there in 1903, the couple was married and eventually became the parents of four children, Harry, Rose, May, and Archie.

Cherniak saved his money to allow him to bring members of his and his wife's families, over to Canada. This included his wife's brother, Charles Rogin, as well as her sister, Sarah, who eventually married Henry Greenberg. Nathan's brother, Samuel, was the first to arrive. They then sent for their four other brothers and Minnie (Minca), their sister. Brothers Samuel, Jacob, and David, eventually changed their names to Schwartz. Nathan, Meyer, and Isidore, however, continued to carry the Cherniak name. Minnie married Hillel Croll and they became the future parents of David, who one day would be Windsor's mayor.

Nathan now had a large family that included the Orechkins, to whom he was related through his paternal grandmother.[34] A thoughtful, spirited individual with a fine sense of humour, he acted as *shochet* between 1903 and 1914. He lost the position due to a disagreement with members of the Jewish community.[35] Trying to find a new source of income, he peddled a little in the countryside, taught Hebrew in his spare time, and opened a small grocery store on Monmouth Road that was run by his wife. He later had a large shop at the corner of Marentette and Wyandotte Street East and eventually went into business with his brother, Samuel Schwartz. When that partnership did not work out, he joined Reuben Madoff at his store at the corner of Riverside Drive and Goyeau Street. That association did not last either and Nathan again went into business on his own, starting a men's wear shop that grew into a small department store by the middle 1920s.[36]

Isidore Katzman was another one of Windsor's Jewish butchers. He and his wife had come from Mogolov in west-

The first permanent resident, Wm. Englander, standing (middle) before his store and the sign that reads, "W. Englander, Groceries & Meat, Butter, Eggs & Poultry" (1898).

ern Russia. Isidore had been born there in 1868 and Lottie, née Jaffe, was five years younger. They had seven children. Sophie was the eldest and became the wife of Mr. Rogin (likely a relative of Mrs. Nathan Cherniak); two of their sons died during childhood in Russia (Saul, at the age of 3 and Milton, at 11). Daughter Rose married a Mr. Berger, while Sally married a Mr. Matlen. The two remaining Katzman sons, were Abe and Harry, the latter of whom died in 1973. Isidore had come to America in 1904. A year later he opened a butcher shop in Detroit that he operated until 1912, when he decided to go into the wholesale meat business in Windsor. He bought Samuel Abrahamson's Mercer Street store in 1921,[37] continuing as a *shochet* until his retirement in 1942.[38]

Another butcher during the early days was Eric Valensky. Nicknamed "Orke", he changed his first name to Aaron. He and his brothers, with the exception of one remaining in England, adopted "Williams" as their new family name. Born in 1860,[39] Orke married Aaron Meretsky's sister, Gishe (Jessie), who was nine years his junior. Having emigrated to Canada with other Meretsky family members, the couple had seven children: two sons (Edsel and Ben) and five daughters (Alty, Dora, Libby, Edith, and Mary).[40]

Orke Williams was a very religious man. Having been persuaded to become a butcher, he probably was the first to use a section of William Englander's store for his ritual slaughtering and for the sale of kosher meat.[41] Between 1902 and 1933, he lived at 66 Mercer Street[42] (later renumbered 462)[43] and died on December 5, 1938. A man by the name of Lopatin became *shochet* in 1934. Cases revolving around improper slaughtering procedures were again brought before the courts and it would seem that the controversies persisted throughout the 1930s.

The Next Move — Shaarey Zedek

The little Pitt Street synagogue had a property exemption of $1,000 by 1904.[44] Aaron Meretsky had been re-elected president, William Englander became treasurer, and trustees were S. Geller and S. Cohen.[45] The synagogue had

become too small to accommodate its burgeoning population and the decision was made to build a new one.[46] By 1905 Joel Gelber was president and his vice president and secretary was Simon Meretsky. In May of that year, Simon purchased an east end lot at the corner of Mercer and Brant streets, for $900 from a Mrs. James Park.[47] The Pitt Street building was sold to David Meretsky for $1,000[48] and a campaign was begun to raise the estimated $3,500 to $4,000 needed for the proposed cement-block structure that was to be built by Alderman Euclid Jacques.[49] Aaron Meretsky laid the cornerstone and by January 1906,[50] $750 had been collected with the expectation of another $250 later that year. Upon completion of the new synagogue, the builder was paid $3,480. Soon thereafter, a crack was discovered in one corner and the congregation threatened to sue the builder.[51] Shaarey Zedek likely opened its doors in time for the High Holidays in 1906. Simon Meretsky, Aaron's son, was elected president and Isaac Weingarden was elected secretary of the congregation, with Rabbi Morris Gitlin appointed as its spiritual leader.[52] The battles among the membership did not stop. For instance, Barney Kaplan accused Simon Meretsky of using insulting language in the vestibule of the new house of worship. The case was settled out of court with Meretsky donating $5 to the synagogue and Kaplan paying all court expenses. Following a dispute in 1908, the position of president remained open until the election of an Essex farmer, A. Orechkin.[53] That caused dissension again, splitting the membership into two separate factions,[54] one led by Jacob Meretsky, who favoured retaining Morris Gitlin as its rabbi, and the other led by William Englander, who advocated the appointment of S. Schumann, a rabbi from Chicago. Rabbi Schumann refused to accept the position, however, because of threats made against his life.[55]

In 1910, Isidore Orechkin succeeded A. Orechkin as president. Samuel Schwartz acted as vice president, Charles Kovinsky and Michael Noble were first and second trustees, respectively, Nathan Cherniak was secretary, and Samuel K. Baum was treasurer.[56] By 1911 Windsor's estimated Jewish population had reached a total of three hundred. Isidore

Shaarey Zedek Synagogue, Brant Avenue.

Orechkin had been re-elected president of Shaarey Zedek; E. Subulski, vice president; and Joel Gelber, treasurer, with J. Orechkin and Peter Meretsky serving as members of the board of directors.[57] Nathan Cohen, who had been elected secretary in 1908 was re-elected to that position.[58]

Rabbi Morris Gitlin, at that time, expressed a desire to move to Detroit.[59] He claimed it would give him the opportunity to study with other rabbis in a more Orthodox environment.[60] However, it is more plausible that this very religious man decided to leave Shaarey Zedek because he had

59

grown tired of the constant infighting that made solemn worship virtually impossible. He apparently remained in Detroit until his death in February 1931.

The tension among the membership only grew worse with the arrival of Rabbi Gitlin's successor. Samuel Abrahamson was not an ordained rabbi.[61] Some argued that he was no more than a *shochet* and soon raised the ire of everyone. Aaron Meretsky accused him of using insulting language and others strongly resented the fact that he dared to question the propriety of some of the ladies in the congregation.[62] There also was trouble between Samuel Abrahamson and his brother Aaron, who accused Samuel of insulting Aaron's wife, Hanna, implying that she had not been "pure" before Samuel had married them. Subsequently, Aaron swore an affidavit to negate his brother's claims. The arguments between them deteriorated to such an extent that Aaron was fined $7.75 for disturbing the peace. As he apparently could not raise the money, he was given the option of spending twenty-one days in the Sandwich Jail.[63] It is not known whether the sentence was ever carried out.

In 1912 Aaron Meretsky became president of the congregation, with Nathan Kaplan serving as vice president,[64] and Michael Meretsky and Morris Katzman as first and second trustee, respectively. One of the new leader's first acts was to dismiss Samuel Abrahamson, with whom he frequently had rows that were so severe that they required court settlement.[65] More trouble ensued when the deposed rabbi opened a store in town. Apart from defiantly serving customers on the Sabbath,[66] he was resentful of the power wielded by Aaron Meretsky. Samuel Abrahamson complained in the following letter published in the *Evening Record* of November 16, 1912:

> The undersigned begs to say he was Rabbi in the Jewish colony for three years and had no trouble in court until Mr. Meretsky got the Aldermanic bee in his bonnet. He wanted me to use my influence with the Jewish people to help elect him. But because I was candid enough to remind him of his shortcomings from an educational standpoint and not to seek the office, trouble started right there. Since that time, Alderman Meretsky has tried to make me feel his majestic might. I stopped the church business and started a grocery and dry goods store, with which I have been able to make a living. I want to be left alone, but Alderman Meretsky has become so proud that he wants to see everybody bowing down before him or else running away. [67]

Those who had attended Shaarey Zedek as youngsters attested to that confrontation and other unpleasant encounters. In view of the perpetual bickering and the explosive atmosphere that prevailed at the corner of Mercer and Brant streets, they still wonder today how religious services could have been conducted at all.

The same year, 1912, Aaron Meretsky invited Reverend Harris Wolenske, formerly from Great Britain and New Haven, Connecticut, to come to Windsor to perform the marriage of his daughter, Tibe, to Michael Burnstein. Subsequently, Wolenske became the rabbi of Shaarey Zedek,[68] as well as its religious teacher.[69] This scholarly gentleman was warmly received by the congregation and remained its spiritual leader until at least 1917.[70]

Aaron Meretsky continued as president of Shaarey Zedek until 1914, when Joseph Loikrec took over, with Joseph Kovinsky and Nathan Cohen remaining as treasurer and secretary, respectively, until 1916.[71] Also in that year, Cohen and Loikrec were presented with gold medals in appreciation of their services to the congregation.[72]

The Beginning of a Jewish Cemetery

When a Jewish resident of Windsor died, funeral services were usually held at the home of the deceased. In the absence of a local cemetery, burial took place in Detroit. Janisse Brothers, a local Christian funeral home, made all of the arrangements. Following the establishment of Shaarey Zedek in 1906–7, however, religious Halachic practices — practices according to Halacha, the collective corpus of Jewish law, traditions, and customs — could be performed in the basement of the synagogue before transferral of the casket to Detroit for internment.[73] The general inadequacy of these procedures and more particularly, those encountered following the death of a child, aroused the concern of Jerry Glanz, a 26-year-old Russian immigrant.[74] In 1914, shortly after coming to Windsor, he decided to look after Jewish funeral arrangements. He remained the community undertaker until his death, when his son, David Glanz, took over the function.

Aaron Meretsky purchased land for a Jewish cemetery on Pillette Road, in 1917. Although acting as an agent for Shaarey Zedek, he held title to the land for a good number of years.[75] The first person to be buried there was a child by the name of Philip Jaffe, whose funeral took place on April 15, 1917.[76] Less than a week later, Joseph Kovinsky's mother-in-law, Rachel Sobelsky, died. She was interred at the Pillette Road Cemetery on April 22, 1917.[77]

By this time, Shaarey Zedek's tax exemption as a church property was listed at $6,000.[78] The synagogue had no rabbi until 1922, when it called upon D. Golden. He came from Detroit with a seven-voice choir to conduct High Holiday services.[79] In 1928, Peter Meretsky became the synagogue president with Rabbi Ashinsky from Detroit carrying out the various religious functions. In 1932, Aaron Meretsky was again chosen as president of Shaarey Zedek, a post he held until the end of his life.

One Divided By Two — Tifereth Israel

During the early years of the twentieth century, another wave of new immigrants began to arrive in Windsor. While the Jewish pioneers welcomed those to whom they were related, they ultimately came into conflict with those who had no such ties. The rift that developed between these two Jewish factions was mainly due to disagreements regarding the leadership of Shaarey Zedek.[80] To the one clique belonged those families who by then had become more affluent merchants (the Meretskys, Kovinskys, Bernsteins, Bensteins, Gellers, etc.). They saw themselves as the backbone of the Jewish community. Despite the fact that they originally had come from the same part of the world and had the same Orthodox background, they wanted their religious services to follow less stringent patterns. The other group (led by such newcomers as the Orechkins and Katzmans) not only favoured preserving the traditions and day-to-day practices they had so recently left behind, they also resented the fact that the members of the more established families continued to retain all the important synagogue positions.[81] Honours were only passed around to those considered of equal status. The clash between these two opposing factions came to a head in 1914, the year Aaron Meretsky was re-elected president. Since the members could not resolve their differences and no consensus was reached, the Orechkin-Katzman clan decided to break away from Shaarey Zedek and form their own congregation. The outcome was the creation of Tifereth Israel, the synagogue was also known as "the Katzman Shul." Nathan Orechkin was elected as the first president, B. Pazner as treasurer, M. Katzman and S. Mossman as trustees, and Samuel Abrahamson as secretary. The latter may have attended services at Shaarey Zedek until 1914 and was listed as its rabbi during the next two years, even though, in the meantime, he had become an active member of the splinter group.

In 1919, the new Tifereth Israel[82] moved into a small bungalow-style building at 48 Mercer Street, only a few doors from Shaarey Zedek.[83] The new quarters were listed with a church property tax exemption of $2,500.[84] The property had an outhouse in the backyard,[85] but the house had only one room on the ground floor, with neither basement nor attic.[86] It was difficult to convert this to a suitable Orthodox place of worship, where men and women could not sit together. After installing the Holy Ark, the room was partitioned so that the men would face the Ark for prayers. The women, who could only enter through the back door, were relegated to a space behind the Ark, where they watched the proceedings through a narrow opening no more than one foot wide.[87] The Orthodox services conducted by the butcher Orke Williams were typically lengthy and the children were permitted to leave the synagogue, rather than having to sit still until the bitter end. Some people clearly remembered playing football and other games on the street outside, or in nearby backyards, while their fathers continued to daven (worship) inside.[88] Tifereth Israel closed around 1925. The building remained vacant for many years until it was re-opened as a mikvah (ritual bathhouse).

While their influence and affluence was increasing, the difficulties between Jews continued throughout the decades of the twentieth century. But the beginning of a permanent settlement began with the establishment of the first seeds of religious life.

Tifereth Israel Synagogue.

The Path Toward Maturity

Statistics clearly indicate that Windsor's total population had surpassed the 12,000-mark by the third quarter of 1901.[89] Accounts regarding the number of its Jewish inhabitants, however, are conflicting, varying somewhere between 132 and 200 in 1900, but reaching 300 in 1911[90] — a marked increase from the sixteen listed by the 1891 census.

Due to Essex County's industrial and agricultural expansion during the first decade of the twentieth century, those Jews who had made Windsor their permanent home had also attained a marked degree of economic stability. Many former peddlers had become respected members of the community, some as well-to-do shopkeepers, while a large number had found prosperity in buying and selling junk. They included Aaron Meretsky,[91] his brother, Jacob, and his son, Simon;[92] Michael Rosen, who had moved from peddling to junk in 1906,[93] and the Kovinsky brothers — Joseph, Jacob, and Samuel[94] — who had gone into the business shortly after 1900. Max Bernstein, who had been a junk and scrap-iron dealer before the turn of the century, in 1904 became the manager of R. Bernstein and Sons — a firm named after his wife, Rebecca, and their son Albert.[95]

William Englander was still operating his grocery business at 122 Windsor Avenue.[96] Former peddler, Herman Benstein, who had purchased Charles Hawkins' grocery store at No. 54 Pitt Street, at the corner of McDougall in February 1902,[97] two years later acquired the two adjacent locations at Nos. 56 and 58 Pitt Street. He subsequently turned these acquisitions into a general department store.[98]

Even before the turn of the century, other former peddlers, including Solomon Glazer[99] and Isaac and Benjamin Jacobson become second-hand dealers.[100] Isaac Weingarden, the first to open a business of this type in Sandwich, started another one, known as "The Model Store," in 1905,[101] while Schwartz and Cherniak operated a clothing business at 31 Sandwich Street West.[102] Samuel K. Baum and his brother-in-law, Ben Brody had opened a home furnishing business in 1904.[103] Using such ingenious promotional methods as offering a fan to every lady who visited their shop,[104] they managed to improve their enterprise sufficiently to allow them to take over an entire building complex eight years later.[105] Jacob Meretsky's son, David, also thrived. He publicized his shop by placing advertisements such as the following in the *Evening Record*: "Laurentian Stoves and Ranges are the best. Old Stoves Bought, Sold and in exchange — David Meretsky, 51 1/2 Pitt Street East. Opposite Market Square."[106]

By 1910, those Jews who had been junk or second-hand dealers ten years earlier, were also becoming specialized. Jacob Schwartz's store on Goyeau Avenue started selling hay, straw, wood, and coal,[107] and Kovinsky & Company added coal and wood to its retail operation. Joseph Loikrec began to make boots and shoes on Mercer Street. Benstein and Sarasohn's general store on Pitt Street East enlarged its premises and added boots, shoes, clothing, china, and dry goods to its grocery stocks.[108] Schwartz and Kaplan opened a shop at 82–84 Wyandotte Street West,[109] and Samuel Schwartz began operations on Glengarry Avenue.[110] While Jacob and Simon Meretsky continued to sell junk,[111] David Meretsky went into the carpet and house furnishing business together with Joel Gelber, a newcomer.[112]

Since conditions in Eastern Europe had further deteriorated, a new group of Russian-Polish Jewish immigrants began to arrive in Windsor during the early years of the twentieth century. While their own, now better established brethren, reluctantly accepted them, they were spurned by the town's Christian inhabitants who, already feeling uneasy about the ever-increasing presence of minorities from many different lands, were afraid they eventually might deprive them of their jobs. Anyway, knowing little about "Hebrew" habits and customs, they were partially amused by these Jewish newcomers' strange dress and language but found their lifestyle totally bewildering.[113] Since they did not know what to make of them, they, ultimately, lumped them together with the Blacks and Chinese, who earlier had settled in Windsor.[114]

The so-called "Jewish Colony" was located in an area bounded by Mercer, Pitt, and Assumption streets, close to the old Market Square in the eastern part of town, a few blocks from the Detroit River. Individuals familiar with that part of Windsor, remember it as a very rough neighbourhood, where everything was in constant turmoil, where life may have provided a degree of camaraderie, but was not without its tensions. Since the people were living in very crowded conditions, and everyone had to struggle hard to earn a meagre livelihood, tempers often flared and fights were the order of the day.[115]

It would be foolish to imply that the Jews among them were saints, even though the majority, ultimately, became good citizens. They not only argued among themselves, but also had squabbles with their Christian neighbours, who, at times, would take them to court, mostly for insignificant infractions.[116] The Jews, in turn, would launch legal actions against them, frequently to claim damages, but often just to air their grievances against large firms who, they felt, had done them harm.[117] As many of them spoke little or no English, they likely were glad to avail themselves of the services court interpreter William Englander had to offer.[118]

These court appearances were not restricted to new immigrants. Even the most established citizens would go before the judge, since the Jewish general thinking seemed to have been that legal action would redress all errors, and winning the case would further elevate his standing in the community. The court, therefore, became the battleground for all forms of retribution. Although these lawsuits mostly dealt with minor and inconsequential violations, and routinely could be resolved by a magistrate, they were taken very seriously by those who felt their honour had been scarred, if for no other reason than the blatant notoriety they seemed to evoke.[119]

However, because of their frequency, the local press usually made sport of these cases, considering them a form of entertainment. Yet, when reporting those involving Jews and Blacks, they would emphasize both the plaintiff's and the defendant's race and colour in the most derogatory terms while, at the same time, failing to mention these individuals' names.[120] The importance of a given situation was, therefore, minimized, since a charge dealing with smuggling or petty theft, generally, was described as something that had been done "both to and by Jews."

The most unfortunate cases were those pitting Jew against Jew. Usually involving suits for damages, thefts, false claims, breaches of contract, broken promise, domestic strife, and assault charges, they also included operating without a proper license, violating an existing by-law, underselling goods, or such lesser offences as mud slinging and using insulting language. Among those who, periodically, appeared in these court battles were such prominent Jewish citizens as Max Bernstein, Aaron, Kate, and Simon Meretsky, Jacob Goldberg, Louis Brown, Maurice Rosen, Herman and Dora Benstein, Nathan Cohen, Aaron Katzman, J. Croll, Benjamin Pazner, and others.[121]

In addition to violent arguments and fights, there were many other misfortunes that plagued the Jewish colony. Stores burned down or were broken into, people were injured in accidents, some got caught in elaborate and somewhat dubious money-making schemes, as found-ins during raids on gambling houses,[122] or smuggling goods across the border from Detroit.[123] Yet, despite these recurring setbacks, many others persevered, continuing to work long hours to make an honest living.

Some measure of success regarding Jewish legal rights was attained in 1910. To assuage the Jewish custom of drinking wine at weddings, the attorney general ruled that, since it could be interpreted as an essential part of a religious ceremony, no special license was required for such feasts. And, when the minister of customs, the Right Honourable J. D. Redi, decided to lift the 25 percent duty on unleavened bread for the Passover festival, Jews felt that this respectful recognition of their religious practices would henceforth allow them to enjoy more cordial relations with other branches of government.[124]

For the Jewish merchants, conditions had further improved by 1920. In the junk business, many, including Benstein & Meretsky, Michael Meretsky & Son, and Meretsky & Meretsky, had formed new partnerships,[125] while A. Gold, Joseph Kovinsky, and Louis Subelsky were operating individually in the same field. In men's furnishings were H. Meretsky and M. Merson, and Cherniak & Company, who sold boots, shoes, and clothing on Sandwich Street.[126]

Samuel Schwartz and Isaac Weingarden had moved to the same street and, after remodelling their store in 1912, made additional improvements four years later. J. Gelber's furniture and Meretsky & Gitlin's furniture, housewares, and carpet business also grew.[127] Others in that field were Jerry Glanz, who had become the owner of Windsor Home Furnishings; Hyman Greenberg, and Aaron Abrahamson, who had added dry goods to his stock. Joseph Orechkin, and Nathan and Max Kaplan were in dry goods,[128] while Max Rosenberg had opened a store on Mercer Street selling coal and wood.[129]

Retail grocers were Samuel Abrahamson, Louis Brown, Peter Caplan, Abraham Center, Cheifetz & Company, Hillel Croll, Henry Greenberg, Meyer Katzman, Kaplan & Schwartz — who also carried dry goods — the Mossman Brothers (on Wyandotte Street East), Orechkin, Charles Rogin, Sam Samberg, D. and E. Schwartz, and Aaron Williams.[130] Herman Benstein, having added dry goods and clothing to his inventory, , erected a new building in 1917 at the corner of Pitt Street and McDougall Avenue. In Ford City, Abraham Adler had opened a bakery, while Barney Hurwitz[131] had started a men's wear store; butcher shops were operated by Isidore Katzman, Levine, and Enkin.[132]

The following Jewish storeowners belonged to the Border Cities Retail Merchants Association that had been organized on April 25, 1919:

Joseph Loikrec	Abraham Adler	E. Orechkin
Charles Kaplan	N. D. Cohn	E. Schwartz
Meyer Katzman	Baum & Brody	O. Orechkin
Dubensky Bros.	Meretsky & Gitlin	Cheifetz & Co
Hymen Shore	Cherniak & Co.	H. Meretsky
Solomon Samberg	S. Schwartz	S. Abrahamson
B. Bernstein	Chas. Rogin	S. D. Sumner
Gelber Furniture*	A. Weingarden	M. Meretsky & Son
M. Katzman	Wm. Levine	H. H. Samuels
A. Katzman	Jacob Schwartz	

*Joel Gelber became president of the Border Cities Retail Merchants Association in 1923.[133]

Although most of these merchants had lived in the "Jewish Colony" at the turn of the century, by 1920, several had moved into other, predominantly Gentile neighbourhoods. Since many had purchased valuable properties or erected impressive buildings there, their assets now could be measured in ways other than the ever-increasing sizes of their stores.[134] By 1912, Nathan Cherniak and Herman Benstein had each erected two-storey frame homes, costing $2,000 and $2,900, respectively.[135] Although Simon Meretsky could not write his name and signed all documents with an "X," he nevertheless had become most suc-cessful in real estate, owning land, buildings, and theatres — properties individually valued at between $20,000 and $25,000.[136] Others involved in similar acquisitions, as well as in construction projects, were Aaron Meretsky, Joseph Kovinsky, S. K. Baum, Charles Rogin, Louis Kaplan, Samuel Schwartz, and Joseph Loikrec.[137]

In the socio-economic stratum, business and property ownership were only two facets of Jewish successes. Although none of the sons of the early pioneers had, as yet, entered the legal profession, by 1920, a few of them had become physi-cians. Max Bernstein's son, Albert was the first Windsor Jew

Louis Kaplan Feed Store and Coal Yard (n.d.).

to attend the Detroit College of Medicine. Following his graduation in about 1906, he set up a medical practice in Detroit.[138] Dr. S. Gelber, son of Joel, after graduating in 1909, moved to Denver, Colorado;[139] Dr. David H. Weingarden, son of Isaac, joined the staff of Detroit's Grace Hospital in 1914;[140] Abraham Kovinsky, son of Joseph, after graduating in 1915, set up his medical practice in Detroit,[141] while Dr. Isidore Cherniak's career as a physician began in 1917.[142]

The names of those Jews who reached financial and academic prominence have been preserved in the annals of the Windsor community. However, since we have no written records of the many who barely eked out a living, we know little about them and their stories are hardly ever told. Yet, we must not lose sight of the fact that, while labouring on hundreds of tasks, they too raised families to the best of their abilities. Their contributions, therefore, must be measured by their dedication, in general, to Judaism, and specifically to the growth and development of Windsor's Jewish community.

Chapter 4
Widening the Horizon

Windsor in the Era of the Great War

The Border Cities entered the teens with great expectations. An announcement was made in 1913 that Ojibway had been selected as the site of the US Steel Corporation's Canadian plant. The prospect of twinning autos with a similar steel industry made many in the area almost giddy. Through interests allied with the Canadian Bridge Company, the Essex Terminal Railway extended a line to the site and Ojibway was incorporated as a town, the next Border City. A real estate boom developed causing the price of the adjacent farmland to soar to $1,500 an acre. Ojibway lots were sold to purchasers all over the continent; speculation was rampant.

Skilled labourers, organized in artisan or craft unions, were merging into trades and labour councils and becoming a potential political power in the community. By 1918, they would produce a progressive platform, run a slate of candidates for City Council, and elect a third of the councillors. Industrial workers, perhaps basking in the promise of mass production and Henry Ford's $4-a-day wages in Canada, would have to experience tougher times before

taking similar action. Ford's paternalism towards his workers was expressed through a Sociological Department whose investigators made regular home visits to ensure that they lived up to his conception of family values. His English Language School, supplied by the company and staffed by volunteers, provided many new immigrant workers with an opportunity to learn the national language and prepare for citizenship. The village, which had arisen around the Ford Works, achieved town status in 1915 and was seen as the coming community in the area.

Following the war, 1919 was the year of strikes in Canada — the Winnipeg General Strike being the most famous. In Windsor, the SWA (Sandwich, Windsor, and Amherstburg Railway) strike of that year was considered by the most conservative elements in the city as "Bolshevik inspired" and needing the full weight of heavily armed military forces to quell the impending threat to the established order. Gas and Water Socialism was at its height following the creation of Ontario Hydro in 1906 and in numerous instances of municipal ownership of energy sources, mass transportation, and other infrastructure and services. The citizens of the Border Cities voted for public ownership of the SWA, which was accomplished in 1920 under the prompting of Ontario Hydro's "Power Knight," Sir Adam Beck.

The Great War broke out in 1914 and Canada dutifully joined the British Imperial contingent. Windsor's industries provided important war materials such as trucks and ambulances, shells, ammunition, and uniforms. The community came together in support of the war effort in a number of ways: Victory Loans, patriotic funds, and sewing and knitting woollens and warm clothing. Peace brought returning veterans to bask in the heartfelt gratitude of their communities through a series of civic receptions and church services. Canada's new international status, marked by membership in the League of Nations and the International Labour Organization (ILO), had been earned by great sacrifices both at home and abroad.

Windsor's Jews had not gone to war, but the community did their part in supporting the war effort. Of more importance, perhaps, were the consequences of peace. In 1917, the Balfour Declaration gave British support for a permanent home for refugee Jews in Palestine. Zionism had always been popular among a certain segment of the Jewish population and this issue brought deep feelings to the surface.[1]

The Beginning of Diversity

The initial struggles of any pioneering group intent on survival are usually dramatic. Windsor's budding Jewish community was no exception. Its members, no longer able to insulate themselves entirely from their surroundings, had learned to interact with their non-Jewish neighbours. Yet, mindful of their solid commitment to family members and to others in their extended community, they methodically laid the building blocks for a cohesive society.

Shaarey Zedek, their first synagogue,[2] had been the place where they had worshipped together, learned, debated, and often quarrelled. Although it had, initially, served as a unifying force, successive events proved that it was not an ivory tower in which everyone spoke with one voice. If conflicting opinions had brought about a parting of the ways — the emergence of Tifereth Israel as a separate religious entity[3]— that split, eventually, led to the development of numerous other Jewish organizations and facilities that allowed all those able to take advantage of them to freely express a variety of thoughts and viewpoints.

The Importance of Education

Since Jews have been reading and studying sacred texts for centuries, they always have been known as the "people of the book." Regardless of how poor they were or how often the whims of rulers in the various European countries where they tried to settle forced them to move from place to place, Jewish parents always instilled in their children that knowledge was something they could take with them wherever they went. Education was a means for attaining security.

Although these children had attended parochial schools that taught Jewish subjects exclusively, when they came to North America they were compelled to enroll in secular institutions.[4] In Windsor, seven public schools and one collegiate institute existed prior to 1901. School taxes were levied on all ratepayers, with the Protestants paying 60 percent and, in the absence of a Separate School Board before 1901, Catholics were assessed 25 percent, while the remaining 15 percent was borne by the various local industries.[5] Also in 1901, night school classes were started at the Central School, founded in 1871. These classes were discontinued six months later as only 5 percent of all eligible students took advantage of them and attendance was both poor and irregular.[6] The vacated Central School premises subsequently became Windsor's new City Hall.[7]

In about 1905, several new public schools were built, including Dougall Avenue, King Edward, and St. Anne's Separate School. The Jewish children attended Tuscarora, Park, Mercer, Assumption, Wyandotte, and Dougall,[8] and despite the fact that a good number of them were recent immigrants who had just learned to speak English, their enrolment was considerably higher proportionately in comparison to that of the Gentile population. Many won prizes during oratorical, poetry, and essay competitions, as well as receiving awards at commencement exercises.[9]

Although a particularly memorable "success story" of a different kind has been told about the newly arrived Simon Meretsky who, despite his expulsion from school for using bad language, managed to become a wealthy man, most other pupils did very well scholastically.[10] An indication of their intellectual prowess is the appearance of so many Jewish names on honour rolls,[11] together with the high marks the majority received in examinations — the results of which were regularly published in the local newspaper. That these students' achievements evoked a certain amount of envy and anti-Semitism is borne out by the following bold and surprisingly enlightened editorial in the *Evening Record* of June 11, 1911:

President Taft has shown himself a man above racial prejudice by twice rebuking those who have displayed bigoted opposition to the presence of Jews. On one occasion he tendered some peppery expressions on rejection of a Jewish applicant by a New York Club. The president's latest broadside was provoked by treatment of a Jew who sought a military commission and was unfavourably reported on by some numb-skull clothed with authority.

There are peanut-minded gentiles who profess to be astonished at the progress the Jewish people are making and their remarkable faculty for amassing money.

It must be admitted the Jews have solved the problem of taking care of themselves. They are loyal to their race, they stand by each other, they support their widows and orphans, the hand of charity is never withheld, and yet they do not display in their philanthropy the same stupid race hatred that they encounter from the so-called Christians.

The Jewish boys and girls succeed wonderfully well in the Windsor public schools and in the Collegiate. They are taught and trained to acquire just a little better proficiency and just a little more knowledge than the other children in order that when they attain the profession they seek they will be sufficiently well equipped to overcome the handicap of an unjust and unfair racial opposition. They appreciate more than anyone else that nothing succeeds like success, and their success comes because it is deserved.[12]

Most of the written records about pre-1900 Jewish education have unfortunately been lost, so we have had to rely on the somewhat sketchy and often unreliable recollections of a few former students who told us that, since no formal Hebrew school existed in Windsor before 1906, pioneer parents too busy trying to earn a livelihood spent little time worrying about their children's religious training. Apparently, the younger ones picked up what they could at home, while the older ones sporadically attended private lessons given by transient *melameds* from Detroit. Others were taught by resident *shochetim* or by members of the community deemed to be equally knowledgeable.[13] Former students also recalled that regular classes were available long before permanent locations existed. Classes were held in a room behind Abrahamson's butcher shop, across the street from Shaarey Zedek,[14] or in the basement of the newly constructed Tifereth Israel synagogue at the corner of Mercer and Brant Streets. The teachers they remembered were Nathan Cherniak, Isaac Kaplan, Harris Wolenske[15] — who held classes in his home on Sabbath afternoons — Morris Gitlin,[16] a Mr. Cohen, and another man named Richardson, who used to teach in Ford City.[17]

Classes were comparatively unstructured and set up in such a way that one teacher could instruct every age group at the same time.[18] The *melameds* taught all the students how to daven, made the boys learn their *maftir* (Torah reading), as well as preparing them for their bar mitzvah.[19] Since the strap or cane was used frequently, some old-timers vividly could recall the "lickings" they got for failing to pay attention.

By 1914, Hebrew school enrolment had become large enough to warrant more classes. Strongly supported by Samuel Geller and Jerry Glanz, the quality of instruction also improved with each passing year. Since it was wartime, the *Evening Record* of November 12, 1915, made special mention of the prayers offered by sixty Jewish students for the welfare of the British armed forces.[20] Dated December 2, 1915, another item dealing with public examinations, pointed out that the Detroit rabbis who conducted them insisted that all the children translate Hebrew texts into English.[21] Early in 1916, Joel Gelber, Reverend Abrahamson, and I. Rosenberg served as judges at graduation exercises, awarding prizes to Eva Croll, Harry Schwartz, Kate Mossman, Lily Waldman, Ida Snider, and David Orechkin[22] — all pupils of teachers Samuel Landy and Max Rosenberg. In that same year, the students put on a Purim play with Leo Croll, Rose and Milton Meretsky, Ida Brown, Sadie and Ben Baum, and Edith Abramson in the cast.[23]

Sports, Social, and Cultural Activities

Apart from excelling in educational endeavours, the younger Jewish set also got involved in countless sports activities. In 1912, Harry Cherniak won the twenty-five-yard dash and Tibe Orechkin came first in the needle-and-thread race.[24] In 1917, Samuel K. Baum was president of the local curling club and, following that year's cross-country races, in which Leo Croll, Jacob Geller, David Greenberg, and William Weingarden participated, Leo Croll[25] was crowned champion athlete of Windsor, winning the juniors' medal in 1918.[26] As rugby had been a very popular sport by 1916, Edsel

Meretsky became a substitute player on the Collegiate Institute team, while I. Meretsky played backfield a year later.[27] Other Jewish boys, including Israel Modlinsky, David Croll, Erwin and I. Bert Meretsky, and David Greenberg joined the team in 1918;[28] those who distinguished themselves received a letter from the school praising their athletic abilities. During that year, David Croll and Israel Modlinsky were on the reserve basketball team;[29] Croll and David Greenberg also became active soccer players in 1919.[30]

Many Jewish adults began to take time out from work to attend social events, such as their children's piano recitals[31] at the end of each school year, card parties, teas, and dances, as well as the occasional political meeting.[32] While most of these functions were held in and around Windsor, families affluent enough to travel often ventured further afield. When they returned from their trips, any adventures they may have had were usually reported in the social column of the *Border Cities Star*.[33]

Parents anxious for their children to marry used a variety of methods to find suitable partners for them. Although they mostly introduced them to each other at local gatherings, some sent their sons and daughters to the homes of friends or relatives in other Canadian or American cities, hoping they would meet their prospective spouses there. Peter Meretsky's mother and father likely were among those who even condoned advertising for a potential mate, since a notice of that type appeared in the "personal" column of a 1901 newspaper.[34] If these and other matrimonial searches resulted in engagements and weddings, they usually were celebrated in style by the entire community.

War Relief and Charity

Between 1914 and 1918, the Windsor press made no specific mention of any Jews from the region having enlisted in the armed forces. This omission was likely due to the absence of records indicating deaths on the battlefield, although several oral histories have cited the names of Jewish soldiers who served in the Canadian or American armies.[35]

Since aid and general relief were vital during World War I, the members of Windsor's Jewish community directed their energies not only toward support of the war effort but also toward assisting Jewry in war-torn Europe.[36] Having collected money in 1905, when the catastrophic events in Russia threatened the safety of the families they had left behind, they again came to the rescue of stricken Jews in 1917[37] by starting the Relief Fund, of which Samuel K. Baum was a trustee.[38] The Jewish organizations that also got involved in philanthropic causes included the Ladies Aid Society, one of the earliest women's groups. Associated with Shaarey Zedek, and started by Mrs. Michael Meretsky, Mrs. Ruben Jaffe, and Mrs. Rubin, Jerry Glanz's mother-in-law, its members took care of local indigent Jewish families,[39] doing all they could to help them. While under the presidency of Mrs. Simon Meretsky, who held the post for almost a decade, the society also raised funds for the synagogue, as well as for Palestine.

Another organization that looked after Windsor's poor and needy Jews was the Hebrew Women's Club. Its membership, about eighty strong, also gave money to the Hebrew Fund, the Red Cross, and, later, to the Palestine Fund. Mrs. M. Meretsky was the club's president in 1916; her slate of officers included Mrs. Nathan Cohen, vice president, Mrs. Rae Kaplan, secretary; and Mrs. Simon Meretsky, treasurer. She and Mrs. Baum took food and clothing to those who had fallen on hard times, while Mrs. Samuels and Mrs. Janosky visited the sick, frequently bringing them flowers.[40]

In 1917, Windsor's Young People's Hebrew Association organized a tag day to aid Jewish war sufferers. Apart from the City Council, which contributed $300, some of the other donors were newsboys Archie Zeitlin, Leo Dropkin, and Morris Graber, as well as Abe and Sam Kovinsky. An editorial, published in the *Border Cities Star* solicited generous support for that particular fundraising drive:

> Though it is not the custom of the Jewish people to go outside of their own race and ask aid for their suffering brethren, the need of relief for Jewish families in Europe suffering through the war has become so imperative that, in spite of the bountiful offerings that have been made since the outbreak of the war, they now find themselves unable to feed the hungry mouths of Europe who cry to their more fortunate brethren in America for bread and sustenance. The Jewish citizens of Windsor, under the auspices of the Young People's Hebrew Association, have secured permission from the Council to hold a tag day on Monday. It is hoped there will be a generous response.[41]

Windsor Jews also were actively involved in the work of the Canadian Jewish Congress; as early as 1915, Shaarey Zedek had sent delegates to its conventions, and members again met in 1919 to elect those who would attend the upcoming Montreal meeting. Despite charges of irregularities involving ballots cast by students below the legal voting age of 18, the election was declared valid.[42] Isidore Cherniak and Max Rappaport emerged as the delegates, having been chosen from a slate of seven candidates that included Miss B. Levin, Joseph Loikrec, Mr. Rosenberg, H. Zeitlin, and Simon Meretsky.[43]

In April 1920, another drive was organized to raise funds to aid Jews in Central and Eastern Europe. Chaired by Joel Gelber, the local Jewish committee included Samuel Schwartz, Joseph Becker, Michael and Simon Meretsky, Herman Benstein, Joshua Gitlin, Joseph Kovinsky, M. Cherniak, N. Benelya, and Hadassah president, Miss B. Levin.[44] Prior to the selection of the teams who would canvass Jewish as well as Gentile citizens, local dignitaries — bank managers, ministers, Rotarians and members of the Chamber of Commerce — heard a stirring five-minute address by Herbert Jones, Toronto campaign director of the Canadian Jewish War Relief Fund.[45] The campaign ultimately raised more than $9,000. In November 1920, a meeting was held to discuss another drive to raise $10,000 for the support of Jewish orphans. Chaired by S. K. Baum, who also took on the role of treasurer, it was attended by M. Rappaport, J. Kovinsky, and Simon Meretsky, as well as by representatives from various local Jewish charities.[46] Tag days to collect money for starving Russian Jews were held again in 1921 and 1922.[47]

Among the numerous other charitable organizations active in the Border Cities were the Jewish Benevolent Society, which provided financial assistance to indigents; Junior Hadassah; the Young People's Group; Aleph Zadik Alpha; and the Naomi Girls, who looked after the needs of the community's younger members. They all sponsored the ever-popular dances and plays, as well as other social, cultural, and religious functions.[48]

The continuing desire of people to emigrate from Europe prompted a nucleus of Windsor Jews to engage in different kinds of philanthropic endeavours. They not only fixed papers for illegal aliens but, once permission had been obtained to remain in Canada,[49] they were provided with initial living allowances, an action that resulted in the creation of a loan society that became the more formalized Essex Co-operative Credit Society Limited on February 8, 1929. From then on, the Hebrew Ladies Free Loan Association's fundraising activities came under the jurisdiction of the new institution that, setting the maximum amounts of loans and deposits at $1,000, eventually helped the many newcomer families who required financial assistance.[50]

Resourceful Windsor Jews also participated in numerous underground operations. They smuggled immigrants across the Detroit River, frequently via Boblo Island, from where access to the United States was relatively easy.[51] During the waiting period, they would provide these people with food and find temporary lodgings for them, sometimes in the basement of Shaarey Zedek or in the homes of local Jewish families. These covert actions went on for many years, their urgency increasing even further with the onset of World War II.[52]

Making Political Waves

During the war years, several Jewish businessmen became interested in politics. The first to declare his candidacy as alderman in the 1915 municipal election was Samuel K. Baum.[53] Born in Austria in 1881, he had immigrated to New York in 1894. Only 13 years old at the time, he had made his living selling newspapers and shining shoes. He had then moved to Toronto and, in 1902, arrived in Windsor, where he peddled dry goods from door to door. He married Tilly Brody[54] and two years later went into the carpet and house furnishing business with his brother-in-law, Ben Brody.[55]

Although Samuel K. Baum lost the 1915 election, he nonetheless found himself on Council, since he had been asked to fill the vacancy created by Alderman Frank H. Mann's sudden death.[56] Appointed to the finance, public works, market and property, and religious committees,[57] Baum served on Council for the balance of the year, together with the indomitable Aaron Meretsky. Although he was subsequently defeated, he automatically assumed the seat left vacant by Alderman Frank Mitchell's resignation in April 1915.[58] Throughout their joint term in office, the relationship between these two Jewish aldermen was decidedly rocky.[59] They clashed on numerous occasions, likely because Baum, who was in his thirties, appears to have been more progressive than the decidedly conservative and much older Meretsky, who was then in his early sixties. In 1916, after renewing their candidacies, they both competed vigorously, extolling their respective virtues and merits in a series of poignant campaign advertisements. Alas, Aaron Meretsky was the only councillor who was not re-elected.[60] And, although Baum did win his seat on Council and even became chairman of the light committee, as well as a member of the market and property, parks and street opening committees,[61] his participation gradually waned. He withdrew from politics before the next election was called, having decided to pursue various business interests in Windsor and Detroit.[62]

In 1917, David Meretsky, Jacob's son, announced his candidacy for City Council.[63] His aggressive campaign, mounted just a few days before the election, apparently paid off, since he not only won a seat, but was immediately appointed to the coveted light, parks, and street opening, market and property, and patriotic committees.[64] However, unlike his uncle Aaron's term in office, his was quite uneventful. His record showed that, apart from sponsoring one petition for a motor bus line,[65] he backed only one other motion proposed by Samuel K. Baum: to hold a tag day to aid Jewish war sufferers.[66]

David Meretsky ran for re-election in 1918 and again a year later, but was defeated both times.[67] However, his cousin Simon, eldest son of Aaron and Katherine Meretsky,[68] gained a seat on Council in 1918, taking fourth place in the final tally.[69] As an alderman he was anything but dull. In fact, he caused a great deal of controversy during the years he was in office. Although illiterate, this very enterprising young man, who had shined shoes and worked as a peddler to earn his own money, became a committee representative for the Third Ward as early as April 1910. He also was instrumental in encouraging the city to contribute $20,000 toward the purchase of land and equipment to create a new factory district in the city.

Following his election, Simon Meretsky not only served on various committees, but actively supported such worthwhile projects as providing additional funding to the Children's Aid Society,[70] as well as the improvement of the local transportation system. Having failed to get Council's approval, especially for the latter, he did not hesitate to express his frustration in the following passionate letter:

> Editor the Record:
>
> I, Simon Meretsky, wish to state to the ratepayers of Windsor, in return or what they have done for me in the last election, that my whole object in running for alderman was because my whole heart is interested in this city's welfare and the betterment of our citizens. My main aim was to get better street car service in this City. Citizens, you have voted for municipal ownership! The next largest vote was to do something immediately to get better car service at once. I want to tell you that a movement has been going on and we are trying to do something for you immediately, which is what you have asked me to do. An offer has been made to the Council by the Sandwich, Windsor and Amherstburg City Engineer's office for the benefit and further development of our City's interests, and I, for one, thought we were getting a square deal....
>
> Three months have elapsed since you elected your alderman and as yet nothing has been done. I will tell you why. Most of the aldermen have their own automobiles and do not need to use the street cars and they do not care how long it takes you to get any place or whether you have one car line or none. It would be satisfactory to some of them as long as their own comforts are looked after. I want to tell you that I have been trying to accomplish something for you. But no, someone in the present council is trying to feather a nest for himself and may come out for Mayor next year, and the only way to get elected is by knocking the Sandwich, Windsor and Amherstburg Railway. I, for one, think it is a shame for anyone to try to prevent the double tracking of London, Ouellette and Wyandotte Streets as the citizens want it, and it is offered to you. An offer was made to you two years ago to lay a track on Erie Street. The people in the east end of the City could have reaped the benefit of having a car line on that Street. Today we have paid approximately between $40,000 and $50,000 for the paving of that Street. "Well, we thought that Simon Meretsky would do something for us" — I have tried, and I

want you to know that I have tried to do my best to protect the citizens' interest.
[signed] Ald. Simon Meretsky,
Windsor, April 5, 1918[71]

Simon's letters caused a great deal of consternation within Council ranks. Since its members viewed his actions as disloyal and contrary to established rules, they voted to reprimand him. Coming to his own defense, he addressed another letter to the editor of the *Windsor Record*. Published on April 16, 1918, it stated in part: "I have been elected by the people of Windsor to work for the interests of the people, and I can truthfully say that there have been plans lying in the City Engineer's office re better street car service for the citizens of Windsor for the last 3 1/2 months...."[72]

Photo courtesy of the Windsor Star

Simon Meretsky.

By then the adverse publicity, spread by the councilmen who continued to criticize Simon Meretsky's behaviour, had reached the taxpayers. Now wary of his motives, especially, in view of his substantial property holdings, they failed to re-elect him in 1919.[73]

The Ford City Community

Following the Ford Motor Company's introduction of a guaranteed minimum daily wage of $5, a large number of people settled in a new community that became known as Ford City. Jews also had moved there, but since it was too far for them to reach Windsor on foot to attend services at Shaarey Zedek and because they were forbidden to drive on the Sabbath, they began to think about forming their own congregation.[74] Believing that Ford City's burgeoning car industry would ultimately make it the centre of economic activity, they were convinced their Mercer Street brethren would eventually join them there.[75]

The moving spirit behind the new synagogue project was Barney Hurwitz. To provide a suitable place for religious services and a Hebrew school, he even vacated his living quarters behind his men's wear store on Drouillard Road, moving his family to a flat on the upper floor of the same building. In 1917, he became the congregation's first president; Sam Samberg was elected treasurer, and Harry Shore its secretary.[76] Religious classes, attended by the children of the approximately ten Jewish families, were first taught by Mr. Richardson and later by Mr. Perlmuter, with other teachers from Windsor occasionally helping out.[77] The school outgrew its existing quarters after about a year or so. Barney Hurwitz, an influential member of the local school board and a substantial taxpayer, was able to obtain a larger room at the Belle Isle Avenue School, which later became the Riverview Hospital on Riverside Drive until it was demolished in the late 1990s).[78]

The congregation, although still without a rabbi, continued to hold religious services in the flat behind Hurwitz's store. However, on March 23, 1925, Abraham Adler paid

$900 to Nicholas Palahnuk for a parcel of land on Hickory and Charles streets, which he subsequently sold to Barney Hurwitz.[79] Abraham Mechanic was the builder of the new synagogue,[80] a brick structure estimated to cost $12,000[81] that was finally completed for $18,000. In August 1925, the cornerstone was laid for the house of worship that was to bear the name Tifereth Israel, the same as the one that had operated on Mercer Street. Among those attending the ceremony were Judge Harry B. Golden, Rabbi Leo Franklin of Detroit, and a Mr. A. E. Brown.[82] Mrs. Aaron Meretsky donated a Torah[83] and Barney Hurwitz was re-elected president.[84] He, Abram and Fanny Adler, Samuel Samberg, and Sam Katzman became the trustees of the Ford City Hebrew School.[85] Following an ownership transfer to themselves, this property was registered as a religious institution and/or school on March 31, 1926.[86]

Although written records regarding Tifereth Israel's activities are non-existent, some verbal accounts have provided useful information about the many weddings and bar mitzvah ceremonies that were celebrated there, as well as about the religious services that were by then held on a regular basis, led at times by rabbis from Detroit. Other officiants were Esser Kamenkowitz[87] and I. Perlmuter[88] who, together with Hyman Mosner, taught at the school, as well.[89]

In 1927, Abraham Levine became the congregation's president; Mr. Cantor, vice president; Abram Adler, treasurer; and Sam Katzman, secretary.[90] In the course of that year, Mrs. Jacob Meretsky donated another Torah,[91] and a ladies auxiliary was founded, known as the Daughters of Israel, under the respective presidencies of Mrs. Goldman and Mrs. Tabachnick.[92] The social teas and other functions arranged by Tifereth Israel's members kept it financially sound, at least for a while.[93] However, overall attendance gradually declined when the Jewish population moved out of Ford City, which eventually changed its name to East Windsor. In 1934, Barney Hurwitz again became president. Although the synagogue continued to hold services and run its school, the founders' aspirations to make it the centre of Jewish communal life really never materialized. The other religious institutions, which were more centralized, became the established Jewish institutions because of their proximity to the majority of the Jewish population. Tifereth Israel continued to survive for many years in spite of being away from the majority of the Jewish population.

The Birth of Zionist Fervour

The idea of establishing a Jewish national home in Palestine had occupied the minds of World Jewry long before 1897, the year when Theodor Herzl organized the First Zionist Congress held in Basle, Switzerland.[94] In Windsor, Zionism first found expression in 1904 when Max Bernstein, in his attempt to start a Zion lodge, assembled some twenty-five Jews at his home. Following a brief address by a speaker, they elected S. Shapiro as president, a Mr. Barnett as vice president, Nathan Cherniak as financial secretary, and Max Bernstein as treasurer; F. Fisher, Joseph and Julius Kovinsky, Sam Bernstein, and J. Sovolsky became members of the board of directors.[95] Although the lodge invited prominent speakers to lecture on Zionism, its activities were, on the whole, sporadic. The signing of the Balfour Declaration on November 2, 1917, however, provided new impetus for Zionist ideals, reaching full entrenchment in 1918, when three young Windsor Jews — Abner Weingarden, Harry Meretsky, and Monte Rosen[96] joined fifteen other recruits from Detroit, who were leaving to fight in Palestine. A town rally, sponsored by the B'nai Zion Society, was organized to give the population a chance to bid farewell to these local heroes.[97] The following story, prominently featured on the front page of the *Windsor Record* edition of May 15, 1918, vividly described the event:

> Unique in the annals of Windsor's war history was the departure Tuesday noon of the Jewish recruits who are now en route to Palestine. It has been some months since there was any kind of a military send-off and this was a distant event, especially in Hebrew circles. The enlisted men, who had

signed up with the British recruiting mission in Detroit, numbered about 18 and included 3 Windsorites, A. Weingarden, son of I. Weingarden, and proprietor of the store at the corner of Ferry and Sandwich Sts.; Harry Meretsky, son of Mike Meretsky, and Monte Rosen. They appear about in the center of the picture, close to Sergt.-Major Russell, who was in the machine-gun section of the "fighting 18th," and wounded. He was in charge of the party that proceeded from the ferry to C.P.R. Station, acting under orders from Captain Brooke Baxter, attached to the British recruiting mission.

On the left is the Piper Sergt. Dickie, of the Chicago depot, whose appearance reminded downtown Windsor of the days of the 241st kilted battalion. In the crowd that marched to the station were Mayor Tuson, Ald. Simon Meretsky, ex-alderman Baum, ex-alderman Aaron Meretsky and prominent Jewish residents, several of whom had their autos decorated with flags and bunting. One of the patriotic Hebrews carried a banner that read: "For Palestine; Land of our fathers; sons of Maccabees; join the Hosts of Israel."

The spectacle of these descendants of Abraham, Isaac and Jacob going off to war in the year 1918 after the birth of Christ to fight in Palestine for the recovery of the Holy Land left a profound impression in the minds of those who attended the send-off and gave the Jewish boys the parting word of encouragement, "Good-bye and good luck to you." The send-off was arranged by the Windsor Society of B'nai Zion (sons of Zion). The flag of Zion and the Union Jack were presented to the boys with stirring words of appeal for their protection and support. The B'nai Zion Society is appealing urgently to the young Jewish men to rally to the support of the several Jewish battalions that are to aid the Imperial Army in regaining the Holy Land and securing a lasting and honourable peace for the birth place of our present civilization.[98]

Windsor delegates attend the first Zionist Congress (n.d.). Pictured left to right are Aaron Meretsky, Jacob Schwartz, and Barney Hurwitz.

Photo courtesy of Michael Sumner

Photo courtesy of Michael Sumner

Windsor's first Jewish Zionists leave for Palestine in 1918.

Influenced by the events of World War I and the resulting world situation, the Jews of Windsor continued to be inspired by the dream of regaining Palestine as a future home for World Jewry. Members of the local Hadassah group, which had likely been active since the beginning of World War I, not only held dances to collect funds for Jewish war relief but also knitted socks for the soldiers who had gone to Palestine.[99] The Zionist cause was further promoted by the Hebrew school students,[100] as well as by the members of the Young Judean Club, a group that, after choosing Mr. I. Rosenberg as its general organizer, elected Mrs. L. Rosa as

its president, Miss Feldman as vice president, Miss I. Baum as secretary, and Mrs. May Cheifetz as treasurer.[101]

Many other Windsor Jews actively participated in Zionist activities. In February 1921, Oscar Lehrman and Samuel Schwartz were delegates to the seventeenth Zionist convention in Montreal;[102] in May of that year, Aaron Meretsky, Jacob Schwartz, and Barney Hurwitz represented the Windsor community at a special three-day Zionist Congress meeting in Toronto.[103] Three weeks later, Barney Hurwitz was made chairman of a committee that would raise $10,000 for Palestine; vice chairman was Samuel Schwartz, S. K. Baum, treasurer, (also a delegate to the 1922 Zionist convention in Ottawa and elected officer of the Canadian Zionist Organization), and H. Kolkol, secretary. Others belonging to the group were Max Cheifetz, Oscar Lehrman, H. Bercuson, Aaron Meretsky, H. Zeitlin, J. Mossman, A. Abrahamson, J. Loikrec, and J. A. Glanz.[104] He and I. B. Levin, representing the Western Ontario Division of the national and executive committees of the World Zionist Congress attended its Montreal convention in January 1926.

During the 1920s, Windsor's Jewish community heard many prominent speakers. They included Zionist world leader, Dr. D. Rubelsky, who, together with the noted Jewish writer and lecturer, Dr. Levin — considered one of the movement's founders — asked that financial assistance be given to those engaged in the struggle for Palestine.[105] In May 1921, Dr. Chaim Weizmann, president of the World Zionist Congress, and Albert Einstein were scheduled to speak in Detroit.[106] Even though Einstein's appearance was cancelled at the last minute, some two hundred people from Windsor turned out to attend the function.[107] Keren Hayesod started the United Jewish Appeal in March 1926. At its inaugural meeting, Border Cities' Zionists were asked to raise $7,000 to meet the demands for the settlement of a flood of new immigrants.[108] Samuel K. Baum and I. B. Levin were put in charge of the campaign, assisted by J. Gelber, secretary; J. A. Glanz, treasurer; and Hadassah's Frances Geller, the group ultimately collected $6,500.[109, 110]

In October 1926, prominent members of Windsor's Jewish community, anxious to improve their fundraising expertise, invited David A. Brown, chairman of the American United Jewish Appeal (UJA), to tell them about the national Palestine campaign he had organized in the United States eighteen months earlier. Following Brown's talk, Jerry Glanz was elected chairman of the Windsor campaign, with Benjamin Brody serving as treasurer, and Jacob Geller as secretary.[111]

They were soon recognized as competent and dedicated fundraisers; J. A. Glanz became a national director of the Zionist movement in 1927, and on the local level, I. B. Levin was elected chairman, with Joseph Loikrec, treasurer,

and Jacob Geller, secretary.[112] In the years to come, these local drives were even better organized. By 1929, for instance, after David A. Croll was named to lead one of these drives, he appointed various support committees. J. Kovinsky, Simon Meretsky, J. Gelber, D. Caplan, J. A. Glanz, Maurice Nathanson, and Nathan Cherniak were on the finance committee; Louis Kaplan became chairman of the pledge committee, assisted by Jacob Geller, Samuel Harris, Joseph Becker, Robert Cohen, Bernard Kaplan, I. M. Cherniak, and Sydney Nathanson; Rabbi Lebendiger, who headed the programs committee, was supported by Samuel Mossman and J. Gitlin. Also involved in that particular relief effort were Hadassah members Mrs. David Meretsky, Miss Frances Geller, and Mrs. Isaac Cohen.[113] The activities of these and other Zionist organizations further increased during the 1930s: they met regularly and not only sponsored lectures by speakers who could outline the situation in Palestine, but also invited others who, in light of Adolf Hitler's 1933 ascent to power, could keep them informed of the problems facing European Jewry.[114]

The Talmud Torah

While Shaarey Zedek had been the focal point of Windsor's Jewish elite since the early years of the twentieth century, by 1916, Agudah B'nai Zion — primarily a Zionist organization — had begun to arouse interest among certain local intellectuals.[115] Although Orthodox in their religious persuasion, these people were less insistent on continuing the shtetl ideology that had hitherto so forcefully controlled their lives, and more inclined toward the formation of a congregation with a decidedly Zionist orientation. Despite the fact that the Ford City congregation, Shaarey Zedek, and Tifereth Israel all had facilities for training their young, they readily supported Agudah B'nai Zion when it proposed to build a new school. In 1918, after sufficient funds had been raised at dances, concerts, and other social functions, a property was purchased at the corner of Tuscarora and Aylmer avenues that would become the site of the new institution, to be named Talmud Torah. Estimated to cost about $20,000,[116] it was to house a Zionist centre and a place of worship, as well as the school, whose plans, drawn up by architect J. C. Pennington,[117] called for four classrooms with a large auditorium, estimated to cost $35,000.[118]

Agudah B'nai Zion contributed $1,500 toward the school project. Joseph Meretsky personally donated $500. During the 1918 Yom Kippur services, held at the I.O.O.F. Hall on Wyandotte Street in Walkerville, another $500 was raised, with an additional $300 donated for the relief of Jewish war sufferers.[119] Louis Kaplan's contribution of $800 earned him the honour of laying the cornerstone for the Talmud Torah building. The dedication ceremonies held on a Sunday afternoon in August 1919 were attended by Mayor Winter and other local dignitaries.[120] On December 1, 1919, a $15,000-mortgage was contracted between Agudah B'nai Zion and the mortgagee, Robert C. Struthers; Max Cheifetz, the society's president, signed the deed.[121] Present at the official opening, which took place on December 20, 1919, were members of Parliament; the mayors of the Border Cities, F. W. Jacobs, W. C. Kennedy, and J. C. Tolme; and Rev. Dr. Abramowitz of Montreal, as well as other prominent Windsor citizens.[122]

Talmud Torah at Aylmer and Tuscarora Avenue.

The Talmud Torah had been established in part to satisfy the needs of those members of the community who had become fervent Zionists and in part for those Jewish immigrants who, feeling rejected by the elite pioneer families, wanted to have a gathering place where they could express their own, distinctive identities. Although the religious services were Orthodox, the teachers at the school, while following a curriculum that included Hebrew as well as other Jewish subjects, tried to incorporate newer ideas and use more modern methods of instruction than those espoused by the older synagogues.[123]

Once the building had been completed, Talmud Torah got involved in numerous Zionist activities. In May 1920, it sponsored a thanksgiving service to celebrate the taking over of the Palestine Mandate by Great Britain.[124] Apart from hearing an address by a speaker from New York, invited guests witnessed a grand parade of one thousand participants, including Talmud Torah students, members of the Young Judea Social Group, the Junior Judean Club, Hadassah, the Jewish Ladies Aid Society, and various other Zionist organizations.[125]

Indicative of the numerous monetary contributions Talmud Torah received are the many entries recorded in its Golden Book. One of the first to commemorate a special occasion with a donation was Jerry Glanz who, on his son Albert's third birthday, gave $50 — half to go to Talmud Torah and the other half to be paid into the Jewish National Fund.[126] In November 1922, $1,400 was collected at the Glanz's home to celebrate the birth of another son.[127] In fact, there was an opportunity to give money to the Talmud Torah at every social or religious function, such as at ritual circumcisions (Mandlebaums, Mossmans, David Kovins, Harold Taub), and bar mitzvah ceremonies, and many other occasions. Some school funds were raised at a banquet for the Defenders of the Blue and White, and at a Junior Hadassah meeting. It is likely that certain sums went toward the support of sports activities for Talmud Torah students, since their Defenders Baseball Club was regularly able to compete against other schools in the city, as well as hold annual awards banquets.[128]

Photo courtesy of Sara Kirzner

Talmud Torah students.

The Zionist movement brought many prominent people to Talmud Torah. Guest speakers during the 1925 Passover services were Dr. Schwartz and Harry Brevis, both of Toronto, as well as Milton Sumner, a senior seminary student at the Rabbi Isaac Elchanan Seminary, whose topic was "Jewish Ideals."[129] Philip Slomovitz, editor of the *Jewish Herald*, and H. Isaac, superintendent of the United Jewish Hebrew Schools of Detroit, spoke at a library night in November 1927.[130] A year later, Rabbi Leon Fram, assistant to Rabbi Leo Franklin of Temple Beth El in Detroit, spoke on the subject of "Jewish Education."[131] In 1929, when Tel Aviv's mayor David Bloch came to Detroit, he also was invited to visit Windsor. Greeted by Alderman Joshua Gitlin, on behalf of Mayor Jackson,[132] he addressed a Talmud Torah gathering to plead for support of the Histadrut; in response, the community raised over $500.[133]

In addition to supporting these and other worthy causes, Talmud Torah had to cover its own operating expenses. To raise funds it held a banquet in 1928 and, after advising the guests that the school needed $6,000 to meet its financial obligations, its president, Dr. I. M. Cherniak, introduced as the speaker of the evening Rabbi Israel Schulman, who proceeded to address them in Hebrew.[134] Concerts, festivals, and picnics were occasions for similar campaigns, such as the $8,000 drive organized in 1930 by S. K. Baum and D. D. Caplan.[135]

Although Talmud Torah records are incomplete, we do know that H. Zeitlin served as treasurer between 1922 and

1924, that Moss Mossman acted as secretary in 1924, and that Abraham Center became treasurer, with H. Subelsky as secretary, in 1925.[136] Jerry Glanz must have served on the 1933 Talmud Torah executive, since his name appeared as the recipient of moneys collected at various celebrations, held during that year.[137] Records about the Talmud Torah's teaching staff are equally inadequate. However, those that do exist reveal that William Barnett had become the school's principal by the mid-1920s. Former students Edsel Benstein, Harry and Oscar Schwartz, and Michael Sumner also remembered Rabbi Joseph Cross as their instructor during early morning classes.[138] Others teachers were S. M. Smullin, D. Lerman, and I. Singerman in 1930–31,[139] while B. Isaacs, who simultaneously, served as superintendent of the United Hebrew Schools of Detroit and Windsor, was principal of Talmud Torah during that term.

After Tifereth Israel on Mercer Street had closed its doors in 1925, some of its members returned to Shaarey Zedek, while others joined the Talmud Torah which, by then, had become known as Agudah B'nai Zion. The two-hundred-member congregation and its executive, composed of S. Mossman, M. Soble, O. Lehrman, P. Meretsky, and I. M. Cherniak, now decided it ought to have its own spiritual leader.[140] In 1928, therefore, the organization appointed Rabbi Israel Schulman, who had recently arrived from Palestine. However, since they were unable to pay him a large enough salary, he had to supplement his income by operating a small soap factory on Brant Street. Although Rabbi Schulman had initially only been hired for a two-year period, he continued to serve Agudah B'nai Zion for ten more years — until his death in 1940.[141]

Jewish Public Library and Peretz Shule

Between 1922 and 1923, the Windsor Arbeitering (Workmen's Circle), in conjunction with Politzeon, an organization considered ultra-left wing, founded another new school. Named the Jewish Public Library, it was housed in a frame building at the northeast corner of University and Parent avenues. Since most of the parents of the children who made up its student body had come to Canada after the Russian Revolution, their political leanings were largely left wing — some even considered them anarchists.[142] And, since these so-called "Yiddishists" were also non-religious, they were primarily interested in having only secular subjects taught at the school.[143] In 1930, a split occurred in their ranks, with the members of the one faction expressing a desire to separate.[144] They made an agreement with the other faction to receive payment for their share in the Parent Avenue property. Signed by Jewish Public Library president, Charles Rogin, as well as by M. Rappaport, H. Wayne, I. Alexis, W. Bekenstuz, and H. Beren,[145] it relieved them of all their financial responsibilities, allowing the Jewish Public Library to continue on its own, which it did until 1937.[146]

In 1934, after excluding from its ranks the left-wing element, on whom it looked with disdain, the dissenting group founded the I. L. Peretz Shule. The school was named for Isaac Leib Peretz, a modernist Yiddish-language author and playwright who stood at the cultural centre of pre–World War I Yiddish Warsaw. An early devotee of Haskalah, the Jewish Enlightenment, Peretz tempered his secular views of education with his writings expressing Jewish ideals grounded in Jewish tradition and history. Peretz saw the world as composed of different nations each with its own character. His writings were said to arouse the Jewish will for self-emancipation and resistance, but unlike many of his fellow intellectuals, Peretz rejected the cultural universalism of Marxism.[147] Led by Max Madoff and others, the school was enthusiastically supported by parents who wanted a fine, secular type of education for their children.[148] Under the guidance of a Mr. Drachler, their first teacher, twenty-three students attended classes, first in the little house on Parent Avenue and, later, in a double house on Erie Street that had been purchased with the help of the Arbeitering. Mr. Bluestein taught there in 1939 and former students also remembered teachers Mrs. Malke Yuzpe and the short, red-haired Mr. Kligman, who stayed on as principal for many years.

Besides raising funds to celebrate a simcha, the school usually charged a fee of thirty-five cents to anyone wishing to attend their various meetings. Such prominent Detroit speakers as Dr. Hayim Zhitlovsky, Mr. Hershbain, Mr. Vineberg, Mr. David Einhorn, and other outstanding Peretz Shule members gave lectures.[149]

Existing records indicate that the school operated a Mother's Club. Two of its chairmen were Chaver Bogen and Chaver Cheifetz, while Messrs. Madoff, Byer, Gordner, Forman, and Parnes are listed among its slate of elected officers.

The Primrose Club and B'nai B'rith

The Primrose Club began operations on November 21, 1923. Founded to provide social and recreational facilities for Windsor's Jewish business and professional men, its premises were located at 415 Ouellette Avenue. They housed a billiard room, a library, meeting and card rooms, lounges, and an entertainment hall.[150] Samuel K. Baum was the club's first president, N. Rotenburg, the first vice president, and Maxwell Schott, the first secretary treasurer. In 1924, J. A. Glanz succeeded Baum; Robert G. Cohen took over from Rotenburg; Jack Gelber, David Caplan, and Saul Rotenberg were members of the entertainment committee, while Schott retained his post as secretary-treasurer.[151]

Yet, even before the Primrose Club was established, its members had been approached by visitors to the city, who were trying to arouse their interest in the work done by B'nai B'rith, a fraternal organization whose programs seemed more appealing to them than those offered by the Primrose Club. It was not surprising that B'nai B'rith soon became its logical successor. The Windsor Chapter received its charter on March 15, 1925, electing Jerry A. Glanz as its first president. Maxwell Schott, who held the post until 1928, was succeeded by Robert G. Cohen, who served during the 1929–30 term. In 1930–31, Dr. Louis Perlman took over, followed by Mr. M. Silver. Other presidents were M. Levine (1933–34), Ben Matthews (1934–36), Harry Cherniak (1936–37), Bernard D. Caplan (1937–38), and Milton Meretsky (1938–40).[152]

Photo courtesy of the Windsor Star

Windsor's chapter of B'nai Brith celebrated its fiftieth anniversary in 1975. The oldest and longest members (from the left, Harry Meretsky, Robert Cohen, and Maxwell Schott), toast each other at the joint installation of officers. A ceremony and dinner was held at Shaar Hashomayim Synagogue to both mark the investment of the newly elected executive officers and honour those who had built the lodge a half century ago. Mr. Cohen and Mr. Schott were original members.

Around 1928, after B'nai B'rith had established a Ladies Auxiliary, Dr. M. Levine's wife became its first president, Mrs. Hyams its vice president, Mrs. I. Cohen its financial secretary, Miss H. Hurwitz its recording secretary, and Mrs. M. Silver its treasurer. Continuing to further B'nai Brith's humanitarian causes, the group ran numerous impressive programs. [153]

Prominent Jewish Religious Leaders

Before dealing with the major shift in Windsor's religious institutions during the mid-1920s, it might be appropriate to mention the significant roles played by two of Windsor's spiritual leaders.

Esser Kamenkowitz served Windsor's Jewish community as *chazan* (cantor) and *shochet* for more than a decade. Born in Lithuania,[154] the son of a wealthy banker, he was an educated man who had received a doctorate from the University of Vilna. When he came to the United States, he tried to make a living as a *chazan* and *shochet* in various cities. He then decided to settle in Windsor with his wife and seven children.

Well remembered for his beautiful voice, Esser Kamenkowitz was a man of medium height. He sported a moustache and sometimes a beard, and was a little on the stout side.[155] Serving Shaarey Zedek for many years, he then had disagreements with some of its directors, which induced him in 1924–25 to move to Ford City, where he ran a grocery and butcher store.[156] He occasionally led religious services at Tifereth Israel and performed wedding ceremonies and other rabbinical functions in the Windsor area, which brought him into conflict with Abraham Able, another itinerant teacher, rabbi, and *shochet*.[157]

Abraham Able came from a long line of rabbis. Born in Dgisno, Poland in 1892,[158] he had arrived in the Border Cities in 1924, bringing with him his wife and children — one son and four daughters[159] — one of whom eventually married a son of Esser Kamenkowitz.[160] Since Able was closely associated with Talmud Torah, people remember him well as a man about five feet, five inches tall, with red hair, a red beard, a ruddy complexion, and a shrill voice.[161] Although somewhat nervous and excitable, he was apparently quite a pleasant individual.

On December 1, 1926, Esser Kamenkowitz died suddenly. Interviews with his son — who incidentally had changed his name to Sockley Kamin and was the man who married one of Abraham Able's daughters — revealed the near-starvation existence the family had had to endure after their father's death, and how little financial help his mother received from the Jewish community.[162]

That tragic event should have ended the rivalry between Kamenkowitz and Able, allowing Able, who was then only 35, to freely perform all rabbinical duties for many more years. However, on May 30, 1927, he too suddenly died.[163] Although the loss of these two men within the short period of six months left a great void in Windsor's Jewish community, it also made its leaders realize that the time had come to make some fundamental changes in the way their religious institutions were run. One of the innovations they implemented around that time was to appoint one rabbi who could serve the entire community. The man they chose for the position was Aaron M. Ashinsky. Born in Russia in 1866, he had studied for the rabbinate in his hometown of Raigrad, Lonza, before immigrating to the United States. He first had settled in New York, and then lived in Detroit for seven years before moving to Montreal, where he had stayed for seven more years. In 1901, he had gone to Pittsburgh, where he had remained for more than twenty years, before returning to Detroit to serve Congregation Emanu-El.[164] Following Rabbi Ashinsky's appointment toward the end of 1926 as chief rabbi of Windsor, David A. Croll wrote in an article for the *Border Cities Star*, "Since the Jews of Windsor have so far been without any rabbinical guidance whatever, they consider themselves more than honoured to be taken under the wing of such a personage." [165] Rabbi Ashinsky has been credited with founding the Zionist movement in Canada. However, his greatest achievement was likely the establishment of the Pitt Street Institute.

The Jewish community had weathered the storms and dissension among themselves, and had established a religious, social, and educational society. Although a complex Jewish community could not be entirely harmonious, it was able to cope with the demands of the time and to prepare for the new challenges that lay before them.

Chapter 5
Good Times/Bad Times

Windsor in the 1920s

The years immediately following the victorious conclusion of World War I promised to bring great prosperity to the Border Cities. New people were attracted to them because it was inexpensive to live there and their industrial and business enterprises flourished since prices for goods and services were steadily rising. Windsor's population passed the 50,000 mark and its level of new construction ranked second in Ontario. Housing was in great demand; jobs for skilled tradesmen and unskilled construction workers were plentiful. By the late 1920s, the collective population of the Border Cities approached 100,000 and optimists were predicting a doubling of that number.

As usual, the auto industry led the way in manufacturing value and jobs. Two dozen lesser-known companies joined the Big Three and the auto parts industry was growing daily. In 1926 the Liberal government of Mackenzie King changed the rules of the game — the auto branch plant economy that had been built on the reality of a high protective tariff of 35 percent, which made it profitable for US companies to establish plants and build automobiles here.

Such vehicles were considered Canadian and were eligible for inclusion in the Imperial Preference plan, allowing members of the Empire to obtain trade advantages over foreign competitors. As the bulk of Canadian production went into the export market abroad, this was a major incentive. King's government, seeking to reduce the price differential charged to Canadian auto buyers as against their American counterparts, reduced the tariff to 20 percent on the majority of autos sold in Canada. To encourage Canadian industry, especially the auto parts sector, the government set targets for Canadian content beginning at 50 percent. Companies complying would be rewarded with additional tariff reductions on remaining imported materials. Auto employment peaked in 1928. The opening of the Bridge and Auto Tunnel at the end of the decade marked the triumph of the automobile age.

With growing population demanding better health care and education, Grace Hospital opened in January of 1920 and Metropolitan Hospital in 1925. Existing school facilities were strained, and the crowded conditions led to additions and new schools. Kennedy Collegiate opened in 1929 on the edge of Jackson Park and St. Mary's Academy relocated from the site designated for the auto tunnel in the centre of the city to the cornfields of South Windsor, a solitary harbinger of the suburban expansion that was anticipated.

The Border Cities Chamber of Commerce reached the pinnacle of its influence in the 1920s, advancing progressive ideas and bringing prominent speakers to the city. City Council often followed their lead as the Chamber prepared public opinion and effectively argued the case for action. Thomas Adams, Canada's most famous urban planner, produced a master plan for the city near the end of the decade, which made recommendations for such "city beautiful" innovations as a civic centre, tree-lined boulevards, and a city hall square with a landscaped promenade through to the riverfront, where a transportation hub would rationalize all the modes of transportation available to city residents. Jackson Park completed Adam's contribution.

For all of Windsor's positive achievements in the decade, it would always be remembered as a focus for the Roaring Twenties. It was a colourful era, with the city's three race tracks, the Jockey Club, Devonshire, and its companion Kennilworth running full cards and attracting large international audiences. Numerous private bookmaking establishments around the city supplemented legalized pari-mutuel betting at the track. But the real action of the decade — and for many the only real game in town — was rum-running, the transporting of illicit "booze" into the United States. The flow of illegal liquor became so immense that the border was commonly referred to as the "Detroit-Windsor Funnel."[1]

The Prohibition Era

As a port of entry, Windsor was bound to be a focal point of border conflicts concerning American quota restrictions and differences over Canadian–US immigration laws.[2] However, they were minor compared to infractions that occurred after January 29, 1919, when the US Congress ratified the Volstead Act, which meant that the border police also had to deal with the illegal shipments of hard liquor coming into the United States from Canada. It was the time when bootlegging became a lucrative business. Many Border Cities residents lined their pockets "running booze" across the river, while others were charging huge amounts for alcoholic beverages they served to Detroit visitors from the huge stocks stored in their basements.[3] Although Windsor escaped the most violent crimes associated with Al Capone and his fellow gangsters in the US, local newspapers were kept busy reporting the outrageous daily shenanigans of bootleggers during the fourteen years the Prohibition Act was in force.[4] Only when it was repealed in 1933 did the illicit trade finally stop.

During that era, Jews had also amassed huge fortunes, which, in many instances, formed the basis of the affluence some of their descendants enjoy today. Yet, many were caught smuggling the "forbidden fruit" across the river or were charged by the police for keeping it in their homes. These incidents affected the entire Jewish community. It was especially painful when Joseph Kovinsky was threatened with blackmail in 1927,[5] and when they heard that attempts had been made on the lives of some of Windsor's wealthier Jewish citizens. However, it was the kidnapping early in 1930 of Maurice and Sydney Nathanson that really caused a great deal of excitement. The two brothers had arrived from Montreal in 1926, and since they represented certain liquor interests, their activities had attracted the attention of some less than scrupulous local elements. In the end, both brothers were freed. Despite attempts by the community to hush up the entire matter, the *Border Cities Star* reported on January 9, 1930, that a sum of $5,000 had been raised to secure the Nathansons' release.[6]

Legitimate Jewish businessmen equally shared in the good times. In 1920, Simon, son of Aaron Meretsky, already a large property owner and active trader in real estate, became vice president of a company engaged in building theatres in the city. Although Samuel K. Baum was its president and Louis Stein one of its directors,[7] it did not take Simon long to gain control of the entire organization, eventually making him the largest moviehouse owner-operator in the area.[8]

Another commercial area emerging in the 1920s was Ottawa Street, which was well on its way to becoming a real community. The street railway brought customers from a distance and the surrounding residential area filled up with mainly new immigrants. Harry Gray, who had recently arrived from Winnipeg, opened a small department store at the corner of Gladstone and Ottawa Streets in 1925. An Ottawa Street pioneer, Gray invested his money in some excellent real estate on the street. The neighbourhood was a mixture of many ethnic groups: Eastern Europeans, Germans, Russians, Ukrainians, and Italians. Gray was convinced that the success of the street was due to the fact "that intermarriage became common among the different ethnic groups and co-operation helped the community to grow."[9] Ottawa Street would continue to grow during the Depression, with some merchants prospering enough to expand their stores. On the eve of the Depression many new merchants showed their faith by opening their own businesses. Sam Freed opened Freed's Men's Clothing Store in 1929, while Nate Tepperman opened his furniture store a year later on the corner of Pierre and Ottawa Street, in a building that was very inexpensive to rent because it was "close to a graveyard."[10] These last two businesses have been family successes over many generations and still ply their trade in Windsor today.

Although many Jewish merchants prospered during the 1920s, others, many of them older men, went out of business between 1922 and 1928. They included Herman Benstein, Joseph Loikrec, Rubin Madoff,[11] and Schwartz and Kaplan,[12] who closed up shop after many years of operation. In 1922, Isaac Weingarden marked his retirement by holding a big sale, even though he continued to run his shop for another three years.[13] Just as Samuel Schwartz, who had closed his men's and boys' clothing store in 1922, re-established it six years later at its old address at 75 Sandwich Street East, where he remained until 1932.[14]

The Continuing Lure of Public Office

As they had during World War I, in the 1920s some Jewish businessmen began to take an interest in city politics. Some succeeded while others failed. Louis Kaplan, born in 1889,[15] had come to Windsor as a young boy. Working in his father Nathan's fuel and feed business during World War I, filling contracts for hay and oats, he also took an interest in the Jewish community.[16] Louis became a candidate for the position of city alderman, first in 1920 and again in 1922. Although he campaigned vigorously, he lost in both elections. Joseph Kovinsky, who had worked diligently to promote Windsor's industrial growth, was elected to City Council in 1921. Barney Hurwitz succeeded in gaining a seat as trustee on the East Windsor (formerly, Ford City) School Board in 1922.[17] However, when he was accused, during the following year's campaign, of improper conduct involving a property he was trying to sell to the school board, he came in last on the ballot.[18] Yet, he was re-elected in 1924.[19] Although Aaron Meretsky had not been successful in his try for a seat on the East Windsor Council in 1923, he continued to serve as parks commissioner and, in 1928, was even appointed to the post for a three-year term.[20] Charles Rogin, who had run for Council at the same time as Samuel K. Baum and David Meretsky, went down to defeat with them,[21] just as Isidore M. Cherniak failed in his 1925 bid to serve on the Board of Education.[22]

Toward the end of the 1920s, another Windsor merchant became interested in city politics. Joshua Gitlin, born on January 16, 1889, was the son of Morris Gitlin, who had come from Russia with his wife, Bernice, and their six children in 1905.[23] After settling in Windsor, Morris had made a living teaching Hebrew and Yiddish, as well as serving the Jewish community as a *shochet*.

Morris's son, Joshua, who had married Libby, Jacob Meretsky's daughter, opened a new and used furniture store on Pitt Street,[24] in partnership with his brother-in-law, David Meretsky. In December 1927, Joshua was elected alderman, coming in eighth of the twelve successful candidates on the ballot.[25] Mayor Jackson personally congratulated him on his victory, openly expressing optimism about his political future.[26]

Joshua Gitlin became an active and outspoken member of Windsor's City Council. Well known for taking strong positions on financial matters, he tried to save public money by endorsing only those proposals he considered sensible and advantageous to the city. Although he supported the formation of the Ontario Tobacco Pool[27] and the creation of a local weather bureau,[28] his views on other innovations were less positive. While instrumental in promoting a new $185,000 market building, and favouring the construction of a new $1 million city hall, he opposed the T. Eaton Company's bid to open a branch store in Windsor, on the grounds that the proposed site required extensive alterations to Tuscarora Street that would be too costly. Challenging Gitlin's stand, one of his fellow alderman accused him of serving his own interests by trying to keep out the large department store that might jeopardize his business.[29] Gitlin never shied away from dealing with issues he considered unjust. On one occasion, he questioned the telephone company's plan to erect poles in certain alleys,[30] while voicing serious objections, at other times, to the use of municipal funds for certain trips by council members.[31] However, since he himself was known to take frequent so-called "business" excursions, his firm stand on expenditures was in direct contradiction to his actions.[32]

Despite his sometimes controversial views, Joshua Gitlin was highly respected as an alderman and regarded as a worthy representative of the Jewish community.[33] Although he contested the November 1929 election, he lost his seat — he may have been one of the first casualties of the Great Depression that was about to descend on the country. Commenting on his defeat, the *Border Cities Star* expressed the hope in its December 3 editorial, that he would run again in the following year.[34]

Jews also began to engage in a number of recreational activities, possibly as a result of these and other business successes. With more leisure time at their disposal, they regularly went on excursions to Toronto and Montreal, or spent their holidays in Florida, California, and even Europe. Indicative of the fact that women had begun to

enjoy a measure of freedom are the announcements in the press of teas[35] and wedding engagements[36] hosted by ladies who were no longer obliged to help out in their husbands' stores and could now participate in the social amenities the city had to offer. With more money available, their children, similarly freed from working in family businesses, attended music[37] and ballet classes[38] and took part in cultural activities — pursuits highly valued by all those striving to belong to middle-class society.[39]

Junior Hadassah of Windsor, circa 1925.

The Shaar Hashomayim

It was during the late 1920s that some members of Talmud Torah and Shaarey Zedek got together to discuss the possibility of amalgamating their two congregations. What they had in mind was the founding of a new religious institution whose ideology would be more in keeping with current trends — less traditional than Shaarey Zedek, but more religious than the mainly Zionist-oriented Talmud Torah. Since they also were anxious to gain greater acceptance in the wider community, plans were made to build a house of worship, whose elegance and style could not help but impress their non-Jewish neighbours. Further impetus came from the Nathanson brothers, Sydney and Maurice, who had just come from Montreal and were former members of its venerable Shaar Hashomayim.[40] One of the ultimate objectives was to add a community centre to the new structure. They sought to attract members of Windsor's Jewish elite, who through their growing affluence and prestige were becoming an increasingly visible presence in the city.

Considerable sums of money were required to get the project underway. Revenues had to be skimmed off those of Shaarey Zedek and Talmud Torah. This action not only decreased the financial support these older institutions had hitherto enjoyed, but also severely decimated their leadership. As a result, some difficult years followed. Although they began to flounder badly, they somehow managed to function, largely due to the resolve and dedication of their membership.

In December 1928, Jack Gelber announced that a site for the new synagogue had been purchased on Giles Boulevard. Almost simultaneously, a slate of provisional officers was elected to handle the building's construction details. Headed by Samuel K. Baum, it included Maxwell Schott as secretary and Benjamin Brody as treasurer.[41]

To assist with the fundraising, the group retained Rabbi Samuel Sachs of Congregation Goel Tzedek in Toronto, and also brought in Rabbi Israel Lebendiger, the leader of a congregation in St. Louis, Missouri. Born on April 15, 1886, near the Polish town of Pinsk, Rabbi Lebendiger had come to America in 1904. After graduating from Columbia University with a Bachelor of Arts degree, he took rabbinical studies at the Jewish Theological Seminary of America. Several years later, in 1933, the degree of Doctor of Hebrew Literature was conferred upon Rabbi Lebendiger by that Conservative-oriented institution. Married on April 10, 1921, he and his wife, Carrie, had one daughter, named Ruth, who, born in Detroit on November 7, 1929, eventually married Ted M. Shuster.[42]

It was Rabbi Lebendiger's eloquence as a speaker that persuaded the Jews of Windsor to lend support to the new synagogue. On December 14, 1928,[43] he addressed Talmud Torah members. Using strong words, he told them, "We do not realize the value of the synagogue until a catastrophe occurs, which might have been averted had we observed what the synagogue offers us, just as we fail to realize the worth of our mother until she is gone." Less than a week

Photo courtesy Of the Windsor Star

Windsor's first Jewish Orthodox Synagogue, Shaarey Zedek (Gates of Righteousness) after being redecorated for the beginning of the Jewish New Year. Pictured above with Rabbi B. Orlanski, who is giving the Bible instruction, are (left to right) Michael Wiesberger, Lew Orlanski, and Irving Cohen.

later, he was named spiritual leader of the new congregation that was to be known as Shaar Hashomayim.[44]

Five committees were set up to guide the synagogue's construction through its various stages. Indicative of the enthusiasm among those involved, was the fact that some individuals simultaneously served in dual and even triple capacities. The project's chairman, Maurice Nathanson, was also on the speakers, campaign, and banquet committees. Other speakers committee members were Samuel K. Baum, who was also on the banquet and campaign committees, and Rabbi Lebendiger, who served on the publicity committee, as well. Provisional officer, Maxwell Schott, was confirmed as secretary. He also served as a member of the publicity committee, together with Jacob Geller and provisional treasurer Benjamin Brody who, concurrently, was on the campaign committee.[45]

Jack Gelber headed the campaign committee, the largest of the five. Other members included: Dr. Isadore M. Cherniak, Nathan Cherniak, Joshua Gitlin, I. Blitzer, David Meretsky, Sydney Nathanson, H. Bercuson, N. Rotenberg, Jerry Glanz, I. B. Levin, L. Greisman, Robert G. Cohen, S. Harris, and William Goldstein — who was also chairman of the building committee. In the latter capacity, Goldstein visited Detroit, Montreal, Minneapolis, and Syracuse to thoroughly study these cities' synagogues. Assistance on the building committee came from the vice chairman, David Kaplan, who also served on the banquet committee. As well, Joseph Becker and Louis Caplan worked with Simon Meretsky, who was a member of the campaign committee at the same time.[46]

The $150,000 fundraising campaign got off to a good start on February 2, 1929, when it was announced at a "smoker" — the first event — that Joseph Kovinsky had given $18,000 to the building fund, a gesture that subsequently earned him the title of "colonel" of Shaar Hashomayim's financial campaign committee. The speaker of the evening was H. Gordon, vice president of Detroit's Congregation Shaarey Zedek. He outlined the functions of a modern synagogue, stressing the importance of young people's involvement in its various social, educational, and athletic activities.[47]

A complimentary dinner held the next day at Windsor's Prince Edward Hotel yielded further campaign contributions from numerous Jewish organizations, including the Shaar Hashomayim Sisterhood. Recently inaugurated at the home of Mrs. Simon Meretsky at 840 Ouellette Avenue, the Sisterhood received congratulations for its efforts from Windsor's Mayor Cecil Jackson, as well as from other prominent local persons.[48] Phi Pi Beta, the local fraternity led by H. Rosen, the Junior Hadassah, the Naomi Girls, and other groups were so successful through the sponsorship of dances and luncheon and dinner meetings, that pledges received by February 1929, totaled $80,000. Some individual gifts were as large as $5,000, but many more were in the $1,000 range.[49]

On March 1, 1929, at Talmud Torah's annual meeting, Maurice Nathanson was elected the first president of Shaar Hashomayim; Jerry Glanz became the first vice president, with David B. Caplan and Joshua Gitlin assuming the roles of second and third vice presidents, respectively. Maxwell Schott continued as recording secretary and Jacob Geller took on the financial secretary's post. Other executive board members were Joseph Becker, Dr. Isadore Cherniak, Robert G. Cohen, David A. Croll, David Meretsky, Louis Mossman, Sydney Nathanson, and Jacob Orechkin.[50]

Windsor architect, Stuart A. Allaster, was put in charge of designing the new synagogue. He had been part of the delegation that had visited Montreal to survey that city's Shaar Hashomayim Synagogue. It was ultimately chosen as the model for the Windsor structure because its grandiose architectural style had made it an indisputable Montreal landmark and the focal point of its Jewish community. Part of the influence came from the Nathanson brothers who were originally from Montreal.[51]

Louis Kaplan, Maurice Nathanson, Joseph Kovinsky, Samuel K. Baum, and David Croll, who also was chairman of new synagogue's constitution and bylaws committee, assisted Simon Meretsky, appointed chairman of the construction committee. After awarding the construction contract to N. R. Ibbeston and Company of Walkerville, Ontario, the group approved the plans for the new building. Estimated to cost $150,000, it was to be in the Byzantine style. Rising to a height of fifty-two feet, it would have a seating capacity for 1,000 persons. A cottage at the rear of the site was purchased in June, 1929, since provision had been made for the inclusion of a small chapel. That added another thirty feet to the required floor area of 78 by 121 feet.[52]

In order that the Holy Ark, housed in the synagogue main building, would properly face in an easterly direction, the entrance, with a broad flight of stairs leading up to three doors, was originally to have faced onto Goyeau Street. However, without architecturally altering the interior, that concept was changed when the planners decided later that Giles Boulevard would be a more prestigious address. As a result of that decision, the Ark, as well as the sanctuary, ended up facing south. As a result, many Orthodox rabbis refused to worship in the sanctuary.

The traditional groundbreaking ceremony took place on June 25, 1929, and was attended by members of Windsor's Jewish community as well as by numerous local dignitaries. Joseph Kovinsky's generosity was further recognized by giving him the honour of turning the first clod of soil with a silver spade.[53] During the construction period, services were held at the Windsor Collegiate Institute. They were led by Rabbi Israel Lebendiger, who also preached at Passover and on other occasions at Shaarey Zedek and Talmud Torah, where Rabbi Israel Schulman was active, as well.[54]

The cornerstone for Shaar Hashomayim was laid in September 1929. Yet, despite prospects for the building's early completion and new attempts to bring about a Talmud Torah-Shaarey Zedek merger, there still was no uniform spirit within Windsor's Jewish community. In fact, by 1930, it had grown to more than 2,500 and a number of new congregations had sprung up. The only explanation for that phenomenon was the Jewish community's general dissatisfaction with existing trends. Those who opposed the new Shaar Hashomayim did so mainly because of its erstwhile elitist stand.

Opposition to the Shaar Hashomayim led some to try to establish another congregation. Some people had joined the United Hebrew Congregation. Organized in June 1928, it was under the chairmanship of Nathan

Joseph Kovinsky is pictured here turning the first sod on the future site of the Shaar Hashomayim synagogue on June 25, 1929.

Photo courtesy of Shaar Hashomayim synagogue

Photo courtesy of Shaar Hashomayim synagogue

Sydney Nathanson (left) laying the cornerstone of the new Shaar Hashomayim Synagogue in September 1929.

Interior view of the Shaar Hashomayim synagogue.

Front entrance of the Windsor Shaar Hashomayim synagogue.

Cherniak with Aaron Meretsky, Harry Cohen, Oscar Lehrman, Louis and Sam Mossman, Herman Zeitlin, Henry Greenberg, I. M. Katzman, Jerry Glanz, S. K. Baum, and David A. Croll serving on the board of trustees. Little else is known about this congregation, but its existence was quite temporary.

Others became members of Congregation Beth El, whose 1928 High Holiday services were conducted by Cantor M. Kaminsky of Toledo, Ohio and held at the I.O.O.F. Auditorium on Wyandotte Street East and, a year later, in a building on Ouellette Avenue under the leadership of Cantor Silverman. According to a 1930 newspaper report, another cantor by the name of H. Z. Cohen "had chanted prayers for the new Ahavath Achin Congregation" at the Graham-Paige Hall at 712 Wyandotte Street East. However, since there was no follow-up to the story, it must be assumed that that particular synagogue did not continue to hold services.[55]

Based on the personal guarantees of Louis Kaplan and Maurice Nathanson, Shaar Hashomayim received a $65,000 mortgage from the Dominion Life Assurance Company in January 1930.[56] The inaugural service was held on February 7 of that year and it was noted three days later that a *Sefer Torah* had been donated by Mrs. Herman Benstein.[57] At the end of the month, City Council decided to levy a yearly tax of one dollar, having advised the congregation that the steps of its new building slightly extended onto public property.[58] Two Friday evening services, the later one led by Rabbi Lebendiger, as well as prayers on Saturday mornings, became regular weekly features at Shaar Hashomayim.[59] Although it had originally been conceived as a Conservative congregation, its members, who still considered themselves Orthodox, were eager to embrace more modern trends. As a result, they not only accepted the inclusion of a few prayers in English, as well as sermons on secular topics, but also condoned a mixed choir for the enhancement of their Friday evening services. The curtain separating women and men was done away with and women were allowed to sit on the same floor, if on different levels, with the men occupying the centre section of the lower level. They also started a children's High Holiday service and, almost immediately, opened a religious school. Unlike the Talmud Torah, which held lessons almost every day, this student group wanted to attend once a week, so the religious school operated only on Sundays.

The Sisterhood, led by Mrs. David Meretsky, became Shaar Hashomayim's first affiliate. She was ably assisted by two vice presidents — Mrs. Maurice Nathanson and

Mrs. Simon Meretsky — with Mrs. J. Gitlin acting as treasurer, Mrs. E. Benstein as financial secretary, Mrs. H. Leon as recording secretary, Mrs. J. Cohen as chaplain, and Mrs. Sydney Nathanson as corresponding secretary. The group continued its fundraising activities, engaging prominent speakers to address luncheon meetings, as well as sponsoring teas, picnics, card parties, dances, and various other social functions.[60]

Toward the end of March 1930, the famous Montreal cantor Reverend Joseph A. Levinsky sang during Shaar Hashomayim's Friday night services. A few days later, he was the principal attraction at a musical evening. Sponsored by Talmud Torah, it was held at Windsor's Capital Theatre.[61] That year, Passover was celebrated in gala fashion, with the noted author and lecturer, Maurice Samuel, addressing a public meeting of Jewish citizens.[62] That event was sponsored by Windsor's very active Zionist Organization, which, at that time, was headed by Philip Benstein; others on the executive were Barney Hurwitz, vice president, Dr. D. Barkoff, secretary, and Joseph Loikrec, treasurer; Samuel K. Baum and Jerry Glanz were honorary presidents and vice presidents, respectively.[63]

In May, in anticipation of the final dedication ceremony, the Border Cities Star reported the re-election of Maurice Nathanson as Shaar Hashomayim's president. First vice president was Jerry Glanz, with David B. Caplan and Joshua Gitlin serving as second and third vice presidents, respectively. Benjamin Brody became treasurer and Maxwell Schott remained secretary, with J. Gelber acting as financial secretary. Other executive members included Joseph Becker, I. Blitzer, Dr. I. M. Cherniak, Robert G. Cohen, David A. Croll, L. Caplan, J. Loikrec, David and Simon Meretsky, L. Mossman, S. Nathanson, J. Orechkin, Dr. L. Perlman, and M. Silver. Honourary presidents of the synagogue, were Joel Gelber, Sr., Samuel K. Baum, and Joseph Kovinsky.[64]

The synagogue's final dedication was held on May 25, 1930:

> Jewish people of Detroit, Toronto and neighbouring communities gathered here Sunday to assist Border Cities Jewry dedicate Shaar Hashomayim Synagogue, the new $250,000 temple of the faith at Giles Blvd. and Goyeau Street, one of the finest edifices of its kind in the Dominion.
>
> Impressive rituals marked the event which was witnessed by nearly a thousand members of the faith and many gentile visitors.
>
> Nearly 100 leaders in the Border Cities, Jewish Circles, visiting Rabbis and distinguished guests participated in the ceremonies, including Rabbi Leo Franklin of Temple Beth El, Detroit, and Rabbi Sachs of Toronto; Maurice Nathanson, president of the local Jewish Congregation; Rabbi Israel Lebendiger of Shaar Hashomayim; Cantor N. Mester of Yeshrum, Montreal; Rev. H. M. Paulin of St. Andrews Presbyterian Church, Windsor; Rev. George Vrooman, Curate of St. Georges Anglican Church, Walkerville; Mayor Cecil E. Jackson, Edmond G. Odette, M. P.; Mrs. Sadie Peterman, representing the Women of Mariam Chapter of Hadassah; Mrs. Sam Farber, Mrs. M. Levine, Dr. Louis Perlman, Max Schott, Sydney Nathanson and Joseph Kovinsky.
>
> The ceremonies started at 2:30 o'clock with Max Schott, secretary of the Congregation, as conductor. An impressive feature was the entrance of Rabbi Lebendiger and Cantor Mester, followed by 11 elder members of the congregation who were honoured by being chosen to carry the Torah and sacred Scrolls.
>
> Those were Joseph Kovinsky, Joel Gelber, Simon Meretsky, Joseph Loikrec, Michael Nobel, J. Orechkin, Lewis Mossman, Joshua Gitlin and A. Barash. They marched to the platform where 11 of the younger

members of the congregation relieved them of their burden, an act symbolic of the young Jews carrying on and perpetuating the faith of their fathers.

The younger members who received the scrolls were Archie Cohen, David Caplan, L. Kaplan, M. Schott, H. Cherniak, W. Rackow, Meyer Barash, B. Mathews, H. Meretsky and B. Kovinsky.

The honour of unlocking the ark and placing the scrolls therein was bestowed upon Joseph Kovinsky as a tribute to the exceptional generosity of himself and his wife, whose donation of 18 thousand dollars toward the building gave impetus to the movement which made the synagogue possible.

As a tribute to their untiring effort and liberal contributions, beautiful loving cups were presented to Maurice and Sydney Nathanson.

The presentation of the huge loving cup to Maurice Nathanson, first president of Shaar Hashomayim congregation, was made by secretary Max Schott, while Dr. Louis Perlman tendered the congregation's gift of appreciation to Sydney Nathanson.

Beautiful floral gifts were also given to Mrs. Maurice Nathanson and Mrs. Sydney Nathanson by the Women of the Congregation; Mrs. Levine, in a fine presentation address, placed a large wreath of roses in the arms of the wife of the congregation's president, while a similar wreath was given Mrs. Sydney Nathanson by Mrs. Sam Farber.

Secretary Schott, in presenting the cup to president Nathanson, said: "Windsor Jewry has indeed become richer spiritually and morally by the presence of Mr. Maurice Nathanson. He took an interest in and responded generously to every worthwhile cause in the community. But the work he did in putting up our beautiful synagogue and centre, a monument of pride and glory for the Jewish people of the Border Cities, has endeared him to all the Jews who will remember him with feelings of love and affection. Our new edifice will be a constant reminder of his generosity and public spirit."

In receiving the cup, Mr. Nathanson spoke briefly of the untiring activities of the congregation of Shaar Hashomayim in making the new synagogue possible. He told how the Jewish men, young and old, of the community had given unstintingly of time, effort and money and extended his thanks and that of the congregation to the women for their able and noble work.

"This synagogue will always be the pride and glory of this community. Yes, it will be more than that," he said. "It will be the pride and glory of the Jewish people of Canada and, in closing, let me extend our deepest thanks to all who had aided financially for their assistance and cooperation.

"You people who are assembled here today are to be congratulated on this magnificent building," he said. "Your work is well done. On behalf of the city, I want to thank and congratulate you gentlemen and your ladies on the glowing success you have achieved in giving this community so beautiful a building.

"The people of the city of Windsor appreciate it. And we desire all Jewry on the Border to appreciate it. See that your children attend its services and see that you attend yourselves. Back up your officers and make this great synagogue a powerful, living, vital thing; an ever-lasting monument for the glory of yourselves, your church, your city and, above all, for the glory of the Supreme Being above."

Rabbi Lebendiger told of the struggle of the Congregation in the building of the Synagogue. It could only be accomplished by united people aided by strong men, strong in faith and strong in purpose. "And God gave us those strong men," he said, "or you would have no synagogue, and so it is in all walks of life. Faith in God and strength of mind and character will overcome all obstacles and crown with success all worthwhile enterprises. By this synagogue you show that you mean to be Jews and want to be Jews."[65]

In August 1930, Max Freiman was appointed cantor of Shaar Hashomayim. He had trained in Berlin, Germany, served in Poland, and, subsequently in US congregations in Youngstown and Cleveland, Ohio. It did not take long for everyone to appreciate his vocal talents, especially, his chanting of prayers during services, together with the twenty-voice choir, ably led by Maurice Goldman.[66]

Windsor in the 1930s

The crash of the New York stock market on October 29, 1929, signalled the beginning of the Great Depression. The prosperity and growth of the 1920s gave way to a decade-long Depression that was not overcome until World War II. Automobile production plummeted and the Border Cities suffered some of the highest rates of unemployment in the nation; as much as a third of the work force lost their jobs. Fifteen thousand cross-border commuters were denied access to the United States and most were thrown onto Windsor's unemployment rolls. Local property taxes fell while relief costs soared, leaving municipalities in a dilemma — feed their needy and bankrupt the community or refuse and face the consequences. Private charities were overwhelmed and desperate citizens, many for the first time in their lives, turned to their governments for aid. Most requests were respectful and mass meetings and marches peaceful; however, as conditions deteriorated, relief strikes took on an angrier mood and street protests occasionally became violent.

David Croll, a Russian immigrant from modest beginnings who symbolized the diverse and multi-ethnic community that Windsor was becoming, was elected mayor in 1930. Over the next four years, he chose to put the people's needs before the city's finances, developing a reputation as a strong and caring advocate of social welfare. An "open door" mayor, Croll never shirked the difficult decisions with which he was faced. But with most of the financial assistance coming from the senior levels of government, local initiatives to refinance or restructure municipal welfare policies were limited. When Liberal leader Mitchell Hepburn requested Croll run for a seat in the provincial legislature he agreed to contest the Windsor-Walkerville riding. Croll swept into power with the victorious Liberals and was soon rewarded by Hepburn with not one, but two, cabinet posts — welfare and municipal affairs.

As minister of municipal affairs, Croll was able to indulge his plan to amalgamate the Border Cities. On July 1, 1935, the four Border communities became the City of Windsor. Henceforth, one mayor and council would represent the border communities and with their combined assets and resources, a successful restructuring of the municipal debt was now possible.

With capitalism in crisis, the desperate conditions of the 1930s provided fertile ground for discontent and alternative visions for the devastating economic situation. The Communist Party of Canada, working through the Worker's Unity League and other front organizations, provided leadership and an ideological explanation for society's ills. Tim Buck, the party's leader, was no stranger to Windsor during this period. From the Prairies came the Cooperative Commonwealth Federation (CCF), a social-democratic alternative to the traditional two-party system with a platform of social justice and public ownership of key sectors of the economy. Made up of a coalition of farmers, labour, and intellectuals, the party campaigned locally and many municipal candidates identified with it and proudly adopted its platform. Windsor social worker Olive Jane Whyte was successful candidate for City Council in 1935 — our first woman councillor — and served as member of the Board of Control for the rest of the decade.

Croll's successor as mayor in 1935, George Bennett, was also a CCF member. As president of the local Trades and Labour Council (TLC), Bennett represented skilled labour

The Hon. David A. Croll is shown turning away after signing the oath of office as minister of public welfare and municipal affairs, in Government House in Toronto, while Mr. C. F. Bulmer, clerk of the Crown in chancery, is slotting his signature.

in Windsor. The Labour Temple provided a central meeting place for two dozen locals and the TLC had been active in municipal elections since 1918. It now appeared that labour would become involved in more senior politics at the provincial and federal levels. Unfortunately for Mayor Bennett, the amalgamation and restructuring of the municipal debt was carried out under the direction of the province and its agent — the Windsor Finance Commission — that severely limited the powers of the new local government. A frustrated mayor and council vehemently voiced demands for a return to Home Rule until the province relented. However, the province replaced the Windsor Finance Commission with a locally elected Board of Control, whose powers mirrored those of the earlier body and served as a check upon municipal spending by mayor and council. Ironically, it would be left to returning Mayor David Croll in 1938 to carry on the Home Rule struggle for municipal fiscal independence.

Industrial unionism was also emerging in this period. Unskilled workers had never had the luxury of organization until mass production produced new industries that could not be contained within the traditional crafts but required organization of the whole industry. The Trades and Labour Congress in Canada and the American Federation of Labour in the United States were collections of trade unions. The emerging auto industry, big steel, and resource areas such as mining required a new form of organization — the industrial union. Recognizing this, the AF of L accepted the creation of a subordinate group, the Congress of Industrial Organizations (CIO) under John L. Lewis of the United Mine Workers. As industrial unionism spread, the first United Auto Workers (UAW) local in Canada emerged out of a sit-down strike in the Kelsey-Hayes automotive plant in Windsor in 1936. The more famous General Motors strike in Oshawa followed in 1937 and it ended David Croll's ministerial career in the Hepburn government. Croll had been given a third cabinet position — minister of labour — where he earned an even greater reputation among the labouring classes. Searching for a less confrontational system of labour management relations than strikes and lockouts, he introduced legislation creating an alternative system of settling labour disputes. Premier Hepburn had neither the patience nor the faith in labour that Croll had when the famous Oshawa GM strike broke out. The workers were demanding union recognition as a local of the UAW. Fearful of industrial unionism creeping into Ontario, Hepburn ordered police and military contingents to break the strike. Croll's opposition resulted in his dismissal from cabinet. Although he retained his provincial seat, Croll returned to Windsor to successfully run for mayor again in 1938.

Windsor's reputation as a transportation centre was transformed in the 1930s. The Sandwich, Windsor, and Amherstburg Street Railway (SWA), municipally owned since 1920, found itself in financial difficulty, requiring the closing of some interurban lines and struggling with a growing deficit and deteriorating equipment. The Ontario Hydro Commission's management agreement was terminated in 1934, and a locally appointed committee of three struggled on. In 1937, a decision was made to abandon the streetcars and replace them with buses, which were considered more modern, flexible, and efficient. (And more appropriate for the auto capital!) The last streetcar ran on May 7, 1939. The Auto Tunnel and Ambassador Bridge limped along, both carrying huge construction debts, but both managed to survive the decade. Not so with Windsor's historic ferries which ran for the last time in 1938, victims of the Depression and of bridge and tunnel competition.

As war clouds started to gather, economic conditions in Canada began to improve. Military preparedness stimulated an economy that had long been under-utilized. Within a few short years, factories would be operating twenty-four hours a day and unemployment would give way to labour shortages as the threat of war would once again loom on the horizon.[67]

Holding On

Windsor's Jews, like the rest of the community, were holding on. They had ended the successful decade of the 1920s with pride in their achievements, new community institutions, and a new synagogue, Shaar Hashomayim. The community had undertaken a heavy debt load, which was increasingly difficult to carry. Perhaps less directly affected by unemployment than most, Windsor's Jewish merchants and small businessmen struggled to maintain their enterprises. Some of the Old World skills and experiences of many of the Jewish merchants and their understanding of the value of extending credit and dealing with hard times were of great value.

At inception, Shaar Hashomayim had envisaged adding to its synagogue a community centre that would attract the elite to its amalgamated Talmud Torah/Shaarey Zedek membership. However, by the mid–1930s, conditions both during and in the aftermath of the Great Depression forced them to welcome everyone into their ranks. Shaar Hashomayim became the dominant force in Windsor's Jewish community, replacing Talmud Torah as the favourite meeting place for young and old. While the larger gatherings took place at the city's hotels and auditoriums, the synagogue became the venue for such smaller lively events as talks by Rabbi Lebendiger, musical evenings with the cantor, dances, children's plays, and some cabaret performances.

In 1931, two new Shaar Hashomayim organizations were formed. The first, known as the Daughterhood, was under the leadership of Rose Glanz, with Florence Gitlin as vice president, Clara Zeitlin as recording secretary, and Marion Burnstine as corresponding secretary. Other members of the executive were Doris Meretsky and Vivian Becker.[68] The aim of the other new group — Shaar Hashomayim Men's Club, under the presidency of Bernard D. Caplan — was to involve the synagogue's male members in its affairs.[69]

In the same year, the Shaar Hashomayim Sisterhood re-elected Mrs. David Meretsky as its president, with Mrs. Simon Meretsky, Mrs. Maurice Nathanson, Mrs. Sydney Nathanson, and M. Silver acting as vice presidents, and Mrs. B. Baum and Mrs. A. C. Solomon as recording and corresponding secretaries, respectively. Mrs. Joshua Gitlin was treasurer, Mrs. B. Simon was chaplain, and Mrs. S. Faber served as auditor. Committed to raising funds, the group organized and ran bazaars and carnivals throughout the decade.[70] A Shaar Hashomayim Junior League under the presidency of Ruth Sumner was started in 1932.[71]

To allow community activities to continue during the lean 1930s, when money was far from plentiful, many Shaar Hashomayim members enrolled in other organizations requiring their assistance and support. In 1931, Mrs. David Croll became president of Hadassah and Mrs. E. Benstein headed the Women's Auxiliary of B'nai B'rith.[72] Many younger members belonged to the Naomi Girls, who continued to hold dances and perform plays, often in conjunction with junior members of Detroit's Temple Beth El.[73] The AZA Boys' Club, one of the most active Zionist groups, kept teenagers busy with sports activities, parties, and dances, often in conjunction with the B'nai B'rith Girls.[74] Planning these events around the synagogue, they and other organizations not only helped raise funds for Shaar Hashomayim's survival, but also provided much needed assistance to Palestine and certain other relief groups.

Early in 1932, as financial problems persisted, Shaar Hashomayim could no longer afford to retain Rabbi Israel Lebendiger and was forced to end their relationship. From November 1932 to the end of 1934, guest readers, cantors, and lecturers came for special programs to fill the void left by Rabbi Lebendiger's departure. Max Freiman continued as cantor, at least for a while longer, while Rabbi Harold Rosenthal, a native of Detroit and a graduate of the Rabbi Isaac Elchanan Yeshiva, was asked to conduct High Holiday services that year.[75] A year later, Rabbi J. Meisels occupied the pulpit with Cantor Abraham Barkin, who was supported by the Shaar Hashomayim choir, chanting the prayers.[76]

In 1934, Jerry Glanz became president of Shaar Hashomayim. His slate of officers included L. Adelman, Joshua Gitlin, Benjamin Brody, and I. Blitzer as vice presidents, David Meretsky as treasurer, Maxwell Schott as financial secretary, and Milton Meretsky as recording secretary.[77] That year, it finally became possible to engage another rabbi. The man chosen by the congregation was Nahum Schulman. His effectiveness as a speaker was not only recognized during the High Holiday services, when Cantor Hyman H. Cohen officiated, but also when he addressed a mixed group of Jews and Gentiles at a civic function. His impressive performance soon led to his final confirmation as Shaar Hashomayim's spiritual head.[78]

Rabbi Nahum Schulman was born on the outskirts of Warsaw on November 23, 1909. His father had gone to the United States at the end of World War I and, after sending for his wife and children, had settled in Terre Haute, Indiana. Nahum Schulman had graduated from the Hebrew Theological College (an Orthodox seminary), as a rabbi, and had served a Chicago congregation before coming to Windsor. As soon as he had taken over Shaar Hashomayim, however, he realized that its membership was not strictly Orthodox. He condoned, at least for a while, the mixed choir, as well as the late Friday evening services, but eventually phased out both institutions as part of his campaign to gradually bring them back to their roots. He decided to continue the synagogue's popular guest speaker program and invited rabbis of Orthodox, Conservative, and Reform persuasions, including David Cederbaum,[79] Leon Fram,[80] Benjamin Goldstein,[81] Maurice Eisendrath,[82] and Leo Franklin,[83] to address the congregation members. Over the next few years, they also were privileged to listen to Rabbi Schulman's weekly talks. On these and other occasions, such eminent cantors as Hyman Cohen, David Shkolnik, Irving Miller, Hyman Bernstein, and M. Kaminsky delivered the musical liturgies.[84]

Although Shaarey Zedek and Talmud Torah had so far resisted all merger efforts, some rapprochement took place in 1936, when Shaarey Zedek agreed to transfer control of its cemetery to Shaar Hashomayim for the fee of one dollar. Jerry Glanz continued to maintain these burial grounds for a token payment and, since he and Aaron Meretsky were two of the synagogue's trustees, they were actually able to retain complete control over them. Even though that may have evoked some criticism, Glanz's contributions throughout the decade could not be ignored, especially his covert efforts to help so many Jewish families gain access to the United States.

For obvious reasons, little information about these operations has come to light. It is known, however, that Jerry

Glanz was instrumental in obtaining naturalization papers for those Jewish immigrants who could not gain legal access to Canada and for whom entry to the United States was difficult, at best.[85] With the help of several friendly border officials, he, and later Rabbi Nahum Schulman, would whisk their human cargo from Detroit to Windsor, where they would hide them in homes or at Shaarey Zedek, while preparing their passports and other essential documents, so that they could "legally" return to the United States. In 1929, Michael Sumner, a former rabbinical student, apparently joined the effort. So that proper travel papers could be issued to immigrants, searches for their personal records had to be made either in Europe or Asia. Several non-Jews also assisted in the operation and, thanks to their help, it was possible to save the lives of thousands of Jews, who would have met with certain death had they been deported to their homelands.[86] Since Jerry Glanz was also very involved with the Hebrew Immigration Aid Society and in 1930 headed the B'nai B'rith welfare committee, he handled the deportation cases that were brought to his attention with equal proficiency. These activities, along with the work done by established Toronto and Montreal organizations, continued even after the end of World War II, when a wave of displaced persons and concentration camp survivors sought access to Canada and the United States.

In addition to being the president of Shaar Hashomayim for more than a decade,[87] Jerry Glanz became president of Talmud Torah in 1936. By then, however, the future of Talmud Torah was in jeopardy. Shaar Hashomayim was still in desperate financial straits and could neither absorb the older institution, nor lend it much support. The Talmud Torah did recover to some extent, when many parents, realizing how much Jewish education had deteriorated because of Shaar Hashomayim's inability to meet its financial obligations, began to take an interest in the educational opportunities offered at the Talmud Torah.

The concern for Jewish education helped establish the I. L. Peretz Shule, which in 1930, had separated from the Jewish Public Library Group.[88] The Peretz group attempted to exclude the left-wing element, whom they looked upon with disdain. The Peretz Shule rejected the Shaar Hashomayim's religious emphasis and also the Zionist bent of the Talmud Torah. Preserving Yiddish culture and Jewish traditions was the main goal of the Peretz supporters.

There were twenty-three students attending classes taught by Mr. Drachler at the I. L. Peretz Shule. The premises were subsequently moved to a double house on Erie Street, purchased with help from the Arbeitering. Malke Yuzpe and short, red-haired Mr. Kligman, who served for many years as both teacher and principal of the school, taught countless Windsor students. The Peretz Shule also had their own officers and the minutes indicate that meetings were held on the first and third Mondays of the month. Several officers elected over the years were Messrs. Bogen, Cheifetz, Madoff, Byer, Gordner, Forman, and Parnes.[89]

In 1934, the Shaar Hashomayim executive called a meeting to discuss making the synagogue a centre with facilities for all Jewish community organizations. A few years later, in 1938, a loose structure had developed that became the basis for a new community centre, separate from the Shaar Hashomayim.

By 1939, the Shaarey Zedek and Tifereth Israel in Ford City were still continuing to operate; the latter still running a school, which was slowly declining as the Jewish population moved out of the area. The Talmud Torah had been strengthened and became the major educational facility, with the Shaar Hashomayim school operating on Sunday. The Shaar Hashomayim became the established synagogue in the community, although the Shaarey Zedek held on to some pioneer families who preferred the old synagogue to the new one.

The Depression was ending and as the year 1939 drew to a close, the world had to face the new crisis of World War II. However, as soon as war was declared, Windsor became a leader among Ontario communities. Not only was the machinery in place to switch to the looming wartime economy, but also, its Jewish community was well prepared to cope with the influx of immigrants anxious to escape Hitler's murderous hordes.

Chapter 6
The Honourable David A. Croll:
Profile of a Public Servent

There is no doubt that the Depression brought severe hardships to people everywhere. Unable to find gainful employment and solve a myriad of problems on their own, they turned for help to governments, hoping their elected representatives would come up with imaginative solutions.

It was fortunate for the citizens of Windsor that, at the beginning of these difficult times, an idealistic, young Jewish lawyer by the name of David Arnold Croll entered their civic arena. Born on March 11, 1900, in the Russian capital of Moscow, he was the eldest son of Hillel and Minnie (Minca) Croll, née Cherniak, who had five other children — four boys and one girl. Leo, two years younger than David, eventually became a physician, Sam and Maurice became dentists, and Cecil became a lawyer; their daughter, Evelyn, graduated from the University of Michigan as a dental hygienist.

David's father, Hillel Croll, had been a cattle buyer. He left his native Russia in 1906, arriving in Canada penniless and unable to speak one word of English. David recalled how his father came to settle in Windsor:

My father was on his way to Detroit where his brother was living at the time. When he got to Windsor it was Friday, and he wouldn't ride on Friday. He was an observer. Always a religious man. He wouldn't go any further so he stayed in Windsor that night. And he stayed the next day. And then he just stayed in Windsor. He had a mother-in-law in Windsor but he wasn't coming to stay with her. His brother was principal of the Hebrew Schools in Detroit and that's where he was going. That's how I became a Canadian. If my father had arrived in Windsor on a Thursday or a Monday I would've been an American. I might even have been an American Senator like my nephew Carl Levin.[1]

Talking about the family's early days in Windsor, David recalled:

My father settled near the shul [synagogue] like everyone else. Two years later, my mother, my brothers and I joined him. We first lived at 800 Goyeau Street. The shul was a block to the south on Mercer Street, a block down and a block over. Then we moved to Brant Street, only two doors away from the shul, and later to Glengarry Street, at the corner of Wyandotte, next to a button factory. I attended Dougall Avenue, Mercer Street and Tuscarora schools, before going to Central Collegiate, which then was called Patterson.

As a youngster, I sold newspapers to support myself. I worked at the newsstand too, for maybe five or seven years. In 1924, I graduated from the University of Toronto and, a year later, from Osgoode Hall Law School. For me, 1925 was a banner year. I was called to the bar, became the Secretary of the Essex West Liberal Association, and married Sarah Levin of London, Ontario. The first two years we lived in various places we rented — on Pelissier Street in Windsor, in an apartment out on London Street near Sandwich — before buying a house at 521 West Giles Boulevard."[2]

David and Sarah had three daughters — Eunice, Constance, and Sandra Ruth. He first joined the law firm of Sheppard and Sheppard, and then opened an office in 1929 with partners Snider and Kelly.[3] Having positioned himself in the active centre of the Liberal Party and ready to enter politics in 1930, he declared his intention to run for mayor. The Honourable Paul Martin, a former member of Parliament for Windsor, remembered his first encounter with Croll:

I first met Dave Croll when we were both attorneys in Windsor. I had come to Windsor in the fall of 1930, just about the time when he announced he was going to run for mayor. I didn't know anything about Windsor and I met Croll as one meets other lawyers. I thought it was rather exciting for a young lawyer to meet the man who was going to run for mayor of the city where I was going to practice. I was one of the very few lawyers who actually gave open support to him. I campaigned for his election. I liked the way he was going to try and help people who needed relief in a city where unemployment was so high. I thought he was a natural politician. I liked his philosophy.[4]

David Croll's platform had wide-ranging appeal. Endorsed by business, labour, and minorities, his campaign advertisements stressed the importance of innovative action to meet the community's needs at the height of the Depression. Among his recommendations were the appointment of an advisory committee to represent all classes and creeds in the city; the establishment of the first free legal-aid bureau, re-organization of the city's social services department, the setting up of a municipal coal yard, the lowering of gas company rates, and the protection of small borrowers against those who charged exorbitant interest.[5]

Croll ran a well-organized campaign, successfully resisting the onslaught of anti-Semitic inferences and remarks that sometimes were hurled at him by the five candidates who opposed him. He handily won the mayoralty race, beating his nearest rival, George J. Hanrahan, by more than 1,000 votes.[6] Commenting on the election, the *Border Cities Star* called it:

One of the most interesting mayoralty races in years — and certainly one of the most difficult to judge….

The election result has several outstanding points. To start with, it represents a triumph of youth and aggressiveness. Mr. Croll is just 30 years of age. He has had no aldermanic or other public office experience. He is able, determined, and courageous, and yesterday he demonstrated to his opponents the benefits that can be derived when a candidate has a well-organized campaign.

Secondly, the *Star* regards the results as a commendable example of the fact that racial and religious tolerance abounds in Windsor. Mr. Croll was attacked in some quarters, we regret to say, on the ground that he happens to be a member of the Jewish faith, also that he was born near Moscow, Russia. The result of the vote shows what the people of Windsor don't think of facts of that kind.

Again it has been demonstrated that the federal or provincial political affiliations of a mayoralty candidate are given little consideration by the voters. In both the federal and provincial fields, Windsor has gone strongly conservative in the last two elections. Yesterday it elected as mayor a young man who has been actively identified with the Liberal Party ever since he came out of school. And, incidentally, the second candidate is also an outstanding Liberal.

The people of Windsor, there is cause for believing, will have every reason to be pleased with their choice. The *Star* has known Mr. Croll ever since he commenced the practice in Windsor some years ago, and it frankly admires those progressive qualities that have brought him forward so rapidly. It is difficult to think of any young professional man who has made as much progress in so short a space of time. He is a credit to the city, to his family, and to the great and historic race from which he sprang. He is an outstanding example of the kind of opportunity that Canada offers youth who come to her shores and work. The little Russian immigrant boy, without money and without influential friends, finds himself, at the early age of 30, a leader in his chosen profession and Mayor of one of Canada's leading cities. That is what we call an achievement!

Now is the time for all good citizens to get together in a co-operative, mutually helpful spirit. The Mayor for 1931 is, as we have said, young and vigorous. He has ideas and initiative. The responsibility he has assumed is a serious one but, by the same token, the opportunity is great. We have reasons to expect big things from David Croll.[7]

Praise and endorsement of the mayor-elect did not stop hostile forces from trying to destroy him. Among them was Clyde Curry, one of the defeated candidates, who declared that Croll was ineligible for the office, alleging that gamblers had supported his campaign, and that corruptive activities had taken place during the election.[8] In response, City Council passed a resolution, ordering an investigation of all voting practices.[9] Before the election, Curry also had made sure that he would retain his aldermanic seat. That move, which had been supported by other members of Council, was designed to keep out Joshua Gitlin, another Jew, who would have been next in line for the post had Curry vacated it.[10]

In the end, Croll's popularity won out and he even gained the support of many former rivals. Ironically, the invocation ceremony of Windsor's first Jewish chief magistrate, which took place just before Christmas 1930, was performed by a Catholic priest instead of a rabbi.[11]

In his inaugural address, delivered on January 5, 1931, Croll stressed, above all, the need for harmony among members of council. To attract new industries to the city, he advocated a tax-rate reduction, consolidating existing by-laws, and setting up a new welfare department. He also pro-

Photo courtesy of the Windsor Star

David Croll.

about continuing the investigation, but insisted on bringing his complaints against Croll before Osgoode Hall in Toronto. When none of them could be substantiated, the enquiry was dropped. Yet, Curry, incapable of accepting defeat, persisted in harassing the mayor throughout his first administration, accusing him, among other things, of "giving away the city" and of keeping "Reds" on the city's payroll. Astonishingly, despite his antagonism toward Croll and Jews, in general, Curry managed to maintain his own popularity and position on Windsor's City Council. The mayor was undaunted by these scurrilous attacks[13] — equally ignoring criticism coming from other quarters, he concentrated on fulfilling his campaign promises to promote the cause of the common man. Here is what he had to say about ameliorating the effects of the devastating economic situation:

> The first thing I did when I was mayor was to establish a welfare department. The Great Depression had just come upon the country and the governments had made little provision for the people who had been thrown out of work. We, in Windsor, were particularly hard hit because the Americans closed their border to 10,000 Windsorites who crossed over every day to work in Detroit. They were left on the doors of the city and the Americans said, "Well, go to Croll. He'll have to feed you." And Croll did feed them. It broke our city, we couldn't pay our debts, but we repaid them in later years. But we made provision to the best of our ability, for everyone who was in need. Food, clothing and shelter were our Number One priorities.[14]

posed a number of local improvement programs and, to provide new sources of income for the city, recommended that the provincial government share gasoline, automobile licence, and liquor-store revenues with the municipality.[12]

The new mayor's first few months in office were anything but productive. With the spectre of an election enquiry hanging over him, he had to spend much of his time opposing it, if for no other reason than to deplore its high price, since the preliminary work already had cost the taxpayer $6,000. His chief adversary, Clyde Curry, not only remained adamant

In his quest to create employment for people, Croll not only canvassed factories, supported the sale of work tickets to attract jobs, but even asked the working wives of city employees to relinquish their jobs so that unemployed men could take their places. To assist the needy, he also established a community welfare fund, obtained provincial relief money, and received an allotment of army clothing for distribution among Windsor residents.[15]

Less than one month after his election, he made good on his campaign pledge to set up a advisory body that could assist the mayor on a number of civic matters. He appointed a fifteen-member board that consisted of businessmen — among them Samuel K. Baum, then serving on City Council, and Jerry Glanz — manufacturers, workers, and women.[16] Since the mayor was anxious to have staff that could competently deal with the numerous requests for assistance, one of the board's first duties was to hire a director for the city's social services department.[17]

Between pushing for expansion of social programs and keeping administrative costs in check, the young mayor's task could have been compared with that of someone performing a precarious juggling act.[18] Provincial and federal assistance was decidedly limited. With receipts accounting for only 60 percent of the amounts owed to the city and expenditures exceeding income, the young mayor had little money for essential services. In April 1931, despite his hard fight for a tax cut, he had to agree to a half-mil tax increase, as well as to the forced sale of homes belonging to those unemployed whose taxes were more than three years in arrears. In light of the city's $308,000 deficit, he had to abolish the five-cent bus fares he so vigorously had fought to sustain.[19]

Relief for the unemployed remained the main issue throughout Mayor Croll's term in office. Since more drastic measures were required to provide funds for those in need, he not only asked city employees to give up between 1.5 and 10 percent of their paychecks, but he contributed 30 percent of his own annual salary of $3,300.[20] Although his first term can be characterized as a constant struggle to provide the basic necessities for Windsor's residents, he also tried to build for the future by promoting such projects as school construction, a new post office, improvement of streets, more parks, and even the purchase of land for a municipal golf course.[21]

Since labour and other influential factions continued to support him, he was ready to take on the challenge of a second term. Again opposed by Alderman Clyde Curry,

who never stopped criticizing the incumbent's policies, and by mayoral candidate Lemaire, David Croll outflanked them both, winning the 1932 election by 11,000 votes over Curry's tally of 4,000. Highlighting his past accomplishments, the *Border Cities Star* of December 6, 1932, stated:

> We have spoken of the personal tribute to Mayor Croll. It was indeed wonderful, one to stir the heart of every man and every woman who believes in the gospel of fair play, human kindness, racial and religious freedom and tolerance. The people gave their answer to those who opposed the Mayor because he happens to be a Jew, because he happens to have been born in Russia, because he has lifted himself up from obscurity to the highest position in the city. The Star is exultant over this phase of the election. It glories in the fact that Windsor has once more demonstrated that it has no use for bigotry, for attempted social distinctions that reek with superciliousness for attempts to set class against class, race against race, faith against faith. Windsor is a cosmopolitan city. It is interested in men and their achievements.[22]

In his first public address, following the election, Mayor Croll told the people of Windsor, "We have got to stop being panicky and try to see something in the philosophy of life in other people. I think that if we hold up our heads we will make definite progress in 1933 in the higher purpose of life, as well as in a material way."[23]

During City Council's opening session, after summing up the difficulties encountered between 1931 and 1932, the problems caused by unemployment and by declining tax revenues, Mayor Croll pointed to the progress that had been made, expressing the hope that world-wide conditions would improve sufficiently to trigger an upturn in the local economy. He assured Council members that, thanks to the added revenue gained through the beneficial Liquor Control Act, he expected the city to meet its fiscal obligations in the coming year. Mayor Croll then urged them to adopt his tax installment payment plan that, despite his proposal to reduce property taxes, could make the city's finances far more stable, since it would, at least temporarily, protect home owners from foreclosures.[24] Understandably, as soon as the 1933 session got underway, the mayor was faced with the same problems as before — rising costs, declining revenues, and the ever-present plight of the unemployed. He fought the Windsor Hydro Commission's attempts to raise rates for street lighting, cut by 3 percent the semi-annual interest paid on debentures and, while proposing a 25 percent reduction in taxes, consistently appealed to Windsor's taxpayers to pay their share.[25] Although he advocated decent wages for workers, especially for women, whom he considered unjustly underpaid, he visibly upset city employees by suggesting they take a cut in salary. On the other hand, he tried to get government funding for a new City Hall, proposed opening the border between Canada and the United States for commuters, and even forced the investigation of questionable Police Commission practices. To generate additional municipal revenue, he tried to persuade companies to locate in Windsor and, to make it a more attractive convention centre, supported the sale of beer and wine in local restaurants and hotels. Despite council members' opposition to some of his ideas, he continued to champion the cause of average citizens, and of the poor and the unemployed. In one instance, he even intervened on behalf of a few local families, when he discovered that they had to live in substandard conditions when the government, in its attempt to provide them with jobs, had moved them to Northern Ontario.[26]

By 1933, David Croll had become a highly visible public servant. Acting like a parent proud of his children's accomplishments, he found time to attend picnics, parades, and rallies, despite his busy schedule. In 1934, still fighting for the city's survival, he had to defend a tax-rate increase from 29 to 33 mils. While continuing to be plagued by wage disputes, he was also forced to deal with the numerous complaints brought against the Hydro Electric Commission, the Board of Control, the Board of Trade, and the War Veterans' Administration, as well as against some Children's Aid Society officials, accused of providing improper care.[27]

David Croll's life changed dramatically in the fall of 1934, when he decided to represent the constituents of Windsor-Walkerville in the forthcoming provincial election. After running a vigorous campaign, he won a seat as Liberal member in the government of Premier Mitchell Hepburn. Soon appointed minister of welfare, municipal affairs, and labour, he continued to perform his duties as mayor, turning over his ministerial salary to the City of Windsor.[28]

Early in his mayoral term, Croll had proposed the amalgamation of Windsor, Walkerville, Sandwich, and East Windsor into a single municipal entity. Believing that it would not only help alleviate the towns' adverse financial situation and consolidate their efforts to find jobs for people, he was also convinced that such a coalition would trigger industrial growth and promote better governing practices. David Croll's foresight was acknowledged and his dream was on its way to becoming reality when plans for the unification of these municipalities were announced in December 1934. When it actually went into effect on July 1, 1935, the *Border Cities Star*, renamed the *Windsor Daily Star* to emphasize its own change in status, gave a lot of publicity to this landmark event. Here is what David Croll had to say about it:

> But my greatest accomplishment as mayor was the amalgamation of Windsor. There were a lot of hard feelings in this, it was harsh, but it had to come. I brought an inevitability forward by ten years.
>
> The people were living in Windsor. The plants were in Walkerville. The taxes were in Walkerville. We were educating the children, providing homes, and Walkerville was getting all the money. I said, "This has to stop." The border people realized it. They were for it, too. But they had a pretty tight

little group in Walkerville that didn't want to give up. They fought it all the way to the Privy Council. And lost. But I had to do it. And I did it.

I was in a little bit of a bind. Walkerville was my riding. And when I arrived there, I had said I would not amalgamate them unless I consulted with them first. Well, I got into office, looked behind the scenes, and saw some dirty work. I had the guy (an official) charged and convicted, and then said to them, "My promise no longer holds true. I've got to amalgamate you. But I'll tell you one thing, I'll come back to you and you can vote against me if you want to." I did come back. They didn't vote against me.[29]

By the end of 1934, after David Croll had declared he would not seek re-election as chief magistrate of Windsor, he also had been made a King's Counsel, an honorary distinction conferred by the monarch on senior members of the legal profession.[30] Continuing to serve the Ontario Legislature as minister of welfare, he could well remember his involvement with the famous Dionne quintuplets:

I was Minister of Welfare and as minister, all children in Ontario who needed assistance came under my coverage. And as such, one morning, they were on the verge of exporting the Dionne quintuplets to the World's Fair in Chicago, and I had to stop it quickly. So I took control of the quintuplets in the name of the Crown. I was the Crown's representative in Ontario and I took charge of the situation and that's the way it was. No one had ever done it before but I had no other course.[31]

David Croll remained in the cabinet, holding the same three ministerial portfolios — welfare, municipal affairs,

and labour.[32] Although he had to grapple with many major problems, he also received high marks and accolades from his party, his constituents, the press, and several organizations for instituting a provincial health care plan. He changed the Ontario tax structure. As well, he worked on housing and minimum wage legislation.[33] On April 14, 1937, he resigned his ministerial post, following a bitter clash between Premier Mitchell Hepburn and the Attorney General Arthur Roebuck over the General Motors strike in Oshawa.[34] Paul Martin praised Croll for the position he took and relates,

Dave Croll left the cabinet over a very important social issue — the right of labour to engage in collective bargaining. He was opposed to Hepburn's totalitarian methods regarding the UAW's strike at the General Motors plant in Oshawa. Well, that made Croll even more popular.[35]

David Croll continued as member of the provincial parliament and, in 1938, one year after being re-elected in his riding of Windsor-Walkerville, decided to again seek the office of Mayor of Windsor. Here is how he described his election campaign:

It was much dirtier. The motor manufacturers were getting to the point where they were going to have unions in their shops, and they were determined to fight that in every way they could. They didn't call me a Communist. It wouldn't have held. But the Communists wouldn't let me win by acclamation. They brought in one of their own people to run against me. Then they apologized to me. "Dave," they said, "we don't want to do this, but it's the only way anybody will ever know we're alive." Of course, they were badly beaten every time.[36]

Croll focused his new platform on seeking industrial peace, condemning wildcat strikes but supporting the working men's rights to fight for better wages. While Windsor's sitting Mayor Wigle tried hard to retain his seat, charging his opponent with poor performance as a former legislator, Croll gained many supporters and, ultimately, won the mayoral race by a wide margin.[37]

His victory meant that he again would play a dual role, as he was still a member of the provincial legislature. Many problems left over from the previous administration had to be solved at the beginning of his 1939 term. Not only did he have to find money for relief and provide adequate municipal services, but he also took on the additional responsibility of chairing the city's Utilities Commission.[38] Plunging into these jobs with the same enthusiasm and tenacity he had shown before, he had the pleasant task of acting as host to King George VI and Queen Elizabeth when they visited Windsor during the summer of 1939.

When World War II broke out in September, David Croll joined the Essex Scots Regiment of the Canadian Army and, while in the reserve, turned over his mayoral duties to the councilman next in line. Commenting on his decision to enlist, the Honourable Paul Martin had this to say:

> Croll wasn't very popular with the "silk stocking" crowd, the wealthy of Windsor, the people of class and background, who hadn't been his supporters. So when the war came and he decided to enlist as a private, some of them weren't too happy. I don't think it was anti-Semitism as much as it was a dislike of his liberal policies and politics. There were people who said to me, "Why should he be in the army?" And I said to them, "Why shouldn't he be? Isn't it important for leaders to lead in that way as well as in others?" But he went through the war as a private, only receiving the rank of lieutenant-colonel at the very end and against the wishes of some people who even had been opposed to his getting into the regiment. But that made him a worthy and strong man and gave him a stature that was quite unique.[39]

When David Croll was finally called to active duty, he made his exit as Windsor's illustrious mayor, without completing his last term of office. While serving overseas with the First Canadian Army, the Second British Army, and the 12th United States Army, he wrote a handbook on dispatch riding that eventually became the standard for the Canadian Army.[40]

At war's end, Croll served as member of the Allied Military Government. Shortly before returning from Europe in 1945, he accepted an invitation to run in the upcoming federal election as the Liberal Party's candidate. He accepted and, following his discharge with the rank of lieutenant-colonel, contested the seat in the riding of Toronto-Spadina. He won the election and, after becoming a member of the Federal Parliament, was active on several House of Commons standing committees — External Affairs, Labour, Public Accounts and Veterans Affairs. He also served on special committees, such as those dealing with defence expenditure, immigration, housing, and the Bill of Rights, and became chairman of the committee that looked into the review of the Bank Act. Re-elected in 1949, and again in 1953, David Arnold Croll was appointed to the Senate on 28 July, 1955. In 1956–57, he was a delegate to the United Nations and, subsequently, a UN observer on several occasions.

Senator Croll lost no time in advocating a larger role for the Senate in the work of parliamentary committees, and he initiated a number of inquiries that led to government legislation. Among those were:

> The Truth in Lending Bill (first introduced in 1960) that sought to compel those selling goods on credit to disclose interest rates clearly and understandably.
> In 1966, he was chairman of the Senate

Photo courtesy of the Windsor Star

In May 1940, members of the Windsor City Council rallied around Mayor Dave Croll at the conclusion of last night's session to wish him well before he left with the Essex Scottish Regiment. Left to right around the mayor are E. W. Lancaster, Arthur J. Reaume, Norman D. Eansor, Ray Dugal, Arthur L. Mason, E. L. Waterman, W. Ernest Atkinson, Thomas E. Raycraft, and Cyril Cooper. The mayor was a private in the regiment he had joined the previous fall.

Committee on Aging, which reduced age for pension entitlement progressively from 70 to 65, and provided in addition for supplementary assistance for those in need. In all, there were some ninety recommendations, the vast majority of which have been accepted.

In 1967, he initiated the study on consumer credit and was co-chairman of the Joint Committee on Consumer Credit.

As chairman of the Senate Committee on Poverty, he undertook the first comprehensive study of poverty in Canada. The report, published in November 1971, called for a Guaranteed Annual Income by using the negative income tax method, so as to put a floor under all families as well as individuals. The report has not only become a "bestseller," but its content has prompted an unparalleled dialogue on poverty in Canada.

Senator Croll chaired the Special Senate Committee on Retirement Age Policies, dealing with those who are compelled to retire at 65 years of age. The report, entitled, *Retirement Without Tears*, was tabled in the Senate on April 15, 1980.[41]

Many honours came to the Senator. As mentioned, he was a delegate to the United Nations in 1956–57, and he has been a United Nations observer on other occasions. The City of Windsor honoured him in 1956, and in that same year he received the B'nai Brith Humanitarian Award. In 1961, he was awarded the US National Community Service Award, and in 1962, in Montreal, he was honoured by the Council of Reform Congregations. Senator Croll was a member of many prestigious organizations, including the Canadian Bar Association, the Essex County Law Society, the York Law Society, and the Freemasons. The Honourable David Croll summarized his career as follows: "I've made my contribution for the betterment of Canadian life. That's what I meant by being free and doing what I wanted to do. I've had an input on social welfare in this country. I know that's an understatement but that will be my footnote in history."[42]

Regrettably, Senator Croll's wife, Sarah, passed away in 1987. In 1990, the 90-year-old gentleman still was maintaining a law office in downtown Toronto and, when we had the pleasure to be received by him during that year, we could not help but be impressed by his spirit, wit, and charm. As a tribute to his remarkable career, Senator David A. Croll Square, located adjacent to City Hall Square in Windsor, was dedicated on July 24, 1990, by Mayor John Millson. At the dedication, Senator Croll said, "I've always belonged to Windsor, and today I can say a part of Windsor belongs to me."[43]

When he died on June 11, 1991, the *Windsor Star* wrote in their lead editorial about Senator Croll's remarkable career:

> Few individuals have selflessly given as much to their country and to their community as Senator David Croll. For six decades, Senator Croll weaved his concerns and compassion into the political and social fabric of Canada and he left an indelible imprint. What is most remarkable about Senator Croll is not that he spent nearly all his adult life devoted to public service, but that he never lost sight of his original agenda — to fight for social justice and champion the interests of the disadvantaged.[44]

Besides leaving a lasting legacy of achievement, Senator Croll accumulated a number of "firsts" to his name. He was the first Jewish mayor of Windsor, the first Jewish member of Ontario's provincial cabinet, and the first Jewish Senator.

PART III

Chapter 7
War and Peace

Windsor in the 1940s

Wartime needs dominated the period 1939–45 and the remaining part of the decade was given over to the desire to return to normalcy and to resume the growth and prosperity that Depression and War had interrupted.

Canada went to war with the rest of the British Empire in 1939; Windsor's citizens responded with enthusiasm but suffered one of the worst tragedies of the war in the failed Dieppe Raid of 1942. Windsor's wartime production made it a major player in the allies' "Arsenal of Democracy." No civilian automobiles were produced after 1942, when the full capacity of Windsor's industrial might turned to war. A variety of strategic products from trucks to universal carriers were mass-produced by the thousands. It was a time of shared sacrifices, of rationing, of war bonds and victory drives.

Forgotten were the jobless days of the Depression; unemployment was non-existent and labour shortages caused concern. More women went to work, although they were still not treated or valued equally. Union organization was aided by government involvement under its wartime powers. Ford was unionized in 1942 and Chrysler followed the next year. Near the end of the war, an attempt by management to restore its pre-war dominance culminated in the Ford '45 strike, a ninety-nine-day strike that enshrined union recognition, the right to collective bargaining, union security, and check off of union dues. Judge Rand's decision established the ground rules for post-war labour relations and brought both sides under the law. The UAW under Walter Reuther's leadership reflected larger Cold War concerns as Communists and leftists were drummed out of leadership positions. Although the CCL declared the CCF as the political arm of labour in Canada in 1943, the left seemed politically ineffective after a brief surge at mid-decade.

Following the war, veterans returned and civilian auto production resumed. Concerns about regressing into another Depression were countered by optimism based upon pent-up demand and the need to rebuild a war-torn world, and a promise and hope engendered by a social safety net — Family Allowances and Unemployment Insurance — that the country would never return to Depression days. At the same time, that post-war future also included the problems of refugees and the homeless. The world's Jewry, traumatized by the Holocaust, redoubled efforts to establish a homeland, which was created in 1948 with the support of the United Nations. Both refugee problems and the successful establishment and security of Israel would affect Windsor's Jewish community, as it joined with world and North American Jewry to provide the necessary financial support.[1]

The War Years 1939–45

World War II broke out on September 1, 1939, when Hitler's forces invaded Poland. Two days later, Great Britain and France declared war on Germany, with Canada following suit on September 10, 1939.

At the outbreak of war, close to 700,000 men and women joined the various branches of the Canadian Armed Forces. Although Jews at that time accounted for only 1.5 percent of Canada's population, 10,712 enlisted — 4,843 in the army, 4,439 in the Royal Canadian Air Force, 269 in the navy, and 1,161 as trainees — a number that represents 6.08 percent of the then total number of the country's 11,506,555 inhabitants.[2]

Windsor Men Serve

The citizens of Windsor responded in large numbers to the Canadian government's call to arms. Those who had enlisted in the Essex Scottish Light Infantry Regiment took part in the disastrous August 19, 1942, Allied commando raid on the German-held French resort town of Dieppe, where the regiment suffered heavy casualties. Fewer than 10 percent of the 553 men who had embarked on the mission returned to England's shores; 121 had been killed in action or had died of wounds, while the Germans had taken 382 prisoners.

Of the Jewish Canadians who had participated in the Dieppe raid, seven were killed in action, one was wounded, seven were declared missing, and six became prisoners of war.[3] Jewish servicemen also were part of the Canadian contingent that had gone to Hong Kong to help defend its British garrison. Many of them became prisoners of war when the Japanese took Hong Kong at the end of December 1941, shortly after their attack on Pearl Harbor.[4] At the beginning of 1943, 150 Windsor Jews were serving in the various branches of Canada's armed forces.

Aiding the War Effort

Canada's civilian population cheerfully accepted such wartime constraints as the rationing of tea, sugar, butter, and meat. And, starting in January 1940, they also helped finance the war effort by purchasing Victory Loan Bonds. Having heeded Prime Minister Mackenzie King's appeals, nine such campaigns yielded an astonishing $8.8 billion by the end of the war. Windsor people also donated money, food, and their time to various volunteer organizations. As a result, the Canadian Red Cross was able to daily pack carloads of foodstuffs for shipment overseas, and the Active Service Club could provide meals, overnight accommodation, and entertainment for the enlisted personnel stationed in the city. And to relieve the acute labour shortage at harvest time, many local school children used their summer vacations to lend a helping hand to farmers.

Soon after the outbreak of hostilities, large numbers of factory workers who had been forced to leave Windsor during the Depression returned to fill the jobs in the city's automobile manufacturing plants when they switched from passenger cars to making army trucks, ambulances, gun carriers, and machine guns. To provide accommodation for this augmented labour force, the Canadian government initiated several building projects that, by the end of the war, had created some 3,500 new dwellings, making Windsor the largest recipient of wartime housing in Canada.

Windsor's Jewish civilians did not lag behind in their contributions to the war effort. As Shaar Hashomayim had become the focal point of their activities, the Sisterhood, under the guidance of Mrs. Ben Yuffy, was actively engaged

A World War II photo of Jewish Windsor men who died in the war. The photo is hanging in the offices of the Windsor Jewish Federation.

in assembling and shipping "comfort boxes" to Jewish servicemen overseas.[5] Frances Geller solicited materials, rented a number of sewing machines and led tireless Hadassah volunteers in generating the Jewish contribution to that particular aspect of the war effort.[6] Shaar Hashomayim's news sheet not only regularly reported on their activities and promotions, but also started to reprint soldiers' letters written to their families back home.[7] Regrettably, the news sheet also had to publish expressions of sympathy to those members who had lost a son, a husband, or a brother. In such an interconnected group, the hardships and losses suffered by individual families were felt throughout the entire community.[8]

New Rabbinical Leadership

In the summer of 1942, Rabbi Nahum Schulman decided to leave Shaar Hashomayim, explaining,

> Despite the fact that I was happy in Windsor and so well settled that I could have remained there all my life, I wanted a change. I had reached a point where I, generally, had become convinced that, despite my usefulness to the community, a new face was needed to better appraise the issues and concerns confronting its members. I also wanted to get back to the United States to serve a community that would be more of a challenge than Windsor was. It no longer represented that challenge for me.[9]

In September 1942, members of Shaar Hashomayim welcomed Rabbi Benjamin Groner as their new spiritual leader. Born in Chicago, Illinois on August 3, 1915, he had completed his early education in his hometown before enrolling at Chicago's DePaul University's College of Law, where he received his Bachelor of Arts degree in 1936. Although admitted to the Illinois bar, he abandoned his plan to become a lawyer, opting instead for a rabbinical career. Benjamin Groner received his *s'micha* — was ordained as a rabbi — in 1938, having studied in Chicago at Hebrew Theological College — it later moved to Skokie, Illinois — and at Telshe Yeshiva–Chicago. After serving a congregation in Salt Lake City, Utah for one year, he accepted a position at Chicago's High Park Hebrew Center.[10] When that institution experienced financial difficulties it had to let him go and he became Shaar Hashomayim's rabbi, a post offered to him by its president Jerry Glanz.

Photo courtesy of the Windsor Star

Rabbi Benjamin Groner, left, greets Cantor Samuel Kantarof of New York City, one of the foremost tenors in Jewish religious music, who arrived in Windsor in May 1947 to officiate at services marking the holiday of Shavuot. All three synagogues conducted special services and Cantor Kantarof took part at Shaar Hashomayim.

Rabbi Groner described the state of Windsor's Jewish community during and after the war, especially the roles played by the city's various religious organizations. Here are excerpts from that conversation:

> I would say that the main difference between Shaar Hashomayim and Shaarey Zedek, (the Mercer Street shul) and the Tifereth Israel

(the East Windsor shul) was that the latter two congregations had fewer members and, therefore, did not employ rabbis on a full-time basis. I know of no rabbi who served them during my tenure but do remember an English-speaking fellow by the name of Rosenkranz serving the Shaarey Zedek (the Mercer Street) congregation for a while. As the leaders of these synagogues were mostly immigrants, their membership was basically Yiddish-speaking, whereas Shaar Hashomayim's, primarily led by native-born Canadians, was about 90 percent English-speaking. Those belonging to Shaarey Zedek and Tifereth Israel were mostly immigrants who, initially, may have felt more comfortable at these older synagogues, mainly because they could continue to worship in the spirit of the shtetls they had left behind. However, over time, many of them were sort of dragged to the Shaar Hashomayim by their children who, having grown up in Canada, wanted to take part in services that were conducted in English.

After being at Shaar Hashomayim for a while, I began to sense that what the congregation wanted was a well-organized and dignified religious service. For example, if prayers were scheduled for 9:00 a.m., the members expected them to start at that time, in contrast to the older synagogues, whose timetables sometimes were a bit helter-skelter.

I stayed in Windsor until the middle of 1949. During those years, I established good relations with my co-religionists, as well as with many Gentiles in the community. Among the outstanding people I met at Shaar Hashomayim I especially remember Archie Cherniak, a highly principled

man, Harry Rosenthal, a dynamo in the Zionist movement, Milton Meretsky, Maxwell Schott, Ben Brody and Mike Sumner — all dedicated men who were seriously involved in synagogue affairs and interested in promoting the well-being of the community.[11]

Following the tradition established by Rabbi Nahum Schulman, Friday evening services started at 8:30 p.m., whenever Shabbat began before 6:00 p.m., with Rabbi Groner delivering the sermon and Cantor A. A. Rosenfeld chanting the liturgy.[12] However, a few years after Benjamin Groner had become the congregation's spiritual head, the Friday evening services were dropped, mainly because of a decline in attendance and because Cantor Rosenfeld, whose home was in Detroit, found it difficult to regularly travel to Windsor for services. In their place, Shaar Hashomayim began Oneg Shabbos — Friday evening celebrations that were attended by young and old and intended to be family affairs.[13] The liturgy was sung by cantors, hired on a temporary basis, until September 1947, when Nathan Adler became Shaar Hashomayim's cantor for about a year. There also were chats by Rabbi Groner, community singing, and the serving of refreshments provided by the Sisterhood.[14]

In a *Bulletin* editorial entitled "A Word About Friday Night," Rabbi Groner commented on the nature of these Friday evening services:

> About fifteen years ago, the practice of holding late Friday evening services, in order to draw into the synagogue people who might not otherwise come, became very widespread among American synagogues. Some congregations found that the innovation met with enthusiastic response while others had different experiences. Today the glamour of this particular service seems to have worn off, generally speaking.[15]

At that time, however, the focus of attention for the Jews of Windsor, as well as for all communities around the world, was concentrated on the war effort rather than on any other endeavour. This is how Rabbi Groner described the mood of his own congregation:

> From the time I came until 1945, the general tenor consistently was one of tension and anxiety, concerning, I shouldn't say concerning but implicit in the on-going attempts for the successful prosecution of the war. Everything in the community, whether it was fundraising or organizing the different facets of community life, had as its frame of reference the military picture overseas. But the community maintained a very energetic program within that background involving the different organizations in the community.[16]

Jewish Education

In many respects, Windsor's Jewish community matured under Rabbi Groner's leadership. This is what he had to say about the various religious schools:

> The Peretz School provided religious education for the children of the Yiddish-speaking parents attending the Mercer Street shul. As Shaar Hashomayim did not have a Hebrew school in the 1940s, most of the children of parents worshipping there went to the Aylmer Street Talmud Torah. Although it was more Zionistically oriented than the Peretz School, the basic curricula for both schools were similar. They included studies of the Bible, the Siddur, Chumash, Jewish history, etc. However, the Peretz School's program was almost exclusively conducted in Yiddish and Talmud Torah's used English and Hebrew as its languages of instruction.
>
> There may have been occasional tensions between the older synagogues and the two religious schools. However, I was not aware of any conflict between them and the Shaar that, basically, was interested in the education of all Jewish children, and cared a great deal about the welfare and progress of both the Peretz School and Talmud Torah.
>
> During my ten years as rabbi of Shaar Hashomayim, relations between the Hebrew School [Talmud Torah], on the one hand, and the Peretz School on the other, were very cordial and, whenever they had a public function or a dinner we were always invited to attend. I always made it a point to tell the administration and leadership of the Peretz School that I was happy to help them with the structure of their curriculum. I also was ready to provide such educational services as preparing their boys for bar mitzvah, as they were just as eligible to take them as the boys who attended the Hebrew School [Talmud Torah].[17]

The Jewish Community Unites

Despite ideological differences among Windsor's Jewish communal factions, the war was creating a unity of purpose for all the people, which made them realize the need for a new structure that would give them the comfort and strength needed to overcome the fears and concerns manifest in the war. These various factions, aware of the importance of coming together as one people, soon recognized that there were benefits to publishing a single community bulletin, to combining their fundraising efforts, and to unifying several organizations, such as youth groups and others, under one umbrella.

That unification process truly began in January 1943 with the creation of *Windsor's Jewish Community Bulletin*. Archie D. Cherniak, in an attempt to further his own vision of a united Jewish community, not only became its executive director but also volunteered to put out the first edition, as there was no professional available to perform the task.[18] As his first editorial explained:

> The *Bulletin* is not for any one group or organization. It is for the whole community. It will urge no particular viewpoint. It will do its one job — keep the community informed of what is going on. All suggestions will be given due consideration. May it play its part, however small, in the great task that confronts mankind — the task of building a better and happier world.[19]

In the *Bulletin*'s masthead, Rabbi Benjamin Groner's name was listed as its editor; Mrs. Ben Yuffy's and Michael Sumner's both appeared as "Associates," while Archie Cherniak was described as the person "in charge of publication."

Continuing the work started by the synagogue's wartime news sheet, the *Bulletin* gave extensive coverage to the comings and goings of the Jewish military men serving at home or overseas. And, apart from local news, the paper also carried a great deal of "thumbnail" information about events occurring in the Jewish world at large. Despite the fact that its editorials dealt with a wide variety of topics — Judaism, anti-Semitism, etc. — it was Jewish immigration to Canada that evoked some of the most incisive comments. In an editorial entitled, "Another Job for Our Community," Michael Sumner attacked the government's poor record in that regard:

> We must, together with the rest of those Canadians who see eye to eye with us, pool

our efforts to dispel prejudice against immigration.... Heaven and earth must be moved so that some of our brothers who will emerge from the European holocaust may find a haven of refuge here. Secondly, we must be prepared to take responsibility for those who can be brought here. Third, we must have expert workers to cope with immigration problems both in Canada and in the United States.[20]

Although Shaar Hashomayim sponsored the *Bulletin*, the paper devoted considerable space to the activities of more than thirty other local Jewish organizations. Commenting on the success of that policy, Michael Sumner believed it represented "a difference of emphasis on interest rather than a difference of interest," and that "viewed from a standpoint of communal partnership," every one of these groups fitted "into a pattern of basic unity."[21]

Possibly due to the constraints imposed by the war and the various institutions' efforts to avoid duplication, it soon became apparent to everyone that the services offered to members of Windsor's Jewish community would have to be amalgamated. To bring about "unanimity with regard to Kashrut," Shaar Hashomayim, after much discussion with Shaarey Zedek and the Tifereth Israel Congregation, reached an agreement in March 1943 to set up a joint Va'ad Hakashruth.[22] Trying to find common ground on such other matters as the Talmud Torah and youth activities, Shaar Hashomayim's representatives again met with these organizations on June 14, 1943.[23]

Although unifying the administration of Kashruth had caused a bitter struggle, it ended in the summer of 1944 after the arrival from Fredericton, New Brunswick of Rev. J. Bornstein. He not only became Windsor's new *shochet* and its first resident *mohel*, but also took on the role of part-time teacher at Talmud Torah, which, by then, was under the supervision of Rabbi Benjamin Groner.[24]

Talking about other butchers who had served Windsor's Jewish community in the past, Rabbi Groner remembered,

There were three full-time butchers — one of them was Ben Williams, another was a fellow by the name of Lopatin, and there was a third one whose name I don't recall right now [Rotman]. There also were two *shochetim* — one called Yudel Mark and another one by the name of Eliahu Oppen. These men were part-time *shochetim* as well as part-time teachers, like *shochetim* sometimes were in small communities where the *shochet* also was a teacher or vice versa. And that impressed me tremendously when I first came there [to Windsor], of course, from the point of view of religious observance.[25]

Another unifying force was a new organization that, ultimately, became the United Jewish Welfare Council of Windsor. The foundation for it had been laid in 1939 when a small group, headed by Milton Meretsky and Norman Ramm, had organized the Jewish Welfare Fund, mainly to avoid multiple fundraising efforts.[26] However, the Council's more recent success was largely due to the efforts of Archie Cherniak, Michael Sumner, and Harry Rosenthal.

On July 8, 1943, the United Jewish Welfare Council of Windsor held a meeting at Shaar Hashomayim Synagogue. Chaired by Harry Rosenthal, it had been called to approve recommendations submitted by its constitution committee headed by Milton Meretsky. It was decided that any group with "not less than ten dues-paying members" could elect one representative to sit on the Council's Board of Governors. Any individual could become a member by simply supporting the annual fundraising campaign with a minimum contribution of $15. Funds derived from these drives would be apportioned to all charitable organizations, including educational and religious ones.[27]

Windsor Jews were able to speak with one voice once fourteen local groups had accepted the constitution of the Jewish Welfare Council of Windsor that held its first meeting on October 18, 1943.[28] Having set a target of $36,000, it raised over $20,000 at its kickoff dinner at the home of Simon Meretsky.[29] The success of that fund drive and of the Council's efforts to boost attendance so that even greater results could be achieved, prompted organizers to hold subsequent dinners in other private homes. [30] Suffice it to say that campaign goals were reached each year thereafter, raising the targets of Windsor's Jewish community as its requirements and worldwide needs increased.

At a Jewish Welfare Council meeting held on November 3, 1943, Harry Rosenthal was elected president. Apart from expressing his appreciation for the honour bestowed upon him and, after thanking the retiring officers for the splendid work they had done, he urged the Board of Governors to "set aside their personal antipathies and work for the common good at this time when the Jews of the world are in such distress."[31] Ever anxious to broaden the Council's mandate, Rosenthal began planning for future activities pertaining to anti-defamation, Palestine, refugees, and Jewish veterans' rehabilitation. For the Jewish community to survive he believed, such tasks would have to be carried out by a centralized agency.

Michael Sumner, another strong supporter of amalgamation, conveyed his interest in expanding the United Jewish Welfare Council's role by publishing the following editorial in the *Bulletin*'s March 30, 1944, issue. In it he summarized the past history of the Welfare Fund — the Council's predecessor — from the end of the 1930s until the formation of the unified organization:

> Up to 1937, Windsor Jewry was doing very little in the way of raising money for overseas charities. The only sizeable contributions were made to the Zionist causes. In 1938, for the first time, Windsor acknowledged its responsibilities to the needs for overseas relief by running a campaign for the Joint Distribution Committee.
>
> Up to that time, the only attempt to run a joint campaign was made in 1937. At this time an arrangement was made

whereby the United Palestine Appeal and the *Gewerkshaften* [unions] would work together on a single campaign.[32]

The fact that attitudes toward women were beginning to change was reflected in the *Bulletin*'s November 10, 1943, editorial. Entitled "Male Autocrats" and signed "L. Z.," it stressed the "complete lack of female participation" at the Community Council's previous meeting, deploring the fact that "although a good proportion of the attendance was made up of the fair but resolute sex, the only two times when a timid female voice attempted to make itself heard it was diverted by a bombast of masculine oratory that fairly shook the rafters of the sturdy synagogue."[33] (According to the minutes of that meeting, it took place at Simon Meretsky's home on November 24, not on November 3, 1943.) It appears that the Jewish Community Council did take note of the editorial's blunt words six months later, when it added an amendment to its constitution stipulating that "not less than three women" were to be appointed to its executive.[34]

By the beginning of 1944, the Council's executive had approved a plan to look into making Shaar Hashomayim the United Jewish Welfare Council's permanent home. It also had voted to take over the publication of the *Bulletin* "on a regular basis, funds for its operation to be solicited as previously."[35]

At a meeting held on May 18, 1944, the Board of Governors finally realized the need to broaden the Welfare Council's role. It, therefore, added the following amendment to its constitution: "It shall also be the purpose of the United Jewish Welfare Council to organize, sponsor, direct and carry on any activity essential to the well-being of the Windsor Jewish Community." In addition, the Board recommended that the Council's name be changed from "United Jewish Welfare Council of Windsor" to 'Windsor Jewish Community Council." Another proposed constitutional amendment was the clause that "any member of the executive missing three consecutive meetings of the executive may be disqualified and replaced by the Board of Governors."[36] All the proposed amendments were carried with overwhelming majorities.[37]

Archie Cherniak, whose dedication had been largely responsible for the formation of the Community Council, was asked to serve as its executive director on a voluntary basis until February 1945, when the Council's executive proposed hiring a professional to look after the Council's various branches. It also was suggested that he and a secretary be paid $8,000 a year. However, when that subject came up for discussion at the I. L. Peretz Shule's March executive meeting, its members were opposed to hiring a director because the $8,000 he and his assistant would be paid was "around twenty per cent of the sum total the Council raises each year." Instead, they suggested hiring "a girl who can do this work and pay her around $25 per year."[38]

Stung by the Peretz faction's criticism but determined to hire a professional by September 1945, the Community Council's Board of Governors approved an executive director at a salary of "no more than $5,000 per annum." At that time, the motion passed with a recorded vote of twenty-five in favour and fourteen against.[39]

In November 1945, Dr. Irwin W. Lefkowitz, who had served as executive director of the Jewish Welfare Board and of United Service Organizations in San Antonio, Texas, became the Council's executive director with a salary of $4,500 per annum.[40] Archie Cherniak continued on a voluntary basis until Dr. Lefkowitz's arrival in January 1946.[41]

Providing an office for Dr. Lefkowitz had been a priority some time prior to taking up his post. It was Simon and Milton Meretsky who, ultimately, put their premises at 327 Ouellette Avenue at his disposal with Michael Sumner donating a desk and a chair, Harry Rosenthal, a typewriter and a mimeograph machine, and Archie Cherniak promising to supply stationery and other office supplies. Ultimately, Miss Leiderman was hired as Dr. Lefkowitz's secretary at a salary of "between twenty and twenty-two dollars per week."[42]

Jewish Welfare Youth Council Formed

The Jewish Welfare Youth Council was formed early in 1944, bringing together ten local youth organizations, including

AZA (Aleph Zadik Aleph), Junior AZA, Junior Hadassah, B'nai B'rith Girls, Young Judea, Amicae Sorority, Elie Boys, Boy Scouts, and the Kappa Delta Phi Sorority.[43] The male high-school students had their own group. However, as there also was a need to bring together Jewish women between 19 and 25, B'nai B'rith Young Women was formed. [44]

Reporting on the activities of the Jewish Youth Council, a letter written by William G. Weingust and published in the December 1944 *Bulletin*, criticized the "skepticism and indifference" of the "powers-that-were," adding that "if the Jewish community needed anything," it was a youth centre where its children "could obtain clean, healthful fun and relaxation, both physical and mental." It appears that the Youth Council did subsequently obtain "more spacious quarters," as Weingust went on to thank the "individuals and organizations who, by their energy and enthusiasm, have made possible the leadership and support for the project."[45]

When Shaar Hashomayim's Sisterhood became an auxiliary of Talmud Torah in January 1945, one body could handle all the communal tasks, especially after Talmud Torah had become part of the synagogue's Sunday school.[46]

Realizing the need for a facility that could serve the youngest members of the community, Shaar Hashomayim announced the establishment of a nursery school in September 1945. Four staff members were hired to care for the approximately twenty-five children between the ages of 3 and 5.[47]

While efforts had been made in the past to draw together diverse groups, many Jewish organizations, anxious to meet their budgetary needs, still held their own banquets, concerts, and other social events. To help with the fundraising, it was not unusual for rabbis from Detroit, both those representing the Conservative and later also the Reform branches of Judaism, to be asked to address various Windsor community functions.[48] And to collect money for Jewish education, the students of the I. L. Peretz Shule would perform plays as part of their annual concert program.[49] As such drives largely depended on the generosity of certain community members, *Bulletin* editors were not averse to publishing in its pages both the donors' names as well as the amounts they had contributed. These lists appeared regularly in print, not only following the annual Welfare Fund Campaign and the drives of other organizations.[50]

The Open House

With anti-Semitism being an ever-present concern among Jews the world over, Rabbi Groner decided to do his part to help create a better understanding between Windsor's Jewish and non-Jewish communities. In the spring of 1944, he organized Shaar Hashomayim's first "Open House," planning to invite members of local churches, unions, service clubs, and fraternal and women's organizations to visit the synagogue so that these groups would have a better understanding of Jewish rituals and customs.[51]

The idea of the open house was first broached by Michael Sumner, who was very active at Shaar Hashomayim in early 1944. He felt that there were so many non-Jewish people in the community whose knowledge of Jewish life currently was so distorted, either out of ignorance, prejudice or coming from some other source, that it was very important to find a vehicle that we in the Jewish community could use in a dignified way to sort of bring to a much higher and much more accurate level the knowledge our non-Jewish friends and neighbors had about Jewish life.

Early in 1944, after a great deal of preliminary discussion, we arranged to have what we called an "Open House," which simply meant that we would invite interested people in the community, specifically, non-Jewish people, to come into the synagogue, look around and ask questions about what they saw. By those means, we would try to bring to them a first-hand, clear-cut picture of the way Jewish life should be viewed.[52]

Before initiating the Open House that was to be held on May 21, 1944, Rabbi Groner had accepted every invitation to address church groups, Rotary and Lions clubs, as well as other civic organizations. To publicize the event, he sent letters to local Catholic and Protestant clergymen, asking them and their parishioners to come to Shaar Hashomayim. He also placed paid advertisements in the *Windsor Daily Star* and was instrumental in preparing a booklet for distribution to all the guests who had been invited to the event.

Between three and four hundred people had been expected at the Open House, but when 4,000 showed up, they had to be taken around in shifts.

Photo courtesy of the Windsor Star

Mr. Morris Tabachnick, left, president of the Shaar Hashomayim Synagogue, and Rabbi Benjamin Groner, look at the tables of the law; embroidered on the covering of the Ark, as they make last-minute preparations for the fourth annual Open House on June 6, 1947.

Photo courtesy of the Windsor Star

The congregation of Shaar Hashomayim Synagogue opened its doors to the public to observe Brotherhood Week in February 1962. Pictured from the left are Charles A. Cohen, president of congregation; Rabbi Samuel S. Stollman, and Saul Nadvan, cantor.

Photo courtesy of the Windsor Star

Wide interest was shown at the annual Shaar Hashomayim Synagogue open house that attracted people from all faiths in June 1951. Following a lengthy talk on the fundamentals of Judaism and an explanation of the various symbols of the synagogue, Rabbi Samuel S. Stollman answered a variety of questions asked by members of the audience. Shown above, explaining some of the points of interest to two of the several Protestant clergy who attended, are Rabbi Stollman and Dr. Louis Perlman, president of the synagogue. From left to right in the group shown in the foreground are Rabbi Stollman, Dr. Perlman, Rev. Gladstone Wood of Riverside United Church; Mr. Don F. Brown, MP for Essex West, and Rev. Donald MacRae of St. Paul's United Church. Beside Rabbi Stollman is the ornamental crown from the Torah.

Reporting on the event," the *Windsor Daily Star* stated that "even the most optimistic hopes of those in charge of arrangements" had been exceeded. "Four times the synagogue was crowded to capacity by Christians during the afternoon, while Rabbi Benjamin Groner gave a half-hour lecture on the symbols, furnishings and the plate-glass windows in the synagogue. At the close of the lectures, the visitors crossed the platform within the synagogue to view the Torah, the ornaments and other symbols of the Jewish faith."[53]

Because of the many requests for copies of the booklet distributed at the Open House, the *Windsor Jewish Community Bulletin* later reprinted the following passages:

> The Jew is not a newcomer to Windsor. As far back as 1810 there are records of Jewish settlers. In 1891 there were sixteen Jews living here. Growing with Windsor, the Jewish community is estimated to be 2,800.
>
> In the last war, as in this one, our young men have done and are doing their share.
>
> We feel that we are rooted in this community historically and practically. We, too, have our contribution to make to the common weal. We shall never fail to live up to our responsibilities as citizens in full measure.
>
> Not the least of these responsibilities is that of building a society and a world which is worthy of the tremendous sacrifice our fighting men are making.
>
> We ask no greater privilege than the opportunity of joining our Christian brothers in this task. All those who worship God, whether in church or synagogue, must work together toward a common end if we are to have a Godly and an upright society.[54]

Following the Open House, Rabbi Groner received a letter from Army Chaplain Sydney K. Mossman, who was the first person born in Windsor to become a rabbi.

Rabbi Sydney Kenneth Mossman was born on April 15, 1913, attended Kennedy Collegiate where he graduated with highest honours. He attended DePaul University Law School in Chicago and earned his rabbinic training at Hebrew Theological College in Skokie, Illinois, where he received his *s'micha*. He served congregations in Hammond, Indiana and Nashville, Tennessee, and served for many years at Shearith Israel Congregation in Atlanta, Georgia.

In his letter to Rabbi Groner, dated June 9, 1944, and posted in England, Rabbi Mossman commended Rabbi Groner on his efforts, calling the Open House "a great gesture [that] perhaps might do much to dispel some of the incredible nonsense believed about our synagogue." In conclusion, Rabbi Mossman stated, "As much as I don't believe we should live a Gentile Judaism, still, I do believe that, in some measured manner, we must cooperate with them and, at the same time, let them know something about us."[55]

Commenting on the success of the Open House, Michael Sumner stated, "It is the belief of the committee in charge that this affair will have untold value for the Jewish Community of Windsor in the goodwill type of public relations achieved."[56]

The Shaar Hashomayim executive subsequently decided to hold such Open Houses on an annual basis. In the years that followed, each one met with similar success, resulting in untold benefits for the synagogue, in that it had managed to establish itself as an extremely community-oriented organization.[57]

War Comes to an End

Until 1943, the war had not gone well for the Allies, especially after Denmark, Norway, Holland, Belgium, Luxembourg, and France had one by one succumbed to the superior might of the Nazi onslaught. The tide began to turn after the Allied landings on the beaches of Normandy on June 6, 1944. The Essex Scottish Light Infantry Regiment, having taken part in what became known as the D-Day landing, ultimately distinguished itself, together with other Canadian regiments by being the first troops to enter the town of Dieppe as liberators on September 1, 1944.

Although the Normandy landing precipitated the end of the war in Europe, it also unleashed a monumental refugee problem. Canadian Jews, therefore, welcomed the announcement by Saul Hayes, national director of the United Jewish Refugee and War Relief Agencies, that 275 Jews who had fled to Spain and Portugal had been satisfactorily settled in Canada. About the same time, the Jewish Telegraph Agency reported that a vessel carrying the first 570 Jewish refugees from Yugoslavia, Greece, and other Balkan countries had safely reached Palestine.

By the end of 1944, Jews all over the world rejoiced when it became evident that the collapse of Germany was imminent. Nonetheless, the events of the war could not help making them even more aware of the importance of Palestine, which, by then, had absorbed more than 300,000 Holocaust survivors. To develop greater immigration opportunities, they called for the acquisition of new land, the establishment of new agricultural settlements, and the expansion of industries in what ultimately became Israel — the Jewish homeland. Although obtaining adequate funding for these vital endeavours was not an easy task, Windsor's comparatively small Jewish population raised $24,623 by the end of 1944, placing them sixth on the list of Canadian cities in terms of contributions to Palestine.

Forty-two thousand Canadians did not return to their hometowns at the end of hostilities. To honour the memory of the brave young Jews who had fought and died for their country, The Royal Canadian Legion's Balfour Branch No. 362 presented a special plaque to Windsor's Jewish community on Remembrance Day — November 11, 1949.[58] It was inscribed with the names of those who had been killed in action: Lawrence Allen, Samuel Berger, Arthur Cherkinsky, Joseph Cherkinsky, Leonard Feldman, Louis Feldman, Carl Rosenberg, Meyer Schwartz, Jacob Silverstein, Benjamin Soloway, and Maurice Strosberg.[59]

Joseph Brennan had been taken prisoner following his part in the Dieppe Raid and was left so badly disfigured that it affected him for the rest of his life.[60]

The war in Europe was not officially over until May 8, 1945. Yet even before Germany's unconditional surrender, Canadians were getting ready to observe the day that would become known as VE–Day. The following letter, written to Rabbi Groner by Windsor's Mayor Arthur J. Reaume indicates that preparations for victory celebrations had been underway for more than two months prior to the end of hostilities:

February 26, 1945

Dear Rabbi Groner,

Some time ago, a committee was appointed to consider the manner in which Windsor should observe the cessation of organized resistance on the part of Germany.

The committee met at the City Hall on February 5th, 1945, and came to the decision that, as the cessation of organized resistance might still leave months of fighting ahead, and there still remained the problem of defeating Japan, any celebration, holiday or work stoppage would be most inappropriate. Rather it should be a time for renewed effort, re-dedication to the task of dealing with our remaining enemy, and a time when all persons should attend divine service in their own churches.

It would, therefore, be appreciated if you would arrange to have your place of Worship open to the public, as soon as cessation of German resistance is announced, so that members of the congregation may offer prayers of Thanksgiving. We would also ask that you arrange to hold an Evening Service at 7:30 p.m. on the day on which the announcement is made, or at the same hour on the day following, if word is received too late to permit arrangements to be made on the actual day.

ARTHUR J. REAUME, Mayor[61]

Even before World War II came to an end, the Allies had been keenly aware of the need to create an international body that would prevent the recurrence of similar conflicts. Representatives of fifty countries met in San Francisco between April 25 and June 26, 1945, to draft a Charter for the United Nations.

A few weeks earlier, Saul Hayes, executive director of the Canadian Jewish Congress, had advised Harry Rosenthal, president of the Windsor Community Council, that he would travel to San Francisco as part of a joint British-American Jewish delegation to put forward the following requests:

- The establishment of an authority that would confer status upon stateless Jews;

- The appointment of UNRRA (United Nations Relief and Rehabilitation Association) personnel, who would understand the special religious and cultural needs of Jews under UNRRA's program;

- The restoration to the Jewish Agency for Palestine of funds and property confiscated from Jewish owners, who no longer were alive, "so that these resources may be used to provide houses and futures in the Jewish National Home."

Additional Canadian representation for Jewish interests was made on July 17, 1945, at a meeting of the Big Three — Great Britain, the United States, and the Soviet Union — at Potsdam in Germany. Although their agenda primarily dealt with determining the fate of defeated Nazi Germany, the Canadian Palestine Committee, the Christian Council on Palestine, and the Zionist Organization of Canada saw that conference as an opportunity to gain Great Britain's support for "a new freedom" that would allow the "disinherited and tortured Jewish refugees of Europe" to enter their ancient homeland of Palestine "without sufferance." Consequently, these agencies presented a brief to Norman Robertson, Canadian Undersecretary of State for External Affairs, urging him to bring their recommendations to the attention of British Prime Minister Clement Attlee.[62]

On August 16, 1945, one week after Japan had sued for peace following the United States' atomic bomb attacks on Hiroshima and Nagasaki, Windsor people finally were able to celebrate the end of World War II. After a VJ–Day rally in Jackson Park, the mayor sent a letter to Rabbi Groner, thanking him "for the part you so ably played in the service and celebration..." and for the work done by his synagogue that, "throughout the dark, dark days of war probably was the greatest of all the organizations in keeping the spirit of the people up and making them realize that without the assistance and guidance of Almighty God our future would be none too bright."[63]

The White Paper

The euphoria of victory celebrations was cut short in the fall of 1945, when Jews learned of Great Britain's decision to continue the restrictive immigration policy contained in its 1939 White Paper that limited to 1,500 persons a month the number of refugees permitted to enter Palestine.

In response, prominent Zionists dispatched strongly worded appeals to Jewish groups throughout the Western world, asking them to protest against the British move. Rabbi Jesse Schwartz, executive director of the Canadian Zionist Organizations, also sent a telegram to Jewish community leaders on September 28, 1945, urging them to organize a series of mass meetings to arouse public indignation.[64]

Similar protests were launched by CCF [now, NDP] member of Parliament for Winnipeg, Stanley H. Knowles, who on October 2, 1945, called upon fellow House of Commons members to support the abrogation of the White Paper. The cause that denied access to Palestine to thousands of destitute European Jews also was taken up by CCF leader M. J. Coldwell, by its national secretary David Lewis, by A. R. Mosher, president of the Canadian Congress of Labour, and by Percy Benough, president of the Trades and Labour Congress of Canada.[65]

Windsor Jewry responded by holding its own protest rallies as well as a mass meeting at the Windsor Arena on October 4, 1945. Jointly sponsored by the Jewish Community and the Zionist councils, it urged participants to pass a resolution along the following lines:

> Continuation of White Paper policy by British Government spells a death knell for tens of thousands of Jews who have survived Nazi atrocities, and who refuse to return to their former homes and scenes of horror and persecution, and who appeal to Great Britain and the world conscience to open the gates of Palestine to them to make their liberty final and true.
>
> The resolution should also call for fulfilment of the pledge of the Balfour Declaration and Mandate endorsed by fifty-two nations. Announcements should be inserted announcing the meeting and inviting the entire community, Jews and non-Jews, to attend. The Zionist office will take care of expenses of advertisements.[66]

The meeting was well attended by Jewish as well as Gentile citizens who, rallying in solidarity with their Jewish brethren, raised funds to show their wholehearted opposition to the terms of the White Paper. According to Michael Sumner, they also heard Rabbi Groner deliver "the finest speech of his career" that created "an understanding for our problems among the clergy and laity alike."[67]

Commenting on that protest meeting in his 1945 year-end review, Rabbi Groner called it perhaps "the most significant in the entire Jewish community." He also said, "The great hall was packed to capacity with almost every adult Jew in Windsor in attendance, in addition to hundreds of Christians whose presence was an eloquent testimonial of their sympathy and friendship for the Jewish cause. Ministers of all denominations and civic leaders from every walk of life addressed the mammoth crowd."[68]

Arising From the Ashes – 1946-1950

The years immediately following World War II were challenging years for all Canadians. As industries began to revert to peacetime production, Jews too wanted to actively participate in the country's post-war reconstruction, as well as in the development of its export markets. However, by then, their attitude toward Canada's institutions had changed from one of "apprehensive defensiveness to one of positive affirmative action."[69]

Windsor's Jewish community emerged with great fortitude and resolve from the conflict that had threatened to destroy all of World Jewry. In a poignant editorial, published in the *Bulletin*'s August 23, 1945, issue, Harry Cherniak, the recently elected president of the Jewish Community Council, reminded them of the new challenges that lay ahead. Here are excerpts from that editorial:

> Windsor's Jewish Community stands today at almost 3,000 men, women, and children. Among us are all types — all financial classes — various ideologies.... We have many assets — three synagogues, our Talmud Torah, and the Peretz School. We have many organizations and also a Community Council. In the main, with a few exceptions, our people give generously

for Jewish causes. Should we be satisfied? The answer, it seems to me, is definitely, no.

The officers of our present institutions will be the first to admit that a much better job can and should be done. Many individual societies could and should have better programs and attendance. Our Community Council has made progress, but is far from its goal.... Congregation Shaar Hashomayim has made marvelous strides in the past few years — but its directors feel much more can be done. Our community youth program is handicapped by lack of buildings. Talmud Torah should have more attendance and the interest of parents. The cemetery problem is still unsolved. Every once in a while, each of us, I am sure, dreams of the day when we can have a community centre for Windsor. Intense interest and energy in raising funds for the relief and rehabilitation of our distressed brethren in Europe is still an urgent necessity.... The Palestine problem clamors for an early solution. Nationally and locally, we will be faced with many post-war problems — re-establishment of soldiers in civilian life, and many others.

Will these problems be solved? The answer lies with you and you and you — the large majority of Windsor's Jewry, who have been passive Jews....

Many men, it seems to me, think they have done their share for the community if they live within the law, support their families, and give a little, now and then, on request. Hasn't it occurred to them that no credit is due anyone for making a living and supporting his family? Even the animals do that....

With summer almost over, a new season of work and activity begins for us all.... Why not pick your spot to do a job this year?... The head of any organization will welcome you, and see that you get something to do that will be constructive and worthwhile, and of benefit to the community.[70]

By the end of 1945, Windsor's Jewish organizations were busily planning for the future. Just as support for the men in uniform had been their primary focus during the war, the present concerns were to help returning soldiers become acclimatized to civilian life. They also were called upon to provide homes and a chance to earn a livelihood to those refugees who, after escaping the horrors of the Holocaust, had made their way to Windsor.

A New Future for Shaar Hashomayim

Over the years, Shaar Hashomayim's membership had risen from 40 to 225 families. Having cast off its elitist image, its membership now included people from all walks of life, not only the well-to-do who, some believed, had been the synagogue's mainstay in the past. The congregation also seemed to have resolved earlier conflicts between those who regarded Shaar Hashomayim as purely a place to pray and others who had recognized its wider communal functions.[71]

In a November 1945 meeting attended by the greatest number of members ever, Jerry A. Glanz was re-elected as the synagogue's president. The executive felt that since he had been the one to suffer the most under its debt, he should be honoured in the year when its mortgage burning would take place.[72] Only two years earlier, the Shaar's mortgage debt had totalled $60,000. The exceptional achievement of retiring that debt in 1945 was achieved through a fundraising campaign headed by Archie Cherniak and the building fund committee[73] that climaxed with a memorial service for Joel Gelber, a recently deceased member and one of Shaar Hashomayim's staunchest supporters.[74]

A fitting tribute to the remarkable Jerry Glanz is the following humorous profile that appeared in the *Bulletin's* April 5, 1945 edition:

HONORABLE MENSCHEN
2. JERRY GLANZ
XRAY BY EMJAY

It all started one day in 1914, when Jerry took a boat ride from the Detroit side of the river and, on arriving in Windsor, saw that our small Jewish Colony was ripe for many communal improvements. So he decided to stay awhile and see if he couldn't help. And since then, it's just been one meeting after another.

It took no time at all, after checking through the Customs and Immigration Department, before he interested a group of Windsorites into organizing the Talmud Torah. And no sooner was it started on its still tortuous path before he was instrumental in organizing the first Windsor Zionist group in 1915.

Finding that he had a few more evenings a week to spare and, because Windsor lacked any sort of fraternal society, he became a member of the Detroit *Pisgah* Lodge of B'nai B'rith in about 1920. And then, thinking it would be a splendid idea to inoculate the Windsor boys with the spirit of benevolence and brotherhood, he obtained a charter for a B'nai B'rith Lodge and was rewarded with its first presidency. Later on, he organized the ladies into forming the B'nai B'rith Auxiliary and was the moving spirit in the forming of the first AZA (Aleph Zadik Aleph) group.

In spite of being an acting member and counsellor in these and other organizations, he found that time hung heavily on his hands between Mincha and Maarev. So he helped organize the first Windsor JDC and was its first president with Moe Stone handling the Shekels.

Because of the influx of many European refugees after the First World War and the need for aiding them to settle in Canada, he became active in setting up a Jewish Immigration Aid and was later honoured by becoming the Dominion vice president.

Some time during that period, Jerry went into the furniture business. And it is this column's contention that he did so only to provide seating accommodation for the many people who came to him seeking counsel and aid. His store has been a clearing house for people of all walks of life, with their problems and troubles ranging from inquiring as to the location of Mercer Street to seeking advice as to how to get rid of a mother-in-law, and others as to how to acquire one. It is said that Mr. Anthony of radio fame was troubled with a personal problem and contacted Jerry for advice and what's more — took it!

That noticeably erect carriage of Jerry's when sitting or standing can be traced to him having occupied the straight-backed president's chair at the Shaar [Hashomayim] for over twelve years. And, after leaving that honoured position, President Roosevelt is said to have sighed with relief, having run second best up to that time.

The biggest blow to Jerry's generous spirit is the lack of panhandlers during these lush times, who used to stop in regularly for their dime for a cup of coffee. So

Jerry is now forced to seize on any casual visitor who may drop into the store and personally conduct him across the street for a cup of coffee.

The organizations mentioned here are only a few of the many that Jerry has been actively associated with in their inception and growth and we could go on like this until the next issue of the *Bulletin* (even if it came out on time), but we're holding up the presses with the result that our backs are breaking. In conclusion, let's doff our hats to the man who always doffs his jacket when there's a job of work to be done.
EMJAY[75]

Those elected as Shaar Hashomayim's vice presidents included Harry Cherniak, Jacob Orechkin, Jacob Katzman, and Bernard Kaplan — all progressive young men who, in the words of Michael Sumner, were "dedicated to the ideal of expanding the synagogue and its services to the community." Much to the delight of those present, the financial statement read by auditor Irving S. Goldin, revealed substantial surpluses in each of the synagogue's operations.[76]

The burning of Shaar Hashomayim's mortgage was indeed the most important event to take place in the summer of 1946. Co-sponsored by B'nai B'rith, the celebration took place during the weekend of June 7–9. Beginning with a Saturday morning service, it concluded with an evening dance in honour of the Jewish war veterans. Many local dignitaries attended the event, including His Worship Mayor Arthur Reaume, Lt. Col. David Croll, as well as other high-ranking officers in the Royal Canadian Legion. Shaar Hashomayim President Jerry Glanz mentioned some of the hardships the congregation had faced in the past, explaining that "we were left with a large mortgage and other liabilities amounting to approximately $125,000" when the Great Depression came and "it was only by hard work and severe strug-

Photo courtesy of the Windsor Star

When the congregation at Shaar Hashomayim succeeded in paying off the mortgage for the synagogue, they arranged a ceremony on June 9, 1946, to burn the mortgage. In this picture, David Meretsky, left, one of the original mortgage guarantors, and Jerry Glanz, a founder of the synagogue, prepare the urn for depositing.

gling that we were able to reduce these liabilities and keep up our maintenance. Now I can say that my work has been completed."[77]

The actual mortgage burning took place after a dinner on Sunday night, when the 350 invited guests assembled in the synagogue's chapel were given an opportunity to watch each original guarantor light his piece of the mortgage document from a candle and deposit the ashes in a silver bowl. That bowl, ultimately, became part of Shaar Hashomayim's treasured memorabilia.[78]

The Jewish Community Council Moves Forward

With their war work behind them, the members of Windsor's B'nai B'rith Lodge, under the presidency of Maxwell Schott, turned their attention to such activities as the rehabilitation of returned Jewish servicemen. Assisted by the Jewish War Veterans' Branch of the Royal Canadian Legion, they formed a veterans' committee to make available much-needed funds and housing to the former Jewish servicemen. Its long-range plans even included guidance counselling, as well as the allocation of money to those wishing to go into business and/or purchase a home.[79] A year later, Windsor's Jewish war veterans changed the name of the "Jewish Branch 362 of the Royal Canadian Legion" to "Balfour Branch 362, The Royal Canadian Legion."[80]

In March 1946, Windsor's Jewish Community Council took over publication of the *Bulletin* that had been published by Shaar Hashomayim since 1943. It was decided to put Archie Cherniak in charge of finances and to let others besides the executive director write the *Bulletin*'s editorials.[81] Other innovations implemented several months later included the creation of a no-charge service column to help individuals looking for employment and a place to live; the listing of items in the "Personals" column according to subject matter; and to print in each *Bulletin* "Rabbi Groner's request for community cooperation in sending material to him."[82]

The Council's executive director, Dr. Irwin W. Lefkowitz, who had come to Windsor in January 1946, left less than three months later because his wife could not stand the Canadian climate. He was replaced by Louis Lieblich, who starting the job on April 1,1946.[83]

Louis Lieblich was born in 1908 on New York City's Lower East Side. He brought to his new task not only a unifying spirit, but also such impressive credentials as a Bachelor of Arts degree from Cleveland's Western University and an Master's degree in social work from the University of Chicago. Talking about his four years spent in Windsor, Lieblich said,

After working in Pittsburgh for a while and serving in the United States Army during World War II, the Council of Jewish Federations referred me to the Jewish Community Council of Windsor. Almost as soon as I had arrived in the city, I fell in love with it and its people. I especially remember Mike Sumner and Milton Meretsky, who were the first to introduce me to the community. What great guys they were!

At first, my office was at the back of Harry Cherniak's store until we moved to new premises in the Palace Theatre Building. Although my title was Executive Director, I did everything — counselling, setting up a family service, raising funds for various causes, budgeting, and even editing the *Bulletin*.

I also made sure that the smaller Jewish communities of Leamington, Chatham and Kingsville took advantage of the services offered by our Council. Not only did we distribute copies of the *Bulletin* to them, but we invited their young people to participate in the activities of our Youth Council. We also were able to arrange with the Jewish Vocational Service of Detroit a complete vocational guidance service for our high-school students.

When I left in 1950, I was succeeded by Morris B. Seidelman as the Community Council's Executive Director and editor of the *Bulletin*. I truly enjoyed the time I spent in Windsor. During the four years I was there, I may have taught the people I worked with something about fundraising and social work. However, in principal, I learned a lot more from them, particularly what it meant to be a Jew. What struck me most about them was that they were, what

I would call, honest-to-God Jews, the likes of whom I never had met before. And, I also would say, that I never ran into anyone in the whole damned town who wasn't a good Zionist or not interested in building up this comparatively little community.[84]

Another sign that Windsor's Jewish community was moving ahead was Harry Cherniak's passionate editorial in the *Bulletin*'s June 5, 1946 issue. In it he reminded members that, even though Shaar Hashomayim's mortgage had been retired and the community was debt-free for the first time since anyone could remember, this was not the time to rest on their laurels. Asking them to consider the need for a Jewish community centre, he pointed out that they could afford to build a very substantial and efficient building "if the majority will agree we need it," and to give as generously to it and in proportion to the amounts that had been given to the synagogue building fund and the Council's Welfare Fund. Mr. Cherniak explained that such a centre "should be paid for in large gifts from the capital of each of us rather than from income," assuring his readers that it would become "an extension of our own individual homes" and "enrich the lives of all of us." In the same editorial, he also mentioned the need for a new cemetery and that help was required for "our distressed brothers in Europe and for building up Palestine as a National Home."[85]

However, at that time, Jewish education was the community's first priority. Before long, the Jewish Community Council announced plans for a summer day camp for young children between the ages of 7 and 13. The program included athletics, arts and crafts, swimming, dancing, drama, and singing. However, those responsible for carrying it out also wanted to provide lessons in Jewish culture and traditions that, they felt, could be "painlessly" imparted to the children.[86] The Peretz Shule continued to teach Yiddish, Hebrew, History, Bible, Yiddish, and Hebrew literature. The Institute of Jewish Studies, under the guidance of Rabbi Groner, Joseph Kligman, Michael Sumner and Louis Lieblich, was drawing up plans to teach adults.[87] And

the Talmud Torah had six classes, led by Leah Levine and Malke Yuzpe, and a bar mitzvah class under the direction of Reverend Bornstein.[88] During the war, Shaar Hashomayim had taken over "direct management and operation of Talmud Torah." However, the final integration of the two institutions only occurred in 1946, which, according to the synagogue's president Joshua Gitlin, made it possible for "the expense of education [to be] spread out among the entire membership."[89] With the two schools now under the supervision of Rabbi Groner, he called the amalgamation "a most worthy experiment, worthy of emulation in other communities." He also felt that the success marking this venture "speaks well for the earnestness and devotion of the individuals who strove diligently to carry the scheme through to fruition."[90]

The status of all Canadians was officially changed on January 1, 1947, when the Canadian Citizenship Act came into effect. Enacted by the House of Commons on June 27, 1946, it conferred a common citizenship on all persons living in Canada, regardless of whether they had been born in the country. Windsor's Jewish community celebrated the event by proclaiming the week of January 5, 1947, "Citizenship Week." Special services were held at Shaar Hashomayim that included the dedication of Canadian and Palestinian flags that, subsequently, became an integral part of the synagogue's adornments. The Jewish Community Council, in collaboration with Shaar Hashomayim, contributed religious and other secular objects to a cultural group exhibit set up at Patterson Collegiate.[91]

Yet anti-Semitism still persisted in and around Windsor. Joseph Eisenberg, who later became the Community Council's executive director, remembered seeing racist signs as late as 1949 all along the Lake Erie beaches — in Colchester and in Leamington. But he was especially offended by one that read "No Jews or Dogs allowed" that stood in front of the Blue Haven Motel in Amherstburg. "That one really upset everyone, " he said, "especially the Jewish war veterans who felt that they now were equal partners in the Canadian mosaic." Mr. Eisenberg recalled that a Jew bought the motel and ultimately gave it to the B'nai

B'rith. Another billboard that had caught his attention was the one that was visible to anyone driving into Walkerville: "Walkerville founded in 1868 and crucified by David Croll in 1936." It is worth noting that Walkerville also had a clause in its property deeds forbidding Jews from purchasing homes in that community.[92] Displays of overt anti-Semitism continued for quite some time in Canada, until Parliament passed a law in 1970 making the promotion of hatred against identifiable groups a criminal offence.

Other Jewish Organizations

In the fall of 1947, Michael Sumner succeeded Harry Cherniak as president of Windsor's Jewish Community Council. Hoping to represent most Jewish organizations in the city, he soon realized that many of them preferred to retain their own leadership and to conduct their own programs and activities. Among them were Shaar Hashomayim's Sisterhood, the B'nai Brith's Men's and Women's chapters, Hadassah's Lillian Friedman and Kadimah chapters, Junior Hadassah, the Herzl Chapter of AZA (Aleph Zadik Aleph), the Jewish Boy Scouts and Girl Guides, Shaarey Zedek Synagogue, Mizrachi, the Pinsker and the Progressive Aid societies, Talmud Torah, the Photography Club, the Jewish National Fund, Hoshnosas Orchim, the I. L. Peretz Shule, the Peretz Mothers' Club, the Jewish-Russian-Ukrainian Farband, United Jewish People's Order, the Gewerkshaften Committee, the Pioneer Women, the Hebrew Ladies' Aid Society, Balfour Branch 362 of the Royal Canadian Legion, Poele Zion, and the Chana Senesh Club.

The meetings and gatherings of all these organizations were held either at Shaar Hashomayim Synagogue, at Talmud Torah, or at the I. L. Peretz Shule. Although the *Bulletin* regularly reported their activities, it hardly ever mentioned Tifereth Israel, the East Windsor synagogue. Events at Shaarey Zedek also were seldom reported, despite the fact that those taking place at the Detroit synagogue bearing the same name received coverage on several occasions. With the *Bulletin* clearly in default regarding reportage on these two congrega-

tions, it was not surprising that the members of Shaarey Zedek refused to accept the Jewish Community Council's membership offered to them in the fall of 1947.[93]

At that time, community unity also was challenged by the diverse opinions held by different groups on Va'ad Hayeshivot. However, it was decided in October 1947 to allow contributions and allocations to these Orthodox religious institutions to be channelled through the Community Council.[94]

Michael Sumner.

Photo courtesy of the Windsor Star

Windsor Welcomes Jewish Orphans and Other New Faces

Early in 1948, the community turned its attention to rescuing those European Jewish orphans who had been fortunate enough to escape the Holocaust. The fact that they were able to come to Canada was due largely to the Canadian government's new and more relaxed immigration laws, permitting 9,892 Jews, out of a total of 125,414, to enter the country.

Of the 399 orphans who had arrived by 1948, sixteen found homes with Jewish families in Windsor.[95] Here is what Michael Sumner remembered about meeting them at Toronto's Union Station:

> They were nice kids but none of them was under 18. One boy comes up to me and says, "I'm afraid they are going to send me back. I am supposed to be an orphan, but my parents are still alive." I told him, "Forget it, you'll live long enough here to bring over your parents." Then a girl and a boy came up to me. She was crying. "What's the trouble?" I asked. Pointing to the young man at her side, she said, "He and I are going to be sent back because we are married." I assured her that once they are in Windsor the town people will be glad to welcome them as a married couple.[96]

It was fortunate that the Jewish Community Council was able to raise sufficient funds to help these newcomers adjust to their new surroundings.[97] But when their numbers grew to 1,000 nationally and Windsor Jews were asked to provide homes for many of these additional orphans, the Canadian Jewish Congress expressed displeasure at the lack of support it had received from them.[98] An April 1948 *Bulletin* editorial, entitled "A D.P. Camp or a Canadian Home?" even accused Windsor's Jewish community of doing only a "partial job," in this regard, although it did make a point of noting "that was something it was not

accustomed to doing."[99] Some of the orphans ultimately went to the United States; others settled in Toronto or elsewhere in Canada. According to Community Council Executive Director Louis Lieblich, all of them had stories to tell that "would curl your hair."[100] Recalling his involvement with settling these orphans in Windsor, he said,

> In 1948, after the government had allowed 1,000 Jewish orphans to come to Canada, I supervised the placement of sixteen of these children in Windsor homes. I found the work very rewarding. Although the Jewish community bore all or at least part of the cost of maintaining them, local doctors provided free physical check-ups, and many Windsor merchants donated clothing and other necessities.
>
> These youngsters quickly adjusted to their new surroundings. They attended Rabbi Chaim Weinstein's special Talmud Torah classes and were receiving English lessons at the W. D. Lowe Vocational School.[101]

Some of the newcomers may have entered the Peretz Shule since enrolment reached 112 in the fall of 1948.[102] At the end of January 1949, it reached 130[103] and, by the end of the 1949 school year stood at 137 with 71 boys and 66 girls.[104]

In connection with the welcome received by other newcomers, an editorial in the July 18, 1948, *Bulletin* praised "those people in our community who have, without fanfare, gone out of their way to be of service to our newly arrived brethren. Receiving these former victims of the Nazis has been an opportunity and a privilege. They will enormously aid our community by adding to its ranks and infusing new spirit into its Jewishness."[105] Louis Lieblich, especially, remembered "Nancy Faye (Arnold), the first baby to be born to a Jewish immigrant in Windsor. Her mother, Esther Arnold, (née Aranovitz), who had arrived with the first group of DP orphans on January 13, 1948, had gone to live with Mrs. M. Golinker on Goyeau Street."[106]

Although Jewish immigration to Canada declined by 50 percent in 1949, applications for assistance increased as New Canadians requested classes in citizenship, English, and Canadian history. However, what most of them wanted were jobs — any kind of jobs.[107]

Leadership Beyond Windsor's Borders

By 1946, many Windsor Jews had become involved in a variety of causes. When Harry Rosenthal was elected president of the Ontario Zionist region in the fall of that year, it was decided to hold a testimonial dinner in his honour at Shaar Hashomayim.[108] Starting in 1947, many local Jews attended meetings in other Ontario towns, in other Canadian provinces, as well as in the United States. In January, Michael Sumner was one of three speakers at a Conference of the Ontario Region of the Canadian Jewish Congress, Harry Rosenthal chaired a session on education, Harry Cherniak another one, while Norman Ramm and Philip Strosberg represented Youth Council members.[109] Also in 1947, Reuben Madoff became a delegate to the General Assembly of the Council of Jewish Federations and Welfare Funds in Atlanta, Georgia.[110] Accompanying him were Harry Cherniak, Archie Rose, and Louis Lieblich. At the Toronto meeting of the United Jewish Relief Agencies of Canada, Windsor was represented by Eli Goldin, Norman Ramm, Harry Rosenthal, and Milton Sumner.[111] And Windsor Jews rejoiced in 1949 when their city was chosen to host the Regional Conference of the Central Division of the Zionist Organization of Canada.[112]

Community work was not restricted to Jewish causes. In the spring of 1947, Maxwell Schott was appointed for a three-year term as the Windsor board of education's representative to the Windsor Library Board;[113] and a year later, Eli Goldin received an Alumni Award from Windsor's Assumption College.[114] In 1949, Archie Cherniak declared himself as the CCF candidate for the Federal riding of Essex West. Although he won his party's nomination in May 1949, he ultimately lost the election.[115]

Photo courtesy of the Windsor Star

Mr. Archie Cherniak, a Windsor merchant, was victorious in a field of four in a three-ballot fight for the 1949 CCF nomination in Essex West. He ran against Liberal incumbent Don F. Brown, and Progressive Conservative candidate Kenneth W. MacIntyre. Here, Mr. Cherniak receives congratulations from William C. MacDonald, chairman, left and Mr. Arthur Williams, right, CCF MP for the riding of Ontario (Oshawa).

Palestine Assistance and the Birth of the State of Israel

In the summer of 1946 Windsor Jews learned about the many illegal arrests of Jews, the harassment of peaceful Jewish citizens, and the looting of Jewish relief funds and Jewish properties by the British in Palestine, which made them realize that the need to provide funds for Palestine had to take precedence over financing other less pressing projects. A week after a Sabbath attack on the leaders of the Jewish Agency for Palestine, Shaar Hashomayim held a service reaffirming the community's "solidarity with our brethren." In a special sermon, Rabbi Groner upheld "the heroic defence [sic] of Palestine" and protested against the arrest of rabbis and other Jews on that day, which he called "a desecration of the Sabbath."[116]

The *Bulletin* challenged members of Windsor's Jewish community to make their voices heard, as the struggle in Palestine was "a fight no less critical than the one for which so many of our sons and brothers so recently gave their lives."[117]

In the fall of 1947, Michael Sumner and Henry Rosenthal were delegates at a meeting of the Jewish Federations and Welfare Funds in Chicago where "all sessions were suddenly cancelled because Golda Meir was flying in from Israel."[118] Having replaced Moshe Sharett in 1946 as head of the Jewish Agency's Political Department — the chief Jewish liaison with the British — and a member of the executive of the Jewish Agency, Golda Meir now was active raising funds in the United States to help cover the costs of the Israeli War of Independence. Michael Sumner recalled his encounter with the woman who would become Israel's prime minister in 1969:

> She came to Chicago, the weather was chilly and she didn't have a coat. She told us what was going on in Israel. Her son was fighting on one front and her daughter on another one. "It's shaping up into a full-scale war," she said, "and we need arms. Munitions are ready for delivery in Czechoslovakia. But until we can lay the cash on the table we can't get delivery."
>
> As soon as the meeting had adjourned, all the delegates went to the telephone to call their local council members. After telling them Golda Meir's story, they asked them to go to their banks to find out how much money they could get without guarantees. I called Harry Cherniak. "Go to our branch of the Bank of Commerce," I said, "and tell them that we haven't got time to raise money as we are faced with an emergency. Ask them how much credit they could extend to the Jewish community on our authority." After all, we were not yet a formal organization.
>
> I think the bank gave us $35,000. Everybody in Canada and in the United States instantly responded to Golda Meir's plea. The next day, she had bills of credit for about $35 million. And, since the machinery had been set in motion, she and her people went back home knowing that a total of about $50 million would be available for the purchase of arms. That is what saved the Israelis' lives. Because when the British left Palestine, they gave their arms to the Arabs to make sure they wouldn't go to the Jews.[119]

The strongly worded appeals throughout the Western world were finally heeded on November 29, 1947, when United Nations Resolution 181, proposing the partition of Palestine into Jewish and Arab states, passed by a margin of thirty-three to thirteen. Despite the fact that Lester B. Pearson, then Canada's Undersecretary of State for External Affairs, had been instrumental in facilitating support for the resolution in the General Assembly, Canada abstained from voting on it in the Security Council, in deference to Prime Minister William Lyon Mackenzie King's stubborn support of Britain's imperial policy.

To celebrate the passage of Resolution 181, Rabbi Benjamin Groner conducted an impressive thanksgiving service with 1,200 people crowding into Shaar Hashomayim to hear him speak. Windsor's Jewish Community Council also issued a statement, expressing gratitude for the birth of the Jewish state and its appreciation to those nations who had "indicated understanding of the Jewish people." Samuel Bronfman, national president of the Canadian Jewish Congress, reaffirmed his belief in the United Nations' sponsorship of a Jewish state by stating that the decision "comes as a great relief to all those who concern themselves with the problem of Jewish homelessness. It also is of tremendous significance to millions of people of all races and nations...."[120]

Photo courtesy of the Windsor Star

Shaar Hashomayim Synagogue was crowded to overflowing yesterday as Jewish residents of Windsor celebrated in worship the proclamation of the State of Israel in May 1948. The flag of the new country was presented during the service, and resolutions asking for recognition of Israel by Canada and the United Kingdom, and the removal of all arms embargoes to the new state were unanimously approved.

The date, May 14, 1948, will always remain memorable for World Jewry for it was on that day that Great Britain ended its mandate over Palestine, an act that made possible the proclamation of the independent State of Israel and the naming of Chaim Weizmann as its first president and David Ben Gurion as its first prime minister. To celebrate that auspicious occasion, Shaar Hashomayim held a commemorative service on May 16, 1948, that included a sermon by Rabbi Groner and, led by the synagogue's cantor, singing by both its choir and its congregation.[121]

Canada did not recognize Israel until December 24, 1948, only fully conferring its recognition of the new state on May 11, 1949, the day Israel was granted membership in the United Nations. One week later, Avraham Harman was appointed the country's first Consul General in Canada and Michael Comay became its first ambassador to Ottawa in September 1953. Even though Canada opened its first embassy in Tel Aviv that year, its interests in Israel remained in the hands of a non-resident ambassador until 1958.

The Arab countries surrounding Israel not only failed to recognize the new Jewish state but, having refused to acknowledge its very existence, invaded it as soon as its independence had been declared. Jews all over the world immediately went into action. In Windsor, the Community Council, under the chairmanship of Reuben Madoff, organized the Aid-to-Israel Committee that collected food, clothing, linen, bedding, medical supplies, and a score of other essentials for shipment to the people of the embattled new nation.[122] And, in response to urgent pleas for funds, the Council obtained a $50,000 bank loan to be passed on to United Palestine Appeal.[123] The loan was fully repaid four months later, backed by guarantees from a sizeable segment of the Jewish population.[124] Praising the community's generosity, the *Bulletin* commended those who had signed the loan notes, singling out Reuben Madoff and his co-chairmen, Archie Cherniak and Jacob Rash, as the action's prime movers. The paper also paid tribute to Nate Rosenberg, who had donated $10,000 to the Aid-to-Israel campaign — a sum considered "far and away the largest gift in the community's history."[125]

Sometime in 1948, Michael Sumner, the Jewish Community Council's president at the time, received a phone call from Sol Hayes, the executive director of the Canadian Jewish Congress. "There is no time for correspondence," he told him. "We are sending you two Hagganah people. They will ask you to do things and you have the authority to act in our name. But everything must be done *sub rosa*." Michael Sumner later recounted the events that occurred as a result of that phone call:

I knew that the Hagganah was a Jewish underground organization, but I couldn't understand what I could do for them. When the two men came to see me — tall and handsome guys — they wanted to know how fast we could organize a meeting of the top people in our community. "Tomorrow night," I told them.

So I sent telegrams to all our members asking them to come to the synagogue at eight o'clock the following evening. I didn't exactly tell them why. I just said, "Come for a confidential meeting with two Israelis." At that meeting, the two men immediately came to the point. "We want money," they said, "but it has to be given on an informal basis. How much can you raise for us in the next twenty-four hours?" They also told us that (they) couldn't issue receipts for those funds, "because we can't run the risk of them leaving any trails. That's all the information we can give you." They got about $35,000 — all in cash! It was a tremendous show of support.

The next afternoon, while we were waiting for the results to come in, the two guys said to me, "We have a second job for you. We are trying to organize an Air Force for the Hagganah. We know that there are many Air Force people in the United States who have been discharged. You are close to the US border. Can you find someone over there who can find out if we can enlist some of these people?"

I immediately went to see Phil Slomovitz who, at that time, was the publisher of the *Detroit Jewish News and Chronicle*. He got me the auditorium of the Shaarey Zedek and then sent word to some Jewish war veterans asking them to come to the synagogue for a meeting. About two hundred showed up and after I had spoken to them about the problem, twelve men enlisted on the spot that night. Others joined later.

The two Hagganah guys then wanted me to find someone who could travel through the American Midwest recruiting other veterans. "Whoever will do that," they said, "can also be on the lookout for war materiel that could be shipped to Israel." Alec Glanz, the eldest son of Jerry Glanz, volunteered for the job. He took three months off and, using the plane the Hagganah had given him, he flew all over the upper Midwest recruiting men and finding used planes and other stuff that would be useful to the Israelis. He did a tremendous job but never received any credit for it. Someone should recognize that.[126]

Immigration to Israel remained in jeopardy until March 1949, when Israeli Foreign Minister Moshe Sharret went to Washington to ask American and Canadian Jewish community leaders to provide funds to feed, clothe, and house at least 200,000 former DP camp inmates, who hoped to make their homes in Israel. In response to his request, the sum of $50 million was pledged.

Samuel Zacks, president of the United Zionist Council of Canada, had attended the Washington meeting. Following his visit to Windsor, the Jewish Community Council Executive borrowed an additional $60,000 for remittance to the United Israel Appeal.[127] After reporting the loan, a *Bulletin* editorial warned that, unless UIA got $50 million "right now, the gates of Israel will have to be shut, the hundreds of thousands of Jews on the move will have to unpack their suitcases in the DP camps and in the ports of Europe, and turn their eyes away from the Homeland — the land which for many years has held the source of all their hopes and dreams."[128]

Rabbi Groner Leaves Windsor

Early in 1949, Rabbi Benjamin Groner resigned as Shaar Hashomayim's spiritual leader:

> My reasons for leaving…were financial.… The salary that I was then receiving, while it was adequate, represented such a gap between what was standard here and what was available in other congregations. Looking into the future, I knew that the adequacies of the moment would then be hopelessly inadequate.
>
> Ultimately, I got an invitation from a pulpit in Chicago, offering me a salary that was almost double of what I was receiving in Windsor. After consultation with the local officers of the congregation, I was just sort of compelled to accept the invitation.[129]

Reverend Irwin Dubitsky, an Orthodox rabbi who had been the community's *shochet* for many years, temporarily filled in as the congregation's rabbi.[130] However, when Rabbi Samuel Stollman appeared on the scene, a new era began for Shaar Hashomayim and for the Jewish community of Windsor.

Chapter 8
The Stollman Era

Windsor in the 1950s

The 1950s were years of trauma and renewal for Windsor. The new decade opened with great promise for the auto industry. New models featuring innovative styling and sales propelled by sophisticated advertising created high hopes and great expectations. Jobs in the industry peaked in 1949, a major changeover year for the Big Three. The Rand formula had not guaranteed a strike-free environment nor harmonious relations, but it set new ground rules for both labour and management. Labour unions professionalized their staff, adding the lawyers and specialists needed to negotiate complicated benefit packages and multi-year contracts. More centralized negotiations at the national level left local union leaders with the time and resources to expand social services to their members and to participate more fully in their communities. US Senator Joe McCarthy and other warriors of the Cold War indiscriminately branded Communists, socialists, left-leaning progressives, and many East Europeans as traitors or threats to Free World societies. The CCF was ineffective in this atmosphere, but the reorganization of the party as the NDP in 1959 offered hope of a revived social-democratic alternative to the traditional two-party system.

South Windsor's residential construction, on hold since the Depression, had begun to take off — boosted by a suburban population explosion that approached 300 percent between 1941 and 1956. Large-scale developers such as Economy Homes Construction, led by Robert Slutsky, and South Windsor's largest builder, Morris Construction, headed by Jewish entrepreneurs and future mall developers Morris Tabachnick and his son Charles, offered family living at reasonable prices and mortgages. Not to be left behind, Windsor's Jews were leaving their old neighbourhoods for the suburbs. Although they dispersed throughout the newly built areas, South Lawn Gardens near Dougall became the preferred suburban location for Windsor's Jewish elite. By the end of the decade, the city began planning another expansion through annexation of the surrounding suburban communities.

Politically, the decade opened with twin scandals: revelations about Metropolitan Hospital and the Windsor police

Photo courtesy of the Windsor Star

Two officials of Regional Shopping Centres Limited, the Windsor-based development firm, look over plans in 1968 for the complex in the part of the old Devonshire racetrack where the shopping centre would be built. On the left is Charles Tabachnick, president of the company, and on the right is Ronald Elingwood, secretary-treasurer.

damaged the reputation of a city already suffering from image problems left from its lawless rum-running days and from the militant labour reputation it earned in the Ford strike of 1945. Mayor Arthur Reaume's long tenure (1940–54), with his reliance upon ward, ethnic, and labour politics was beginning to wear thin with the business sector

of the city. His defeat in 1954 would lead to a municipal reform strategy aimed at diversifying an economy too reliant on the automotive and related industries, and modernizing municipal government by replacing the old ward system with an at-large council and city manager form of administrative leadership. Under new Mayor Michael Patrick, business leadership was reviving and would play its strongest role since the 1920s, when the Border Cities Chamber of Commerce often led the politicians, administrators, and the community. A 1955 Junior Chamber of Commerce–sponsored study of port facilities and Windsor's future as a seaport anticipated the completion of the St. Lawrence Seaway by the end of the decade. In 1958, the Chamber commissioned the Battelle group of international consultants to provide a blueprint for a revived municipality.

The greatest trauma facing the city was the exodus of Ford assembly operations in 1954, although it proved not as traumatic as first thought. Ford did not desert the city, but rather increased its investment in foundry and other operations; however, jobs were lost and confidence crumbled. The news was devastating to local businesses as well as to workers and their families. In this atmosphere of doom, Chrysler stepped up, announcing that it was staying, that Windsor was an ideal location, and that it possessed the labour force

A group of young men who were following in their fathers' footsteps by taking an active part in store development and promotion are shown examining one of the new city-owned parking lots in the Ottawa St. business district in 1957. From the left are Jerry Freed, Milton Whiteman, Norman Ordower, Sam Vexler, Ruben Heller, and Herbert Gray.

necessary for its future expansion. In future, Chrysler, not Ford, would be Windsor's Home Town Car Company. Windsor's 1954 Centennial, a century after it had achieved village status, gave the community a time for celebrating and toasting the future. Part of the future rested with a renewed interest in the area's youth and their education. New school construction would require the attention and resources of both parents and the wider community. A bequest from the long-established Cleary family providing for a park (Dieppe) and civic centre rekindled the dream of a publicly owned and accessible waterfront as Windsor's signature amenity. And finally, a new study into urban blight and decay by Dr. Faludi resulted in a renewal plan to revitalize the central city.

As Canada's post-war international role expanded, peace-keeping became its main military preoccupation. In 1956 Canadian diplomacy was responsible for finding a solution to the Suez Crisis when British and French troops (joined by Israel) attacked Egypt following its nationalization of the Suez Canal. Minister of External Affairs Lester Pearson won the Nobel Peace Prize for his efforts in defusing the potentially explosive situation and Canada was a member of the UN Emergency Force that kept the peace between Egypt and Israel from 1956 until 1967, when Nasser expelled the UN forces. For Windsor's Jews, Israel was a unifying community force requiring total support. The Hungarian Revolution of 1956 also provided an opportunity for the local Jewish community to pick up its share of the refugee relocation burden. With some one hundred refugees settled by 1958, Windsor's effort equalled that of its much larger Detroit counterpart.

The decade of trauma and renewal ended on a high note in 1959 with the visit of Queen Elizabeth to commemorate the opening of the St. Lawrence Seaway.[1]

Rabbi Stollman's Tenure Begins

The 1950s were years of renewal for Windsor's Jews. New personalities appeared on the scene, among them Rabbi Samuel S. Stollman who as Shaar Hashomayim's new spiritual leader would have a profound impact on their lives.

Rabbi Samuel S. Stollman.

Photo courtesy of the Windsor Star

Describing his origins, Rabbi Stollman explained, "I was born in Russia, where my father had been a rabbi ever since he was nineteen. To avoid being drafted into the Russian Army, he escaped from there when I was two years old and made his way to the United States."[2]

The Stollman family settled in Detroit, Michigan where Samuel spent his early years. He attended high school and junior college in Chicago, as well as taking classes at the city's Hebrew Theological College before going to New York City. There, he enrolled at Rabbi Isaac Elchanan Theological Seminary (RIETS), an affiliate of

Yeshiva University and the Western hemisphere's largest centre for Orthodox Jewish higher learning. At the same time, he attended Columbia University's Teachers' College where he received a BSc in 1945.[3] Rabbi Stollman's *s'micha* took place in June 1947. Just over a year later, he and his wife, Deborah, went to Scranton, Pennsylvania to found the Hebrew Orthodox Day School. He had hoped to obtain a rabbinical post there, but when no such position was offered to him, he looked to Detroit. When he heard that Rabbi Benjamin Groner was leaving Shaar Hashomayim, he applied for the position right away, mainly because it was in Windsor, Ontario, across the river from Detroit, where his father was the dean of the local rabbinate. Speaking affectionately about his father, Rabbi Stollman said, "He and I had a very close relationship and he was also an excellent teacher."[4]

The younger Stollman started his assignment as Shaar Hashomayim's rabbi in June 1949. Michael Sumner said of Stollman's appointment that, "even though he was not the most impressive candidate to apply for the job, he got it because of his father's position in Detroit. It was a matter of prestige for us."[5] November 16, 1949, must have been very special for the elder Stollman because on that day he had the honour to officiate at his son Samuel's formal installation.[6]

Many of the new religious leaders of Stollman's generation were determined to be seen as "modern Orthodox" rabbis. Most possessed degrees in secular education as well as their religious training and many, as Stollman himself would do, taught in (held professorships) colleges and universities. "Modern Orthodox rabbis took an active interest in the education of youngsters determined to rescue that generation from abandonment of its Jewish identity."[7] Whether or not Stollman aspired to be a part of that group, education would be a major priority for the Shaar Hashomayim's new rabbi.

Rabbi Stollman spent part of his first summer implementing a series of innovative projects, such as the reorganization and expansion of Talmud Torah, following a major fire in 1949, with a view to making it Shaar Hashomayim's religious school. On the occasion of the opening of the new school, the following paragraph of a *Bulletin* article is indicative of the philosophy prevalent during his tenure:

> And don't forget that girls are children too! The little girl of today is the young woman of tomorrow with the responsibility of building a home. The education she receives today will determine what kind of Jewish life she will perpetuate in her own home.[8]

Apart from creating a kindergarten for preschoolers, Rabbi Stollman also was instrumental in setting a $5-a-month tuition fee for all departments — kindergarten, elementary, and secondary school.[9]

The following excerpt from one of the new rabbi's *Bulletin* articles, provides a further insight into his ambitious education plans:

> Much of the Shaar Hashomayim's program is geared to the needs of our youth and will be more fully implemented as such in the near future. Our kindergarten, Religious School, Sunday classes, Confirmation Classes for Girls, Nusach, congregational singing classes for boys, the Junior Congregation, the impending Hebrew History classes for the youth, etc., are all aimed at attracting the interest and loyalty of our youth. Not only do we provide Junior services for the younger children, but we are training a number of our Bar Mitzvahs to officiate at the main services in the synagogue. We are doing all this with the hope that we are making the Jewish way of life meaningful and attractive to them.[10]

Rabbi Stollman also introduced Bible classes and classes in philosophy and history in order to establish an Institute for Adult Jewish Studies that would "spell the difference between a static and a progressing Jewish community"[11] To determine the level of people's interest in such a venture, he asked the Jewish Community Council and the Shaar Hashomayim Sisterhood to conduct a survey. It yielded favourable results and the Institute for Adult Jewish Studies became a reality by the end of 1951, with Rabbi Stollman, Joseph Kligman, Morris Seidelman, and James Victor taking on the roles of instructors. Courses offered included Elementary and Advanced Hebrew, Contemporary Jewish Problems, a History Survey, and classes in Jewish Customs and Practices.[12] That same year, Rabbi Stollman also began the Sunday Morning Tefillin Club that offered morning services followed by a discussion period during which bagels and coffee were served.[13]

Community Funding of Jewish Education

The I. L. Peretz Shule had been conducting a full learning program ever since 1934. Although students were taught to read and write in Hebrew, including Hebrew grammar, its curriculum did not include learning how to read from the Siddur — the book of prayers.[14] The school did, however, sponsor a number of impressive social programs, such as annual graduation ceremonies and well — publicized annual banquets.[15]

Not wishing to be left behind, Shaarey Zedek's religious school, under the guidance of Rabbi B. Orlanski, not only taught Hebrew, davnen, Chumash, Rashi, and the Talmud — they presented each of these subjects in English, Yiddish, and Hebrew. Rabbi Orlanski believed that the change in setting and circumstances that had taken place since earlier generations had been trained, required "a strenuous educational effort as a means of self-acceptance as a Jew."[16] Following the creation of the State of Israel, he also held Sunday classes for those young people who had expressed an interest in becoming "acquainted with the history of the Jewish people and the establishment of the Jewish homeland thousands of years ago."[17]

Louis Lieblich resigned as executive director of Windsor's Jewish Community Council to accept a post in San Antonio, Texas.[18] Shortly after his departure, Morris B. Seidelman became the Council's new executive director, being paid an annual salary of $5,500 plus a yearly expense account of $500.[19]

It was at the beginning of Morris Seidelman's tenure when the increased cost of educating the young brought about significant school budget deficits. The Peretz Shule was the first among Windsor's Jewish educational institutions to approach the Community Council for funds when it asked for a subvention in the amount of $5,600. Although that request was immediately rejected because the Council's constitution prohibited financial assistance to religious schools, the considerable communal support for it did prompt its executive to study the matter more closely. After forming a committee to represent all three schools —

Photo courtesy of the Windsor Star

Graduation exercises held at the I. L. Peretz School. The 1960 graduation class and school officials were (from the left in the front row): Allan Levine, Faith Awerbuck, Gail Rubin, Joseph Kligman, the principal, Leslie Wayne, and Rubin Madoff, the president. In the back row (from the left) are Leah Zack, Shulamith Kligman, Revelone Bookman, Helen Melnik, Ida Wexler, Alan Gumprich, and Ellis Fabian.

the Peretz Shule, the Shaar Hashomayim, and the Shaarey Zedek — the executive asked Archie Cherniak and Jacob Rash to look after Council interests.[20]

Originally, Archie Cherniak was adamantly opposed to educational funding because the Council's constitution prohibited granting welfare fund monies to local religious and educational institutions. However, Community Council Executive Director Louis Lieblich pointed out that the majority of American and other Canadian communities "financed local Jewish schools through their welfare funds." And Michael Sumner, speaking for Shaar Hashomayim, wondered whether it would be necessary to exert some control over the educational institutions receiving the money and whether Zionist groups, interested in overseas projects, actually, might object to such funding. Harry Schwartz concluded the debate by informing the Jewish education committee that Shaar Hashomayim would present its own request for financial assistance.[21]

Three months later, during the education committee's May 9, 1950 meeting, Michael Sumner repeated his fears that the Jewish community might be saddled with total financing of the schools. In that connection, he posed the following question: "To what extent will we pay to distinguish between deficit and total financing and what guarantees can be set up to safeguard deficits at the present time?"[23]

Although everyone ultimately recognized the importance of financially supporting Jewish education, it took several more meetings to deal with the "Prohibition" amendment to the Council's constitution. In fact, the Peretz Shule's representatives were so reluctant to accept the amendment knowing that their primary competitor, Shaar Hashomayim, would also ask for financial support, that they went as far as proposing that they receive funding without any of it being made available to Shaar Hashomayim. It must, however, be said that they asked that their proposal be omitted from the agenda of the education committee's annual meeting.

A month later, Michael Sumner, acting on behalf of Shaar Hashomayim, gave "notice of motion" to the Council's Board of Governors that the constitutional amendment to eliminate "the Prohibition against Financial Assistance to local Religious Institutions" be accepted.[24] Further motions were passed in September of that year, stipulating that gifting be part of regular annual allocations, that the local agencies and/or institutions "submit periodic financial statements to the Jewish Community Council," and that no allocation be "more than 40% of the total money raised by the said institution."[25]

Commenting on the passage of the amendment, Joseph Eisenberg, the Council's executive director after 1958, recalled from those involved that "the community was very conflicted at that time, particularly the so-called Shaar people and the Peretz Shule people, the swing-vote decision finally was made by the B'nai B'rith."[26]

Shaarey Zedek's Rabbi Orlanski also went before the Community Council's education committee to request an annual educational allocation. To prove entitlement, he explained that his school, then under the chairmanship of Ben Cohen was divided into three grade levels with three teachers holding classes five to six days each week. He also pointed out that the Shaarey Zedek's weekly expenditure was $35 per student, while its weekly tuition fee was only $10. Speaking about Yeshiva Ner Yehuda, he stated that this Talmudic academy was now on its own, even though it had had some affiliation with his congregation in the past. In response, the education committee asked Rabbi Orlanski to submit regular annual statements, reminding him that, based on its previously established 60/40 percent formula, overall funding must not exceed $6,500.[27] In view of Shaarey Zedek's small student body of fourteen, the committee also recommended that to qualify for the allocation, the required student quota be reduced from twenty-five to ten at all the other institutions.[28]

Apart from annual Welfare Fund campaigns, pressure also was brought to bear on certain community members to donate funds to Va'ad Hayeshivot, the organization entrusted with caring for Orthodox Jewish educational institutions. As these funding solicitations were creating a great deal of conflict, Louis Adelman suggested that $5,000 be set aside for Va'ad Hayeshivot from the Welfare Fund campaign, while Archie Cherniak proposed that, instead of soliciting funds from individuals, each synagogue hold an annual fundraising affair, with the funds so obtained in no way affecting the Welfare Fund pledges. He also stipulated Va'ad Hayeshovit's budget be handled by a committee consisting of Community Council members, as well as the rabbis and representatives from the three congregations — Shaar Hashomayim, Shaarey Zedek, and Tifereth Israel.[29] The purpose of the committee would be to consider requests for funds, to decide on respective allocations, and to raise money over and above the amounts made available by the Community Council.[30] In July of that year, Louis Adelman was elected president of Va'ad Hayeshivot, while Rabbi Orlanski and Rabbi Stollman became its honorary presidents.[31]

Eager to advance Jewish learning and Jewish awareness, the Windsor Jewish community's financial assistance to its educational facilities was in full force by the mid-1950s, with funds being regularly allocated to yeshivot — the Talmudic academies — as well as to a host of other schools. The only time the subject again came up for discussion was in 1954. As both Shaar Hashomayim and the I. L. Peretz Shule had reported deficits for the preceding year, individual subsidies were increased from $25 to $30 per student.[32] Records show that Shaarey Zedek received these subsidies until 1956. However, it must have ceased operations in the following year, since only Shaar Hashomayim and the I. L. Peretz Shule were listed as recipients in 1957.[33]

Early Plans for a Jewish Community Centre

The idea of a community centre had been on the minds of Windsor's Jews ever since the late 1920s. Yet no concrete plans existed to build one, mainly because of a scarcity of funds — first, during the Great Depression, and later during World War II. In fact, such a project was not even considered feasible in the immediate post-war era since all available monies had to be directed toward aiding European refugees and to meeting the needs of the newly created State of Israel.

The first serious attempt to build a community centre had been made in the spring of 1947. By then, Windsor's Jewish community had grown to about 2,800 and its leaders, having recognized the inadequacies of its cultural, social, educational, and recreational facilities, felt it was time to consider the undertaking.[34] Although Council President Harry Cherniak had strongly supported it a year earlier, he did not think it possible to raise the necessary capital for it. But never one to shirk responsibility, he had become involved with the so-called "Committee of One Hundred," that hosted several parlour meetings and had approved the formation of a fundraising committee headed by Harry Vexler and Robert Slutsky.[35] The project came closer to reality when an unofficial Community Centre Campaign opened with eight lead gifts totalling $31,000; an official campaign to raise $150,000 got underway two months later.[36] Supporters were even assured that the funds raised would not affect annual Welfare Fund campaign contributions.[37] However, plans to construct the centre had to be shelved once again, clearly for economic reasons.[38]

All group programs and social events, therefore, continued to take place at the Jewish Community Council's offices at 405 Pelissier Street and, according to Joseph Eisenberg, "in the basement of Shaar Hashomayim as we had run out of rented facilities."[39] Concurring with Eisenberg, Rabbi Samuel Stollman maintained that "the motivating factor in wanting to build a facility was simply the fact that there were certain activities Shaar Hashomayim could not handle."[40]

Despite Rabbi Stollman's apparent interest in a community centre, he was clearly concerned about its intended function and its potential location:

> The actual centre is no more than a hopeful dream at the moment. But whether near or far we shall have to decide on its synagogue relation. Competition with the synagogue will prove disastrous for Jewish life in our community. Every well-advised opinion on the subject...concurs that it must be co-

ordinated as a Synagogue Centre. The sparks of Jewishness today are too few to be further scattered. The Synagogue and Centre must be co-ordinated for the sake of organic Jewish life.… We cannot leave this amalgamation to chance. Let no one think that the rabbi's attitude is a prejudiced one. If the Synagogue suffers because of Centre competition for the interests and activities of the community, rabbis will still be needed,… though their responsibilities will be greatly lightened.… Let not the Synagogue become a museum of Jewish life. We want a living, active reality for now and always.[41]

There also was considerable discussion among the larger Welfare Fund contributors and the members of the Community Council's executive committee whether or not to "clean up those present pledges already made" before embarking on a fundraising campaign for the centre.[42] Yet those attending its April 1950 meeting did establish a committee that would begin planning a capital campaign aimed at raising $50,000 over a five-year period.[43] But when the executive committee again met at the Norton Palmer Hotel in June 1950, it was made quite clear to those present that the campaign must not interfere with the Council's annual fundraising efforts and that "no indebtedness must be assumed."[44]

In other words, the centre's progress and the size of the structure would have to depend on how much money could be raised. In fact, an editorial in the February 1951 issue of the *Bulletin* emphasized that the Welfare Fund's campaign "includes provisions for a community centre fund from those donors whose contributions to the Welfare Fund, this year at least, equals their last gift. Only in that event is a contributor eligible to make a gift to the Community Centre."[45]

As early as November 1950, Rubin Madoff had the foresight to ask his real estate agent to approach the owners of the bungalows adjoining Shaar Hashomayim on Goyeau Street as he felt that these properties could be the site for the future community centre.[46] Existing 1951 records also show that the Community Council Executive had taken out one $2,000 five-year annual lease on them to provide space for the Youth Council and another yearly $500 lease for some office space.[47]

By 1951, the City of Windsor had grown to 217,150 inhabitants — a figure thirteen times higher than a century ago. To meet the needs of the similarly expanding Jewish community, Shaar Hashomayim, in collaboration with Windsor's Community Council, proposed to build an addition to the synagogue. Located on Giles Boulevard, it would house meeting rooms, classrooms and offices to provide space for the synagogue's youth groups, for its newly created religious school, as well as for any future programs.[48]

The underlying motive for the synagogue's expansion may have been to block the plans of those who wanted the centre to be separate from any religious institution. Describing the conflict that existed between these two factions, Joseph Eisenberg stated that I. L. Peretz Shule President Rubin Madoff led the battle to "de-affiliate," while Rabbi Stollman and his supporters wanted the future community centre to be affiliated with Shaar Hashomayim. "There was a big fight, but the forces for an independent centre won and away they went. B'nai B'rith swung [the votes] in terms of it not being part of the Shaar Hashomayim."[49]

In the summer of 1951, Rabbi Stollman took steps to restore to the synagogue to "its rightful place as a House of Study, a House of Assembly, and a House of Worship." He organized the Shaar Hashomayim Men's Club.[50] He was likely also instrumental in requesting that the words *Shaar Hashomayim News* be included in the *Bulletin*'s layout and that its distinctive masthead show his name and that of his cantor, Saul Schenker. Cantor Schenker arrived in Windsor in September 1950 for High Holiday services and he served the community with distinction, having changed his name to Saul Nadvan, until his death on November 3, 1979.[51] He was buried in Israel.

The following poem, which appeared in Rabbi Stollman's bulletin column, but which he did not pen, satirizes the

Photo courtesy of the Windsor Star

Members of Shaar Hashomayim Synagogue pictured here conducting special services for Rosh Hashanah in 1967 are (from the left) Max Levine, vice president of the congregation; Cantor Saul Nadvan; Rabbi Samuel Stollman; Charles Cohen, president of the congregation; and Jackson Rosenzweig, one of the officials in religious services in the congregation. Mr. Levine and Mr. Rosenzweig are holding Torah scrolls and Mr. Cohen is holding the shofar, or ram's horn, that is blown at the new year's service.

conflicting attitudes that existed between the older and the younger members of Stollman's congregation:

NO COMMENT
I go to *shul* thrice daily
And pray loud and strong.
I follow all the *mitzvots*
And therefore do no wrong.
Of course, my growing children
Don't seem to think as I,
They find my way of thinking
Old-fashioned, rather dry.

They want a *shul* with comforts,
A fine and modern school,
With desks in every classroom
And cleanliness the rule.

For this they give their money,
For buildings much too fine;
What's wrong with just a *shtibel*
Like my father's and like mine?

Of course, my *shul* grows empty
With every passing year,
The old folks are departing
Their children are not here.

But I won't waste my money
On building modern schools,
For I, of course, am clever,
My children are the fools.[52]

The Jewish Community Adds a Social Services Role

In response to Michael Sumner's suggestion that Windsor's Jewish community provide social services for its members, the Welfare Council's executive committee conducted a survey to determine how best to proceed in this regard.[53] It then consulted the Council of Jewish Federations and Welfare Funds to find out whether existing services to assist the needy families were adequate. It also created a social services committee that soon reported that "a number of smaller communities with Jewish populations of 3,000 or less provided case work services and supplementary local relief." In response, the Council's executive committee recommended that the Welfare Council not only assume that responsibility but also recommended that relief be provided to those eligible for supplementary allowances given by other agencies, or "to substitute for those allowances where eligibility does not exist." The social services com-

mittee further determined that all these services be rendered by the Council's professional staff and that they be administered by the Jewish family services committee.[54]

Even though Michael Sumner moved acceptance of all these recommendations in October 1951,[55] it took the Council's board of governors another three months to give their stamp of approval.[56]

Windsor Meets National and Overseas Needs

Despite the comparatively small size of Windsor's Jewish community during the 1950s, the Welfare Fund managed to increase its goal year by year. Regional and national bodies, therefore, consistently bestowed high praise on the community for its steady financial support of Israel and for meeting the needs of those Jewish immigrants who recently settled in Windsor.

The National Conference on Israel and Jewish Rehabilitation met at Montreal's Mount Royal Hotel in March 1951 to decide how to solve the immigration and economic problems that continued to plague the State of Israel. At the meeting it was resolved to set aside $5,250,000 as Canadian Jewry's contribution — money that was to be used to bring some 600,000 Jews to Israel within the next three years and to help the country become economically self-supporting.[57]

The quota Windsor's Jewish community was asked to accept was $125,000 — an amount materially higher than that pledged the previous year. At that time, $40,000 had gone to United Israel Appeal; $26,500 to Canadian Jewish Congress and the United Jewish Relief Agency, and $10,000 to youth aliyah. A further $3,500 had been sent to each of the following universities: Hebrew University in Jerusalem, Haifa's Technion, and the Weizmann Institute of Science in Rehovot, Israel.[58] According to Community Council president Milton C. Meretsky's June 1951 report, financial assistance also had been given to various yeshivot in North America and Israel, as well as to the Israeli Symphony Orchestra to help offset the cost of bringing it to the United

States and Canada.[59] Windsor's Jewish community had also donated 3,000 trees to the Jewish National Fund's forest of six million trees that were to be planted in the corridor between Tel Aviv and Jerusalem as a living memorial to the six million Jews who had perished during the Holocaust.[60]

Even though little was known over the years about Shaarey Zedek's fundraising activities, it appears that the congregation had raised $1,000 during the 1949 Yom Kippur appeal to pay for the construction of a four-family apartment building in Israel.[61]

To commemorate the one-hundredth anniversary of the birth of I. L. Peretz, founder of the Peretz schools, their Windsor branch and its affiliate, Arbeiterring, declared 1952 "The Peretz Year" and celebrated it with a special concert.[62]

Talmud Torah Becomes a Funeral Chapel

After Rabbi Stollman became Shaar Hashomayim's spiritual leader in November 1949 — just a year and a half after the establishment of the State of Israel, he had decided to combine religious instruction with studies about Israel. By so doing, he not only took care of Talmud Torah supporters' pro-Zionist leanings, but also brought them to his synagogue as members. Shaar Hashomayim had been able to serve everyone's educational needs in the past, but the additional classrooms and the extra office space resulting from its 1951 expansion made it possible for all the students to be taught under one roof.

As Talmud Torah had ceased to function as a religious school after the 1949 fire, the building at the corner of Tuscarora and Aylmer streets stood empty for a while. Shaar Hashomayim president, Dr. Louis Perlman, suggested that "to dispose of the old building and set up a trust fund with the proceeds was a wise decision, [as we could look] forward to the time when the community will be prepared to erect a community centre."[63] The building was, however, not sold. Before long, it was rented to the Oddfellows' Lodge, whose members met there for years, along with the Jewish Boy Scouts, who met once a week downstairs, until the decision

was made to turn it into a Chesed Shel Emes — a funeral chapel.[64] Commenting on that decision, an anonymous writer stated in a *Bulletin* article, "It is the mark of a well-organized community when it talks almost simultaneously about a community centre and a funeral chapel. The first is to prepare the way for dignified Jewish living and the second is a preparation for dignity and for Jewishness in the extreme eventuality. It is also a mark of traditional Judaism that death is viewed with serenity, calmness and acceptance."[65]

Since the Chesed Shel Emes project had the backing of congregations Shaar Hashomayim, Shaarey Zedek, and Tifereth Israel, as well as of the Jewish Community Council, the latter's Board of Governors wasted no time endorsing a $25,000 campaign to raise the necessary funds to adapt the old Talmud Torah building to its new purpose.[66] By May 1950, the campaign was well underway, with $6,000 pledged and some of that money already paid.[67]

The dedication of the new funeral chapel took place on February 27, 1952[68] — one year and four months after the Chesed Shel Emes committee members had given it their blessing.[69] Each of the three congregations, together with the Community Council, then appointed representatives to sit on the Chesed Shel Emes board of directors and chose Jerry Glanz as director of the Chevra Kaddisha.[70]

By the end of May 1952, when it became clear to the Council's executive committee that running the chapel needed the community's financial support, it approved a one-time allocation of $5,000 to cover operating expenses.[71] Although Chesed Shel Emes continued to have yearly deficits, it did provide proper care to the members of the Jewish community, in accordance with the traditional laws.[72]

A Go-Ahead for the Community Centre

Further delays occurred with regard to actually approving the construction of a Jewish community centre until the fall of 1953, when the Council's executive decided to raise $300,000 in a separate campaign and to proceed on a "pay as you go" basis. It also recommended the establishment of a planning committee that could accept special gifts and memorial donations. Ultimately, everyone agreed that the success of the campaign would be enhanced if the land for the centre could be purchased prior to the start of the campaign. It also was suggested that acquisition of lands around Shaar Hashomayim and their possible rezoning should be investigated.[73]

The kick-off date for the campaign was set for November 1, 1953.[74] Yet, the ever-present needs of the State of Israel again prompted some people to move for postponement of the campaign. The motion failed, but to avoid further conflict, it was decided to run two campaigns — one for State of Israel Bonds and a second one for the community centre.[75]

The second campaign began in November 1953 under the co-chairmanship of Rubin Madoff and Michael Sumner. By then, it also had been decided that the centre would be owned and administered "exclusively by the Community Council with the National Jewish Welfare Board acting as consultant."[76] To mark the official closing of the drive, a mass meeting was scheduled for February 7, 1954, with Lt. Col. David A. Croll as the guest speaker.[77]

When $256,791 had been pledged by the end of March 1954, the success of the campaign was almost assured. The recently constituted community centre planning and site sub-committee could therefore turn its attention to finding a site acceptable to both committee members as well as major donors.[78]

Before long, it became clear that the powers that be were favourably disposed toward a property at the southwest corner of Giles Boulevard and Dougall Avenue that was jointly owned by the Lutheran Church, a private individual, and the City of Windsor.[79] Consideration was also given to two other sites, one facing Goyeau Avenue at the rear of Shaar Hashomayim, and the other one at the southeast corner of Ellis Avenue and Dufferin Place, which had the advantage of being across the street from a lot that could be purchased as a car park.[80] What followed were lengthy discussions about the three prospective sites, as well as about the advisability of separating the new centre from

Shaar Hashomayim or affiliating it with the synagogue.[81] After some months' delay, the planning and site sub-committee presented the following list of possible locations:

- Ouellette Avenue, south of Mario Restaurant to Jackson Park
- Goyeau Street through to Dufferin Place, southerly to Giles Boulevard
- East side of Ouellette Avenue near Pine Street
- Goyeau Street next to the Bell Telephone Building
- The Elmwood Casino
- The old Knights of Columbus Building
- Corner Dougall Avenue and Giles Boulevard
- Goyeau Street at the rear of Shaar Hashomayim[82]

Before it selected any of these sites, however, the sub-committee wanted to determine what type of facility the new centre should be. It consulted William Avrunin, associate director of the Detroit Jewish Welfare Federation, who recommended that it should include a large play area in the form of a gymnasium, a small kitchen accessible to the gymnasium, and two lounges — one for adults and one for teenagers. In addition, there should be an area where adults could meet, possibly a boardroom, an arts and crafts room, and four to six clubrooms that could serve as classrooms. Mr. Avrunin's proposals also included a health club with separate shower and locker facilities for both sexes, as well as a suite of offices and a lobby furnished with display cases for rotating exhibits. Another one of his suggestions was that 60 percent of the community centre's revenues be derived from membership fees and that the health club operate on a for-profit basis.[83]

When Sheppard & Masson, the architects retained for the project, were asked to attend the September 23, 1954, meeting of the planning and site sub-committee, they urged members to "keep in mind that Windsor's sewers were not very efficient, especially in the area bordering Giles Boulevard which was formerly a creek."[84] Regarding the cost of building the centre, the architects' estimate was between $12 and $13 per square foot.[85]

Also consulted at a meeting held later that same day was Leon Spector, director of the National Jewish Welfare Board's Building Bureau, who, according to Council president Harry Vexler, was a trained architect with "extensive experience in the construction of Centre(s) throughout the U.S. and Canada."[86] After touring the various sites, Mr. Spector felt that Jackson Park was the most appropriate one. He did, however, reject the area behind Shaar Hashomayim, describing it as "a deteriorating neighbourhood," and felt that the Elmwood Casino was unsuitable because its asking price was too high and the estimated renovation costs would become too great a financial burden for Windsor's Jewish community. [87] Mr. Spector agreed with the architects and the sub-committee members that "a building along the lines of the Hamilton Jewish Community Centre would be most suitable for our community."[88]

During a third meeting, held even later that evening, the community centre planning and site sub-committee unanimously passed the following resolution:

> Resolved that the sub-committee recommends that the Jackson Park site be acquired, providing all legal obstacles can be overcome, and further recommends that facilities of the new Centre be used for educational purposes by the whole community in the interest of the general economy of the community.[89]

Michael Sumner reported a shortfall in the community centre's pledges that was less than the one forecast at the beginning of the year. [90] A month later, Mr. Sumner, speaking on behalf of Shaar Hashomayim, asked that complete control of the new centre's facilities be given to the synagogue with regard to religious services, that Kashrut and all Shabbat and Holy Day observances be

followed, and that the centre not compete with Shaar Hashomayim as caterer for weddings and other life-cycle ceremonies.[91]

The Jewish Community Council's Board of Governors unanimously passed the motion to proceed with the purchase of the Jackson Park site, not, however, before voting on Michael Sumner's requests. President Harry Vexler ruled him out of order for having made them in the first place and, when Sumner asked for a ruling on the subject, the chairman rejected it.[92]

Although both the I. L. Peretz Shule and the Shaar Hashomayim had expressed an interest in using the classrooms at the new centre, the following item in the minutes of the school sub-committee's October 1954 meeting is indicative of the rivalry that existed between the two institutions:

> It is the opinion of the committee that a physical separation be incorporated into the architectural plans so as to avoid mutual embarrassment among the students of both schools due to differing customs.[93]

It is interesting to note that such a separation occurred many years later when members of the Windsor Reform Congregation Beth El were forbidden to ride to Jewish events in Detroit on the same bus as the students from the Shaar Hashomayim.

By the spring of 1955, Shaar Hashomayim and the I. L. Peretz Shule had actually agreed to "make use of the centre's facilities for educational purposes."[94] However, Shaarey Zedek had not been asked to share the space with these two schools, presumably because it had too few students.

As soon as the major donors had approved the purchase of the Jackson Park site, it looked as if nothing could stand in the way of building the new facility.[95] But plans to purchase the site had to be abandoned yet again when several people in the neighbourhood objected to the rezoning of the property for a Jewish community centre.[96]

Upon recommendations from Windsor's City Council, David Mechanic, chairman of the site location committee, subsequently held discussions with Loblaw Groceteria Limited, which owned the land on the west side of Ouellette Avenue, between Hanna and Tecumseh avenues. Priced at $60,000, it covered an area of 36,000 square feet with a 100-foot frontage on Ouellette Avenue, and a depth of 180 feet extending as far as Pelissier Street.[97] On July 19, 1955, the purchase of that property was approved by all the major contributors.[98]

Early in 1956, the Community Council's executive committee expressed special thanks to David Bennett of Principal Investments Limited and Milton C. Meretsky for their generous financial support, to Dr. C. R. Weber and Benjamin Yuffy of Yuffy & Yuffy, solicitors. Also thanked were the *Windsor Daily Star* for making the public aware of the difficulties faced by the Jewish community, Windsor's Mayor Michael Patrick and his City Council for helping to

Eli C. Goldin, president of the Jewish Community Council, signs a contract for the 1958 construction of the new Jewish Community Centre to be built on Ouellette Avenue north of Tecumseh Blvd. Standing (from the left) are Keith Gosnell of Granite Construction Co. Ltd., Gerald Semord of J. P. Thomson, architect; Harry Vexler, Morris Tabachnick, J. D. Geller, and Milton Meretsky.

locate the site, and David Mechanic for his work on the site location committee.[99]

To assist with the revisions of the Jackson Park plans and to adapt them to the new Ouellette Avenue location, Leon Spector suggested that a committee review the original designs and make specific recommendations. Basing his cost estimates on similar facilities in the United States and Canada, he felt that one campaign was not enough to obtain the funds required for a building estimated to cost about $300,000. As an alternative, he proposed raising a long-term mortgage.[100]

There also was considerable discussion regarding the selection of an architectural firm for the project. Ultimately, suggestions for the possible joining of two such companies in an "associateship" were overruled in favour of appointing J. P. Thompson and Associates.[101]

Better Community Programs

After Morris Seidelman's resignation in 1953, Khayyam Z. Paltiel succeeded him as the Windsor Community Council's executive director with a yearly salary of $6,000. After moving from Winnipeg to Windsor, he started his assignment at the beginning of September 1953.[102] Paltiel came into his own two years later, when he delivered an impressive address at the Council's 1955 annual meeting. After mentioning "the advent of the Community Centre project" and "the need for strengthening our youth work program," he went on to endorse "a social, cultural and athletic program for the young people in our community." He was also in favour of Council President Harry Vexler's recommendation to hire a full-time permanent program director, whose task would be to prepare, co-ordinate, and supervise programs for all age groups, as well as to train part-time volunteer personnel. Paltiel even went as far as to reveal that interviews to engage such a professional had already taken place.

He also expressed the hope that the Friendship Club, a program for senior members in the community that had been initiated by his wife and which he described as "one of my pleasures over the past year," would now become the new program director's responsibility. In that connection, he mentioned other work he had done for seniors, such as providing homemakers and companions for them when they needed assistance, as well as helping place those who required more care into institutions. Outlining his ideas for the future, Mr. Paltiel spoke of his wish to begin a day camp for children,[103] a wish realized in the summer of 1956.[104]

With regard to the settlement of newcomers, Paltiel offered a glimpse into the work being carried out. It not only entailed finding jobs and homes for them, but also providing them with medical and other social services. In that connection, he mentioned that legal assistance had been given to almost one hundred immigrants who had restitution claims against the German government.

Speaking about fundraising efforts, Paltiel noted that efforts on behalf of both the Community Centre and the 1954 Welfare Fund had been under the aegis of the Community Council, while the State of Israel Bond drive had been run by a committee, chaired by Jacob Geller. These three mid-1950s campaigns had yielded a total of $440,000, despite the fact that only 750 families had contributed to them. Pointing out that a unified community campaign would permit the leadership to set priorities, Paltiel stressed the need for the Welfare Fund drive to remain the focus of all fundraising efforts.[105]

In April 1955, the Community Council's executive committee approved a budget of $8,800 for current programs and also endorsed the hiring of a full-time program director at a yearly salary of $4,000.[106] The position was filled by Harold Chetkow, a man who had pursued graduate work in English Literature and Social Group Work at the University of Toronto.[107]

Raising Funds for Israel

In 1948, following the creation of the State of Israel, a new form of Canadian communal expression came into being. Known as the Jewish National Fund's Negev Dinner, it was designed to honour outstanding community leaders and to commemorate significant events in Jewish life. Proceeds from Negev Dinners were originally supposed to gather support for the development of Israel's sterile Negev Desert, an area constituting some 60 percent of all its land. However, as needs grew, these funds had to be diversified to sustain other projects in the newly formed Jewish state.[108]

In 1952, representatives of Windsor's Community Council travelled to Toronto to attend a Negev Dinner in honour of their own native son, Senator David Croll.[109] Also invited were representatives of such Zionist-based organizations as Hadassah's Lillian Friedman and Kadimah chapters, Pioneer Women, Mizrachi, Chana Senesh, Junior Hadassah and Farband, since the Jewish National Fund wanted to establish a presence in Windsor.[110]

Reuben Madoff, a prominent member of the Jewish community and a former president of both the Community Council and the I. L. Peretz Shule, was the chosen honoree for Windsor's first Negev Dinner.[111] Held on December 4, 1955 at Shaar Hashomayim Synagogue, it raised over $4,000 for the Jewish National Fund,[112] but no other Negev Dinners took place in Windsor until 1972, when Morris Tabachnick was honoured.

At the beginning of 1956, when political as well as economic crises again faced the State of Israel, the Zionist Organization of Canada, in agreement of the Canadian Jewish Congress, launched a special Emergency Fund Drive to raise $2 million. These funds were urgently required to settle 45,000 immigrants who had been hastily brought to Israel from North Africa. The Windsor Jewish Community Council executive unanimously approved $50,000 to be earmarked for the Emergency Fund Drive, providing that its 1956 Welfare Fund goal of $112,000 also could be met.[113]

The Emergency Fund Campaign received a major boost on April 23, 1956, when a Special-Gifts Dinner was held at Windsor's Prince Edward Hotel. The event was chaired by Eli Goldin, who proudly presented Samuel Bronfman, president of the Canadian Jewish Congress, as the evening's guest speaker.[114] Later that year, Shaar Hashomayim and the Chesed Shel Emes funeral chapel launched equally successful High Holiday Israel Appeals.[115]

As travel to Israel had become more commonplace by the end of the 1950s, Eli Goldin, Morris Tabachnick, and Harry Rubin embarked on a twelve-day study mission to the Holy Land. Interviewed by the *Bulletin* upon their return in December 1958, "they all stressed the need for cash in Israel, urging members of Windsor's Jewish community to pay their pledges to the 1958 Welfare Fund so that immediate remittance could be made to Israel. Amazed at what had been accomplished in agriculture, industry, and education, they were convinced that if Israel would be allowed to live in peace with its neighbours for another 10 years, it would be a model for the whole Middle East of the way in which people should live."[116]

Three members of Windsor's Jewish community were among the sixteen Ontario delegates who flew to Israel in November 1958 for a twelve-day study tour. Pictured from the left are Morris Tabachnick, Eli Goldin, and Harry Rubin. Their trip was sponsored by the Zionist Organization of Canada.

The Suez Crisis and the Hungarian Uprising

In the summer of 1956, Windsor's Jewry learned that full-scale war had broken out in the Middle East, following the seizure and nationalization of the Suez Canal by Egypt's Colonel Nasser. At the beginning of that debacle, Israel's lack of heavy weaponry and adequate air power had relegated the country to a purely defensive role. The armies of Egypt, Syria, and Jordan, supported by 3,000 Soviet tanks could penetrate Israel's borders, while their air forces, supported by 1,100 Soviet planes, were able to bombard its cities with rockets. However, by the end of October 1956, the tide had turned in Israel's favour. Its armed forces had invaded the Gaza Strip and the Sinai Peninsula and were advancing towards the Suez Canal.[117] At that point, the British and French demanded that both Israeli and Egyptian forces withdraw from the Canal Zone. When Nasser refused to do so, they bombarded the Egyptian bases. And as both the United States and the USSR had demanded an immediate ceasefire, a UN resolution soon forced the British, French, and Israelis to withdraw from Egyptian territory. Stationing troops of the United Nations Emergency Force (UNEF) along the frontier between Israel and Egypt did help to ensure an element of peace, at least for the next decade, even though sporadic border incidents continued. And, even though Israel gained access to the Strait of Tiran when the Egyptian government reopened the canal, no comprehensive Arab-Israeli peace talks followed the Suez Crisis.[118]

Unrest also arose in Europe, especially in Hungary, where students and workers began to rebel against the Communist regime. In the wake of intervention by the Soviet Army that had been called in to crush the rebellion, 200,000 Hungarians, including approximately 3,500 Jews, fled their homeland during the first quarter of 1957. Many of them found refuge in Canada — about thirty of them settled in Windsor.[119] Provided with much-needed relief by the Jewish Community Council, these Hungarian immigrants soon became part of the Canadian mosaic, forming a new constituency of Jews who hailed from a European country other than Poland and Russia, the countries of origins for the majority of Windsor's Jews.[120]

Political harassment of a different kind erupted in the United States in the early 1950s when a nondescript Republican Senator from Wisconsin by the name of Joseph McCarthy began hunting down a host of prominent Americans and wrongfully accusing them of Communist sympathies. For four long years, he and his aides exploited the issue by holding public hearings — the first to be televised. In the course of these interrogations, witnesses were bullied and browbeaten and numerous reputations were destroyed.

The fallout from that turbulent time, henceforth known as the McCarthy Era, also affected Canadians, among them several Jews living in Windsor. Particularly affected were those who belonged to a committee that was helping to raise funds for needy Jews living in Birobidzhan, a Jewish autonomous region thousands of miles east of European Russia, founded by Stalin in 1934 as a "homeland" for Soviet Jews. Other Windsor Jewish residents were involved with the local branch of the United Jewish People's Order, a socialist organization that had tried to improve the lot of workers during the 1920s and 1930s. Since the membership lists of these two groups had somehow fallen into the hands of those aiding the McCarthy witch hunt, half a dozen people from Windsor were "pink-listed," i.e. forbidden to enter the United States. All of them resented having been randomly singled out. Some ignored the ban, while others waited for it to end; one individual even spent time and money trying to clear his name. When the McCarthy Era ended in December 1955, all Canadians again were able to freely cross the border.

The Shaarey Zedek Expansion

Shaarey Zedek's Rabbi Orlanski had left Windsor some time during the mid-1950s. Rabbi Shmaryuhu Karelitz had evidently taken his place and, according to an article in the

Photo courtesy of the Windsor Star

Photo courtesy of the Windsor Star

The contributors' banquet at Shaar Hashomayim Auditorium opened a drive for funds for the new Shaarey Zedek Synagogue being built at Giles Blvd. and Lillian St. Among those present were (from left to right) Rabbi Shmaryuhu Karelitz of Shaarey Zedek; Senator David A. Croll, guest speaker; Rabbi Samuel S. Stollman of Shaar Hashomayim, and Morris Tabachnick, president of the Jewish Community Council.

The new Shaarey Zedek Synagogue on Giles Blvd. was officially opened by Senator David Croll, a former mayor of Windsor. Leading members of the Jewish community who took part in the ceremony were (from left) Cantor Saul Schenker, Rabbi Samuel S. Stollman, Senator Croll, Rabbi S. Karelitz, and Michael Ordon, Chairman.

Bulletin's September 1957 issue, had been that congregation's spiritual leader since January of that year.[121] Shortly after his arrival in Windsor, Shaarey Zedek commenced a vigorous fundraising campaign to provide funds for a new synagogue. To be located on Giles Boulevard East, at the corner of Lillian Street, it was to replace the old Mercer Street building that had been expropriated by the City of Windsor. In a letter addressed to the Windsor Jewish Community Council, Shaarey Zedek's President L. Gordner asked for an allocation of $10,000 "to assist in building those of our facilities, which will have general community usefulness." In fact, plans for the new structure called for "an auditorium with a seating capacity for 350 persons, a fully equipped kitchen, as well as one other room, which will be available for meetings."[122]

Mr. Gordner's request was rejected because the Council's constitution as well as the structure of the Welfare Fund "forbid(s) grants for Capital purposes."[123] Determined to go ahead

Shaarey Zedek Synagogue.

with the project, Shaarey Zedek asked the children of the late Joseph and Annie Kovinsky to unveil the building's cornerstone and, subsequently dedicated the new synagogue in their parents' name.[124]

By the end of the year, only the building's ground floor, comprising a social assembly hall, classrooms, kitchen facilities, a mikvah, and a chapel, had been completed. An intensive campaign, therefore, got under way to raise the $18,000 required to cover the cost of building a second floor that would house the main sanctuary.[125] The new synagogue was completed at the end of 1958 when Shaarey Zedek let it be known that it would be available for "life-cycle celebrations."[126]

The Community Centre Groundbreaking

Due to a multiplicity of fundraising campaigns, community resources were stretched to the limit at the end of 1956, and there was no doubt in anyone's mind that the Community Centre project needed more money. Its fund received a shot in the arm from Windsor's B'nai B'rith Lodge No. 1011, when its members turned over $20,000 — a legacy bequeathed to the Lodge by the estate of the late Saul Goldman.[127] Two years later, the Lodge, under the chairmanship of Al Goldberg, organized a raffle that netted $7,200 for other Jewish causes. These raffles became community events for Jews and non-Jews alike and continued for several decades with prizes getting bigger as revenues grew.[128]

Determined to raise the outstanding $100,000 for the Jewish Community Centre, a team of forty young people, among them Mel Sorffer, Myer Dorn, Herb Gray, and Marty Rosen, got together in February 1957 for one purpose — to approach all those people who had not yet made pledges to the campaign.[129] Six months later Community Council President Eli Goldin asked building committee chairman Harry Vexler to find all those donors who had not been contacted before.[130]

These efforts must have yielded some concrete results because a confident Vexler soon announced that the cen-

tre's long-awaited groundbreaking ceremony would take place on Thanksgiving Day — October 14, 1957.[131] However since balances of 40 percent were still needed to complete the project by March 1, 1958, he suggested holding a series of "parlour meetings in homes" to track down the approximately three hundred families who had not yet made their pledges.[132] For the project to proceed as scheduled, the Council's board of governors also approved a Canadian Bank of Commerce loan of up to $225,000.[133] Although that loan was guaranteed by funds raised annually from the Welfare Fund Campaign, the mortgage on the building still required some personal guarantees.[134]

On May 16, 1958, Council President Eli Goldin announced that the contract for the $342,747 structure had been awarded to Granite Construction Company. He also paid tribute to Harry Vexler, Morris Tabachnick, Michael Sumner, and Rubin Madoff for the exemplary way in which these men had guided the project over the preceding four-and-a-half years. The members of the Council's executive committee then added their thanks, commending Eli

The cornerstone of the new Jewish Community Centre was laid in October 1958 by Rubin Madoff, past president of the Jewish Community Council. Pictured from the left are Mayor Michael J. Patrick, Eli Goldin, and Mr. Madoff.

Goldin for his efforts to further the project.[135]

On October 13, 1958, one day before the groundbreaking ceremony, the community centre's cornerstone was laid and duly dedicated.[136]

Personnel Changes 1957–58

When Community Council program director Harold Chetkow resigned on June 11, 1957, to take up a position in the United States, he was replaced by Montague (Monty) Pomm.[137] Born in England, the 33-year-old Pomm had left his homeland in September 1957 to "seek his fortune" in Canada, working first as the Community Centre's program director and later as its assistant executive director. During his tenure he initiated a number of very successful programs for young and old, such as Jewish Book Month and Jewish Music Month, which used the talents of the local symphony orchestra as well as of artists living in Windsor and Detroit. Other ventures included the Adult and the Junior Friendship Club, physical education classes, and theatre workshops. However, what Monty Pomm described as his "most significant program," was named BBYO (B'nai B'rith Youth Organization), a youth program involving teenagers from both Windsor and Detroit.[138] Both the BBG (B'nai B'rith Girls) and AZA (Aleph Zadik Aleph) boys were very active organizations, holding social, educational, and religious programs. The annual Sweetheart-Beau Dance was one of the highlights of the year.

On June 25, 1958, Khayyam Z. Paltiel, the Windsor Community Council's executive director, tendered his resignation to study for a doctorate at Hebrew University in Jerusalem on a Klausner Fellowhip.[139] He was replaced on October 1, 1958, by Joseph Eisenberg, who had accepted the position at a salary of $8,700 per year plus a $500 car allowance.[140]

Mr. Eisenberg was born on Staten Island, New York, served in Europe for four years during World War II and upon his return to the United States first worked as a program director in Staten Island, New York, then in Bayonne, New Jersey, and later in New Britain, Connecticut as executive director of the Jewish Federation. Eisenberg "I had three opportunities: one was San José, California, the other was Peeksgill, New York and the third was Windsor, Ontario." He accepted the Canadian job because "I thought it might be nice for my kids to experience a foreign country for a couple of years."[141]

Special Events of 1958

In January 1958, Windsor hosted the Seventeenth Regional Conference of the Canadian Jewish Congress. The prominent guest speakers at that three-day meeting were His Excellency Arthur E. Lourie, the newly appointed Israeli Ambassador to Canada, Canadian Jewish Congress Director Saul Hayes of Montreal, and Dr. Stuart E. Rosenberg, rabbi of Toronto's Beth Tzedek Synagogue, one of North America's largest Jewish congregations.[142]

To plan the celebration for the State of Israel's tenth anniversary, Windsor's Jewish Community Council established a committee, headed by Meyer Dorn, the president of B'nai B'rith Lodge No. 1011. Events planned for the occasion included a dance, a major rally with a prominent Israeli speaker, a commemorative religious service, and a variety show staged by local groups. While almost all the events took place at Shaar Hashomayim, one program sponsored by Mizrachi was held at Shaarey Zedek and included a speech by Rabbi Karelitz.[143]

To mark the successful conclusion of the 1958 Israel Bond Drive, a gala night took place at Shaar Hashomayim on November 9, 1958. George Jessel served as the master of ceremonies and it was up to this well-known star of American radio, television, and the Broadway stage to introduce the evening's guest speaker — the Honourable Paul Martin — a prominent Windsorite, a former minister of national health and welfare, and the recipient of the 1956 Canadian Council of Christians and Jews Brotherhood Award.[144] Having just returned from a study trip to the Middle East, Mr. Martin regaled his audience with a vivid

In April 1958, as part of the events to commemorate Israel's 10th anniversary, the Windsor Jewish Community Council held a cabaret dance in the Shaar Hashomayim Synagogue. In charge of planning were Mr. Myer Dorn (left), anniversary committee chair, and Mr. Monty Pomm, a member of the committee.

account of his visit to Israel. The following is an excerpt from Volume II of his autobiography, *A Very Public Life*, that reflects his impressions of the country:

In 1958, Israel was a tourists' paradise, scat-

tered with relics of the past; [my wife] Nell was very moved by the hallowed places. We also explored the modern Israel and saw the benefactions of Canadian Jews — refugee centres and forests — as well as the state-run armaments factory. In Tel Aviv and Jaffa, one sensed the new state's vigour and promise. In the north, we drew close to the Mount of Beatitudes and passed by Safad, a small and ancient Galilean community.

Israel has its paradoxes. It was truly polyglot, but ferociously nationalistic. Orthodoxy and modernism, and the all-pervading influence of the Old Testament, were equally present. The nation had a foreign policy derived from the demands of the moment, but it brought with it stormy decisions and great courage.[145]

A Dream Becomes Reality

The year 1959 not only represented a milestone for Windsor Jews but was also the fruition of a fifteen-year dream — the opening on January 1 of their very own community centre at 1641 Ouellette Avenue.[146] Although the official key-presentation ceremony did not take place until April 19, 1959, the Council immediately moved all its activities that, until then, had been scattered throughout the city to the new premises. And it did not take long for an operating committee to be appointed: Phil Strosberg took charge of athletics; Barney Madoff and Dr. Maurice Adelman of youth and adult activities, respectively; Leona Schott was chosen to look after the Golden-Age programs; while Michael Sumner headed the library; and Sidney Lazarus, the day camp.

Jewish families, as well as single men and women, soon became members of the Community Centre that boasted a health club, a leisure-time concept that still was considered novel in 1959.[147]

A move, unprecedented in the history of Windsor's Jewish community, was to name the new building after Philip Bernstein, a man who had donated $75,000 toward its completion, but had only recently returned to the city after several years' absence.[148] To further honour him, the

Setting the scene for the contribution tea of the Lillian Freiman Chapter of Hadassah in June 1959 at her apartment is Mrs. Milton J. Kovinsky. The proceeds from the affair went toward a hospital in the Port of Eilat in Israel.

Community Council sponsored a testimonial at the Centre auditorium on November 22, 1959. Members of the Lillian Freiman Chapter of Hadassah acted as hostesses for the event and Lawrence Freiman, National President of the Zionist Organization of Canada, was the evening's guest speaker.[149]

While Jewish Community Council members were basking in the success of their newest venture, Shaar Hashomayim was about to "modernize and expand the facilities of the Synagogue."[150] Although its campaign to raise $300,000 for that purpose only got underway at the beginning of November 1959, pledges of $87,050 already had been received a week later. The donated funds were to be used to provide additional seating in the synagogue's main sanctuary and in the balcony, for an enlarged and modernized social hall and improved kitchen facilities, and for air conditioning in the main sanctuary and in the social hall.[151]

Not to be outdone or left behind, the I. L. Peretz Shule spent $2,200 to purchase a half-acre of land on Memorial Drive — a street today called Ypres Boulevard.[152]

Shaar Hashomayim Celebrates Rabbi Stollman's Tenth Anniversary

On the occasion of the tenth anniversary of Samuel Stollman's tenure as rabbi of Shaar Hashomayim, Michael Sumner paid a heart-warming tribute to him in an article that appeared in the *Bulletin*'s May-June 1959 issue. The following are excerpts from it:

> During those ten years [Rabbi Stollman] has laboured — some of you will remember that we had decided we wanted a shirt-sleeve Rabbi — with a persistence that has gotten wonderful results. When he came we had only the structure of a synagogue. In ten years he has breathed life and activity into that structure. The Men's Club, the Religious School, the T'filin Club, the Mr. and Mrs. Club are visible tangible activities well known to everyone.
>
> But less tangible are the many influences on individuals and groups in and out of the Jewish community. It is not by accident that the Congregation has developed a core of younger men to give it leadership. It is not by accident that there has been developed in the Congregation the will and the enthusiasm for an expansion project that will encompass the needs of Jewish religious education, as well as of our basic social and congregational requirements.
>
> Nor is it an accident that strong loyalties have been built up toward our Jewish tradition and the synagogue; so much so

> that the money niggling that used to be the headache of the past has been replaced by a spirit of generosity....
>
> In the light of the influence he has had on the community, it does not now seem too much to hope that the next decade will see many of his seeds bear fruit. A community which develops the habit-pattern of synagogue attendance; an all-day school for the effective education of our children; the acceptance by an increasing number of young families of kashruth — that tradition which makes of a home a synagogue; more intelligent understanding of the meaning of Jewish tradition by young and old; these are all goals toward which Rabbi Stollman labours diligently and determinedly....[153]

The year 1959 also marked the two-hundredth anniversary of Jewish settlement in Canada. On that occasion, the Canadian Jewish Congress issued a Proclamation of Faith and Thanksgiving that stated in part:

> From many lands, our people have come to these hospitable shores in search of religious and political freedom and economic opportunity. Thanks to these advantages, we have taken our place with our fellow citizens in the promotion of the economic, political, religious, social and cultural life of our country. We have come to the aid of the needy among us, and have brought relief to our brethren in countries of oppression and poverty. Our sons have responded to the call of patriotism in peace and war, some receiving coveted awards for their bravery and service, others making the supreme sacrifice.
>
> In this mosaic of Canada we have held

fast to our ancient prophetic ideals. We have been motivated by our steadfast belief in human dignity and human welfare. In this hour of thanksgiving we recall that our generation was privileged to witness the creation of the State of Israel, and we express our profound gratitude for the leadership Canada demonstrated in his historic achievement....[154]

As the 1950s came to a close, the landscape of Windsor's Jewish community had drastically changed. It had a new community centre, Shaarey Zedek had completed its expansion, improvements to Shaar Hashomayim's facilities were underway, and the I. L. Peretz Shule was making ambitious arrangements to accommodate the community's largest student body.

By the end of that decade, a fledgling religious institution had made its first appearance in Windsor. Despite the fact that the Reform Congregation Beth El had few supporters at first and was viewed with considerable suspicion by the other religious institutions, it soon made lofty plans for the future. It was only a beginning....

Chapter 9
Reform Judaism Arrives

Windsor in the 1960s

Windsor entered the 1960s with high hopes of becoming a modern city. An outpouring of reform energy followed Mayor Michael Patrick's victory in 1954 and the city moved toward the future, determined to pull itself up by the bootstraps. The 1958 Battelle Commission suggested a number of reforms such as diversification of its economic base and less reliance upon the auto industry, attracting middle class professionals, cleaning up the city's image and environment, and a host of political changes such as an at-large council and a city manager/administrator. The long years of dominance under Art Reaume and councils interfering with administrative efficiency and modernization were assumed to be over. The emergence of the University of Windsor and St. Clair College reflected co-operation between industry and education, and the newly established university brought together Roman Catholic, Anglican, and United Church colleges that contributed to the wider university environment as well as to the broader community. At the same time, Windsor was in an economic recession in the early 1960s; unemployment levels were high. Attempting to produce the

wide variety of makes and models demanded by the market had resulted in inefficiencies and prevented the implementation of economy-of-scale savings.

With the Auto Pact of 1965, the auto industry jettisoned its historic tariff protection, which had been largely responsible for the establishment of a branch plant industry in Windsor, to experiment with free trade. Although the pact represented only sectoral free trade in autos and auto parts and provided a safety net for Canadian autoworkers, the trend toward continental free trade and globalization was unmistakable.

Windsor could no longer be contained within the old forms and borders and the Annexation of 1965 brought the nearer suburbs — Riverside, Ojibway, and Sandwich East — into Greater Windsor. On the East Side, Tecumseh and St. Clair Beach successfully rebuffed Windsor's advances and Windsorites continued to flee the central city for the suburbs.

As the nation approached its centennial in 1967, official bilingualism and biculturalism were being challenged in a number of ways as Quebec demanded cultural independence, Canadian students and youth demanded changes, and New Canadians demanded a place in the sun. In a climate of cultural diversity, groups became more assertive about preserving their cultural heritage. How to retain their culture, how to be both Jews and Canadians, was a question Jews had been grappling with since their arrival. Multiculturalism became government policy by the end of the 1960s. Ethnic diversity helped mute prejudices and supported the growth of tolerance, but racism and discrimination still existed. Jews had long been recognized in the struggle for civil rights and actively supported a number of causes. The hopes and expectations for Lyndon Johnson's "Great Society" were dashed as Windsor's Jews shared with the rest of their fellow citizens the disappointment and despair at watching Detroit burn in the 1967 riots.

In contrast to the American experience in Vietnam, which was tearing the country apart and driving many of its young men to Canada, Windsor's Jews could exalt in Israel's total victory in the 1967 Six Day War. The tiny nation's larger and more defendable borders offered the hope of greater future security.

Divorce laws were liberalized as the government got out of the nation's bedrooms in 1969. The traditional family remained the ideal, but single-parent households, blended families, and remarriages were on the rise. The women's movement and participatory politics — the catch phrase of student activists — heralded a new secular society in which war and materialism challenged traditional religious values and the post-war consensus of the 1950s.[1]

Mayor Michael J. Patrick proclaimed September 23–29, 1956, Business Women's Week. Pictured with the mayor, displaying the poster for the week, were (left) Mrs. Leone Schott and Mrs. G. L. Hamilton of the Windsor Business and Professional Women's Club.

Reform Arrives

Under Rabbi Stollman, the Orthodox synagogue, Shaar Hashomayim, had dominated the Windsor Jewish community since 1949 and refused to bend to wishes for a more modern but still Conservative synagogue. Stollman's Orthodoxy was unchanging — as an astute guardian of the past traditions, he intuitively knew that once change had begun, it would be unstoppable. While Stollman stood fast, others argued for full participation outside the shtetl and engagement with wider society. Reform and change were in the air and the Jewish community of Windsor was no less affected than other Canadians. Pressure from youth, from the US, and from Reform Judaism heralded a new day. The inherent patriarchy of Orthodoxy could not contain the emerging demands of women, who were now better educated and more worldly, and demanding a place in the active world outside the home, nor an assimilated middle class who were quite comfortable in the new world environment in which they and their predecessors had prospered and flourished. By the 1960s, Reform Judaism had been winning out in the United States and in many parts of Canada; Reform arrived late in Windsor but the time seemed auspicious for its success.

The story goes that before Rabbi Samuel S. Stollman was hired as Shaar Hashomayim's new spiritual head in 1949, Michael Sumner asked Rabbi Stollman's father, then the dean of Detroit's rabbinate, "Rabbi, I don't know how long we are going to continue as a strictly Orthodox synagogue as there may come a time when the membership will demand that women and men be allowed to sit together. Not that they'll want a change in the services or anything, but how would your son feel about such a thing?" The elder Stollman laughed and said, "Well, your question is not surprising. I must tell you that in my day I had to make similar decisions. But I can't guarantee whether my son will do one thing or another." [2]

His son left no doubt about where he stood as rabbi of Windsor's leading Orthodox congregation:

> When the first "dissidents" broke away from Shaar Hashomayim to found a Reform Congregation, I asked them if their objection to traditional seating was the reason for their departure from the Synagogue. They answered me quite candidly that "family" or mixed seating was not the real issue. They did not want their children or themselves, for that matter, be instructed in Shabbes observance, kashrus or other Mitzvot. Their ideology was not traditional and, therefore, they wanted a "liberal, reformed or progressive" congregation with all the experimentation and latitude that it represents. I was thankful to them for setting the record straight. It was clear that even if the Shaar had compromised on seating (which would have meant the end of my association with the Synagogue), the pressures for further change would not have diminished. [3]

Surprisingly, when Rabbi Stollman arrived at Shaar Hashomayim in 1949, he did not reject the existing mixed seating in the synagogue's balcony on the grounds that "the arrangement with most of the Rabbis who came here was to accept the status quo. In other words, we were not going to go down or up or change in any way." [4]

It was clear, however, that as an Orthodox rabbi he could not have allowed any compromises to the laws governing traditional Judaism, even though most Shaar Hashomayim members were more Conservative in their personal practices than strictly Orthodox.

In the 1950s, there certainly were more than a few individuals at Shaar Hashomayim who had a definite interest in reforming the synagogue's practices. It is quite possible, therefore, that they used the issue of mixed seating throughout the synagogue as the basis for discussions about eventually forming a more liberal congregation. In that connection, Robert Cohen, who was Shaar Hashomayim's president from 1951 to 1953, recalled that "we wanted a Conservative synagogue and he [Rabbi Stollman] wouldn't go for it." [5]

Rabbi Stollman's position on mixed seating was clear, but those who wanted a change were equally unrelenting. Robert Cohen remembered a religious committee meeting during which the subject was to be addressed:

> Well, Rabbi Stollman knew my thoughts on mixed seating and the thoughts of several of the other boys. But when we met and nothing was said about it all evening long, I said to him, "Look, Rabbi, I don't want to hurt your feelings and you don't want to hurt mine. But we have come here to talk about mixed seating." That was when Rabbi Stollman said to me, "Yes, you have a point." But the boys who supported a more conservative approach to Judaism did not

agree. "What do you mean?" they said to the Rabbi, "You can't talk about mixed seating here. This is a religious meeting."

But we did sit down and we spoke about mixed seating for a while until Rabbi Stollman picked up a kind of bible [or more likely a Jewish text] and started quoting from it some old old-time rabbonim, who claimed that if a Jew has to sit in the temple with goyim he just as well might not go there at all. And when he quoted several other little things from that book it kind of hurt my feelings. So I got up and walked out of the meeting.[6]

Emotions ran high after that, setting the stage for a breakaway congregation. However, before taking the final step, Arthur B. Weingarden and Larry Greene went to see Rabbi Stollman one more time, hoping to discuss with him the possibility of liberalizing Shaar Hashomayim. But he was not prepared to take any steps to accommodate them, suggesting instead that they remain at Shaar Hashomayim and observe as much of its Orthodoxy as they chose to observe. According to Arthur Weingarden, "as this would not have provided us with the spirit and practice of the Judaism we sought, we were determined to proceed with the new synagogue."[7] Corroborating Weingarden's recollections about the meeting with Rabbi Stollman, Larry Greene explained:

Things were done at the Shaar in ways we were not happy with. Mixed seating was not the only change we wanted. Another one was aliyot [paying for the honour of being called to the Torah]. Art [Arthur Weingarden] and I also had expressed a desire to be part of the Rabbi's couples' group but only if reforms were made that would be consistent with a Conservative congregation. But Rabbi Stollman refused to make the changes we asked for. We,

therefore, told him that we probably would try to form our own group, one centred on Reform or liberal principles that were more agreeable to us.

His answer was that Reform was not the way to practice Judaism, that it would never take hold, and that we would be disrupting the peaceful existence of the Jewish community of Windsor.

I still believe that if Rabbi Stollman had offered us some type of compromise solution to Orthodox practices, a liberal congregation never could have been formed in Windsor.[8]

While several members wanted changes at the Shaar Hashomayim, Rabbi Stollman could not deviate from Halacha as an Orthodox rabbi. Any presumption was ludicrous! Defending his implacability on Orthodox values, Rabbi Stollman said that mixed seating was not the only reason people wanted to practice Judaism from a different perspective but rather, "people wanted an excuse for not coming to shul." He believed the movement away from traditional Judaism "resulted in a kind of insecurity in people — an attempt to convey to the public, 'I am as modern as you are. I am not backward.'"[9]

Fully aware of the repercussions his actions had caused, Rabbi Stollman felt that "by being intransigent about mixed seating, I even helped to establish the temple. And if there is credit to be given for that, I should get a great reward."[10]

Joseph Eisenberg, Windsor Community Council's executive director between 1958 and 1989, was certain that the establishment of a Reform Congregation in Windsor had hurt Rabbi Stollman "because he felt it was [only] a personal rejection of him, not a religious attitude. He also was hurt that Beth El happened because some people thought it would make a noise but won't last. So the rabbi kind of lashed out from the pulpit, scathingly calling it 'the other place' as a last resort. He lost a lot of good people and I think he took it personally."[11]

Educational Institutions Retain their Independence

Soon after the new Jewish Community Centre had opened in Windsor, the acrimony between Shaar Hashomayim and the I. L. Peretz Shule intensified when it was suggested that the two educational institutions should operate on the premises of this new facility. Both rejected the idea and each of them launched campaigns to attract the ever-increasing number of students to their religious schools. Their requests for the Community Council's executive to approve the construction of their own educational facilities required the Council's Board of Governors to take a position on consolidation[12]:

The suggestion has been made in some quarters that the Shaar Religious School and Peretz School should function in the Windsor Jewish Community Centre instead of operating separate facilities.

Since such a suggestion could damage the building fund campaigns of the two educational institutions, the Council, the Synagogue, and the Peretz School deem it advisable to express their official stand on this issue.

Prior to the building of the Community Centre, the Community Council set up a committee to investigate the feasibility of housing the schools in the centre. The result of this committee's deliberations was the decision that, in the light of the realities as they existed and now exist, the purposes of Jewish education in Windsor would only be served by maintaining separate facilities.

It must be recognized that the problems of Jewish education transcend its purely economic aspects. Any respect for the curricula and autonomy of the schools, which their devoted supporters strive to uphold, must prevent any action being taken to interfere with the full freedom of both schools. It is our conviction that no formula can be developed which would enable the two schools to occupy the same building without impeding their freedom and their proper academic atmosphere.

It should be the intention of the community to encourage and strengthen the educational endeavours by the existing institutions. It is in the total community interest that all community institutions should flourish since no single institution can now, or ever, serve the total needs of a community as large and as varied as ours.

We call on all organizations and persons to give their unqualified support to the legitimate functions of all of our institutions, and to abstain from unstudied proposals which might interfere with the support of any of our campaigns or institutions.[13]

Thanks to the divergent religious philosophies held by Shaar Hashomayim and the I. L. Peretz Shule, both were able to retain their own schools, even though the latter, as a more cultural educational facility and less of a religious one, would have fit nicely into the framework of the Community Centre's mandate.

Shaar Hashomayim's $300,000 expansion-fund campaign was well underway by January 1960 with donations reaching $125,000. The plans called for a new religious school annex, an enlarged and modernized social hall and kitchen, additional balcony seating and air-conditioning.[14] After purchasing a house and a lot at the end of 1960, the Shaar Hashomayim had sufficient land to build its own religious school. The plans were to "remove the house and reroute the alley through the lot into Windsor Avenue. This new outlet will make possible the closing of the alley on Giles Boulevard and its transfer by the City to the Synagogue to be used in conjunction with the lot already cleared (formerly 155 Giles Boulevard) as one continuous piece of land for the erection of the new Religious School."[15] When Louis and Rachel Kaplan donated $36,000 to the synagogue's $110,000 building fund, the time to erect the actual building had arrived.[16] Construction took place over the next four months and to celebrate its completion and dedicate the school — henceforth to be known as the Louis and Rachel Kaplan Shaar Hashomayim Religious School — a Shabbat service was held on January 30, 1965, followed by a ceremony on Sunday afternoon, and a banquet later that evening.[17] Louis Kaplan passed away that year, but the Louis and Rachel Kaplan Shaar Hashomayim Religious School continued his legacy. Within the school, a chapel was named after Joshua Gitlin and his wife, Libby, and dedicated on April 3, 1966.[18]

Six young Jewish students graduate in June 1961 from Grade 8 of the Shaar Hashomayim religious school. The students, who received their diplomas at a special service at the Shaar, are (from the left, front row) Sandra Center, Terri Strosberg, and Phyllis Shapiro; in the back row (from the left) are Martin Mock, Joe Fruchter, and Michael Gordner.

Photo courtesy of the Windsor Star

The Status of Three Congregations

The plans of Windsor's Jewish institutions suffered a setback in the mid-1960s, when gloomy economic times descended on the city.[19] However, at the end of the decade, Shaar Hashomayim did manage to raise sufficient funds to carry out their renovation plans, especially after the Zalev family presented the synagogue with a special gift of $35,000. The gift enabled the synagogue to spend $150,000 to refurbish its auditorium and improve its kitchen facilities.[20] The formal dedication of the hall, henceforth to be known as the Charles Zalev Social Hall, took place on December 7, 1969, a date that happened to coincide with Shaar Hashomayim's fortieth anniversary.[21]

Although Shaarey Zedek's building had been completed some years earlier, a sum of $30,000 was still needed to pay off its mortgage. To relieve the heavy burden resting on the shoulders of its original founders, the synagogue initiated a Dollar-a-Week Building Fund Plan, whereby donors automatically would become chartered shareholders and eligible for a full Shaarey Zedek membership.[22]

However, the Dollar-a-Week Building Fund Plan was not successful, and as the cost of building the new synagogue seemingly had exhausted the small congregation's resources, Shaarey Zedek's board had no choice but to dispense with the services of its spiritual leader, Rabbi Karelitz. Deploring his departure in June 1962, Michael Sumner praised the rabbi for having "almost single-handedly built the new Shaarey Zedek Synagogue, never for a moment losing sight of the needs of the community as a whole." He also commended him for having been "realistic in his approaches to community problems, striving to maintain harmony and to bring his own Congregation to awareness of the whole community's needs." Sumner expressed regret that "the $30,000 still owing on the mortgage of a building that represented a $175,000 investment should have forced Shaarey Zedek's leadership to dispense with the Rabbi's services. The loss will be the community's as well as their own."[23] After Rabbi Karalitz had left Shaarey Zedek, its congregation did not have permanent rabbinical leadership

until Rabbi Joseph Krupnik assumed the position in 1992. During the long interim, under the guidance of President Norman Hurwitz, it did carry on in its own fashion, hiring a *baal tefillah* — a leader of prayers — or other individuals to conduct services, and inviting guests to speak at its functions.[24]

Little information is available to chronicle the activities of Tifereth Israel as the *Bulletin* seldom mentioned the synagogue's name, other than to publish a list of donations for Siddurim in November 1963, as well as mentioning certain other donations in its April 1964 and March 1969 issues.[25] Over the years, attendance at Tifereth Israel steadily declined as its members went, one by one, to their "eternal rewards." In the beginning of the 1970s, so few were left that services ceased and the synagogue was forced to close a few years later.

Preparing to Form a New Congregation

At Detroit's Reform Temple Beth El, it was customary for the rabbi to invite the younger members of his congregation to his home after Friday evening services to have the opportunity to discuss his sermon with them. Arthur Weingarden remembered attending one of these get-togethers in the late 1950s. At a luncheon at the Statler Hotel in Detroit, members of his Windsor group asked Rabbi Richard Hertz and Rabbi David Baylinson to advise them how to go about starting a Reform congregation in Windsor. Reportedly, the rabbi had simply replied, "Just start."[26]

That brief encounter led to the formation of a Steering Committee for Liberal Judaism and a meeting on December 22, 1959, at Detroit's Temple Beth El for the purpose of "organizing a Reform Judaism Movement in our city of Windsor, Ontario, Canada."[27] Present at that meeting were Rabbi David Baylinson of Detroit's Temple Beth El and members of the newly formed steering committee — Mr. and Mrs. Harvey White, Mr. and Mrs. Larry Greene, Mr. and Mrs. Arthur Weingarden, and Dr. and Mrs. Lee Brown.

The primary goal of the steering committee was to have a congregation established by Rosh Hashanah of the year

1960. And, providing there was sufficient "stimulation and enthusiasm," its members also wanted to be able to hold their first religious service on February 19, 1960 — a service they hoped would be conducted by Rabbi Baylinson with the help of the scrolls and prayer books he would bring along from his congregation.[28] However, before that first service could take place, the members of the steering committee wanted to explain their intentions to Windsor's Jewish community. To do so, they were planning to distribute literature, bearing the slogan "Come Worship with Us," to describe the new congregation. They also wanted to personally contact all the people on their list of forty tentative members, as well as those on their list of "unaffiliated families in Windsor." After the first service, they were determined to have on hand "a complete list of interested and committed families" and have in place "a committee of elders in the community."[29]

The steering committee met again five days later, on December 27, 1959. Having assembled at the home of Arthur and Madelyn Weingarden, its members decided to move the date of the first service to the second week of March 1960. Until that time, they were planning to take couples for discussions to any of the three Reform congregations and to attend Friday evening services.[30]

The committee contacted Rabbi Bernard Baskin, head of the Canadian Council of Liberal Congregations (later, the Canadian Council for Reform Judaism), as well as Rabbi Baum, the director of New Congregations of the Union of American Hebrew Congregations in New York,[31] to ensure that the Reform movement's national and regional bodies were aware of all these plans.

They suffered their first setback at the end of January 1960 when Windsor's Jewish Community Council refused its request to hold religious services at the Jewish Community Centre. However, the Council's board of governors did assure the new group that other space, if available, would be provided, at the same time suggesting that it become a member of the Jewish Community Council as soon as possible.[32] Working hard to enlist support for the new congregation, the steering committee held parlour meetings in various homes, inviting guest speakers such as

Rabbi Baylinson of Detroit and Rabbi Baskin of Hamilton to explain Reform Judaism to prospective members.[33] Rabbi Richard Hertz of Detroit's Temple Beth El attended one of these meetings on March 11, 1960, and expressed his desire, as well as that of his board, that the name of the new congregation be Temple Beth El Windsor, deeming it "a great honour" if that name indeed were adopted.[34] Complying with his wishes and, following approval by its members, the steering committee formally adopted the name Congregation Beth El of Windsor. The letterhead on its new stationery showed Arthur B. Weingarden as chairman, Bernice White as secretary, Morris Menkin as head of the finance committee, Larry Greene as public relations officer, and Madelyn Weingarden as membership chairman. Harvey White was put in charge of religious affairs, Marcia Menkin and Shirley Swartz of the Sisterhood, and Syril Greene and Gertrude Weingarden of education, while Maurice Berkovitz, Archie Cherniak, Jack Greene, Frank Bear, Elliot Swartz, Max Weingarden, and Dan Weingarden became temporary officers of the various committees.[35]

Beth El's early services were held at Windsor's Southwood School on Cabana Road. By April 1960, the congregation also had started a religious school. It had four classes of nineteen children, ranging in ages between 4 and 13, who were taught by volunteer teachers — all of them members of Beth El.[36]

Beth El Makes Its Debut

After joining Windsor's Jewish Community Council, the time had come for Congregation Beth El to have its own spiritual head. When Harvey White, Arthur B. Weingarden, and Dan Weingarden heard that Sherwin T. Wine, the assistant rabbi of Detroit's Temple Beth El might be available, they met with him to ask whether he might be interested in serving their congregation. He agreed to do so, but only on weekends, as he was planning to study for his doctorate. Rabbi Wine was born in Detroit, Michigan on January 25, 1928. Having received his BA and MA from the University of Michigan, he attended Cincinnati's Hebrew Union College, graduating from there in 1956.

Rabbi Wine was hired in June 1960 at a weekly salary of $100 and started his new assignment following a garden party given in his honour.[37] The following are excerpts from a letter in which he described his efforts to further the development of Windsor's Congregation Beth El:

> I stayed with the Temple until June 1964.… During that time, we laid the foundation for a functioning congregation — services, a newsletter, committees, adult education, as well as lecture — and community — outreach programs.
>
> Establishing a Reform temple in Windsor was not easy. Many issues had to be dealt with — the hostility towards us by many members of the Jewish community, (especially by the leaders of the Shaar), the arguments among liberal and conservative reformers whether yalmulkes or no yalmulkes should be worn, finding money, and developing a core leadership to sustain the congregation.
>
> The early years were the years of the volunteers — from teachers to choir members. Despite the challenges, these pioneer times were exciting and inspiring. We were building from scratch, at times, in a hostile community. However, with leaders such as Arthur B. Weingarden, Max Weingarden, Larry Greene, Bob Cohen, Bill Silver and Harvey White, the bonds of friendship were intense in the early years, creating the warmth of a Temple family.[38]

Beth El's first general membership meeting was held on June 28, 1960, when approval was given to the congregation's constitution and the decision was made to hold the current year's High Holiday services at Windsor's Cleary Auditorium on Riverside Drive. During the meeting, donations for prayer books were solicited and those in attendance also acknowledged Joseph and Lillian Finkel's generous gift of a Torah and its accessories, as well as thanking Dr. David Weingarden for presenting the temple with an organ.[39]

By that time, Beth El's membership had grown to twenty-nine registered members and the number of students attending its religious school had risen to thirty-five. Seven teachers were conducting the regular lessons, while Rabbi Wine had taken on teaching the bar mitzvah classes.[40]

Temple Beth El was now looking for a more permanent home. Although several sites had been considered for purchase, renting Simon Meretsky's house proved to be the best immediate solution.[41] After signing a twenty-two-month lease at a yearly rent of $1,200, payable in twelve monthly installments of $100, the congregation moved to its new premises at 1172 Ouellette Avenue.[42]

In late summer 1960, Temple Beth El was holding regular religious services and by September of that year had formed a choir led by Elliot Swartz. Its members included Ruth Katzman, Lillian Hart, Joyce Head, Marilyn Baker, Esther Goldstein, Bill Silver, and Martin Goldberg, with

Photo courtesy of the Windsor Star

Home of Simon Meretsky that became the first home of Congregation Beth El.

Ruth Tribute acting as music director and organist. Jack Baum was chosen to blow the *shofar* — the ram's horn — on the High Holidays.[43]

Beth El's board of directors also held discussions with Rabbi Baum, director of new congregations of the Union of American Hebrew Congregations that ultimately led to the Temple's affiliation with the body that served all Reform congregations.[44] Another major issue that required Beth El's attention was obtaining burial grounds for its congregation.

Until the early 1960s, Shaar Hashomayim's cemetery on Pillette Road had served the needs of its congregation as well as those of the community as a whole. The site, originally owned by Jerry Glanz, had been turned over to the Shaar Hashomayim, even though the home at 2618 Pillette Road, adjacent to the cemetery, was not sold to the synagogue until 1967.[45]

The impetus for setting aside a portion for Congregation Beth El came from Michael Sumner who proposed to the Shaar Hashomayim board that "they set aside a portion of the Shaar Hashomayim Cemetery in order to allow the families to be buried in the same place."[46] Beth El and Shaar Hashomayim established a dialogue with regard to the Pillette Road Cemetery, but discussions dragged on for some time before an agreement was reached regarding the appropriate manner in which both congregations could use the burial grounds and the Chesed Shel Emes Funeral Chapel. When a meeting was finally called for April 26, 1961, Shaar Hashomayim condoned certain compromise solutions such as permitting Beth El members to use a funeral home other than the Chesed Shel Emes Chapel, even though *tahara* (the washing and ritual purification of the deceased's body) could only be performed at that chapel. Burials could be delayed to permit out-of-town mourners to attend; embalming was acceptable; wearing *tachrichim* (burial shrouds) was mandatory, but they could be concealed under clothing; the use of *kippahs* (skull caps) and *talisim* (prayer shawls) by both the deceased and the mourners was optional, and families were permitted to leave the cemetery prior to the lowering of the casket.[47]

It would be seven long years, until April 29, 1968, before Shaar Hashomayim representatives agreed to set aside a section of the Pillette Road Cemetery as Congregation Beth El's burial ground and to allow the temple to follow its own funeral service rituals at the Chesed Shel Emes Chapel. Even though control of the cemetery, as well as of the chapel, remained in the hands of the Chesed Shel Emes Burial Society, it was decided to let one caretaker look after the needs of both synagogues at the cemetery to avoid duplication of services and cut down maintenance costs.[48]

Matters came to a head in 1967 during Rabbi Shelley Waldenberg's tenure at Beth El. At that time, an incident occurred involving the congregation's first burial at the Pillette Road Cemetery. Arthur Barat, who served as president of Congregation Beth El, related the story as follows:

> Rabbi Waldenberg had asked me to meet him at an apartment above a store on Wyandotte Street. When we got there, we saw a sick lady lying in bed. She told us that her name was Gracia Paquay, that her husband had been killed during World War II, that her son, who lived in England, was a convert to Judaism, and that she, herself, was about to embrace the Jewish faith. Handing me a cheque, she said to me, "I want to be buried in a Jewish cemetery. Please take this. It is all the money I have in my bank account."
>
> When I later visited Mrs. Paquay in the hospital she showed me her certificate of conversion. Soon afterwards, she died and her body was taken to the Chesed Shel Emes Funeral Chapel. Although we had informed Rabbi Stollman what we had done, someone from the funeral home telephoned us and said, "There's a goy (non-Jew) here; get her out."
>
> The night before her burial a meeting was held in the Shaar Hashomayim funeral

chapel. Then we all went in the rain to the southern part of the cemetery, filled with construction debris, to plant a stick marker on a line. Incidentally, as part of the agreement with Rabbi Stollman to keep Beth El's burial grounds separate from those of Shaar Hashomayim, Beth El had committed itself to replace the marker with a wall just wide enough for a coffin to pass through.

The next day, we buried Mrs. Paquay in a grave beyond the line where we had placed the marker, having been given permission to inter her nowhere else but in the farthest corner of the burial grounds. It was the very first funeral service to be held by Congregation Beth El.

Nine months later, when we unveiled her tomb stone, we handed $650 to Don Clark, the monument maker. That was all the money we had left of Mrs. Paquay's funds. He accepted it as full payment for his work.[49]

Beth El Moves to Permanent Quarters

As Beth El's membership had grown to sixty-six by September 1960, it was decided to look for larger quarters.[50] According to its president, Arthur B. Weingarden, "the leadership provided by Rabbi Wine and the enthusiastic support of the large majority of our members was a certain recipe for growth and we were soon looking for land upon which to build a permanent temple."[51] In December 1960, he appointed Max Weingarden as head of the building committee, entrusting him with the task of looking for a suitable site.[52] He also put William Silver in charge of the building fund campaign so that he could raise the necessary money to finance the project.[53]

Over the next six months, the building committee submitted a number of proposals to the Beth El board. As all of them were rejected, Martin Goldberg moved that consideration should be given to a certain group of lots priced at $12,000 that were located at the northwest corner of Mark Avenue and the Third Concession in the Township of Sandwich West. Despite the fact that Elliot Swartz seconded the motion, it once again was defeated, likely because the board was reluctant to purchase a property without having the required funds in hand. Several other motions failed, but the fact that the board had decided to take a long-term option on the Mark Avenue lots seemed to indicate its definite interest in moving forward with the project.[54]

Beth El's first fundraising event took place on June 28, 1961, at the home of Max Weingarden. Twenty-two members came to hear the evening's speaker, Rabbi Bernard Baskin, and pledged a total of $12,000. Two weeks later, during Beth El's general membership meeting at Harvey White's home, Hy Muroff proposed "that the congregation accept the generous gift of $12,500 donated by Max and Dan Weingarden and their families for the purchase of the land on 3rd Concession between Mark and Glenwood Avenue upon which will be erected the House of Worship, Social Hall and School for this Congregation." The motion passed unanimously.[55]

At the groundbreaking ceremony for the new temple on October 22, 1961, greetings were received from Mel Sorffer, the president of Windsor's Jewish Community Council, and from a Sandwich West Township representative.[56] Actual construction was to commence in May 1962 and the board already had decreed that costs must not exceed $87,000, but it took close to six months before the plans were approved and the architectural firm of Pennington & Carter was commissioned to design the building.[57] Temple Beth El's dedication ceremony took place on November 11, 1962. It began with a solemn Torah procession that was led by President Robert Cohen and followed by the kindling of the eternal light and a consecration prayer delivered by Rabbi Bernard Baskin of Hamilton's Temple Anshe Shalom. Building committee chairman Max Weingarden, acting as the formal presenter, symbolically handed the temple over to Robert Cohen, who accepted it on behalf of the congregation. The highlight of the service was a stirring address by Rabbi W. Gunther Plaut, senior rabbi of Toronto's Holy Blossom Temple. Rabbi Sherwin Wine's reverential response followed and, to complete the dedication ceremony, the congregation rose to recite a stirring declaration of faith in unison.[58]

Photo courtesy of the Windsor Star

Rabbi Sherwin T. Wine officiated at the October 22, 1961, groundbreaking ceremony for the new Temple Beth El that was built on 3rd Concession Rd. at Mark Avenue. Pictured from the left are Arthur B. Weingarden, president of the congregation; Frank Crowe, deputy reeve of Sandwich West, and Rabbi Wine.

Beth El's Struggle for Acceptance

Thanks to the tireless efforts of Beth El's enthusiastic supporters, the congregation moved quite quickly to establish itself as a viable religious institution and an integral part of Windsor's Jewish community. Gaining acceptance among its members was another matter. Even though most of them were not Orthodox in their practice of Judaism, they did favour a more traditional approach in keeping with the upbringing they had received in Eastern Europe. While Detroit's Jewish community was enjoying a vibrant Reform movement, largely because its members were primarily of German origin, many Windsor Jews viewed the new temple as a radical institution that wasn't really Jewish. Beth El members, therefore, had to tolerate being called goyim — Gentiles — who had rejected the tenets of Judaism. According to Joseph Eisenberg, "There was almost an imprimatur of *treif* — unkosher — put on it."[59] An indication of Beth El's near ostracism by Windsor's Jewish community was the omission of its name and that of its rabbi from the High Holiday greetings published in the September 1961 issue of the *Jewish Community Council Bulletin*.[60] But the fact that so many people — especially, the adult children of parents who were firmly entrenched in Shaar Hashomayim — had joined the Reform congregation was a clear indication that there was indeed interest in this non-traditional observance of Judaism.

A degree of acceptance was gained at the end of 1963 when the Jewish Community Council granted Beth El's religious school the same yearly subvention that the city's other Jewish educational institutions had been receiving.[61] However, that allocation was then and remained very small for some time to come, mainly because neither Rabbi Wine nor his successor Rabbi Waldenberg were compensated for the time they spent teaching. Three years later, when Congregation Beth El asked the Council to change its allocation procedure, that request was denied on the grounds that any alteration to the existing formula would equally affect the other schools.[62] It took a full year before the Council's board of directors adopted the following recommendation:

Officers of the Temple Beth El were installed on November 11, 1962, at special ceremonies featuring the lighting of candles to symbolize their dedication to Judaism. From left, Mrs. Harvey White, secretary; Dan Weingarden, treasurer; Harvey White, vice president; Arthur B. Weingarden, president; and Jack Greene, vice president.

That the salary of Temple Beth El's principal be calculated at $2,500 per annum for administration and at $7.00 per hour for formal teaching time. And that those instructing Bas and Bar Mitzvah students be compensated "at a comparative rate for similar teaching at the other two institutions."[63]

Taking the Pulse of a Community

After three years as executive director of the Jewish Community Council, Joseph Eisenberg raised several troubling issues in his 1961 *Annual Report*. One was the decline of Windsor's Jewish population at an annual rate of 6 to 7 percent, resulting from "many of our young people going away to university and college and not returning to Windsor" and from "some of our elder statesmen moving on to what we hope is a happy life hereafter." Last but not least, the decline was due to the "low birth rate among the Jews in Windsor." Concerned about the reality of an aging population, Eisenberg called upon community leaders to "plan before and not react to crisis after."[64]

Offsetting Eisenberg's concerns was a list of the Council's successes over the past twelve months, such as the youth program, Camp Yomee, that had been filled to capacity every year. In the field of adult programming, successes included the Friendship Club; courses in bridge, Hebrew, physical education, and social dancing; and the critically acclaimed plays performed by those attending drama classes. In regard to social events, a New Year's Eve Ball, an Israel Independence Day commemoration, a Yom Ha-Shoah observance, and a choral performance had helped fill everyone's community calendar. Eisenberg also praised the family service the Council was providing to those who required immediate emotional and financial support.[65] By the end of 1961, the Council's board of governors had even approved the funds to build a swimming pool adjacent to the Community Centre.[66]

Apart from the programs offered by the Jewish Community Centre, there was no shortage of other organizations people could join, such as Shaar Hashomayim, the I. L. Peretz Shule, Shaarey Zedek, and Congregation Beth El. Several other groups were offering programs tailored to their particular mission within the community. They included the Pinsker Society, the Balfour Branch 362 of the Royal Canadian Legion, B'nai B'rith, as well as Histadrut — Israel's Federation of Labour — whose annual fundraising campaigns had been headed by Morris Tabachnick for many years. To honour him for his efforts on the Federation's behalf, a medical clinic in Atlit, near Haifa, was named after him and he was invited to come to Israel to attend its dedication.[67]

In the summer of 1965, the Federation of Jewish Women's Organizations was formed, replacing the League of Jewish Women, an organization that had never really succeeded. This new organization, headed by Leona Schott and

Approximately 125 delegates from Windsor and from several Michigan cities gathered in Windsor in May 1961 for a youth leadership conclave of the Great Lakes Council of the B'nai Brith Youth Organization. Making use of the lounge facilities of the Windsor Jewish Community Centre for some photographic work are, from left, standing, Arnold Weiner, Marty Cohen, and Duke Howitt; from the left, seated, are Pacer Berman and Marc Samrick; and manipulating the camera is Larry Blenn. The conclave was one of four held annually, and the third meet hosted by the Windsor youths since the centre opened two and a half years previously.

Betty Verk, brought together such groups as B'nai B'rith Women, Windsor's Hadassah Council with its five chapters (Aliyah, Chai, Lillian Freiman, Eva Goldberg, and Shalom), the I. L. Peretz Mothers' Club and Study Club, the Batya Miriam Chapter of Mizrachi, the Pioneer Women chapters Ada Maimon and Kinneret, the Sisterhoods of Shaar Hashomayim and Beth El, and Shaarey Zedek's Ladies' Auxiliary.[68] The task of this new women's federation was to "coordinate, stimulate and initiate programs and projects for the benefit of the entire community."[69] Although running the annual Welfare Fund campaign was its prime responsibility, it also was called upon to schedule the many

Photo courtesy of the Windsor Star

Eli Grad, director of Shaarey Zedek Schools of Detroit, was the speaker at the seventh annual Jewish Book Festival at the Jewish Community Centre in November 1962. His topic was "The contribution and impact of the Bible on Western Culture." Pictured from the left are Mel Sorffer, chairman of the program; Mr. Grad; and Joseph Kligman, principal of the I. L. Peretz Shule.

Photo courtesy of the Windsor Star

Members of the Windsor Jewish Community Council's summer day camp are shown here in a Sabbath play. The camp director was Ben Levine. Shown here (from the left) are Harold Shore, Larry Lando (standing), Lonny Rudover (kneeling), and David Pasikov.

community events in such a way that they would not clash with one another. Other worthwhile projects included publishing a community directory that listed all its member organizations, as well as organizing a "welcome wagon" to assist new families settling in Windsor and provide volunteer services for the whole community.[70]

Another project that helped bring together all the women in Windsor's Jewish community was the yearly one-day Hadassah Bazaar. Started in 1967 under the guidance of Eva Goldberg and hosted by the members of all the Hadassah chapters, it was the largest event ever attempted in Windsor. And, as it became better known throughout the city, it grew even larger with each passing year, eventually becoming Hadassah's major fundraising instrument for all its Israel projects.[71] At the end of 1967, Hadassah's various Windsor chapters formed the Hadassah Council under the leadership of Ruth Hurwitz. Its mandate was to further

expand the annual bazaar, put on fashion shows, and co-ordinate various other fundraising events.[72] Over time, however, the size of the bazaar was dramatically scaled down and gradually came to an end when those who had worked on it for many years could no longer expend the Herculean efforts required to carry on. Although the Council's executive director, Joseph Eisenberg, had praised the Hadassah

Kicking the water of the Jewish Community Centre's swimming pool with all their might are some of the 161 day campers involved in the Centre's 1966 summer program. The children here are being coached by Mel Schwartz, the pool's senior instructor. In the background some older day campers cool off in the water.

Bazaar in the past, describing it as "magnificently successful," and, "completely involving," he also feared that it had "upset the equilibrium in the community."[73]

While Windsor's yearly campaigns had brought in considerable funds in support of local needs, as well as providing support for Israel, Joseph Eisenberg complained in 1963 that fundraising had actually "lost its punch, had lost its glamour." He warned the community that "unless we can recreate fever pitch, the normal attrition that takes place will leave us with tremendous facilities but without funds to operate them."[74]

In an attempt to increase gifting levels to the Council's annual Welfare Fund campaign, a decision was made to publish in the *Bulletin* not only the names of those who had contributed to it, but also the amounts each person had given. The purpose of that measure was not only to provide an incentive to Fund donors to increase their gifts, but also to encourage those who had not yet been listed to become contributors.[75] The first appearance of donors' names, in the *Bulletin*'s October 1964 issue, prompted Council president Sidney Lazarus to remark, "When the Centre was built, our Welfare Fund Campaign totalled

Photo courtesy of the Windsor Star

The newly formed Federation of Jewish Women's Organizations held its first program for women community leaders at the Jewish Community Centre. Pictured from the left chatting over coffee before the program are Mrs. Gerald Verk, first vice president; Mrs. Meyer Ordower, second vice president; guest speaker Dr. Susan London, head psychologist at IODE Hospitals; and Mrs. Harry Slopen, the program committee chair.

$107,000 — since then, this is what has happened! 1960 — $95,000; 1961 — $91,000; 1962 — $88,000; 1963 — $87,000; and to date for 1964 we have $78,000."[76]

Another donors' list was published in 1965, but the list was scrapped the following year after the Council's board of directors received a letter from Beth El chairman Arthur B. Weingarden in which he strenuously objected to having his name listed in the *Bulletin*. He also indicated that unless the practice was stopped, he would drop his pledge to the Welfare Fund to the bare minimum required to sustain his membership and give the remaining amount to another charity.[77]

Reacting to Mr. Weingarden's complaint, the Council decided to stop showing the giving levels in the *Bulletin*, but to continue publishing the donors' names. The feeling was that this was one way of bringing the entire community's capabilities to the attention of individual members and "to stand as an acknowledgment of those who gave and as a reminder for the others."[78] The practice of publishing donors' names in the *Bulletin* continued for a while and

Mrs. Charles D. Solovich, left, past president of B'nai Brith, was the guest speaker at the annual donor luncheon of the Windsor Chapter of B'nai Brith held on March 22, 1967. The general convener of the event — an important one on the social calendar — was Mrs. Harry Bornstein.

then was dropped, only to resurface with dire consequences in the wake of the 1973 Yom Kippur War.

In 1966, Montague Pomm resigned his position as the Council's assistant executive director, just as Elliot Rubin, a part-time caseworker, left the Council's employ at the same time. Although Joseph Eisenberg deplored the loss of these two competent professionals, he realized that without addi-

Throngs of people poured into the Cleary Auditorium on May 15, 1968, to get first crack at the bargains offered at the annual Hadassah Bazaar. One of the most popular booths was the baked goods sale. All the items were donated by members of the Hadassah, and there was something for everyone.

tional financial assistance he would be unable to continue existing Community Centre programs or to develop new ones. Having begged for funds in vain, he reluctantly advised Windsor's Community Council members that he henceforth would have to rely more on the efforts of volunteers.[79]

Another request for funds was put forward a year later by Michael Sumner, chairman of the Council's committee on housing for the aged. After submitting plans for a communal living facility for seniors, he informed the Council's board of directors that provincial legislation would provide a grant of $5,000 per bed and cover 80 percent of the deficit per resident. However, to be able to proceed with the project, a minimum of forty residents was required.[80] Given the relatively small size of Windsor's Jewish community, it was therefore possible to give a complete accounting of all persons over 65 years of age, instead of just taking a sample.[81]

It took many more years before Michael Sumner's dream could become reality. His legacy will live on, how-

Photo courtesy of the Windsor Star

The annual Hadassah bazaar (this one was held on May 27, June 6, 1970) combined the bargains of the Parisian flea market with the excitement of Petticoat Lane, and included an art exhibition along with many other features. Shown above at the Windsor Art Gallery are Mrs. Gerald Freed, co-convener of the event (seated) choosing the school art to be displayed. Assisting her (standing) from the left, are John Andrews, curator of education, Windsor Art Gallery; Mrs. Merton Bernstein, chair of the art display, and Garnet Humphries, art co-ordinator for the Windsor Board of Education.

ever, as a stalwart supporter of the cause to provide adequate care for the elderly in Windsor's Jewish community, along with his contributions to both Shaar Hashomayim and Windsor's Jewish Community Council.

Another first for Windsor's Jewish community was the formation of a Chevra Kaddisha in September 1967.

That group of "accredited Jewish persons, who had deemed it their religious and moral obligation to attend upon the deceased members of the Jewish faith in accordance with the Orthodox Jewish custom and ritual," included Jacob Rosenzweig, Sam Strosberg, Louis Berger, Hymie Rosenbaum, and Manuel Burk.[82]

Ominous Signs for a New Generation

During the 1960s, the assimilation of young men and women raised particular concerns among some elders who thought it threatened the survival of the Jewish people. One of them was Joseph Eisenberg who, as a responsible leader of Windsor's Jewish community, felt obliged to broach the subject in his 1963 *Annual Report*. The following are excerpts from his message:

> Our whole life from 1933 on — some 30 years — the fruitful years for most of us, has been concerned with the vital life's work of saving remnants of those of our people who were decimated in Europe. What we must do at this time is once again reinforce the concept that, unless we build stronger communities where we are, we will be in no position to help strengthen communities overseas....
>
> My concern is not with the education of the youngster from nursery school through Bar Mitzvah but with the youth from 13 to 20. We find they are dropping out of formal Jewish educational circles at a time when Jewish education is the most meaningful and the most necessary part of their lives. I think this is a vital concern because, if we are to maintain a commitment to Jewish life, it must continue to be instilled, indoctrinated, educated and learned through the major formative years of adolescence. I think this whole area is a primary concern that communities will have to face.[83]

In an earlier *Bulletin* article, Rabbi Stollman had written about using education as a means to confront the problem of inter-dating among adolescents. He also stressed "the need in our community for a concerted effort not only to continue to offer the social activities so important to our youth but also to give them more Jewish ideological and religious contents."[84] Another suggestion to further Jewish education for adolescents came from Joseph Kligman, principal of the I. L. Peretz Shule. He recommended that a mental hygiene course be made an integral part of the curriculum. That course would include "the areas of mental hygiene principles, the generic development of personality, the self, and the self-concept with particular emphasis on all areas of adolescent growth with an understanding of Jewish moral values and the value of the preservation of the Jewish group." He also felt that an adequate knowledge of a Jewish individual's people was essential to his or her wellbeing.[85] And in defence of the I. L. Peretz Shule's emphasis on Yiddish and Hebrew, Kligman pointed out that "without at least partial use of Yiddish and Hebrew, in addition to the language of the country, no second culture is possible." He maintained, "when a Jewish child answers a question in Yiddish and Hebrew, he is symbolically answering the roll call of the Jewish people. Every Jewish word is a 'social contract' with the Jewish people."[86]

The views of Beth El's Rabbi Sherwin Wine differed to some extent from those expressed by Messrs. Eisenberg, Stollman, and Kligman. He felt that "while institutions like the Community Centre are important for promoting Jewish social contacts, their effectiveness is limited because they can never replace the public school as the major setting of teenage activity. The challenge to our leadership is not to find new ways to shield our children from the outside world but to present a meaningful and attractive Judaism that can survive and grow in the open competition of an integrated society."[87]

The exchange of ideas among various community leaders had led to the establishment of a Teen Institute, a first for Windsor. Sponsored by the Jewish Community Centre, this series of lectures was designed to help parents better understand the psychological dynamics of their teenaged sons and daughters.[88] The program not only sparked the interest of the Jewish Agency, but also that of several other North American Jewish communities, who all had been looking for ways to research and serve the needs of Jewish teenagers.[89]

The 27th anniversary of the I. L. Peretz School was celebrated in December 1960 with a banquet and concert at the Shaar Hashomayim auditorium. Pictured from the left are Harry Rubin, chairman of the event; Rubin Madoff, president of the board of directors; Morris Brodsky, board member, and Joseph Kligman, principal.

Funding for religious education moved further forward toward the end of 1964, when all the proceeds from the successful B'nai B'rith Blue Haven Foundation Raffle went to Windsor's three Jewish educational institutions.[90]

Education for adolescents again came up for discussion in 1965, when Sidney Lazarus, the Jewish Community Council's new president, expressed the following views on the subject: "Now, individually the schools in the past have tried to organize something of a high school education. For one reason or another it hasn't succeeded and we felt that, through the auspices of your Community Council and with combined efforts, something could be done to foster con-

tinued education."[91] The result of his appeal was the formation of the High School Institute of Jewish Studies. It was a
co-operative program for those students who were willing
to attend a series of Sunday afternoon lectures to be delivered by Rabbi Stollman, Rabbi Waldenberg (Rabbi Wine's
successor), and the I. L. Peretz Shule's new principal, Morris
Becker.[92] However, it took several more years before similar
programs became available to post–bar and bat mitzvah
students on a regular basis.

Changes at Congregation Beth El

In November 1962, Rabbi Wine advised Beth El's board
that he was planning to look for a new position as of July 1,
1963. He believed that his objectives in Windsor had been
met and that it was time for him to seek something more
challenging.[93] Trying to define the reasons for the rabbi's
decision, Arthur Weingarden explained that "in his fourth
year with us, Rabbi Wine's religious philosophy began to
change and he began meeting with like-thinking people in
the Detroit area. He did not impose his thinking on our
congregation and, when he saw that his direction was not
compatible with ours, he advised us that he would be leaving us at the end of that year."[94] Rabbi Wine remained with
Congregation Beth El until June 1964 and following a dinner at the Elmwood Casino in his honour, left for Detroit,
where he established a new movement that became known
as the Society for Humanistic Judaism.[95]

Rabbi Sherwin Wine's successor was Rabbi Shelley
Waldenberg, who, after attending Rabbi Jacob Joseph Yeshiva
in New Jersey, graduated with a Master's degree in Hebrew
Literature from New York University. He also held a Doctor
of Divinity degree from Cincinnati's Hebrew Union College
and had pursued graduate studies at Oxford University in
England. Prior to coming to Windsor, Rabbi Waldenberg had
served as a US Army Chaplain in Germany.[96] On the occasion of his ordination as Beth El's new spiritual leader, he
expressed these thoughts:

For me, Judaism does not begin and end
with reforming, abolishing or changing.
I am too overwhelmed by the accumulated cultural, historic and moral wealth
of all past generations of Jewish creativ-
ity. My primary concern is to make this
wealth of heritage comprehensive, meaningful and exciting.[97]

A New Home for the I. L. Peretz Shule

At the end of 1959, the I. L. Peretz Shule had purchased land
for its new building on Memorial Drive — now Ypres Avenue
— and by March 1960 an architect had been brought in to
draw up the plans. Estimated to cost between $125,000 and
$150,000, the school would have "four classrooms, a kinder-
garten room with a convertible room, when necessary, a
library and a stage."[98] However, Morris Brodsky reported a
month later that, in addition to the rooms mentioned, the
building would have a large auditorium that could seat 250
people and "a room for the principal."[99] And when Harry
Rubin became chairman of the building committee, he
announced that it would cost another $40,000 for land "to
build the shul building the way we want it."[100] Following a
fundraising campaign that yielded $17,000 and after putting
the old Erie Street building on the market for $32,000, the
leaders of the Peretz Shule felt that they had the capital
needed to go ahead and hired the architectural firm of J. P.
Thompson and Associates to draw up new plans.[101]

It soon became clear to the Peretz Shule board that a
move to Memorial Drive was not in its best interest. First and
foremost, the street bordered on Walkerville, a Windsor suburb known for not allowing either Jews or Blacks to purchase
homes and settle in the community. Secondly, the families of
most of its students either were in the process of moving to
South Windsor to be closer to the new Jewish Community
Centre or were living too far away from Memorial Drive.

The I. L. Peretz Shule's principal Joseph Kligman retired
in 1963. Having been its guiding spirit ever since its incep-

tion, he was succeeded by Benjamin Abay, a Montrealer who had been the principal of Calgary's I. L. Peretz Shules.[102] At the beginning of his tenure, the members of his board learned of a private house adjacent to the Windsor Jewish Community Centre that its owner, Dr. Clifford Weber, had offered to sell for $65,000. The Council was not interested in purchasing the property at that time, as it did not wish "to further encumber itself with financial obligations."[103] Despite the fact that the I. L. Peretz Shule was very keen to acquire it, it is puzzling why it sent the following rather restrained and almost self-effacing note to the Council:

> Inasmuch as the I. L. Peretz Shule is in the process of selling its building and ultimately will be building and, inasmuch as the Community Council has expressed interest and concern, it was wondered if there would be any suggestions forthcoming at this time.[104]

The Council chose to ignore the Peretz enquiry, extending instead an invitation on March 18, 1964, to all the Jewish schools asking them to make use of the Community Centre's facilities. Congregation Beth El declined the invitation, even though accepting it would have meant alleviating the crowded conditions in its classrooms, and Shaar Hashomayim wanted to explore "the question of space, rental fee and administrative set-up." The I. L. Peretz Shule, on the other hand, seemed interested at first, but eventually decided not to accept the invitation.[105]

On July 9, 1964, after selling its Memorial Drive land, the I. L. Peretz Shule acquired the Weber house on Ouellette Avenue at a cost of $58,000. Even though the building had to undergo extensive renovations, the school finally had the space it needed in a location that was easily accessible to all its students.[106] Benjamin Abay retained his position as the school's principal until the fall of 1965, when Morris Becker took over from him.[107]

The members of the Community Council executive may have erred in their judgment not to purchase the Weber

I. L. Peretz Shule, at the corner of Tecumseh Avenue and Ouellette Avenue.

property when it was offered to them. However, they had made a wise move when they allowed the I. L. Peretz Shule to buy it because it was easier for the Community Centre to have as its neighbour a secular Jewish institution than a religious one. Besides, Council executive director Joseph Eisenberg may have speculated at the time that if school ever closed its doors, its building would automatically become an integral part of the Community Centre.

In January 1969, Professor Block, founder of the Hebrew Day School in London, Ontario addressed the members of Shaar Hashomayim Men's Club with a view to interesting them in opening a similar school in Windsor.[108] Rabbi Stollman supported the idea because he felt that a school with a curriculum that included civic studies as well as conversational Hebrew and Torah classes would expose both elementary and high school students to all "the facets of Jewish tradition."[109] Before long, a day school steering committee was created and, in March 1969, Dr. Joseph Rezek, one of its members, reported that twenty-four students had shown an interest in attending the school, while seventeen had actually enrolled. As suitable premises had to be found to accommodate them, the I. L. Peretz Shule was asked to consider allocating some of its classrooms for that purpose.[110] Its board must have agreed because the Windsor Hebrew Day School opened there in the fall of 1969 with Rabbi Hillel Smulowitz acting as its principal.

There is no doubt that the Peretz Shule now was facing competition, not only from the new Hebrew Day School, but also from Beth El, as more and more children switched to these two institutions for their religious instruction. In March 1969, the I. L. Peretz Shule expressed interest in holding an informal meeting with members of Beth El to discuss a school merger.[111] Did the leaders of the Shule already surmised that modernity would ultimately result in

Students at the Hebrew Day School were encouraged to explore various interests as part of the school's attempt to take a modern approach to its subjects. Trying the guitar are (from the left) David Silverman, Gabrielle Bernstein, Susan Frank, and Alan Zekelman, who were all 7 years old.

their demise? Joseph Eisenberg even believed that the I. L. Peretz Shule's willingness to share its facilities with the Hebrew Day School had, in fact, helped postpone its demise.[112] However, as anticipated, the I. L. Peretz Shule did have to close its doors in the 1973.

By contrast, enrolment at the Windsor Hebrew Day School was greater than anticipated with five students attending kindergarten, nine in Grade 1 and seven in Grade 2. And, even though all the parents were pleased with the quality of education their children were receiving, the school was consistently plagued by financial problems and was ultimately forced to close because of internal dissent among the members.

The Six Day War and the Detroit Riots

The Six Day War broke out on June 5, 1967, after Egypt had concentrated large forces in the Sinai Peninsula and closed the Straits of Tiran to Israeli shipping. Israel first tried to solve the crisis through diplomatic channels, having asked Great Britain and France to intervene. When these efforts failed and Israel faced a military alliance of Egypt, Syria, Jordan, Iraq, and other Arab countries, including Algeria and Kuwait, it had no other choice but to embark on military action.[113]

Watching these developments in the Middle East from the sidelines, Windsor's Jews were anxious to show their solidarity with the people of Israel by organizing a community rally on June 1, 1967, with Max Goody, president of the Zionist Organization of Canada, as guest speaker.[114]

The Six Day War came to a successful conclusion at the end of June 1967 with Israel gaining control of the Gaza Strip, the Sinai Peninsula, the West Bank of the Jordan River, including East Jerusalem, and the Golan Heights. And as soon as hostilities had ended, the Community Council's board of directors was asked to initiate a special campaign to raise $250,000 for the Israel Emergency Fund. Although $234,000 was pledged and $212,000 realized, Windsor Jews urged the Council's board of directors to approve a loan for the outstanding amount so that the total

sum requested by the Israel Emergency Fund Committee could be remitted as soon as possible.[115]

In fact, the horrors of war had raised the community's consciousness to such an extent that money for the Emergency Fund came from individuals who had never before contributed to a campaign, and even regular donors felt that the events in Israel necessitated giving beyond their normal contribution levels. The large amounts collected that year, for both the Welfare Fund and for Israel, showed that Windsor's Jews were capable of giving substantially more to these annual appeals than had been previously anticipated. Commenting on the success of this most recent Israel Emergency Fund Campaign, Joseph Eisenberg called it "an enriching experience" because of the "tremendous outpouring of funds, of energy, of leadership, of devotion, of identification with a cause and with a people."[116]

In the enthusiasm of the moment, the Jewish National Fund, under the chairmanship of Rabbi Stollman, finally gained a foothold in the city with an inaugural meeting on October 17, 1968. Rabbi Stollman's reputation in the community made him a logical choice to head the organization in its pioneering period.[117] To start its operation, the JNF placed its familiar blue boxes in every Jewish home, which resulted in contributions of $700 to its first semi-annual collection.[118]

The first to recognize the advantages of centralized campaigning were Hadassah, Pioneer Women, and Mizrachi, Windsor's three Zionist women's groups that, represented by Molly Cohen, Helen Glaser, and Malka Yuzpe, came together under one umbrella organization. Although these three groups henceforth stopped raising money independently for the Jewish National Fund, each of them continued to support its own Israel-based institutions.[119] Kurt Weinberg, executive director of the Jewish National Fund based in Toronto, was the visionary who took the initiative to recognize the long-term fundraising potential in Windsor.[120]

There is no doubt that Windsor Jews had consistently rallied to Israel's cause. However, they also responded to other emergencies, such as the 1967 Detroit race riots, when their neighbours to the North needed their support. According to the *Rearview Mirror* archives of the *Detroit News,*

> unlike earlier outbreaks, these were indiscriminate: mobs torched and plundered black businesses as freely as white ones and burned down a number of black homes. Both black and whites participated in looting, burning and rioting.… Forty-three people lay dead by the time the 1967 Detroit riots ended five days later on July 28.… One month after the riot, a city tally showed 388 families homeless or displaced and 412 buildings burned or damaged enough to be demolished. Dollar losses from arson and looting ranged from $40 million to $80 million.[121]

Commenting on the causes of these riots as well as on the civil rights movement in general, Joseph Eisenberg expressed concern that they had consumed "Jewish community energy, the kind of energy we need for Jewish survival." He also spoke of the price to be paid for a "free and open society when we begin to recognize how much of this energy we need to use and how much more we must find so that creative Jewish living will continue as an entity here today." He concluded his remarks by stating, "I envision the development of the Jewish community in Canada far differently from [that in] the States. I think this is something that will require a great deal of thought and self-examination on our parts."[122]

Anti-Semitism Raises Its Ugly Head

Anti-Semitism seemed to be more prevalent after the Six Day War than before. The phenomenon was not new for Jews, as prejudice against them had existed for a very long time. Many private clubs still barred them from becoming members, just as they, as well as Blacks, still were banned from owning homes in certain Canadian communities.

However, discrimination against Blacks was more clearly defined than that against Jews. For them, it sometimes was less apparent, especially when certain individuals were making disparaging remarks about Jews in the presence of persons whom they did not believe to be Jewish.[123]

After 1962, Canadian Jews thought the law was on their side when making openly racist remarks had become a punishable offence. But there still was a need for vigilance, such as in the case of the publication of a particular pamphlet that contained "virulent Anti-Semitic material." As William Tepperman, chairman of the Council's community relations committee reported, "quick and decisive action" had to be taken to withdraw said pamphlet from the newsstands.[124] In another matter, Windsor's Jewish Community Council had lodged a complaint with the Ontario Human Rights Commission about a certain help-wanted advertisement that stipulated that only "a Christian stenographer" need apply.[125]

Council President Sidney Lazarus also deplored "the resurgence of hate literature in Canada" in the mid-1960s and the fact that the news media was giving too much prominence to the activities of neo-Nazis. Joseph Eisenberg, however, saw the relationship between Jews and Gentiles in a different light. Describing it as the "Five-O'clock Shadow," he said, "Jews are being accepted in the business, commercial world, etc. as equals. But come five o'clock, a shadow seems to fall and we go about our way in our own groups in terms of socialization." He thought that there were two factors contributing to this situation: "the reaction or attitude of the non-Jewish community toward us and, by the same token, we too suffer at some point from Ghetto psychology." Eisenberg felt that one of the real tests lay in the degree of Jewish participation in the general community's activities. On that score, he did think that Windsor's history was a good one.[126]

As another example of the need for Jewish vigilance — as well as of the connections between Jews in Windsor and the broader Jewish community — the Canadian Jewish Congress and B'nai B'rith had asked a few of their representatives to monitor an address by a member of an Arab propaganda group to be delivered at a Windsor meeting of the Canadian Institute of International Affairs. Mindful of the possible anti-Jewish fallout following the Six Day War, the CJC wanted a report on the proceedings that they could trust to be accurate.[127]

These were uncertain times and various manifestations of anti-Semitism continued to arise, but Windsor's Jewish community usually responded decisively and with one single voice.[128]

Solving Problems at Beth El

Rabbi Robert Benjamin succeeded Rabbi Shelley Waldenberg when he left Congregation Beth El to pursue doctoral studies at Jerusalem's Hebrew University.[129] After graduating from Cincinnati's Hebrew Union College in 1966, Rabbi Benjamin had briefly served a congregation in Fargo, North Dakota before coming to Windsor in the spring of 1968.[130]

Right from the start, Beth El's new spiritual leader was devoted to the idea of improving relations with other religious groups in the city and was keenly interested in aiding its underprivileged. Unfortunately, the Beth El leadership wanted a spiritual leader devoted primarily to the needs of the congregation. Since Beth El was quite new, it did not realize that a rabbi's role did include community service. Anxious to publicize his views, Rabbi Benjamin granted an interview to the *Windsor Star* at the beginning of May 1970 in which he admitted that the "congregation and I have a different view of the role of the rabbi." He believed that Beth El "has to be involved more in the flow of society — almost as if no walls existed in the synagogue." He felt that "no subject should be foreign to the synagogue or any other religious organization," and that members should "respond to the needs of society around them." However, he also complained that his congregation had "responded with rejection because they don't want to become involved."[131]

There was no doubt in anyone's mind that Rabbi Benjamin's ideas were different from those held by the majority of his congregation.[132] As he also had become aware of the fact that the publication of his remarks had displeased a number of its members, he wrote the following letter to Beth El president Arthur Barat, one day after his interview had appeared in the *Windsor Star*:

> As you know I have discussed with some members the content of a recent article that appeared in the "Star." A careful reading of the article will reveal that the remarks were not intended to discredit or slander any person affiliated with the congregation. It merely stated that we disagree with regard to the role of the rabbi, a fact that cannot be denied. It is also my opinion that the congregation has not been involved in certain aspects of communal activity. Certainly, no one can deny that I am entitled to that opinion.[133]

Rabbi Benjamin's tenure at Beth El was not only short-lived but created a split within the congregation. Yet as soon as the interview process to find a new spiritual leader had begun, the congregation's membership became one unified force.

Since 1968, Congregation Beth El had been faced with another problem — the expropriation of some of its land to make way for Windsor's new E. C. Row Expressway.[134] Even though it was not slated until 1973, the temple's board of directors advised the city in the fall of 1969 that it was "not happy with the effect the expropriation will have on our property," and asked the city to replace it "in a location as close to where we are as possible so that we can construct a new building."[135]

In 1968, Beth El had become part of a committee comprising Windsor's four congregations that would administer the Va'ad Hakashruth, the group responsible for upholding Jewish dietary laws. Since everyone knew that it would be under Orthodox jurisdiction and supported through an annual fee of $5 per member, Congregation Beth El stipulated that the contribution should not be mandatory.[136]

There is no doubt that Va'ad Hakashruth always had been and would remain under the control of the Shaar Hashomayim, even though Windsor's Community Council was contributing 50 percent of its annual deficit to a yearly maximum of $2,500. The Council also took it upon itself to decide how best to safeguard the supply of kosher meat for Windsor's Jewish population. When Shaffer's Kosher Meat Market opened in 1970, Rabbi Stollman must have been pleased to know that an adequate supply of kosher meat was henceforth assured. He even wrote a note in the Shaar Hashomayim *News* urging everyone to support the new store.[137]

In 1974, Harry Weinstein was the only kosher butcher in the city. However, as his business was not generating the desired profit because fewer people were keeping kosher, he had to ask Shaar Hashomayim to relieve him of the four-cent tariff the synagogue was charging him.[138] In response, the fee was reduced to $1,200 per year.[139]

The Decade Comes to an End

Looking back on the 1960s, there is no doubt that Windsor's Jews had rallied their forces in an exemplary fashion during times of crisis and had diligently worked together to provide vital services to their community. The Chesed Shel Emes Funeral Chapel, the Pillette Avenue Cemetery, and Va'ad Hakashruth had all benefited from joining together, thereby creating a healthy environment regardless of differences in philosophies and the occasional acrimonious jostling for power and influence among the various religious institutions.

As a new decade began, further consolidation of services and the appearance on the scene of new faces helped tip the balance of influence among Windsor's Jews. While the Community Council's leadership had come from the I. L. Peretz Shule, Shaar Hashomayim, or B'nai B'rith during the 1960s, it would largely be drawn from Congregation Beth El in the next decade. And since many institutions would amalgamate or disappear from the scene altogether in the 1970s, a different configuration of players would be called upon to solve the Jewish community's day-to-day problems.

Chapter 10
Consolidation and Realignment

Windsor in the 1970s

The late 1960s and early 1970s were a period of general prosperity. Revenues were buoyant and both the federal and provincial governments were ready to help fund important projects. The announcement of the E. C. Row Expressway and the conversion of an old brewery into a fine art gallery were just a few of the period's accomplishments.

Windsor was much larger territorially and had greater diversity than the pre-1965 city. As time went by it became clear that the at-large council was overly representative of some sections of the city, but did not reflect the views of some other areas at all. Critics charged that the small tightly knit council working closely with a strong manager and a compliant mayor was ignoring the demands of some parts of the community. The West End (formerly Sandwich) and South Windsor felt particularly aggrieved.

By 1975 one alderman who articulated this concern — Dr. Ronald Wagenberg — chaired a special committee to investigate the situation and recommended a return to the ward system and an enlarged council. Members of the existing City Council, the city manager, and government supporters resisted this initiative. The issue went before the electorate in 1977, who voted to re-establish the wards, with a ten-member council elected in five wards. The city manager was reined in, reduced to the position of city administrator, and a more participatory form of government was restored. Indeed, when the Valhalla Inn's prime waterfront hotel project at the foot of Ouellette Avenue met adverse public reaction, council flip-flopped in deference to it and cancelled the project.

Internationally, two events impacted upon the Windsor Jewish community in significant ways: the 1973 Arab-Israeli War once again appeared to threaten the existence of a Jewish homeland in the Middle East and the US détente with the Soviet Union opened up possibilities for more liberal immigration and a new openness to demands for equality and social justice for Jews in Russia.[1]

Amalgamations and Closures

During the 1970s, Windsor's Jewish Community Council wielded considerable influence. Being at the hub of activities and the holder of the communal purse strings, it could bring diverse groups together, as well as raising and disbursing considerable amounts of money for local and overseas needs.

Equally secure was Shaar Hashomayim Synagogue. It had been the Jewish community's leading religious institution since 1929, even though two other synagogues — Shaarey Zedek and Tifereth Israel — had been active in the city longer. And although the newly created Congregation Beth El may have challenged Shaar Hashomayim's position at the beginning of the 1960s and committees had been formed to represent the interests of the two other synagogues, the Orthodox-oriented Shaar Hashomayim retained control over Va'ad Hakashruth, the overseers of dietary laws; the Jewish cemetery; the Chesed Shel Emes Funeral Chapel; and the Chevra Kaddisha, the Holy Burial Society, whose members supervise all Jewish funerary practices.

On the education front, however, the landscape continued to change. For many years, Windsor's Jewish parents had had various choices with regard to their children's religious education. But when the supply of potential students began to dwindle at the beginning of the 1970s, the four Jewish learning institutions had to find new ways to survive in the city's fiercely competitive climate. Dr. Joseph Klinghofer, the educational director of the Canadian Jewish Congress, cited the following statistics for 1970:

Congregation Beth El school	120 students
Shaar Hashomayim school	76 students[*]
I. L. Peretz Shule	35 students[**]
Windsor Hebrew Day School	21 students

[*] This figure includes 9 students in nursery school and 22 in Rabbi Stollman's study group

[**] This compares to 51 students a year earlier[2]

He concluded that, "Four schools are now competing for the 20 Jewish children in Windsor reaching school age every year.[3]

Since each of the schools asked for yearly allocations, the Windsor Jewish Community Council realized that it could not possibly fund all of them individually. Ways and means had to be found to amalgamate some of these schools into a single communal institution. When Windsor's Jewish Community Council suggested to the I. L. Peretz Shule and Congregation Beth El that a merger of all the nursery schools would solve the funding problem, neither of them was interested in the plan.[4] The two schools' negative attitude in merger discussions did not sit well with the Jewish Community Council's board of directors, especially after the board had been asked to also subsidize the Hebrew Day School that had begun operations just a few months earlier.[5] The members of Beth El were opposed to the merger because they thought that by doing away with their Joni Rosenthal Nursery School they would be depriving themselves of a valuable future membership source. And the I. L. Peretz Shule was opposed because, having agreed to share its facilities with the Hebrew Day School, it suddenly felt confident about its survival, even though it had to resort to advertising for nursery school and Grade 1 pupils in the fall of 1970.[6]

By January 1971, the educational situation was becoming serious; remedies had to be found. Encouraged by the Community Council, Beth El and the I. L. Peretz Shule held meetings to discuss the possibility of merging their classes.[7] Already chastened by its difficulty in hiring a principal with an enrolment of only thirty students,[8] the Peretz supporters were faced with the realization that the community's newest educational addition, the Windsor Hebrew School, rather than proving their salvation, was "in serious jeopardy of imminent dissolution."[9] A month later, all the representative schools signed a document agreeing, in principle, to the "formation of an Affiliated Hebrew School System."[10]

But their problems were not over. Anyone who headed Shaar Hashomayim's religious school was, of course, fiercely opposed to the idea of merging with any other religious institution, mainly because it was understood that

Orthodox teachers should be teaching all subjects.[11] Not too surprisingly, merger discussions ended when comments were made that Beth El was not an appropriate place to teach Judaism. Nonetheless, by the time the 1971 school year ended, Windsor Hebrew Day School had indeed amalgamated with the I. L. Peretz Shule.[12] The terms of the merger called for "the combined organization with day and afternoon school programmes" from kindergarten to Grade 4, and the sharing of "administration, teachers, facilities and equipment on the premises of the I. L. Peretz Shule."[13] The Hebrew Day School's principal, Rabbi Smulowitz, became the principal of the new school known as the Hebrew Academy of Windsor.[14]

Sadly, the I. L. Peretz Shule was forced to close its doors forever at the end of the 1973 school year, after faithfully serving Windsor's Jewish community for thirty-nine years.[15] In June 1972, after Rabbi Smulovitz had resigned as the principal of the Hebrew Academy of Windsor, Rabbi Chaim Halberstam was appointed as his successor.[16] His tenure was short-lived, though, because the Hebrew Academy had to close at the same time as the I. L. Peretz Shule.

Another Jewish school, Kadimah Day School, tried to establish itself in Windsor in June 1977. Hoping to rent one room for a full day and a second one for a half-day of classes at the Jewish Community Centre, it agreed to be responsible for "storage space, equipment, telephone, licensing, staffing, operation, insurance and alterations."[17] Windsor's Jewish Community Centre had no objection to housing the new school at the Centre. Its presence there would have had only minimal impact on Congregation Beth El, as nine of the ten students interested in enrolling there would have come from Shaar Hashomayim. In view of existing "harsh economic developments," the Council did warn the Kadimah representatives of the pitfalls connected with operating a school. Although they agreed to arrange their fundraising in a way that would not conflict with "already existing campaigns," they, ultimately, had to abandon plans to open the school because of "lack of response" to their venture.[18]

Another venerable institution that had to close during the 1970s was Tifereth Israel, a synagogue that had existed since the 1920s at 1012 Hickory Road, at the corner of Whelpton Street (formerly Charles Street) in Windsor's East End. Although it had had a membership of about forty Orthodox Jewish families, that number had declined over the years as older congregants died and the next generation moved away from what was perceived as a declining area. The *Windsor Star* published the following vivid description of the synagogue's interior in 1973:

> As one steps inside, they open a time capsule, calling on scenes brought from Europe close to half a century ago and left virtually unchanged these many years. In the middle of the sanctuary, an immense chandelier hangs from a sky-blue ceiling sprinkled with stars. A pair of carved lions and a bright, hand-painted eagle stare down from the Holy Ark. In the basement is a small meeting room once used for daily after-school Hebrew instruction.[19]

Many former members recall the dinners and other social functions held in the small meeting room.

Tifereth Israel celebrated its last High Holiday services, led by Rabbi Spiro of Detroit and Reverend Dubitsky, in the fall of 1970.[20] Shortly thereafter, there were rumours that the synagogue was closing. To dispel them, members of the congregation bravely announced their 1972 slate of officers — Harry Sigal, president; Morris Enkin, vice president; Solomon Sigal, treasurer; Harold Swartz, secretary.[21]

The congregation continued to operate until the middle of the 1970s. But the neighbourhood had fallen on hard times by then, mainly because of the closure of the Ford plant. The synagogue building had been vandalized and stood empty until 1979, when it was bought by Réal Quesnel, the owner of the adjacent butcher shop, who tore it down to make room for his new and enlarged grocery store.[22]

The sanctuary of Tifereth Israel Synagogue in 1973, as it had been for nearly fifty years.

The sanctuary of Tifereth Israel Synagogue.

However, Tifereth Israel will live on in the hearts and minds of Windsor's Jewish community as some of the objects that had adorned its interior were salvaged and given new homes. The "immense chandelier" now hangs in Shaarey Zedek with a commemorative plaque explaining that the Adler family donated it to Tifereth Israel in 1927. The synagogue's Holy Ark and its Torahs, given to the Jewish Community Centre at the time of its dissolution, now grace the foyer of the Peretz House, a residence for Windsor's seniors.

A New Rabbi Comes to Windsor

It was at this point that I had the honour of becoming a part of the Windsor Jewish community as the rabbi of Congregation Beth El, a position I held for almost fifteen years. I began my duties as the congregation's new spiritual leader on July 15, 1970. I was born in Chicago, Illinois on October 7, 1942, the son of Rabbi W. Gunther Plaut and his wife, Elizabeth, and grew up in St. Paul, Minnesota, where my family had settled when I was 6 years old. I received my public and high school education in St. Paul and subsequently attended the city's Macalester College, graduating from there in 1964 with a Bachelor of Arts degree. I obtained my Master's degree in Hebrew Letters from Cincinnati's Hebrew Union College — the Jewish

Institute of Religion — where I was ordained in June 1970. Seven years later, I earned a Doctorate of Hebrew Letters from the same institution.

My installation took place on September 18, 1970, with my father, W. Gunther Plaut, then senior rabbi of Toronto's Holy Blossom Temple, conducting the service and well-known Cantor Jacob Barkin chanting the liturgy.[23] Also taking part in the ceremony was Richard C. Hertz, senior rabbi of Detroit's Temple Beth El, the man who had helped establish Windsor's Reform congregation.

At the time that I assumed my position at Beth El, my congregation comprised eighty-six families. Its future was somewhat uncertain, a state of affairs clearly spelled out to me by Beth El President Arthur B. Weingarden who, during a walk around Windsor's Roseland Golf Course, cautioned me that my annual salary of $16,750 would only be secure

Photo courtesy of the Windsor Star

My father, Rabbi W. Gunther Plaut, was the guest speaker for my installation as rabbi of Temple Beth El Windsor. In the picture, from the left, are Rabbi Richard C. Hertz of Temple Beth El, Detroit; Jacob Barkin, world-renowned cantor of Shaarey Zedek, Detroit; Rabbi Gunther Plaut of Holy Blossom Temple, Toronto; me; and Arthur B. Weingarten, president of Windsor's Temple Beth El.

until the end of my current contract. But I was unfazed by these warnings, as I had set certain goals for myself. I not only wanted to attract new members to Beth El, especially non-affiliated Jews, but was also determined to find new ways to raise money, to strengthen the congregation's religious school, to create new programs, and to become more visible and more active in the community.

My first activities in that regard were to begin the weekly Sunday morning radio program *Religion in the News* in 1971, to become the host of the CBET television show *Religious Scope* a year later, and to start teaching a course on Judaism at Windsor's Assumption College School. Changing my congregation's attitude toward community involvement became one of my unspoken priorities, and it was my hope that heightening my own profile would help me to accomplish this.

Beth El's future was no longer in jeopardy when its membership rose to 110 families by the end of my first year of tenure. I was now free to turn my attention to other matters, such as the temple's choir, who had been singing since the first services were held in 1960. The choir needed some respite, especially as it now was in greater demand to perform at b'nai mitzvah ceremonies and other life-cycle events. In August 1972, at my urging, a soloist was hired who could relieve these tired and overburdened volunteers.[24] The regular presence of a cantor also made sense as a means of enticing more members from Shaar Hashomayim, which had always had one. Beth El's first soloist was a man by the name of Burton Zipser.[25] Next came David Gutman and then Leo Mogil, who was followed in 1980 by Sidney Resnick, a musically talented and very dedicated cantor who remained at Beth El until his retirement in 2001.

Congregation Beth El's celebrated its thirteenth anniversary — its bar mitzvah —during my tenure with events beginning on Wednesday, April 4, 1973. All the members attended, as did some of the guests who had been present at my installation, including Rabbi Sherwin Wine, who regaled his audience with reminiscences about the synagogue's beginnings and his own memories about the time he had spent at Beth El. On Friday evening, April 6, a special Shabbat service took place that featured my father, Rabbi W. Gunther Plaut, as the guest speaker. Concluding the festivities was a dinner dance held later that evening.[26]

Ever since coming to Beth El, I had been aware of the Windsor Jewish community's resentment of Reform Judaism in general and Congregation Beth El in particular. Hoping to dispel these negative feelings, I decided to gradually move away from the classical Reform religious setting to a more traditional pattern of worship. These innovations ultimately paid off as they not only improved Congregation Beth El's image within the community, but also brought about a further increase in its membership.

More Rivalry on the Educational Front

The alignment within Windsor's Jewish educational system drastically changed after the 1973 demise of the I. L. Peretz Shule. Beth El and Shaar Hashomayim were now the only two congregations still operating religious schools and even though their aims may have been similar, they functioned very differently from one another. For example, Shaar Hashomayim's 1973 professional teaching costs were twice those of Beth El's $15,938, which included $9,000 for my salary.[27] In 1974, Shaar Hashomayim had seventy-nine students, but its teaching staff budget had risen to $35,000 while that of Beth El had increased to a mere $19,000 with 108 students. Yet Shaar Hashomayim's overall expenses were twice as high as those of Beth El. The Shaar Hashomayim held classes for 67.5 hours per week for forty-one weeks of the year, while Beth El had a 44-hour teaching week that stretched over a yearly thirty-one-week period.[28]

During the 1970s, Shaar Hashomayim's religious school had several principals. Rabbi Melvin Sacks was in charge at the beginning of the decade and stayed until 1972, when Rabbi Chaim Schloss took his place as head teacher.[29] When Rabbi Schloss retired in 1974, Rabbi Murray Lieberman became the new principal. Licensed to teach in the State of New York, he also served as Shaar Hashomayim's *baal Koreh* (Torah reader), as its *baal tefillah* (reader of prayers), its *chazan sheini* (assistant cantor), and as its executive administrator — all tasks he performed at a starting salary of $17,000.[30]

Rabbi Lieberman remained in Windsor until June 1976. It was during his tenure that enrolment at the Shaar Hashomayim Religious School began to show a slight decline.[31] Rabbi Chaim Gartenhaus, a native of New York City, ordained at the Rabbi Jacob Joseph Yeshiva in 1971, began his duties on September 1, 1976. At the beginning of his first school year, it became evident that Shaar Hashomayim's enrolment had dwindled to thirty-nine students, likely because of its membership's decreasing birth rate and aging population.[32] Following Rabbi Gartenhaus's departure two years later, Reverend Ira Zaidman made his debut at Shaar Hashomayim. He was not only the principal of its religious school, but also served as *baal Koreh*. Staying on until the spring of 1981, his tenure lasted longer than that of any of his predecessors.[33]

As Shaar Hashomayim's student body declined further by the beginning of 1977, the synagogue's board of directors had to reluctantly admit that the prognosis for its school's future enrolment was "not good."[34] To rectify the situation, Dr. Yehudah Lipsitz, the educational director of the Canadian Jewish Congress in Toronto, was consulted. He recommended changing from Ashkenazic to Sephardic pronunciation of the way Hebrew was taught at the school. Implementing this new measure required several lengthy discussions, but the board ultimately adopted Dr. Lipsitz's suggestion.[35]

Despite the fact that Shaar Hashomayim and Congregation Beth El were functioning autonomously, both were receiving annual allocations from Windsor's Jewish Community Council. The Council had realized, as early as 1972, that in order to meet their requests for increases, maintain other communal programs, and satisfy overseas demands for funds, it would have to change its funding formula.[36]

Mainly because Beth El's religious school was larger than Shaar Hashomayim's and was also offering confirmation classes, it asked the Council at the beginning of 1973 to increase Beth El's subvention to include "the Rabbi's salary for teaching, Bar Mitzvah instruction and for administration." The Council's budget and finance committee ignored Beth El's request, but decided to contribute toward the principals' salaries of both Shaar Hashomayim and the Hebrew Academy, whose 1973 budget of $34,416 included $13,500 for the principal's salary.[37]

In the spring of 1974, the Council appointed Morris Brodsky as head of a special committee on school allocation because its members believed that, as a former supporter of the now defunct I. L. Peretz Shule, he was well qualified to direct his energies towards furthering the city's Jewish education. When asked at one of their first meetings to guarantee all school costs from nursery schools up to and including Grade 13, Mr. Brodsky and his committee set the subventions at $25 per student, based on his or her attendance record.[38] Almost as soon as Mr. Brodsky's appointment was ratified, conflict arose between Shaar Hashomayim and Congregation Beth El. Originally, Beth El had requested that three representatives from each institution sit on the Council's school allocations committee and that its chairman be nonpartisan, but as many of its members belonged to the Shaar Hashomayim Synagogue, they were reluctant to share power.

The matter came to a head when Beth El members apparently were treated "with scorn bordering on contempt," during a May 1974 school allocations committee meeting.[39] Anxious to receive what they considered their fair share, Beth El's Ted J. Hochberg, Richard Rosenthal, and Hy Muroff issued the following statement:

> Members of the Board — the undersigned have no intention of returning for another exercise in futility. We, at the Temple, feel that the education of Jewish children in Windsor is a community responsibility, not a question of donation per se from Council. We ask you, is the allocation fair to the majority of those children?[40]

A year later, Congregation Beth El still felt uneasy when Morris Brodsky announced that his committee wanted to begin an educational program for high school students.[41] These plans became reality in the fall of 1975 when the Jewish Community Centre established the Hebrew Collegiate Institute. As an incentive for enrolment at the school, the Centre even agreed to underwrite the cost of a trip to Israel for those students who, after two years of study, had met certain attendance criteria. Beth El continued its confirmation classes, even though it knew full well that the incentives were strong enough to prompt some students to enrol in the Hebrew Collegiate Institute's program.

Although Shaar Hashomayim was pleased that the Community Centre had taken over Jewish high school education, Community Council Executive Director Joseph Eisenberg was less enthusiastic. Having taught at the new school, he described it as "fragmentation and empire building" and "a waste of money," as he really wanted the Jewish Community Council to have more control over all the schools as well as greater influence on the scope of Jewish education.[42]

In retrospect, the Hebrew Collegiate Institute program was a success for three reasons:

1. It brought together students from both congregations.
2. It increased students' knowledge of Jewish identity.
3. It allowed graduates to acquire a deeper understanding of Jewish diversity after spending an extended period of time in Israel.

The school allocation issue dominated the Community Council's agenda almost to the end of the decade. Shaar Hashomayim and Congregation Beth El continued to receive allocations — the former $10,880 by 1977 and the latter $8,886 with the Council supporting up to half of the rabbi's salary.[43] However, when Bernard Putterman became chairman of its special school allocations committee in 1977, he recommended that the allocated amounts be 30 percent of the schools' expenditures, based on the budgeted direct teaching costs, and that these costs be equally shared by both institutions. He also pointed out that the change in the Council's allocation formula had been made "in recognition of the equal value of both schools to the community and their contribution to Jewish education."[44]

Responding to the Plight of Russian Jewry

In 1971, Canada became the first country in the world to adopt an official policy of multiculturalism. The move was prompted by the changes that were taking place in the composition of the country's population and requests from various cultural groups for recognition. The government wanted to acknowledge the contributions made by these groups and signal that, rather than asking them to assimilate, there was room within Canadian culture for the traditions they brought with them.

No such legislation was available to Jews living in what then was the Soviet Union and when Western countries became aware of their plight, they tried to take steps to help them. In Windsor, a rally on behalf of Soviet Jewry was held in City Hall Square on December 30, 1970, with some people carrying placards that read, "Let them live or let them leave," "I am my brother's keeper," and "Break the chains of Soviet repression."[45]

The main communal thrust was focused on aiding those Soviet Jews who had managed to leave their homeland and had found refuge in other countries especially, in Israel. With the need for funds becoming critical, top priority was given to the campaign for State of Israel Bonds, culminating in a tribute on November 17, 1970, to honour its chairman, Harry Zekelman, and his wife, Wanda.[46] In January 1971, Windsor became "the first community in North America to buy bonds communally held for the State of Israel," after the Jewish Community Council had purchased $100,000 worth of the securities.[47] To kick off the April 1971 Israel Bond campaign, Teddy Kollek, then the mayor of Jerusalem, was invited as the event's guest speaker.[48]

When Soviet Premier Alexei Kosygin came to Ottawa on a state visit in the fall of 1971, many Canadian Jews, including rabbis from the various branches of Judaism, travelled to the nation's capital to take part in a protest against the treatment their brethren were receiving in the Soviet Union. I was among them and explained that I was participating in that rabbinical gathering "because I want to stand up for my people in Russia. The time for excuses has passed; now is the time for peaceful action."[49]

By the end of 1971, Windsor's Jewish community had raised funds "in excess of $300,000."[50] And its efforts throughout 1972 involved the launch of another emergency fund campaign in addition to the regular United Jewish Appeal. Regarding the latter, Charles Zalev, chairman of the UJA Men's Division Campaign, reported a 34.1 percent increase over the previous year, while the UJA Women's Division Campaign, chaired by Paula Taub, experienced a 31.6 percent increase.[51]

Despite these positive results, members of Windsor's Jewish Community Council had to devise new techniques to augment the funds required to sustain Soviet Jewry. Their plan, which required approval by 70 percent of the Council's executive, called for donors to "rate" themselves, and if the amount they were prepared to give did not come within 80 percent of the rated amount, the gift would be considered "unacceptable." Council members also stressed that they "would have to be very selective as to what gifts would be turned down." In addition, teams of two would meet with prospective donors and, if they were unsuccessful in obtaining 80 percent of the rated amount, the donor would be canvassed a second time.[52]

This novel fundraising idea provoked opposition from some members of the Council's board of directors. In fact, two of its members, William Tepperman and Morris Baker, resigned because they did not like the tactics being used to raise funds.[53] The fundraising technique angered many others as well and would cause further problems a year later.

Menachim Begin, Israel's future prime minister, was the dignitary chosen to kick off Windsor's 1972 State of Israel Bond Campaign that ultimately raised more than $200,000.[54]

However, the need for financial support became even more critical in October 1972, following the arrival in Israel of some 25,000 Russian Jews. Targets had to be almost doubled, even though North American Jewry had contributed $390 million during the 1972 Welfare Fund campaigns.[55]

At the end of 1972, the Council of Jewish Federations and Welfare Funds issued the following poignant statement:

> The Council of Jewish Federations and Welfare Funds, on behalf of its 230 affiliated local Jewish Federations in 800 cities, expresses its admiration of and support for Soviet Jews who are courageously demanding the right to emigrate and the right to live as Jews, with the full rights accorded other Soviet citizens. We commit ourselves to everything within our power to help them achieve their goals. Soviet Jews must be free to emigrate, to be united with their families in Israel, the United States, Canada, and other free lands.
>
> As is afforded other religious and nationality groups, those Jews who remain in the Soviet Union, must be granted the right to maintain Jewish educational, religious, cultural and communal institutions, the right to study Jewish history, language, and literature, and to have a relationship with Jewish communities inside and outside the Soviet Union.[56]

In 1973, the year Israel celebrated twenty-five years of independence, Dr. Henry Shanfield became chairman of the State of Israel Bond campaign. That campaign was even more crucial for the survival of the Jewish state than previous fundraising efforts because of accelerated Russian immigration and the imminence of the Yom Kippur War.[57]

By the late 1970s, the UJA had sponsored regular campaigns as well as Project Renewal, a drive specifically designed to raise funds for the rehabilitation of some 160 distressed neighbourhoods throughout Israel and for the improvement of the lives of some 300,000 men, women, and children.[58]

A Dispute with the United Church

While Jewish communities throughout North America were deeply involved in raising funds for Soviet Jewry, an issue arose that first caused alarm in Toronto and then had repercussions in Windsor. It so happened that Reverend A. C. Forrest, editor of the *United Church Observer*, had become an outspoken critic of Israel after the 1967 Six Day War. Although he strongly believed that all faiths should dialogue with one another and had written favourably about the Jewish state in the past, it was unclear whether his latest comments were purely anti-Zionist or, in fact, were anti-Semitic. Regardless of discussions as to the one-sided nature of his attacks, his criticism became more and more biting. According to Rabbi W. Gunther Plaut, who was at the centre of the controversy, "[Reverend Forrest] was no longer satisfied to espouse the Arab cause and denigrate 'the Zionists' (a term he soon applied to all Jews), but portrayed himself as a man who suffered greatly for his faith and was being crucified for it."[59]

The dispute heated up further in March 1972, when Reverend Forrest reprinted a *United Church Observer* article written by John Nicholls Booth, a prominent minister of the Unitarian Church. In it, Booth "accused Zionists of manipulating the news, and singled out B'nai B'rith as a Zionist apparatus, which had penetrated deeply into the American government, the communications media and educational institutions."[60]

Windsor's Jewish Community Council became involved in the Forrest controversy, when Reverend Martin Rumscheidt, a University of Windsor professor, and a group of United Church ministers opposed to Reverend Forrest expressed an interest in meeting with members of the Jewish Community Council's Relations Committee.[61] That meeting, held in the spring of 1972, was attended by Bernard Putterman, William Tepperman, Joseph Eisenberg, and Rabbi Samuel Stollman and myself.[62] When asked much later to comment on the discussions that had taken place, I said that the dialogue between members of Windsor's Jewish community and the United Church delegates should continue, even though there had been much "frustration and futility."[63] As a way of possibly ending the dispute, Rabbi W. Gunther Plaut had been asked to come to Windsor on October 25, 1972, to speak at Iona College, an affiliate of the United Church of Canada at the University of Windsor.

Despite the fact that lawsuits had been filed in connection with Reverend Forrest's *United Church Observer* article, the efforts to heal the past wounds resulted in a document signed by the United Church of Canada and the Canadian B'nai B'rith. Accordingly, both parties agreed "to dialogue as the appropriate means whereby points of view can be expressed, reconciliation achieved and understanding established."[64]

The Reverend A. C. Forrest dispute was settled by the time there was a change in the leadership of the United Church of Canada. However, the relationship between that body and Windsor's Jewish community never regained the same degree of rapport it had enjoyed with other Christian institutions.

Windsor Jews Gain Prominence

During the 1970s, many Windsor Jews began to participate in activities outside their own community. In the fall of 1970, Abraham Kellerman from Toronto became Windsor's first Jewish city solicitor, a position he held until his retirement. On September 1, 1972, following a nineteen-year career as a successful lawyer, Carl Zalev became Windsor's first Jewish judge, appointed to the Superior Court of Justice. He retired from the bench at the age of 75 after thirty-one years of loyal service.[65] Significantly, Saul Nosanchuk was appointed a judge of the Ontario Court of Justice on November 1, 1976. Another Jewish judicial appointment was made on March 15, 1982, when Sam Zaltz joined the ranks of the Ontario Court of Justice. Some decades later, on June 20, 2000, Steven Rogin was appointed a judge of the Superior Court of Justice.

In 1974, Dr. Ronald Wagenberg, a professor of political science at the University of Windsor who specialized in teaching Canadian government, national government, US public administration, and municipal government, was elected Windsor City Council alderman, a position he held for ten years. One of his major achievements was to scrap the existing council-manager system of governance in favour of reverting to the ward system with an enlarged council that had existed earlier. The proposal for a ten-member council in five wards won City Council's approval in 1975 and was put in place for the 1977 municipal election. That system has endured to this day.[66]

Henry Shanfield served alongside Dr. Wagenberg on Windsor City Council. Having begun his political career in the former town of Riverside, he served as a councillor from 1976 to1978, and subsequently completed four terms on the Windsor Utilities Commission. Mr. Shanfield later became known as a dedicated and tireless environmentalist. He was a proponent of cycling as a means to preserve the environment and led the fight to save Peche Island from development. In 1999, when the City of Windsor acquired that island, situated in Lake St. Clair a short distance from the Detroit River shoreline, it changed the name of former Kayak Cove to Shanfield Shores.[67]

In 1982, Martin Goldberg was elected to represent Ward 1 on Windsor City Council. While serving his term, he also chaired the energy conservation committee and was a member of the planning advisory committee, as well as a director of the Windsor and Essex County Children's Aid Society and of Huron Lodge, a municipally owned and operated facility for seniors. Following his term on City Council, he became the Progressive Conservative candidate for Windsor West, but did not win the election. He and Eli Goldin were the only two Jewish presidents of the Windsor 1918 Rotary Club.

Among those who became prominent in the pursuit of volunteer activities was Richard Rosenthal, who served as president of the United Way of Windsor–Essex County and

president of the Hospice of Windsor. Ted Hochberg was the founding president of Credit Counselling of Metropolitan Windsor, and president of the Windsor Chapter of the Ontario Association of Credit Counselling Services and of the Better Business of Windsor and Essex County. Arthur B. Weingarden was president of the Windsor Symphony Orchestra, while Harry Zeilig headed the Art Gallery of Windsor. Rochelle Tepperman was an elected member from Ward 2 of Windsor's board of education and chaired the Windsor Police Services Board and the Metropolitan Hospital Foundation, as well as serving as the vice chair of the Windsor Symphony Orchestra and of the Art Gallery of Windsor. Gerald Freed was the president of Windsor's Chamber of Commerce and Chairman of the United Way of Greater Windsor, the Greater Windsor Heritage Foundation, and the Windsor and Essex County Development Commission, as well as being involved in the Art Gallery.[68]

Jewish politicians have occupied prominent positions throughout Windsor's history. Apart from Herb Gray, who was active in federal politics, their involvement in local government clearly shows a greater proportion of representation than Windsor's Jewish population figures would indicate.

Living and Learning

For a small Jewish community such as Windsor's, there was no shortage of programs and activities to satisfy the interests and needs of everyone. For instance, thanks to Arthur Weingarden, an accomplished artist himself, monthly art shows were held at Beth El for young artists to exhibit their work in the temple's Charlotte Flagg Gallery.[69] These art exhibitions not only raised money for the congregation, but also brought into the building those people who normally would not enter a synagogue. Also under Beth El's auspices was the Academy of Jewish Studies, which I started in the fall of 1971. It boasted an impressive roster of instructors, among them Rabbi Smulowitz, principal of the Hebrew Academy, Rabbi David

Jessel, community affairs associate of Detroit's Jewish Community Council, and Yael Tsabar, a teacher from Israel who taught Hebrew evening courses.[70]

On the social front, the Beth El Sisterhood and Brotherhood organized popular annual events such as the Monte Carlo Raffle that gave away as first prize a trip for two to Israel. The brainchild of David Greenberg and Ted Hochberg, it continued for almost a decade. Attracting members from the Jewish community as well as the general public, the event raised substantial amounts of money for Beth El.

Apart from celebrating all the Jewish holidays, Shaar Hashomayim's programs included courses on various subjects offered by Rabbi Stollman, occasional theatre nights, as well as a series of Men's Club and Sisterhood functions that also appealed to the community at large.

Not to be outdone, Shaarey Zedek regularly invited prominent guests to conduct its High Holiday services. The synagogue also held raffles and sponsored dinners, the success of the latter largely due to the untiring efforts of its Sisterhood.

The most ambitious programs were those organized by the Jewish Community Centre, which was kept humming with such diverse activities as basketball and volleyball meets and classes in weight training, swimming, bridge, cooking, and photography. While the Friendship Club was popular among the community's seniors, members of all ages could enjoy performances by the Centre's adult choral group and its Theatre Workshop, as well as the occasional film night. People also came together, year after year, to observe Yom Hashoah — Holocaust Memorial Day — and to commemorate Kristallnacht, that infamous night in November 1938 when gangs of Nazi youth roamed the streets of German towns, breaking the windows of Jewish businesses and homes and burning and looting synagogues. On the fifth day of Iyar, according to the Hebrew calendar, the Centre celebrated Israel's independence, for it was on that day in the year 5708 — May 14, 1948 — that the Jewish state was established. By the middle of the 1970s, in conjunction with the United

Jewish Appeal campaign, Joseph Eisenberg had also begun yearly group trips and brief study missions to Israel. In June 1973, when Joel Verbin became the Jewish Community Centre's program director, his main interest lay in expanding its youth activities.[71] Regrettably, he left two years later, and Sheldon Indig took over the post, vowing to continue the work Verbin had begun.[72] When he left, three years later to become executive director of London's Jewish Community Council, he passed on the torch to Jerry Solomon.[73]

In November 1971, the Jewish National Fund asked the Jewish Community Council to participate in the selection of honorees for the Negev dinners. Even though its executive committee declined "co-sponsorship and involvement in the selection of a candidate" at that time, it did endorse the concept of rewarding those who had rendered outstanding service to the community.[74]

Photo courtesy of the Windsor Star

About fifty senior citizens at the Jewish Community Centre were members of the Friendship Club, which got together every second Tuesday for a varied program of activities. Four of them are seen here, in October 1968, whipping up their latest batch of cookies. Pictured from the left are Mrs. Barash Silver, Mrs. Abe Melnik, Mrs. Walter Lobbenberg, and Mrs. Lena Bookman, the club's president.

Photo courtesy of the Windsor Star

The Centre Theatre Workshop of the Jewish Community Centre prepares a 1966 presentation of How To Succeed in Business Without Really Trying. *Rehearsing for the production are (from the left) Al Orman, Gerald Freed, Aronne Ruth Vexler, Ruth Tribute, and Beverley Alexis.*

After a hiatus of seventeen years, when Rubin Madoff was honoured, the annual tradition resumed with the selection of Morris Tabachnick as the chosen honoree for the June 7, 1972, Negev Dinner that featured Senator Paul Martin as the guest speaker.[75] Although Mr. Tabachnick was a worthy recipient of the honour and everyone agreed that he deserved it, Joseph Eisenberg, executive director of the Windsor Jewish Community Council, expressed the opinion that the Negev Dinner "was bound to be a one-time shot," that its "sure success" could not be repeated, and that "it would die as it had

A hand-printed citation was presented to Rubin Madoff in 1955 for his part in the Jewish National Fund drive at a testimonial dinner at Shaar Hashomayim Synagogue. Pictured from the left are Mr. Madoff, Shalome Gelber, guest speaker, Mrs. Madoff, and Morris Tabachnick, who is shown presenting the scroll to Mr. Madoff.

previously."[76] On the contrary, there is no doubt that the annual Negev Dinner became Windsor's premier social event and one of the Jewish community's most important fundraising functions. Jacob D. Geller was honoured in 1973, having received the Greater Windsor Foundation's "Man of the Year" award a year earlier.[77] The honoree for 1974 was Senator Paul Martin and, even though no one received the JNF tribute in 1975, Rabbi Samuel Stollman was honoured in 1976, just one year prior to his official retirement from Shaar Hashomayim. In 1977, Rose Tepperman became the first woman to be accorded the distinction by the Jewish National Fund. Eli Goldin, whom the *Windsor Star* had named "Mr. Windsor" because of his long-standing service record to both the Jewish and Windsor's civic communities, followed her in 1978.[78] Charles Zalev was the honoree in 1979. [79] These successful dinners continued to be held annually with attendance levels reaching some 1,000 in the late 1990s.

When I was president of the Jewish National Fund, I persuaded Kurt Weinberg, then the executive director of JNF's Toronto Branch, to hire Beth El's secretary, Sharon Kaplan, as a half-time worker for JNF based in Windsor, suggesting that she could service its phone lines from her office on a full-time basis. In 1985, after I had left Windsor and Kurt Weinberg had retired, Sharon Kaplan became JNF's executive co-ordinator. She ran the organization in an exemplary manner and, even after leaving Beth El, continued to work for the Jewish National Fund. The fact that it raised millions of dollars over the years is partly due to Sharon Kaplan's efforts.

The members of Windsor's other Jewish organizations showed equal dedication to raising funds and to serving their community. Belonging to them meant regular attendance at monthly meetings, giving teas in their homes, and sponsoring donor luncheons — all get-togethers designed to collect money for Israel and for other worthwhile causes. Truly remarkable was the fact that everyone supported these functions, even though each one of these organizations constantly vied for new members and to maintain their communal presence. It was therefore not unusual for the member of one group to ask for support from a friend belonging to another group and for that call to be answered without reservation because the one who had made it knew that favours had to be repaid.

Windsor Responds to the Yom Kippur War

A new challenge confronted Windsor's Jewish community in the fall of 1973 when Egypt and Syria, supported by other Arab countries, jointly and attacked unilaterally Israel, trying to force it to surrender all captured lands. The attack occurred on October 6 — Yom Kippur — the Day of Atonement and the holiest day in the Jewish calendar. Caught by surprise, Israel suffered severe losses in human life as well as in equipment.[80]

Once the war had started and blood was shed, Windsor's Jewish community rallied, making contributions to the cause that exceeded the United Jewish Appeal's yields of $217,941 in 1971; $270.734 in 1972; and the slightly higher amount that was raised in the following year.[81]

Officially, the Yom Kippur War ended on October 22, 1973, when the UN Security Council passed Resolution 338, calling on all parties to begin "implementation of Security Council Resolution 242 in all its parts" through negotiations.[82] In the aftermath of the war, Windsor's Jewish community raised over $1 million. Although its 1974 campaign attempted to surpass that figure by setting a goal of $1.1 million, the final results never could match the previous high, a remarkable feat that was never again repeated.

The success of the Yom Kippur War campaign was largely due to the efforts of the Israel Emergency Fund Committee. It was headed by William Hurwitz, who was ably assisted by Sidney Cohen, Gerald Freed, Jacob D. Geller, Eli Goldin, Henry and William Kovinsky, Dr. Bernard Lyons, Milton C. Meretsky, Oscar Posen, Morris Tabachnick, William Tepperman, Charles Zalev, and Harry Zekelman.[83] Some of these committee members were so committed to the cause that they temporarily abandoned their businesses to concentrate all their efforts on raising the necessary funds. Using methods that may have seemed unconventional at the time, they asked individuals to not only pledge a certain amount, but also to pay it immediately. And, whenever they encountered a reluctant donor, they would go as far as to ask Jews in other Ontario communities to stop doing business with him, in some cases even refusing to accept donations they did not deem to be "fair-share giving."

During the 1967, 1968, 1969, and 1970 campaigns, the Windsor Jewish Community Council had approved the publication of lists of pledges and "paid gifts," as well as the publication of honour rolls bearing the names of those who had given to the United Jewish Appeal. Those who did not want their names to appear could write a letter prior to the deadline of the campaign, requesting that they be omitted from these lists.[84]

The publication of the names of contributors to fundraising campaigns yielded both positive as well as negative results. Positive because they may have stimulated increased giving; negative because many people considered the practice offensive. Prior to 1975, it had not caused a major backlash among those whose names were not on the list, but after that time, the hue and cry was deafening, especially when the supporters of the Israel Emergency Fund wanted to publish one list showing the names of "all those who gave their fair share" and another one naming "all those who had not pledged in 1974."[85] Yet the practice continued for several years, albeit with disastrous consequences as many of the listed non-givers refused to even support the UJA. But funds continued to be raised, not only to finance projects within Windsor's Jewish community, but also to help Soviet Jews who had immigrated to Israel. As the needs of the Jewish State persisted, it was easier for Windsor's synagogues to approve an Israel Bond Yom Kippur Appeal in the fall of 1974.[86]

New Attitudes and Changing Demographic Patterns

In past decades, most Jews had worried about their survival and how best to instill Jewish values in their offspring. In the 1970s, Windsor's young families wanted their children to appreciate Judaism and know some Hebrew, encouraging them at the same time to move fully into the Canadian milieu. With more and more young Jews entering the non-Jewish world, the Jewish Community Centre and the various religious institutions emerged as the sole repositories of Jewish values in the city.

There is no doubt that these trends affected the family structures within Windsor's Jewish community. Even though it was less assimilated than that of Detroit, it never-theless had to deal with its share of divorces and mixed marriages at a time when the role of women in society was beginning to change. Whereas only a few women had been in the work force in the mid-1970s, by the end of the decade many more had become wage earners like their male counterparts in addition to fulfilling their traditional roles as homemakers.

In the spring of 1974, when women sought to play a more active role at the Shaar Hashomayim, a certain amount of opposition had to be anticipated. Marten Brodsky, chairman of the synagogue's constitution committee, who was sympathetic to their cause, submitted a "package proposal" to the synagogue's board of directors, asking that "the constitution be amended to allow all women to be officers except president, executive vice president, religious vice president and gabbai [honourary official of a Jewish Orthodox congregation]."[87] Apart from asking for changes in the definition of synagogue memberships, Brodsky also proposed amending the congregation's "constitutional documentation (including charter, if necessary)" so as to be able to entrench "in a substantially permanent manner the supremacy of Halacha."[88]

About six months later, on January 27, 1975, Shaar Hashomayim's board of directors approved Marten Brodsky's proposal. Ratified by two-thirds of the congregation's membership, it allowed women to hold offices within the congregation below the restricted positions originally listed and six women were permitted to sit on the synagogue's board of directors.[89]

Shaar Hashomayim also adopted the motion that the synagogue be "bound by and subject to the requirements of Orthodoxy, as represented by the divine written and oral law of Torah and Halacha."[90] For the time being, at least, the synagogue's Orthodox standards could prevail. However, a move away from strictly "traditional Judaism" would become the subject of much controversy in succeeding years.

Summing up the "many attitudinal and value changes" that had been taking place in the lives of Canadians, Joseph Eisenberg stated in his 1976 *Annual Report* that "as upward-striving immigrant Jews were becoming well-to-do members of the Canadian white middle class… perhaps the most important of these [changes] was the acceptance of 'happiness' as the goal of life." As this standard was being used by parents to rationalize the intermarriage of their children," Eisenberg argued, "upward mobility had become an obsession with 'success.'" In other words, "one could not just be rich, "one had to become super-rich" and make "our institutions and organizations part of the same processes." He also believed that by "helping to 'Canadianize' Jews, the institutions were 'Canadianizing' themselves," many of them becoming "the arenas of the competition for status and power" and symbols of "offices, chairmanships, size and conspicuous consumption."[91]

In the 1931 census, the Jewish population in Windsor was 2,500, the highest level ever attained. Twenty years later, in 1951, it had declined slightly to 2,330.[92] Toward the end of the 1970s, Windsor's Jews also had aged and decreased in numbers with a new generation, born and raised in Canada, creating new alignments for the future. Confirming these demographic trends, Joseph Eisenberg's 1977 *Annual Report* listed 1,831 Jews living in the Windsor area, over 50 percent of whom were 65 years of age and older.[93] The population decline would continue and become a major issue of concern for the Windsor Jewish community in the future. At the same time, it is interesting to note that despite the small size of the Jewish population in Windsor, their influence on the broader community has been such that many non-Jews in the city laboured under the misconception that the Jewish community was actually much larger than it was.

When the I. L. Peretz Shule closed its doors in June 1973, it had offered its property on the south side of the Jewish Community Centre to the Council "for use in providing a geared-to-income Senior Citizens Housing."[94] Four years later, however, the school's ardent supporters had not yet handed over the property in the fond hope that they might be able to reopen the school some time in the future. Since the building had stood empty for quite some time, Joseph Eisenberg chided these dreamers, "Don't sit on that piece of property, you don't have to be landlords," reminding them that "if the tradition of the Peretz Shule as an instrumentality in this community for Jewish education is to mean anything, it must continue as an instrument of Jewish survival." Eisenberg felt that it only could do so, "if there is a translation of what sits empty next door into housing — housing for the elderly."[95]

Eisenberg's strong words may have motivated the I. L. Peretz Shule supporters to let go of the property in the hope that the envisaged seniors' home would indeed perpetuate the school's venerable name. As a result, negotiations between Windsor's Jewish Community Council and the school soon got underway, the outcome of which was a Working Policy Proposal that called for "a residential facility aimed especially to serve Jewish seniors" with a kosher kitchen, a dining room, and a Jewish chapel. It would be owned, built, and operated by a separate corporation, with 50 percent of its board members representing Windsor's Jewish Community Council and 50 percent the I. L. Peretz Shules' Windsor Branch. The proposal also stipulated that the new senior residence was to be administered by Windsor's Jewish Community Council, that it had to be completed within two years of the property transfer to the corporation, and that, failing that, it automatically would revert to its original owner.[96]

The Working Policy Proposal was accepted on September 29, 1977.[97] Following the property transfer to the new I. L. Peretz Property Development Corporation, the Windsor Jewish Community Council applied to Canada Mortgage and Housing Corporation (CMHC) for $10,000 seed money to be used to conduct a feasibility study for the new facility. That survey had the support of the B'nai B'rith women's group.[98]

Although Joseph Eisenberg had never verbalized his long-range plans for the property adjacent to the Jewish Community Centre, his strategy to encourage the I. L. Peretz Shule to purchase it did eventually come to fruition. Ultimately, the site became part of the Jewish Community Centre and, by 1980, was well on the way to being a much-needed residence for Windsor's Jewish seniors.

Rabbi Stollman Retires

In the spring of 1977, Rabbi Stollman expressed a desire to withdraw as spiritual head of Shaar Hashomayim. Even though he was only 55 years old at the time and the synagogue's board of directors had asked him to reconsider his decision, he remained adamant in his resolve, claiming ill health and "the emotional strain in Synagogue matters" as the primary reasons for his resignation.[99] Shaar Hashomayim had no choice but to negotiate a financial arrangement with Rabbi Stollman that provided him with a severance package to be paid over a period of nine years.[100]

To honour Rabbi and Mrs. Stollman prior to his departure from Shaar Hashomayim, and to show appreciation for the couple's dedication to the synagogue and to the community at large, the congregation held a dinner for them on October 23, 1977.[101] A week later, Rabbi Stollman was awarded the title rabbi emeritus, after serving Shaar Hashomayim for more than twenty-eight years.

In an interview with the *Windsor Star* just before his retirement, Rabbi Stollman stated that he had "very much enjoyed preaching, talking and sharing ideas with the congregation," that to be "deeply involved with Judaic teachings" had been "very rewarding in itself," and that he hoped to have been "helpful to many people who needed guidance or assistance." When asked about his future plans, he said that he would continue living in Windsor, teaching English literature full-time at the University of Windsor, and that he hoped to turn his attention to "his other great love — interdisciplinary research and writing." Concluding the interview with the words, "Our home has always been a home for counselling and advice," he added that, "if I could be of any use, from time to time, I would be glad to help, but it would be in a limited way."[102]

Several years after leaving Shaar Hashomayim, Rabbi Stollman was asked why he had retired at a relatively young age. In response, he spoke of having experienced physical signs of stress through the last number of years, especially with regard to the mixed seating issue. "Having accumulated a lot of scars, I became the scapegoat for a lot of things. It was really a matter of health and being kind of burned out." Rabbi Stollman also cited frustration in terms of earning a livelihood and deploring the fact that he had not been making a sufficiently high salary. "As far as I was concerned, it became more and more difficult to educate the children, which was very costly," he said. However, he did concede that he would not have retired as early as he did had there not been "a direction all ready," namely, a full professorship at the University of Windsor, a status he had achieved in 1972.[103]

Joseph Eisenberg agreed that the rabbi's physical well-being and his ability to move into another career had been the two reasons for his departure. He added, however, that "it also meant that he would not have to be involved in the political shenanigans that take place in any synagogue, which I think he had enough of."[104]

Here are some highlights of Rabbi Stollman's academic career during his Windsor rabbinate and thereafter: After entering Wayne State University in 1959, he earned an MA with a major in English literature, a minor in Hebrew literature, and a PhD in English literature. From 1964 to 1966, he taught at Wayne State as an adjunct professor, subsequently, joining the faculty of the University of Windsor. After he became a full professor, he served a three-year term as dean of its Department of English, before retiring in 1988 with the title of professor emeritus.

Rabbi Samuel S. Stollman continued to worship at Shaar Hashomayim and at the same time continued to exert some influence on the Jewish community, albeit in an unobtrusive manner. Whenever he was in the city, he would advise his supporters on particular matters and when asked to provide counsel, he was willing to oblige. When he took a sabbatical from the University of Windsor from September 1978 to July 1979, Rabbi Stollman spent it in Israel.

On Sunday, December 11, 1977, one month after his retirement, Dr. Stollman had the honour to announce that Miss Minnie Slobasky had established a fund in memory of her sister Rachel Kaplan. The income from it was to be used "for special annual projects" that would benefit the Louis and Rachel Kaplan Shaar Hashomayim Religious School, built and dedicated by Rabbi Stollman in 1965. A month later, Miss Slobasky unveiled its cornerstone, appropriately engraved with words to commemorate the creation of the Rachel Kaplan Memorial Fund.[105] She had also given money at the same time to Shaarey Zedek, requesting that the synagogue's chapel be named after her sister.[106]

In May 1978, Miss Slobasky donated $55,000 toward the construction of a new and enlarged Chesed Shel Emes funeral home, again in memory of her sister, as well as of her brother Harry Slobasky, a project further enriched by Morris and Freda Tabachnick's generous gift of $30,000.[107] Since Shaar Hashomayim already had received pledges in the amount of $131,500, it now was able to spend $85,000 on the new chapel to be erected on the site of old Talmud Torah building at the corner of Alymer Avenue and Tuscarora Street, awarding the building contract to Collovino Construction Company.[108] The formal dedication of the Rachel Kaplan Hebrew Memorial Chapel took place on Sunday, September 16, 1979,[109] the establishment and building of which was due in great part to the devotion and dedication of David Glanz in seeing this project through from its inception to its conclusion.

In the fall of 1978, Rabbi Benjamin Z. Holczer accepted the position of Shaar Hashomayim's new spiritual leader. Engaged for one year at an annual salary of $18,000, he was also offered the use of the parsonage as his living quarters.[110] Rabbi Holczer was born in Budapest,

Rachel Kaplan Hebrew Memorial Chapel.

Hungary and immigrated to Canada as a young man. The records show that he had graduated from Montreal's Rabbinical College, that he held degrees in various disciplines, and that he had been ordained at Ner Israel Rabbinical College in Baltimore, Maryland.[111]

During Rabbi Holczer's tenure at Shaar Hashomayim, there was much friction between him and Congregation Beth El. Less than a year after his appointment, a situation arose that could have resulted in permanent discord between members of both synagogues if a third party had not intervened to settle the dispute. Following the death in the spring of 1979 of a Shaar Hashomayim member, his family had asked me as Beth El's rabbi to deliver the eulogy and recite some psalms at the funeral service. Rabbi Holczer strongly objected to that request, however, and it was left up to Shaar Hashomayim's executive and the Chevra Kadisha to resolve the matter as amicably as possible. They decided that Rabbi Holczer would conduct the funeral service and that I would deliver the eulogy, but that Rabbi Holczer would not permit me to read the psalms.[112]

A short time later, another incident occurred that clearly showed Rabbi Holczer's animosity towards Beth El. In that particular instance, he had refused to allow the students from both congregations, who had been invited to attend Detroit's annual Jewish Book Fair, to travel together on the same bus. Of course, both congregations strongly objected to the rabbi's actions. Remembering the ruckus that they had caused among their members, Joseph Eisenberg remarked, "I think from that point onward, both factions suddenly realized this nonsense had to stop. Sure there were points of difference but I don't think there was any bitterness. Of course, the Rabbi left."[113]

In July 1979, Shaar Hashomayim prematurely terminated Rabbi Holczer's contract. About a week later, he sent a letter to President David Glanz informing him that he was seeking other employment. The synagogue's board of directors then drafted a suitable agreement that was duly signed by both parties.[114]

Despite this parting of the ways, a happy event occurred in the fall of 1979, when Shaar Hashomayim celebrated its

Golden Jubilee. Starting on November 10 of that year, Shabbat morning and afternoon services were held with Rabbi Holczer still officiating and former rabbis Nahum Schulman and Benjamin Groner acting as the featured speakers. Rabbi Emeritus Samuel Stollman and Senator David Croll spoke at the Sabbath brunch, while Rabbi Norman Lamm, president of Yeshiva University, was the guest speaker at the Golden Jubilee Banquet later that same evening.[115]

To chronicle the events of this fiftieth anniversary celebration, Michael Sumner was asked to produce a book to be entitled *The Golden Jubilee Book — Congregation Shaar Hashomayim*. He also chaired the publication committee and was solely responsible for publishing this commemorative edition.[116]

Regrettably, Saul Nadvan, who had served as Shaar Hashomayim's cantor for twenty-nine years, died on November 3, 1979, just one week before the start of the Golden Jubilee festivities.[117]

Rabbi Holczer's tenure as the spiritual head of Shaar Hashomayim officially ended on September 1, 1980.[118] His actions may have been divisive at times, but in the long run they still contributed to greater cohesion among all the members of Windsor's Jewish community.

Cemetery Negotiations

Beth El had been struggling to obtain its own burial grounds ever since the early 1960s, but negotiations with Shaar Hashomayim had been painfully slow. Talks between the two congregations dragged on for another four years before an agreement was reached in 1971 that "anticipated the immediate development of the South Sector of the present cemetery to be known as Temple Beth El Cemetery." It did, however, stipulate that a *m'chitsa*, a six-foot-high wrought-iron fence, would have to be erected to separate the two sectors. Shaar Hashomayim was willing to pay $2,615 toward building the fence, estimated to cost $6,115, and two-thirds of the cost to paint it. Beth El, on the other hand, was responsible for paying the balance of these so-called improvements, which included a pedestrian entrance to permit individuals to move from one sector of the cemetery to the other. Fortunately, B'nai B'rith agreed to assist both congregations by donating $2,000 to Beth El and $1,000 to Shaar Hashomayim.[119]

By 1973, Congregation Beth El appeared to have acquired its own cemetery. Several questions remained unresolved, however, such as how to handle Shaar Hashomayim's request to use the Beth El section of the cemetery to bury Shaar Hashomayim members who had not met its Orthodox standards.[120] After a seventeen-year struggle, the boards of both congregations finally approved a cemetery agreement on May 20, 1976. Unfortunately, Shaar Hashomayim's membership rejected it seven months later, an action that prompted some Beth El members to contemplate ending all discussions with Shaar Hashomayim and to look for other cemetery land instead.[121] Ultimately, however, it was decided to consult Shaar Hashomayim President Al Gordner as to what steps could be taken to make the cemetery agreement a reality.[122] Gordner not only wanted assurance from Beth El that the new fence would conform to the laws of Halacha and that members of other congregations could be buried in the Beth El section at non-member rates, he also demanded that Beth El pay for drainage at the cemetery.[123]

The other problem that delayed the ratification of the Beth El–Shaar Hashomayim agreement pertained to the Province of Ontario's 1970 Cemeteries Act, which decreed that religious institutions set aside a certain sum of money for the maintenance of their graves. In the early years, contributions to this so-called Perpetual Care Fund were not universally mandatory, and Shaar Hashomayim's methods of collecting them had been quite lax. Now that they were forced to comply with these provincial regulations and knowing full well that many of its graves had been neglected, the synagogue asked Windsor's Jewish Community Council to contribute to the Perpetual Care Fund, claiming that it considered the maintenance of graves a communal obligation.[124]

The Council's cemetery committee subsequently recommended that payments for non-funded perpetual-care graves be made to a trustee — $10 per grave for a ten-year period — and that the income from that trust be paid annually to the Cemetery Perpetual Care Fund.[125] Shaar Hashomayim thereupon made signing its agreement with Beth El contingent on the Jewish Community Council's willingness to pay that "ten dollars per year, per grave for a period of ten years with a maximum of $3,000 per year," requesting that that amount be put into a trust fund for Shaar Hashomayim.[126]

The cemetery agreement won the approval of the memberships of both congregations and was finally signed in June 1978. It called for the following:

- The erection of a fence to divide the cemetery's north section from the south section.
- Assurance that no cremated or embalmed human remains would be buried in either section.
- Identical fees and other charges to be levied on graves in both sections.
- Each congregation would be responsible for maintenance and operation of its section.[127]

As the cemetery improvements, estimated to cost $13,000, exceeded Beth El's financial resources, the congregation asked for and obtained $1,500 from B'nai B'rith's Blue Haven Foundation.[128]

To legalize the ownership of its cemetery, Beth El had to submit to the Ontario government the signed agreement with Shaar Hashomayim, the deed for the transfer of the land, a land survey, a copy of the cemetery by-laws, and the reconciliation papers from the trust company holding the perpetual-care funds.[129]

The deed for the transfer of land was further delayed when Beth El's Arthur Barat received a letter from H. C. Fletcher of the Ontario government's Consumer and Commercial Relations Department. Dated December 10, 1979, the letter stated that "the cemetery's perpetual-care funds are not being administered by an approved trustee as required by the Act," and that "the annual return on receipt and investment of perpetual–care funds has not been received for the year 1978."[130] Consequently, the final chapter of the Congregation Beth El's cemetery acquisition story remained unwritten by the end of the decade.

Congregation Beth El's Expansion Project

Another problem that had been facing Beth El since 1968 was the impending expropriation of some of its land to make way for the E. C. Row Expressway. As the City of Windsor had not shown an interest in purchasing the synagogue building, the matter had been dormant until 1972, when Beth El's board of directors engaged the prominent Windsor lawyer Leon Paroian to handle the case for them.[131] The argument he put forward was that the synagogue's property would be worth less because of the increased noise levels the proposed expressway was expected to produce, and that future expansion would not be feasible as the City of Windsor was planning to expropriate only the synagogue's frontage. Mr. Paroian suggested therefore that the city purchase the entire site to facilitate Congregation Beth El's relocation.[132]

Negotiations with Windsor's City Council seemed to proceed favourably after Beth El had tentatively approved the city's March 1976 offer to purchase the property for $325,000. Consequently, Irwin (Butch) Rivelis, Dick Rosenthal, Arthur B. Weingarden, Barrie Rubin, and Ted Hochberg, were asked to look for a new building site.[133] In August 1976, however, Max Weingarden, a Beth El founding member and a professional builder, expressed his opposition to accepting the city's offer, maintaining that the land was worth more than originally estimated. He also cautioned Beth El's board that the cost of erecting a new temple would be higher than previously anticipated as the membership would not be satisfied with rebuilding the same structure. He was also concerned about the congregation's $67,000 bank indebtedness, a factor that he felt ought to force Beth El to consider retaining its existing property.[134]

Heeding Max Weingarden's advice, Beth El's board of directors decided to study the matter further, "even if the decision to relocate and sell to the city has already been passed by the membership at large at the general meeting."[135] Less than a month later, however, Arthur B. Weingarden advised the board of directors that the city was no longer interested in purchasing the building and that the offer of $19,000–$20,000 for the land to be expropriated had been rejected.

Expanding the current site therefore became Beth El's only option. Arthur B. Weingarden soon became head of the building expansion committee and, following the establishment of three subcommittees, Sidney Cohen was asked to look into financing the project, and Arthur Barat was to handle the architectural plans, while Nels Katzman agreed to take care of "internal needs."[136] After John Hreno, the architect, had submitted a design plan, estimated to cost $425,000, the building expansion committee asked him to pare it down to between $280,000 and 325,000.[137]

In June 1979, when approval was given for the building expansion fundraising campaign to begin, ten prominent Beth El members were approached for donations.[138] Among them was Harry Rubin and his family, who were prepared to give $100,000, provided that contributions would be received from everyone else in the congregation. Mr. Rubin also insisted that the adjacent house at 2515 Mark Avenue be purchased to provide proper access to the redesigned synagogue building.

By September 1979, Beth El's board of directors allowed the expansion to proceed, provided that sufficient funds had been raised to retire its bank debt and to pay for the Mark Avenue house, as well as for the proposed additions and alterations.[139]

There is an interesting story connected with the way in which the expansion campaign's largest gift was secured. Harold Taub, Bill Silver, and I had made a trip to Toronto to meet with Charles Tabachnick, a former Windsorite who wanted to give something back to the community where he once had lived and still had business interests. When he met the three of us, I showed him the plans for the synagogue expansion. After looking at them briefly, he offered to donate $75,000 with the same stipulations as the Rubins — that is, that the majority of the Beth El membership was willing to contribute to the campaign and that the 2515 Mark Avenue house was included in the project. Much to the surprise of Mr. Taub, Mr. Silver, and Mr. Tabachnick, I suddenly produced documents showing that I had actually bought the house myself. When Charles Tabachnick asked me how I could afford to pay for it out of my modest salary, I sheepishly replied, "I was hoping you would assist us." Tabachnick leaned back in his chair and without a moment's hesitation raised his original pledge to $150,000.[140] With that contribution in hand, the success of Beth El's building fund campaign was reasonably well assured, provided that we could come to some suitable settlement with the province. With the addition of the Tabachnick gift, the congregation had received more than $600,000 by the beginning of 1980, with additional gifts still outstanding.

Congregation Beth El on the Third Concession.

A Shift in the Balance of Power

In 1974, the Center for Jewish Community Studies, an organization based in Philadelphia, Pennsylvania and Jerusalem, Israel, commissioned a series of studies to gather data about the way major Jewish communities functioned in Canada. The outcome of that endeavour was a study written by Ronald Wagenberg and Stephen Mandel of the Department of Political Science at the University of

Windsor entitled, "The Governance of the Jewish Community of Windsor." The study dealt specifically with the power base and structure of the community, thereby clearly reinforcing many of the themes outlined in this chapter and elsewhere in this book.

Based on the responses received in interviews conducted by the authors and the answers given to their questionnaire, the study revealed that Windsor's Jewish Community Council "was perceived to be the most important single organization in the community."[141] What is startling is that organizations such as Hadassah and the Shaar Hashomayim Synagogue were tied in importance with B'nai B'rith, which was mentioned next. The city's various religious schools followed them with Congregation Beth El ranking further down the list together with the Pioneer Women and the various synagogues' Sisterhoods.

The study also showed that "the most important positions in the community" were the executive director of the Jewish Community Centre and the members of the rabbinate. Rabbi Stollman, therefore, was considered one of the most influential people, with the Jewish Community Council president and the presidents of the various other Jewish organizations ranking equally in importance. As a result, the authors concluded, "it is evident that professionals carry a great deal of weight in Windsor."[142]

Individuals who wielded influence and power in a particular organization included Morton M. Bernholtz and Dr. Henry Shanfield, both past presidents of Windsor's Jewish Community Council. Others singled out were Michael Sumner and Charles Zalev of Shaar Hashomayim and Arthur B. Weingarden of Congregation Beth El, while Harry Zekelman and Morris Tabachnick were mentioned as significant fundraisers.[143]

The 1974 study confirmed that the community's balance of power would shift to Joseph Eisenberg, the executive director of the Windsor Jewish Community Council, after Rabbi Stollman's retirement in 1977, even though the rabbi emeritus would continue to exert some influence. And while all Windsor's Jewish Community Council presidents, with the exception of Beth El's Gerald Freed, had come from

the Shaar Hashomayim in the past, the Council's leadership was largely drawn from the ranks of Beth El, following Rabbi Stollman's retirement. Among them were former Windsor Jewish Community Council presidents William Silver, Richard Rosenthal, Ted J. Hochberg, and Dr. Michael Malowitz, who had also been presidents of Beth El, as well as congregation members Harold Taub, Gerald Freed, Alan Orman, Jerry Alexis, Marcey Katzman, Jay Armeland, and Dr. Sharon Horlick.

Joseph Eisenberg, executive director of the Windsor Jewish Community Centre.

Another phenomenon noted in the study was "a shift in emphasis away from religion to Zionism and community non-sectarian power." In that connection, the authors found that "the community was able to unite in the face of an external threat or need," but was divided internally "by certain seemingly insoluble problems."[144]

A series of consolidations, closures, and realignments had taken place in the decade about to draw to a close. However, the day-to-day operations of Windsor's Jewish community remained firmly in the hands of the its Community Council with the Jewish Community Centre expanding its programs to include many more aspects of community development.

Looking ahead, Congregation Beth El's expansion program, discussed in the late 1970s, would be completed in 1983. And the I. L. Peretz Shule building, slated for redevelopment since the early part of the 1970s, would be torn down in the next decade to make way for a high-rise apartment complex that would serve Windsor's Jewish and non-Jewish senior residents.

Congregation Beth El after the expansion had been completed.

Chapter 11
The Right Honourable Herb Gray:
Windsor's Prime Statesman

The story of Windsor's Jewish community would be incomplete without a chapter devoted to the accomplishments of Herb Gray. Just as David Croll left his mark on Canada's political landscape during the 1930s and for half a century thereafter, Herb Gray did so between 1962, when he first appeared on the country's political scene, and 2002, when his parliamentary career ended. No amount of wider responsibilities nor national recognition could ever change the fact that these two remarkable public servants were Windsor's own.

The Grays were Jews from a part of czarist Russia that was commonly called "White Russia" and is today known as the Republic of Belarus. Members of his father's side of the family arrived in Winnipeg around 1900 and anglicized their name Gurarie to Gray. Harry Gray had first come to Winnipeg before World War I as a boy, hoping to go to school and have the opportunity of a higher education, impossible under the anti-Semitic laws of the czarist government. Recalled to Russia to help his mother and unmarried sisters on the unexpected death of his father, Harry was not able to return to Canada until 1925.

When he returned as a penniless immigrant, Gray settled in Windsor because it was close to Detroit, where he had a brother in the grocery business. Harry's first job as a grocery clerk was in nearby Amherstburg. Within a year he opened his own small business selling yard goods in Windsor. There he met Fannie Lifitz, a nurse working at Detroit's Harper Hospital. Also from Belarus, her family had settled in Prince Albert, Saskatchewan around the time of World War I and it was there that she received her medical training. Harry and Fannie were married in Detroit[1] in 1929 and before long he established his small business, Gray's Department Store, at 1407 Ottawa Street and acquired or built several properties along the same street.[2] Herbert Eser Gray, the eldest son of Harry and Fannie Gray, was born May 25, 1931. Leonard (Leo), Herb's brother, arrived four years later, in 1935.[3]

The Grays were committed and proud Jews who belonged to Shaar Hashomayim Synagogue, but they were inclined toward the knowledge and understanding of their culture more than toward enduring the rigours of Orthodox Judaism. They were part of a substantial number in the Jewish community linked to the I. L. Peretz Schule

Gray's Dry Goods and Shoes (n.d.).

who enjoyed a more secular outlook. Harry became a founding member of this secular Jewish school, which he and Fanny supported because it fostered knowledge of Yiddish language and literature, as well as Jewish history, customs, and traditions. "While they considered Hebrew the language of Zionism and of religious ritual, they looked upon Yiddish as the link between the past and the present and as the means for Jews to better communicate with one another."[4] The Grays also encouraged their young son Herb to take an interest in music and, "even though he studied classical piano his adult musical tastes eventually included jazz and rock 'n' roll."[5]

The first school Herb Gray attended was Windsor's Victoria School. He later went to Kennedy Collegiate, where his oratorical skills became apparent when he entered and won the 1949 Western Ontario Senior Boys' Public Speaking Contest. He chose as his topics "Canada, a Growing Country" and "What Inflation Really Means," in which he "outlined briefly the problems of geography and economics which have militated against Canadian nationhood from the earliest times."[6] He spoke eloquently about the greatness of Canada, stressing its "indomitable will to create a separate Canadian way of life and to maintain it against every shock of economics, every pull of diverse

racial origins…." He summed up by saying that "only if all groups worked together to check the pressures of higher costs and higher wages could the inflationary danger be resolved."[7] Herb Gray expressed these same sentiments throughout his political life.

When once asked what single event had influenced him to seek a political career, Gray recalled a rally he had attended in the gymnasium of Kennedy Collegiate. Then Prime Minister Louis St. Laurent was the guest speaker and Gray was so impressed that he decided to join the Young Liberals.[8] Years later, when Herb Gray became government leader in the House of Commons and deputy prime minister, he occupied the same office that his role model Louis St. Laurent had occupied as Canada's prime minister from 1948 to 1957.[9]

After graduating from Kennedy Collegiate, Herb Gray attended the University of Western Ontario for a year before heading for Montreal to enrol at McGill's

Tom Douglas (left), third-form student at Ingersoll Collegiate, above discusses some of the finer points of oratory with Herbert Gray, fifth-form student at Kennedy Collegiate. A few minutes later, Herb Gray defeated Tom for the 1949 WOSSA senior boys' public speaking championship.

School of Commerce, where he pursued the advantages of becoming bilingual. To perfect his French, he boarded for a summer with a French-Canadian family in Quebec City while he took courses at Laval University.[10] After graduating from McGill in 1952, he attended Osgoode Hall Law School in Toronto and was called to the Ontario Bar in 1956. That same year, he returned to Windsor to become an associate member of McTague, Deziel, Clark, and Holland, one of the city's oldest and most prestigious law firms.

As a young professional, Gray was expected to participate in community and civic affairs. He did not disappoint. Before long, Gray also became active in community service work, taking on the 1961–62 presidency of the Windsor Jaycees, becoming a director of Junior Achievement of Windsor, and serving as vice chairman of the 1962 Brotherhood Week Committee. He also was a member of the local B'nai B'rith Lodge and of the Richelieu Club, an international francophone service club devoted to various humanitarian causes.[11]

Herb Gray's interest in Canada's Liberal Party was awakened by St. Laurent during his "last year of high school in 1949 and continued when he went off to university."[12] As a Young Liberal, he attended that party's 1958 Leadership Convention and became a delegate to its 1960 National Policy Convention. Having repeatedly expressed an interest in doing "something constructive and creative,"[13] he began to think about running for Parliament. Paul Martin remembered a 17-year-old Herb coming to his Windsor law office in 1948 to ask him what he could do to get into politics. Although ambivalent when asked whether he remembered that particular episode, Gray recalled spending a lot of time with Paul Martin while articling as a student in Martin's law office and helping him to organize his annual dinner dance, which was considered "one of the biggest political events of the year around here."[14]

No one was surprised when Herb Gray declared himself a candidate for the Liberal nomination in Windsor West on April 20, 1961. Challenged by Valerie Kasurak and

Dr. Tony Wachna, both members of Windsor's Liberal establishment, and businessman John Braithwaite, Gray's quest for the nomination became one of the most fiercely contested political struggles in the city's history. On voting day in February 1962, close to 2,000 people were jammed into the Tivoli Theatre, leaving many standing outside on Wyandotte Street East. Herb Gray led on the first ballot, was ahead again on the second, but only captured the nomination with the required clear majority of votes the third time round.[15] There was no doubt that by nominating Herb Gray the people of Essex West had sent out a clear signal that they preferred the young bachelor to the Liberal Party's establishment candidates.

Herb Gray faced the voters for the very first time when Prime Minister John Diefenbaker called a federal election for June 18, 1962. Even though the Conservatives won that election, Gray captured his riding for the

More than 300 Liberal party supporters attended the ninth annual meeting of the Southwestern Ontario Liberal Association held in Chatham in March 1962. Pictured from the left are Walter Gordon, candidate for Toronto-Davenport and organizer for the Liberal Party of Canada; John J. Wintermeyer, Ontario Liberal leader; the Hon. Paul Martin, MP for Essex East; and Herb Gray, candidate for Essex West.

Liberals with 18,152 votes, defeating the PC incumbent, Norman L. Spencer, by 7,134 votes.[16] His strategy had been to work hard, often rising as early as 5:00 a.m. in order to arrive at the gates of the various manufacturing plants in his riding to deliver his message to the workers coming off night shift and those coming to work in the morning. He would spend the rest of the day knocking on doors, attending tea parties, and meeting people at shopping centres and at the city market.[17] The NDP's Bill Tepperman, a well-known Windsor Jewish businessman, lost that election by 8,381 votes.[18] Reflecting on his first campaign, Gray said, "An interesting sidelight to that first

Windsor businessman William N. Tepperman, 25, was chosen as the New Democratic Party candidate in the Essex West riding at a convention in Assumption High School in 1962. From the left are defeated nominee, Roy Battagello, a teacher at Kennedy Collegiate; Mme. Thérèse Casgrain of Montreal, a vice president of the party and the guest speaker; and Mr. Tepperman.

Photo courtesy of the Windsor Star

campaign was that it was the first election for the NDP. And the NDP candidate was William (Bill) Tepperman, who was the son of Nathan Tepperman, and Tepperman's was the other major business on Ottawa Street. "Our families were very friendly, especially Nate Tepperman and my father."[19]

Sworn into office on September 28, 1962, with his mother present in the Office of the Clerk of the House of Commons, Herb Gray had chosen a bilingual ceremony. The fact that the oath of office was administered in both English and French prompted Leon Raymond, the French-speaking Clerk of the House of Commons, to declare how

Photo courtesy of the Windsor Star

For more than a month prior to the June 1968 federal election, Herb Gray who was re-elected Liberal member for Windsor West, was up before sunrise campaigning at the factory gates. Mr. Gray was re-elected by a wide majority and to show his appreciation, he returned to the gates at Chrysler of Canada plant early in the morning to thank voters.

"very much" pleased he was that a member from a primarily English-speaking part of Canada, had "paid this tribute to our two founding races and cultures."[20]

On October 29, 1962, Herb Gray rose in the House of Commons to deliver his maiden speech. Devoting his opening remarks to praises of House Speaker Marcel Lambert, he went on to admonish the Diefenbaker government for its poor handling of the economy. Claiming that there were 9,000 fewer jobs in Windsor in 1962 than there had been in 1957 when the Tories first came to power, he told the House that "they (the Tories) laughed and still laugh at programs to deal with the threat to jobs created by changing technology, automation and the movement of industry."[21] To prevent plants from moving away from the Windsor area, he urged the government to develop Windsor's harbour where dockage facilities were at a premium, and to encourage subsidiaries of American companies to produce more goods in Canada. Specifically targeting the auto industry, he said, "We must continue to look at all possible ways of increasing the Canadian content in our automobiles," making sure that these auto firms do not "continue importing transmissions, paying the duty and passing the cost on to the Canadian consumer."[22] A few months later he returned to the subject, warning the government that the city's chronic unemployment would continue unless something was done about freight rates that were discouraging industries from locating in Canada.[23]

In 1963, Herb Gray made his first bid for re-election. Stressing the merits of the Liberals' policies on education, he told his constituents that his party was planning to create 10,000 scholarships every year and a student loan program, as well as a retraining program to assist those who had lost their jobs due to automation and other economic changes.[24] He also emphasized the importance of the Liberals' Area Development Program that would provide incentives for industries to locate in and around Windsor making it possible for young people to find jobs in their home communities.[25]

Herb Gray had no trouble retaining his seat on April 8, 1963. Having received 23,165 votes, he had defeated his Progressive Conservative challenger Tom Brophey and the NDP's Trevor Price by substantial margins.[26] That evening, standing on a table at his Ouellette Avenue campaign headquarters, he thanked his joyful supporters for all their efforts, stressing the importance of teamwork as the only way to "put Windsor and Essex County back to work again."[27]

Following the election of Lester B. Pearson's Liberals, there was much speculation that Herb Gray would be offered a parliamentary assistant's post.[28] It never materialized, however, despite the fact that he was professionally and intellectually eminently suited for such an appointment and had proved his worth by conscientiously representing his riding.[29]

A month later Paul Martin, his old mentor, fellow Windsorite, and the new minister of external affairs, asked him to represent Canada at the first Inter-American Conference of Ministers of Labour in Bogota, Columbia,[30] Gray also actively participated in the famous Flag Debate, voting for the adoption of a distinctive national flag that he saw as a unifying symbol for all Canadians.[31] And during the Commons' lively debates on immigration, he expressed the view that an increase in population would help Canada's economy grow, noting that people with "little more than basic intelligence and good health" should be allowed to gain entrance to the country.[32]

When writs for another general election were issued September 1965, Herb Gray was ready to face his constituents for a third time. Running against Dr. Austin L. Dixon, the Progressive Conservative candidate, and Hugh Peacock, the New Democratic Party's nominee, he won handily on November 8, even though the margin of his victory was smaller than it had been in 1963.[33] Prime Minister Mike Pearson personally expressed his wish to assign Herb Gray chairman of the finance, trade, and economics committee, completing a "triple threat" power base for the Windsor/Essex community that also included the influential Paul Martin as a Cabinet minister representing the Windsor riding of Essex East and MP Eugene Whelan of Essex as head of the agriculture, forestry and rural development commit-

Photo courtesy of the Windsor Star

Essex West Liberal supporters had plenty to cheer about when their candidate, Herb Gray a young Windsor lawyer, was re-elected by an overwhelming majority in 1963. After a Liberal victory was assured in the riding the supporters, about 200 strong, marched through downtown Windsor streets.

tee. Both relative newcomers — Gray and Whelan — had gained coveted committee positions.[34]

Now entrusted with bringing about far-reaching amendments to Canada's Bank Act, Gray also got involved with the complex Kennedy Round of trade negotiations that lasted from 1963 to 1967 and ultimately yielded three important agreements:

1. An agreement to reduce by one-third the tariffs maintained by developed countries on industrial products.
2. An "Anti-Dumping Code."
3. An international agreement designed to stabilize wheat prices.

In the late 1960s, Gray also attended the Canada–US Interparliamentary Conferences and meetings of the International Monetary Fund and the World Bank.[35]

Although he was heavily engaged in furthering his political career, Herb Gray did find time for romance during those years. The object of his affection was a young woman by the name of Sharon Sholzberg, a native of the Montreal suburb Ville St. Laurent. She had received a BA from Sir George Williams University, as well as a BSc at McGill, majoring in math and physics. While she was at McGill, she had had opportunities to discuss issues with young law students, which led her to switch to the study of law rather than preparing for a career in scientific research. She also had become interested in politics and, after joining McGill's Young Liberal Club, became a member of the original group that helped the young John Turner win the Montreal riding that included the McGill University Campus.[36]

Sharon Sholzberg met Herb Gray in the spring of 1964 when they both attended a Young Liberals' Convention in Ottawa. He was already an MP, while she was, by then, a first-year law student and president of the McGill Liberal Club. In her third year of law, she became the first woman president of the 15,000-member McGill Students' Society.

A year after her graduation from law school in 1966, Sharon and Herb were married on July 23, 1967, at Montreal's Chevra Kadisha B'nai Jacob Synagogue. When asked to comment on her plans for the future, she said that she hoped to "have some connection with law in some capacity or other and, at the same time, be a housewife and do whatever I can to help my husband in his career."[37] The Grays' son, Jonathan David, was born on October 8, 1971, and their daughter, Elizabeth Anne, arrived three years later on August 5, 1974.

Early in 1968, less than a year after Herb and Sharon were married, the new prime minister, Pierre Elliott Trudeau, called an election. Well prepared to face the electorate for a fourth time, Gray again was nominated as the Liberal candidate. His riding of Essex West had been renamed Windsor West on June 16, 1966, and, as required by the party constitution, he had to undergo the formality of re-nomination.[38] He had no trouble obtaining it and when he launched his election campaign, he asked Sharon to manage it for him. In contrast to other political wives, however, she rarely appeared on the platform with him, consistently making it a habit to remain active behind the scenes.[39]

On June 25, 1968, Herb Gray was re-elected with 16,442 votes — 7,470 more than his nearest opponent, NDP Stuart Ross, and 11,440 more than the Progressive Conservative candidate William J. Waldron, who received 5,002 votes.[40] Pierre Trudeau rewarded Gray for his hard work by appointing him parliamentary secretary to Finance Minister Edgar Benson.[41] In that role, he was expected to assist Mr. Benson with the forthcoming budget, as well as guiding the issue of tariffs through Parliament. Happy to work with the finance minister and supportive of the Liberals' programs to improve housing, fight pollution, and create employment opportunities, he did, however, appear to question their plans to balance the budget. Arguing that budgets were tools to bring about economic growth and development, he did not think that they should be balanced just for the sake of balancing them.[42]

When Herb Gray was appointed minister without portfolio on October 20, 1969, he became Canada's first Jewish federal Cabinet minister.[43] Working in association with the minister of finance, he immediately went to work, successfully steering several government bills through Parliament including an amendment to the Quebec Savings Banks Act, the amendment to the Small Business Loans Act, and a change in the Student Loans Act.[44]

Already well known as an economic nationalist, Gray was concerned about the increase in foreign ownership that he felt was threatening Canada's economy. When asked in the spring of 1970 to address a meeting of the John White Society at Osgoode Hall Law School, he used the opportunity to tell his audience that Canada would have to develop new policies if the country wanted to preserve its sovereignty. These policies would have to be in Canada's interest while, at the same time, not being "unfair to those who invest capital here to the extent that we continue to need it." To stimulate entrepreneurship and technological development, he also urged Canadians to invest more in their own country.[45]

On September 24, 1970, less than a year after becoming minister without portfolio, Herb Gray attained another first for Canadian Jewry when Prime Minister Trudeau promoted the 39-year-old to the post of minister of national revenue. Although he was honoured to have a separate portfolio, Gray nevertheless soon realized how sensitive his new portfolio really was — it touched the life of every Canadian, from the richest to the poorest. Not surprisingly, it was not easy getting his message across at a time when taxpayers' morale was at its lowest point, creating a mood of prevailing instability, and people were talking about a possible middle-income tax revolt.[46] He saw this challenge, however, as very much a continuation of the work that had started when he was first appointed to Cabinet: "I had full Cabinet status from the beginning and this occurred before the existence of a two-tier system in the Cabinet. A minister without portfolio was a minister just as much as a minister with a portfolio."[47]

Herb Gray was asked by Pierre Trudeau to head a special working group of officials to consider and report on the foreign investment issue. His views on the dangers of foreign ownership were confirmed on May 2, 1972, when, following a two-year study, he unveiled a major report on behalf of the government that was officially called *The Foreign Direct Investment in Canada Report*, but became widely known as the Gray Report. Dealing with the costs and benefits of foreign investment, it recommended greater reliance on ad hoc regulations, as well as calling for a tribunal to oversee six specific economic areas: takeovers; new foreign-owned enterprises; licensing, franchising, and investments by existing foreign-owned firms; and external investments by Canadian-owned multinationals. Based on the Gray Report, the tribunal known as the Foreign Investment Review Agency (FIRA) was established in 1974. In essence, it entrusted the Cabinet with making final decisions on questions involving takeovers and transfers of ownership to foreign interests.[48]

Just like the young Herb Gray who had won a public speaking contest way back in 1949, Herb Gray, as the federal minister of national revenue, once again made his position clear: There was a definite need to implement earnestly and persistently what he thought were important safeguards for Canada. He still held that belief in 1992 when he said, "The more that other people own of our country, the more they can tell us what to do."[49]

After almost four years in government, the Trudeau Liberals felt it was time to ask Canadians for a new mandate. When they called an election for October 30, 1972, Herb

Gray knew that its outcome was not in doubt, even though he considered the New Democrats' Paul Forder a formidable opponent. When the results were in, Gray's lead had indeed been reduced to less than 5,000.[50] When Canada's twenty-ninth Parliament met on January 4, 1973, the Liberal government had been relegated to minority status. Since a reduced number of MPs had been elected in Western Canada and certain parts of Ontario, other regions, such as Windsor, would get more than their fair share of Cabinet seats. Eugene Whelan was made minister of agriculture, and Herb Gray was moved from national revenue to consumer and corporate affairs, a post formerly held by Ronald Basford. When

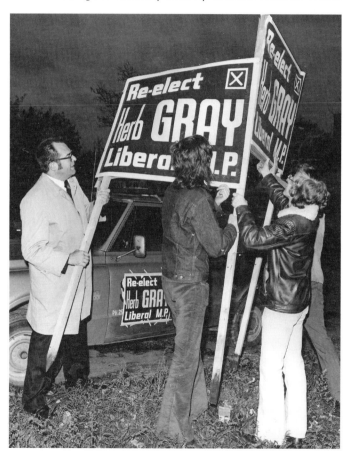

A campaign sign for the re-election of Herb Gray, Liberal MP in 1972.

Basford's proposed Competition Bill had become too controversial for Trudeau, he had replaced him with Robert Andras, who subsequently pulled the bill from the House's roster. After taking over from Andras, Gray prepared a completely new draft bill.[51]

Although Gray's quiet and unassuming manner had won him praise in some circles, others described him as "dull" or "invisible." Despite the fact that he had put forward a "startling flow of changes in the business framework and in consumer protection, for example on product safety," it was said that "the tornado of activity" had been little noticed, because it wasn't being carried out "by a flamboyant minister."[52]

Parliamentary uncertainties and the defeat of the government over the budget made an early election inevitable. When it was called for July 8, 1974, Herb Gray had to face his constituents for the sixth time. He garnered 19,474 votes — more than 56 percent of the total votes cast — and he won his riding by the largest majority ever. His opponents, the NDP's Ron Seale received 10,630 votes and the PC's Bill McKay, 4,466 votes.[53] Despite the fact that the Liberals had been returned to office with a majority, Gray's fortunes changed dramatically on the heels of that election.[54] When he was called to the prime minister's office on August 1, 1974, Pierre Elliott Trudeau advised him that he would be removed from his Cabinet post. Gray remained tight-lipped on the specifics of their discussion and, despite the fact that five other ministers had been dropped at the same time, the press only questioned Trudeau about Herb Gray. In reply, the prime minister told reporters that there was "very high respect towards Mr. Gray, not only from the people, in general, but from myself. I think he is a man of great abilities who certainly has great intelligence and administration."[55]

Once again leader of a majority government and having, so to speak, "rescued" the Liberal Party, Trudeau was likely only too eager to accept Senator Keith Davey's assessment that Herb Gray "a very bright and hard-working guy," but "one of the nameless, faceless mass of ministers," who were "part of our problem."[56]

Trudeau must have agreed with Davey and bought his idea that what the prime minister needed were "sales pitchmen," rather than ministers who promoted the reasoned viewpoints that had been part of the previous government. With his brush cut and decidedly serious demeanor, Gray hardly fit the image of a "sales pitchman." He was generally viewed as someone who was devoid of any real glamour and could hardly compete with John Turner, a politician who not only had good looks but also athletic prowess. In other words, "the Prime Minister and Senator Davey wanted to hear ragtime, and Gray was playing a fugue."[57]

Asked whether he had been forewarned about his abrupt change in status, Gray replied, "That was the main shock of the thing. I couldn't believe that there was such a disparity between what I thought I was doing, confirmed by what other people thought I was doing, and what he (Trudeau) came to think I was doing. I had no inkling."[58] While he remained more or less silent about his discussions with the prime minister, his wife, Sharon, was not afraid to call Trudeau's reasons for her husband's dismissal "awfully superficial," adding that, despite his calm public posturing, "it hurt him very deeply," adding that she didn't know "whether it's a hurt that he'll ever really recover from."[59]

Shortly after losing his Cabinet post, there was speculation that Herb Gray might jump from federal to provincial politics. During the February 1975 Ontario Liberal convention, Party Leader Robert Nixon invited him to become "a senior member of his team."[60] Although he admitted thinking about seeking the nomination in a forthcoming provincial election, he, ultimately, decided to remain in Ottawa.[61] It is interesting to note that several years later Gray was asked by both the federal New Democrats and the federal Progressive Conservatives to leave the Liberal Party to take on a senior position with their respective parties. He obviously never pursued their offers.[62]

At that point in time, Gray's political future seemed uncertain. Considering that he was still a young man in his mid-40s, there was speculation that he might resign as member of parliament to practice law in Montreal. But he called such speculation futile, explaining that he never had been called to the bar in the Province of Quebec.[63]

While the other ministers who had lost their Cabinet posts soon faded into oblivion, Gray found a new role for himself by becoming his own government's outspoken and most incisive critic. He said he was doing so in a constructive way to encourage the government to stick to its Liberal policies. Some Liberals in the House were not pleased to suffer his attacks, but he seemed to relish the opportunity to criticize the party's policies and then see his comments favourably reported in the press. The fact that his name frequently appeared before the public brought about a change in Mr. Gray's image and led some Ottawa pundits to suggest that if the prime minister were to see a "new Herb Gray," as an improved politician with more fighting spirit than before, his chances for another Cabinet post were good.[64]

In the meantime, however, Herb Gray attacked the government for delaying the passage of their consumer protection laws, for its lateness in delivering the second part of the foreign investment control legislation, for being too slow in establishing a new competition policy — the regulation of mergers and monopolies — and for being too secretive about its foreign investment laws.[65]

Yet he never failed to defend and support the citizens of Windsor. Trying to protect them against undue hardships, he quickly intervened on their behalf when Marks & Spencer announced it would lay off employees at its Windsor store. Contacting the Foreign Investment Review Agency, he asked them to determine whether the British company had broken its earlier agreement to provide more job opportunities in the city after buying a controlling interest in Peoples Department Stores, the Canadian chain that previously had owned Smith's of Windsor. Although Gray's *Foreign and Direct Investment Report* was the basis for the FIRA Act, the minister of industry achieved its actual passage.[66] A year later, Gray complained that FIRA was being used "more as a device for facilitating foreign investment rather than reviewing it."[67]

Continuing to take aim at inadequate government policies, Herb Gray urged greater safety controls for freight cars.[68]

He also criticized his party for approving a merger between two US-based retail companies[69] and demanding that the results of a five-year probe into oil-price fixing be disclosed.[70] He challenged the Liberals to do something about rising food prices, deploring their lack of power to control them and recommending that the government set up a national commission on inflation. True to his Liberal roots, whenever he noticed a violation of the Canadian Human Rights Act, he was quick to demand an investigation.[71]

He was clearly willing to take on any matter, however diverse. He had earlier accused the United States of violating the Auto Pact,[72] and now also opposed Air Canada's planned takeover of Nordair,[73] and the giant Thomson newspaper empire's absorption of the Hudson Bay Company.[74] He further succeeded in forcing Exxon Corporation to back down on its plans to divert 25,000 barrels of oil a day from its Canadian subsidiary, Imperial Oil, to its parent company in the United States.

When asked how he felt about being, so to speak, a thorn in the side of his own party's hierarchy, he explained that he was acting "almost the way US senators act, identifying issues and problems, speaking out on them, making them national concerns." He firmly believed that he was expressing the views "shared by a large number of people in the caucus" — "a point of view not only held within the party, but also by small-l liberals and people concerned with social justice."[75]

Early in 1979, it had become clear that the Liberal government was in trouble. The economy was in recession, interest rates were still sky high, and the polls showed that Canadians were dissatisfied with the way Trudeau was handling the economy. In view of these circumstances, the rumour that the prime minister might call an election caused a great deal of consternation in certain government circles. When he did ask Canadians to go to the polls on May 22, 1979, Herb Gray was determined to run again, this time against the New Democrats' Maxine Jones and the Progressive Conservatives' Professor Bob Krause. Gray's past criticism of government actions may have antagonized certain Liberals, but it did not deter his constituents from voting for him in large numbers. His victory was assured as they cast 16,943 votes in his favour, 5,037 more than Maxine Jones received, while Professor Krause finished as a distant third with a total of 5,869 votes.[76]

Nationally, the Liberals lost the election to the Progressive Conservatives and when Joe Clark's minority government came to power on June 4, 1979, Herb Gray had to take his place on the benches of Her Majesty's Loyal Opposition. After five years as a Liberal backbencher on the government side, he became his party's finance critic. Trudeau asked him to be part of a shadow cabinet in that lead role, to monitor and challenge what the Liberals viewed as the potentially destructive economic policies of Joe Clark's government.[77] Gray consequently attacked the Progressive Conservatives for hiking interest rates, neglecting important economic issues, procrastinating in tabling the budget, and for promoting high energy prices.

In retrospect, Gray's appointment as finance critic was the beginning of his return to a leadership role within the Liberal Party, especially after his vigorous attack in the House on a vote on the government's first budget contributed to the defeat of the minority Clark government in December 1979. When a new election was called for February 1980, the Liberals commissioned a series of television spots as part of their campaign strategy. Portraying themselves as team players, they tried to show Trudeau as a leader who ostensibly stood alone. Some of these advertisements even promoted Herb Gray. By extolling his virtues as a finance critic with great expertise in economic matters, they not only kept his image before the Canadian public, but also seemed to herald his return to the top ranks of the Liberal Party.[78]

The polls had been closed for less than thirty minutes when an uncharacteristic grin was seen on Herb Gray's face. And, no sooner had the last vote been counted than it became clear that he had indeed won a landslide victory. He received 19,755 votes from the people of Windsor West — 5,742 more than the combined total of all the other votes cast — he easily defeated the NDP's Maxine Jones (9,785 votes) and the PCs' Ned Griffith (4,107 votes).[79]

Many of the issues Gray had supported since the beginning of his political career were now front and centre of the Liberal platform — job creation, economic growth, social concerns, and the development of a viable industrial strategy. By concentrating on these important issues, Gray felt that his party had finally demonstrated a willingness to listen to the people. But he was especially pleased when Trudeau appointed him minister of industry, trade, and commerce, as well as minister in charge of the Foreign Investment Review Agency. "This is exactly what I wanted to do," he told the Globe and Mail shortly after the election.[80] In addition to being returned as a member of the Cabinet, Gray also was appointed Prime Minister Trudeau's "political minister," for Ontario, whose duties included co-ordinating links between the Liberal party and the caucus.[81]

In view of Herb Gray's long-standing interest in economic nationalism, he reaffirmed his commitment to the cause by striving to make Ottawa "an active player in industrial development rather than just a passive referee."[82] Determined to push for 50 percent Canadian ownership in the oil and gas industry by 1990, he proposed that foreign bids be made public to allow Canadian firms to submit counter-bids. He also felt that the government's real priority should be economic growth and the creation of new jobs, especially for young people just entering the work force. In fact, he strongly believed that spending money to boost the economy and maintain social programs was more important than reducing the deficit, a policy that had been high on the Progressive Conservatives' agenda.[83]

With a likely slump in automotive sales looming large on the horizon, Gray was concerned about the effect it would have on Canadian auto plants, especially in the Windsor area. He was therefore anxious to modify certain parts of the Canada–US Autopact, so that Canada would receive a fairer share of North American automotive production.[84]

But it was his efforts to enable Chrysler Canada to stay in business that truly endeared him to the citizens of Windsor and Ontario. Trying to prevent the automaker from having to file for bankruptcy, he proposed that loan guarantees be provided by the federal government that were tied to commitments from Chrysler to guarantee jobs and adequate production levels in Canada. Gray said that he took part "in a series of negotiations with representatives of Chrysler and the Auto Workers' union." A tentative aid package was worked out at a May 1980 meeting that lasted almost until dawn and included Gray, Chrysler president Lee Iacocca, the Auto Workers' Union representatives, and Ontario Industry Minister Larry Grossman.[85] "We're not just saving Chrysler Canada, but the entire Chrysler Corporation," Gray told reporters when he emerged from the meeting.[86] The deal involved placing what became the highly successful Chrysler Minivan in the Windsor Chrysler assembly plant.

There is no doubt that Gray's negotiation with the unions and his talks with the automaker were among the most important accomplishments of his career.[87] He had prevented mass layoffs and the possible closing of Chrysler. When he heard that the Ford Motor Company was planning to lay off 1,000 workers in Windsor and 1,500 at their Oakville plant, he also initiated talks with them to prevent these plant closings.[88] After only one meeting with Ford executives, however, he abruptly cancelled another one, likely because he considered it futile to proceed with it in light of the prevailing economic situation.[89]

Even though the Chrysler situation had been seemingly resolved, Gray knew that action might have to be taken about car imports from Japan. Alarmed that 1979 sales of Japanese cars had been close to $500 million, while Canadian car sales had totalled no more than $600 million, Gray travelled to Japan to ask Japanese automakers to make direct investments in Canada by building manufacturing plants.[90] He also urged them to purchase more Canadian parts "to meet the urgent adjustment problems of the North American automotive industry."[91]

In January 1982, Herb Gray was appointed minister of regional economic expansion, a post he held along with the position of minister of trade and commerce until September 30 of that year, when Trudeau made him president of the Treasury Board. In that capacity he was supposed to help save Canadian jobs, while at the same time finding ways to cut federal spending. To do the former was difficult during what

turned out to be the country's worst post-war economic recession, while attempts to do the latter doubtlessly did not endear him to many of his political friends. Yet Gray moved ahead, supporting start-up affirmative-action programs for women as well as for handicapped persons, bringing forth guidelines for introducing micro-technology in the civil service, as well as devising methods to speed up payment of government bills. It became clear at that point exactly how opposed he was to free trade with the United States, an idea endorsed by some prominent business figures.[92]

On February 28, 1984, after Pierre Elliott Trudeau had taken his now famous "walk in the snow" that resulted in his decision to step down as prime minister, some thought that Herb Gray would seek the leadership of the Liberal Party. He decided not to do so, endorsing instead John Napier Turner, the man considered Trudeau's natural successor. Endorsed by the Liberal Party in a convention on June 20, 1984, Turner became prime minister, and to reward Gray for his loyalty and support, he re-appointed him president of the Treasury Board and asked him to continue in the influential post of political minister for Ontario.[93]

When Turner called a hasty election for September 4, 1984, Herb Gray was again nominated without opposition. Making job creation the central theme of his campaign, he reminded his constituents, among other things, of the vital part he had played in bringing about the survival of Chrysler Canada.[94]

The Liberals lost that election and during the Progressive Conservatives' massive sweep, Herb Gray was the only Windsor Liberal to retain his seat, having captured 13,625 votes while his NDP rival Paul Forder received 11,503 votes, and PC Martin Goldberg tallied 8,181 votes. Although Gray could not explain the Liberals' countrywide rout, he did pledge to help rebuild his party.[95] He was one of only forty-four Liberals elected in 1984.

When Brian Mulroney became prime minister on September 17, 1984, Gray lost his job as president of the Treasury Board. But thanks to the experience he had gained in his various government posts and, because of the loyalty he had shown John Turner, he became the Liberal leader's right-hand man as Opposition house leader, a position he held until February 1990. Gray continued to fight for the causes he had championed in the past, never failing to attack Conservative government policies in press interviews and on talk shows.[96] He also continued to support John Turner, even though his leadership was challenged (unsuccessfully) at the 1986 Liberal Party convention, in the summer and fall of 1987, and in the spring of 1988, when twenty-two out of thirty-eight Liberal MPs demanded a leadership review. Gray may have realized that he was jeopardizing his own future within the party by continuing to stand by Turner, yet he vigorously defended his action, maintaining that he always had "followed the policy of supporting the leader democratically chosen by the party."[97]

By the summer of 1988, it became clear that a federal election was not far off. After being nominated in Windsor West for the tenth time, Gray was ready to launch yet another campaign.[98] NDP Leader Ed Broadbent, in his attempt to find a high-profile candidate to oppose Gray, had asked former Windsor mayor Elizabeth Kishkon to run in the riding.[99] She turned him down, claiming that she had no political ambitions at the federal level or the desire to wage an election battle against the popular Windsor West MP. "I do admire Herb Gray," she said, "I think most people in the city do. I think we have a hard-working and dependable MP."[100] Paul Forder, on the other hand, having lost to Gray by just 2,100 votes in the previous election, did accept the NDP nomination.[101] The Progressive Conservatives had chosen an Anglican minister, Canon Bert Silcox as their candidate. He surprised everyone when he uncharacteristically focused on the need to aid the poor in his nomination speech, rather than tackling such issues as the Liberals' and New Democrats' criticisms of free trade.[102]

When the federal election was called for November 21, 1988, Herb Gray did his best to appeal to the voters of Windsor West. With its share of new immigrants and a large Italian-Canadian population, it was a riding composed of a broad mix of older and newer residential areas, commercial establishments, and a sizeable manufacturing sector — primarily, the auto industry — for which the City of Windsor is famous.[103] Despite the lively debates among the candidates, Gray soon emerged as the front-runner who ultimately coasted to victory with 23,796 votes, compared to NDP Paul Forder's 12,143 votes, and the Tory Canon Silcox's mere 6,131 votes.[104] The Liberals lost the election, but doubled their seats to eighty-eight.

As soon as the House was back in session, John Turner reappointed Herb Gray as Liberal house leader.[105] When he also made him deputy leader of the Opposition a few months later, however, it was generally believed that the Liberal leader was about to retire.[106] Gray was quick to downplay the significance of the appointment, maintaining that his additional new role was to assist Turner in organizing the caucus, to be "a very effective opposition and holding the government to account." Nor did Gray waste any time in continuing to criticize the government for running up deficits while cutting social programs at the same time. In addition, he also reaffirmed his party's opposition to the Tories' plan to replace the manufacturer's sales tax with a tax on almost all goods and services.[107] Even though he spent a lot of time fighting the proposed legislation, he continued to champion the causes that were dear to the hearts of the citizens of Windsor.

At the beginning of 1990, there was much speculation that John Turner would soon step down as leader of the Opposition, given his strong antipathy to the Canada–US Free Trade Agreement.[108] He eventually did so at the beginning of February 1990, but remained leader of the Liberal Party. The race to succeed him only began in earnest when the Liberal Party executive announced that it would hold a leadership convention in Calgary from June 20–24, 1990.[109]

The resignation by Turner prior to that convention led to Herb Gray's elevation to leader of the Opposition. Consequently, he did not support any leadership candidate, not even front-runner Paul Martin, although he was from Windsor, or Jean Chrétien, the other leading candidate.[110] Not wanting to take the spotlight away from these contenders, Gray was quick to explain that by endorsing one candidate over another he would not be able to effectively carry out his new role as leader of the Opposition, working with all the candidates and their supporters in the House.[111] Herb Gray was unanimously endorsed by the Liberal caucus as the new leader of the Opposition. In February 1990, rising in the House of Commons for the first time since his appointment, he received a standing ovation from all the parties, even though it was noted that the Tory and NDP members were a little slow getting to their feet. With his new job came numerous additional perks — an increase in salary, a car and a driver at his disposal at all times, and the opportunity to move into Stornoway, the prestigious residence of the leader of the Official Opposition. Gray declined the latter on the grounds that he already had a home in Ottawa,[112] but he did use Stornoway for occasional receptions. Congratulating Gray on his new role, the *Windsor Star* of February 9, 1990, editorialized that

The quiet man of Windsor West may work silently but he works well and tirelessly. In both government and opposition, he has distinguished himself as what Parliament Hill knows as a "constituency man." No matter how demanding and time-consuming his other duties, he has kept in touch with his constituents and the triumphs and troubles of his home city. That can be expected to continue as he takes on the heavy demands of his interim job. The interim title and the duties involved are an honour that he deserves, even though he will serve for only a few months. But jobs in life change often and in politics they change even more often.[113]

In his first official speech, Gray pleaded for understanding between French and English Canadians, stressing how proud he was to be able to speak for Canada in both official languages, despite the fact that "my background is neither French nor English."[114] As his new job unfolded, he continued to attack the Tories — on their budget, on their proposed cuts to health care, on their lax pollution laws, and for restricting gas exports. Still concerned about the forthcoming Goods and Services Tax (GST), Gray accused Finance Minister Michael Wilson of making a false promise to pass on to taxpayers the savings from the replacement of the federal sales tax with the GST, a charge Wilson denied.[115]

Last but not least, Gray expressed grave concern about the Meech Lake Accord, the set of constitutional reforms agreed upon on April 30, 1987, by Prime Minister Mulroney and all the provincial premiers. Designed to induce Quebec to accept the Canada Act that created the 1982 Constitution, it included five basic points: A guarantee of Quebec's special status as a "distinct society"; a commitment to Canada's linguistic duality; increased provincial powers in immigration; provincial input in appointing Supreme Court judges; restricted federal spending powers; and restoration of the provincial right to a constitutional veto.[116]

Herb Gray truly blossomed as the Opposition leader and although he was known as a tireless worker, he had certainly never made a name for himself as a stand-up comic. But in the spring of 1990, when he delivered the traditional Opposition leader's speech at the parliamentary press gallery dinner, he became the undisputed smash hit of Parliament Hill. No one had expected a man who was generally described as "Gray Herb," to display so much refreshing good humour. Focusing on his renowned dull image, he mused about what it would be like if he were to run for the leadership of his party. Using "Paint the Town Gray" as his campaign slogan, he thought he would place signs on the doors of the hotel rooms of convention delegates that read, "Don't disturb — I'm with Herb." Naturally, he brought down the house with Prime Minister Mulroney raising ten fingers to indicate that Gray deserved "a perfect ten."[117] The spoof, reported in the *Ottawa Citizen* under the heading, "Herbalmania Sweeps Press Dinner," even got a reaction from Finance Minister Michael Wilson, who congratulated the leader of the Opposition on "the kick-off to his campaign," suggesting that "The Bland Is Strong" might be a better slogan as Gray's standing in the polls apparently had risen substantially. Indeed, after his speech, reporters hounded him, wanting to know whether he would run for the leadership of his party.[118]

On June 20, 1990, when Herb Gray did address the delegates gathered in Calgary for the Liberal Leadership Convention, he reminded them, first and foremost, of the Quebec separatists' threat to Canadian unity. Specifically referring in that context to the dangers of the Meech Lake Constitutional Accord, he predicted that the Tories would become known "as the people who waited until the last minute to roll the dice with the future of this county at stake." Then directly addressing the party faithful, Gray said, "I want to say on your behalf to Brian Mulroney, 'Mr. Prime Minister, your days are numbered!'"[119] That remark was met with chants of "Herb, Herb, Herb," as the delegates rose to their feet to give the interim leader a standing ovation. Encouraged by their enthusiasm, Gray continued, "In fact, if Brian Mulroney listens to the two food tasters he has just hired to follow him around, he will hear those food tasters say, 'Brian Mulroney your goose is cooked!'"[120]

On the day Herb Gray made that speech, he did not yet know that the Meech Lake Accord would die two days later — on June 22, 1990 — when the provinces of Newfoundland and Manitoba failed to endorse it. Although he had doubts about the accord, its failure gave the separatist threat to Canadian unity another life.

The delegates elected Jean Chrétien as their new party leader. Anxious to tour the country to build support for the party for the next six months, Chrétien asked Herb Gray to continue as Opposition leader. He did so, vigorously attacking the Mulroney government and, once the House was back in session, concentrating all his efforts on making sure that Jean Chrétien would become Canada's next prime minister.[121]

Gray's term as leader of Her Majesty's Loyal Opposition came to an end in late December 1990, when Jean Chrétien won a fall by-election in New Brunswick and entered the House on December 21, the day before it adjourned for the Christmas/New Year's break. With pride, Herb Gray remarked, "At one point when I was Opposition leader the Liberals rose in the polls to 56 percent."[122] Jean Chretien appointed Sheila Copps as deputy leader, Dave Dingwall as house leader and Herb Gray as finance critic,

where he continued to chastise the Tories for their financial mismanagement, telling them that although the deficit could not be ignored, fighting the recession was the only way to reduce it. He had not been able to stop the Goods and Services Tax from coming into force on January 1, 1991, but he did however maintain that Canadians would have preferred a fairer system of taxation and lower interest rates as the means to encourage economic growth.[123]

Herb Gray's father, Harry Gray, died in December 1991 at the age of 96. When he delivered the eulogy for his dad, Gray spoke of a man who had maintained a reputation for fair dealing and high integrity during the thirty-seven years he had been in business. "'Nothing is too good for the customer,'" Herb Gray said, "was the motto that guided him throughout his life." When Harry Gray had once been asked to reveal the secret of his success, he said, "Always give the public quality merchandise at reasonable prices with money-back guarantee, and above all advertising."[124] Harry Gray was buried at the Shaar Hashomayim Cemetery in Windsor next to his wife, Fannie Gray, who had passed away in 1987 at the age of 88.

Back in the House of Commons, Herb Gray chided the Tories for spending $2.2 million to fund a Museum of Humour in Montreal and a year later pumping another $3.3 million into the project, while at the same time claiming to have no money for research, the unemployed, or day care. Questioning the need for such a museum, the finance critic quipped, "Canadians may enjoy a world-wide reputation for being stable and practical, but possessing a world-class sense of humour is not a characteristic that comes immediately to mind when describing our fellow countrymen and women."[125]

The Canada–US Free Trade Agreement had been in effect since 1989. However, talks were now underway for a new pact that would eliminate most trade and investment barriers among Canada, the United States, and Mexico. Gray's opposition to the Canada–US Free Trade Agreement was well known, but to support his argument against NAFTA — the North American Free Trade Agreement — scheduled to come into force by January 1, 1994, he cited a study conducted by the US-based International Institute for Economics. It showed that Canada would lose 4,000 jobs under the pact, while the United States would gain 130,000 and Mexico would gain 600,000, and that Canada's trade surplus with the US would drop by $250 million a year for the next four years. In light of these findings, Gray hoped to convince Trade Minister Michael Wilson to break off the NAFTA talks.[126]

On June 18, 1992, Gray's thirtieth anniversary as an MP was fittingly celebrated on Parliament Hill with 160 Liberals attending a reception in the courtyard of the East Block singing Otis Redding's song, "Sittin' on the Dock of the Bay" to the following new lyrics:

> Been sitting now for 30 years,
> And it's done strange things to my rear,
> I watched the Tories rollin' in,
> Gonna watch 'em roll away again.[127]

The organizers of the event paid tribute to his political achievements as well as to his passion for rock 'n' roll with a special video that documented his career with footage set to the "driving rhythms" of Bruce Springsteen, Dire Straits, the Rolling Stones, and other rock musicians. Liberal Leader Jean Chrétien delivered a heart-warming message, recalling the 1960s when he and Herb Gray were young MPs. He told the gathering that they often would eat together, while "he was working on his French and I was working on my English. He succeeded; I did not."[128]

Herb Gray likely was pleased with these accolades as well as with the *Windsor Star*'s June 18, 1992, editorial congratulating him "for surviving in the turbulent world of politics for thirty years and for being a diligent and responsible member of Parliament for all that time."

> That is no easy accomplishment, particularly in an era when the public is not all that fond of politicians and is usually not in the mood to live with them through too many elections. Gray, however, has prevailed in 10 elections and is the longest serving member of the House of Commons. Is his longevity attributable to the fact he carried the Liberal banner? Not entirely. Herb Gray is a decent man and one whose roots remain in Windsor. He has earned the respect of his constituents.[129]

When *Maclean's* magazine later asked him what he thought about his thirty years in federal politics, he optimistically answered, "It is not a bad beginning. But I look on it as a halfway point in the things I want to do."[130]

Without another challenger in sight, Herb Gray again received his party's nod when an election was called for October 25, 1993. This time, his main opponents were the PC's Dan Friesen, the NDP's Professor Emily Carasco, and the Reform Party's Brett Skinner. Gray defeated each of them by the biggest margin of any past election, receiving a total of 27,008 votes compared to Skinner's 4,179, Carasco's 3,359, and Friesen's 1,663. His victory was even sweeter when it was revealed that Windsor voters had elected three other Liberals — Susan Whelan in Essex-Windsor, Shaughnessy Cohen in Windsor-St. Clair, and Jerry Pickard in Essex-Kent.[131]

With the defeat of the Progressive Conservatives, the Liberals were swept into office with a sizeable majority. Kim Campbell, Brian Mulroney's successor, resigned on November 3, 1993, and Jean Chrétien was sworn in as Canada's twentieth prime minister a day later. He subsequently appointed Herb Gray to two senior positions — government house leader and solicitor general. As house leader, he worked closely with the prime minister, overseeing the government's legislative program, getting legislation through Parliament and judiciously negotiating with the opposition parties.[132] As solicitor general, it was his job to try to make good on the promises the Liberals had made during the election campaign, such as the establishment of a National Crime Prevention Council that, together with federal, provincial, and local governments and organizations, would look for common solutions to fighting crime. The solicitor general is responsible for all federal government law enforcement activities reporting to Parliament —

for the RCMP, the Correctional Service, the Canadian Security and Intelligence Service (CSIS), and the National Parole Board — totalling some 35,000 employees, with a budget of close to $3 billion annually. Gray said he was planning to discuss the Council with Justice Minister Allan Rock, as well as looking into such causes of criminal behaviour as unemployment and poverty.[133]

Although Herb Gray carried out these tasks with his usual dedication, he always found time to indulge in his favourite pastime: listening to the music of such rock musicians as Bruce Springsteen, country singer Bob Seger, and others, while doing things in the office, working at home, or driving his car.[134] When asked why he found this kind of music so appealing, he once said in an interview, "I'm interested in what the young people who surround me and whom I represent are talking about and what they are interested in."[135]

His knowledge of popular music certainly had earned him the respect of the media. Why else would the people at Radio Canada, CBC Radio's French-Language Service, have chosen him as the personality on the Hill to best assess in French the contribution that the "King of Rock 'n' Roll" had made to that type of music when they wanted to commemorate the tenth anniversary of Elvis Presley's death on August 16, 1987? And when the Ottawa rock station CHEZ-FM was looking for someone from the Liberal Party to act as a guest disc jockey to play music he or she liked, they also picked Herb Gray for the job. According to one of the station's former disc jockeys, true to his Windsor roots, he played "nothing but working-class rock stuff."[136]

In April 1996, Gray suddenly found himself engaging foes other than his political opponents. After collapsing with what he thought was the flu, he took himself to Ottawa Civic Hospital where after a week of tests, he was diagnosed with small-cell carcinoma of the esophagus.[137] Both sides of the House expressed shock and, as a *Windsor Star*'s editorial noted, "average folks and political pundits alike paused when they heard that Canada's solicitor general and House leader was being treated for a malignant tumour."[138] At the end of August, after a course of chemotherapy, Herb Gray had surgery to remove the site of the cancer. When Gary Fortune, his chief assistant, was asked about his boss's condition and when he would return to work, he confirmed that the operation had been a success and then jokingly told reporters, "He'll probably take the weekend off."[139]

A sign of the relief felt by the people of Windsor that the prognosis for Herb Gray's full recovery was good came a few months later when they greeted him with a spontaneous round of applause during a function he attended on Remembrance Day.[140] Further proof of the high esteem in which he was held in Windsor was the roast given in his honour on February 20, 1997, at Cleary International Centre. A full capacity audience had not only come to raise money for the city's Capitol Theatre and Fine Arts Centre, but also to hear speaker after speaker roast Herb Gray with good-natured humour. When his turn came to respond, he did not disappoint those present. "After a health problem, people often say "They're 'glad to be here; they're glad to be anywhere. But for me that wouldn't be accurate. I'm only glad to be here with you."[141] Just over a year later, on April 3, 1998, he was the guest speaker at the Canadian Cancer Society's sixtieth anniversary dinner. Commenting on his miraculous recovery, he told those gathered for the event, "It's not easy to discuss these things. But just as I found that other people's messages to me helped provide hope and encouragement, people have told me that they were helped by the way I faced my difficulties."[142]

The 1997 spring election provided the following stellar results with Herb Gray retaining his seat (21,877 votes),[143] in comparison to a field of candidates such as Tom Milne (NDP — 9,411), Jeff Watson (Reform — 5,295), Dan Friesen (PC — 2,452), Richard Warman (398), and Robert Cruise (199). After that election, on June 11, 1997, Jean Chrétien appointed Herb Gray as Canada's first full-time deputy prime minister. Following the swearing-in ceremony at Ottawa's Rideau Hall, he was ready to take up his new duties, which included leading the government in Question Period in the House, chairing Cabinet, and responding in caucus while the prime minister was absent, working on party strategies, chairing government committees, and making sure that good relations were maintained between cabinet members and the Liberal caucus.[144] He continued to chair the central Cabinet committee, the special committee of counsel that maintained oversight of the government's legislative program and made decisions that were to be implemented by regulation. During Question Period, he also had a chance to demonstrate what a past master at stonewalling he really was. By applying his dry wit and low-key demeanour, he not only managed to deflect most of the Opposition's unpopular questioning, but also was able to defuse controversies arising in the House at other times.[145] It was said that when John Turner was the leader of the Liberal Party, his aides, desperate to divert attention from yet another leadership crisis, would send out Herb Gray, the so-called "antithesis of controversy," to joust with the likes of such high-powered television hosts as the late Barbara Frum.[146]

When Jean Chrétien called a federal election for November 27, 2000, most people felt that he was "throwing the dice." However, contrary to expectations, the Liberals won big, easily retaining their parliamentary majority in the House. Even though the NDP's Joe Comartin had defeated the Liberal incumbent Rick Limoges in Windsor's Lake St Clair riding, Herb Gray chalked up a total of 20,729 votes in this his thirteenth consecutive election victory. His Canadian Alliance opponent Jeff Watson obtained 8,777 votes, the NDP's John McGinlay received 6,080 votes, and the Progressive Conservatives' Ian West got 2,116 votes.[147]

Herb Gray was not surprised when he was informed that he would have to undergo surgery to replace a leaky heart valve in late summer of 2001. He had been aware of this condition for some years. Fortunately, he recovered quickly from the ordeal and soon was ready to resume his duties,[148] including sitting on the special Cabinet committee that dealt with post–September 11 security issues.

But he was truly surprised by the event that occurred in January of the following year. Summoned to the prime minister's residence at 24 Sussex Drive one hour after his return from a trip to Israel and Jordan, he was told by Jean Chrétien that he forthwith would be relieved of his duties

as deputy prime minister. Even though he had expected a Cabinet shuffle following Industry Minister Brian Tobin's unexpected resignation, he certainly was not prepared for its outcome. He expected to remain in his post at least until after the fortieth anniversary of his first election as a member of Parliament. Gray said, "My objective was always not to set a record for length of service but for the quality of service."[149] He further said,

> As Deputy Prime Minister, among my responsibilities was the creation from scratch, of two special federal departments. One was a department to carry out the federal government's program to mark the new millennium, the Year 2000 and this was done at the request of the Prime Minister. The special department set up was the Millennium Bureau of Canada, which provided partial funding for over 1,700 projects across Canada, big and small. The Prime Minister also asked me to try and bring about a solution to the issues of thousands of claims filed in courts across Canada by former students of the now closed, Indian residential schools.[150]

Herb Gray set up a special, small department to coordinate a strategy and negotiations for this purpose.

Unfailingly loyal and discreet to the end, Herb Gray never discussed the conversations he had had with the prime minister. But many of his supporters were furious with Chrétien for treating Gray in such an insensitive and shabby manner. In an attempt to make good on what appeared to have been a slight toward a dedicated public servant, the prime minister asked the governor general to bestow upon him the title of "The Right Honourable." This is a distinction normally held by sitting and former prime ministers, sitting and former chief justices, and governors general. Herb Gray resigned his House of Commons seat, refusing to accept a Senate appointment or return to the role of backbencher.[151] He opted instead to be the Canadian Chair of the International Joint Commission, an international body dealing with trans-boundary water issues and trans-boundary air and water pollution concerns all along the Canada–US international boundary from one ocean to the other. As a long-time defender of the environment, his views were well known. In fact, he had expressed them in an article published in the *Windsor Star*, in which he praised the work done by ERCA, the Essex Region Conservation Authority, in connection with the Detroit River cleanup, the Trans-Canada Trail, and the Assumption and Centennial Park shoreline improvements in Windsor. Committed as ever to saving the environment, he now looked forward to doing the job with the help of expert staffs in Ottawa, Washington, and Windsor as well as hundreds of experts appointed to more than nineteen IJC boards and task forces.[152]

Herb Gray's past performance as a member of Parliament had been exemplary. He set a record by winning thirteen consecutive elections.[153] He also set a longevity record of 14,389 consecutive days of service in the House of Commons, beating by one day the record held by John Diefenbaker. Gray also became the third-longest serving MP ever, Wilfred Laurier having served from January 22, 1874, to February 9, 1919, — forty-five years — although his service was broken between October 8, 1877, and November 28, 1877, and between July 11, 1896, and July 30, 1896. And then there was Graham Haggart, the Tory minister for railways and canals — predecessor of the minister of transport — who served from October 12, 1872, to March 13, 1913.[154]

When Herb Gray's tour as MP and Cabinet minister came to an end on January 15, 2002, it was brought home to the people of Windsor and Canada what they had lost. Having served their community for many years, his untiring devotion had been immeasurable, especially his contribution in the case of Chrysler Canada. Not only had he been instrumental in averting the company's bankruptcy in 1980, thereby saving more than 10,000 jobs, but indirectly he also had helped its parent company qualify for US government assistance. As the MP for the riding of Windsor West, he had stayed close to his constituents at all times, yet he never failed to make himself available to the countless other citizens of Windsor and Canada who regularly streamed to his office to ask for his help.

Over the years, Herb Gray did receive recognition for his efforts. When he was named the honoree for the Jewish National Fund's 1980 Negev Testimonial Dinner, 340 members of Windsor's Jewish community gathered on July 23, 1980, at Shaar Hashomayim Synagogue to pay tribute to their favourite son. Former Windsor MP Paul Martin Senior was the keynote speaker on that occasion and, when he mounted the rostrum to deliver his address, he told the people of Windsor that they were "honouring a resolute, dedicated, sincere young man," who had emerged into the top ranks of Canadian statesmanship.[155] In a telegram read during the event, then Prime Minister Trudeau called Herb Gray a man who had "no peers as a defender of human rights," praising him for his "hard work and high principles."

On December 2, 1998, he received B'nai B'rith Canada's 1998 Award of Merit at a gala event where he was feted as a "Man of Integrity."[156] In 2001 he was the dinner honoree in Ottawa; in 1998 he was the Israel Bonds Dinner honoree in Ottawa; and the Ottawa Branch of the Magen David Adom (Israel Red Cross) of Israel placed his name on one of its ambulances. He received an honorary doctorate from the University of Windsor in 1983. In 1987 there was a dinner in Windsor attended by some 1,200 people to mark his thirtieth year in the House of Commons. At this time he was presented with a sitting with the world-famous portrait photographer Josef Karsh of Ottawa. The resulting photograph is displayed on the wall of the government lobby in Ottawa between the photographs of John Turner and Jean Chretien because he, like them, served as leader of the Opposition in the House of Commons, although unlike them he did not go on to be prime minister. He was the 1998 honoree of the Commonwealth Jewish Council. He received a special award from the Canada Israel Committee at the 2002 Parliamentary dinner attended by 1,500 people, including the president of Israel and Prime Minister Chretien. McGill University bestowed an Honorary Doctorate of Laws on June 13, 2003.[157] It should be noted that earlier in the spring of 2003 he received an honorary doctorate from Assumption University of Windsor and an honorary doctorate from the Catholic University of Lublin in Poland.

An era came to an end on May 13, 2002, when the voters of Windsor West went to the polls to elect a successor to the seat left vacant by Herb Gray. Rather than electing Richard Pollock, another Liberal, they chose the NDP candidate Brian Masse. Capturing 40 percent of the vote compared to Pollock's 35 percent, the philosophy of this former city councillor was more likely in line with that of the majority of people living in Windsor West, often described as the riding of the "lunch bucket crowd."

So why had they stuck with Herb Gray for almost forty years? Having polled more than 54 percent of the vote in the 2000 general election, more than 30 points above his closest rival, he not only had been their senior voice around the cabinet table, but also their popular local hero who, they felt, had been poorly treated by Jean Chrétien when he forced him to relinquish his post as deputy prime minister only a few months shy of his fortieth anniversary in Parliament. During his almost forty years as a member of Parliament, Herb Gray indeed has made Canadian history. He was the first Jew to receive a Cabinet appointment, the first to be appointed as deputy prime minister and the first person to hold that position on a full-time basis. On May 8, 2003, the Canadian government bestowed the honour of Companion of the Order of Canada in recognition of Herb Gray's illustrious political career, an honour that is restricted to 165 living Canadians. Gray said, "I am continuing in a different form of full-time public service as Canadian Chair of the International Joint Commission."[158]

The City of Windsor, Canada as a whole, and the Jews of Windsor are truly blessed that a man of his calibre had decided to devote most of his professional life to serving the people.

PART IV

Chapter 12
The Bicentennial of Windsor Jewish Life

Windsor in the 1980s

The city stood at a crossroads in the 1980s, which began with Chrysler's near bankruptcy and ended with the production of the minivan, one of the most successful vehicles in automotive history. Only a nearly superhuman effort on the part of Herb Gray, Lee Iaccoca, the unions, and governments at several levels had saved Chrysler and ended the economic pall that had descended upon all sectors of the community. As Windsor's centennial approached in 1992, it seemed a time for taking stock, for peering into the future. There was much that had not changed over the past century. Windsor remained a blue-collar, working-class city highly dependent upon the auto industry and its accompanying suppliers. It had always been subject to boom-and-bust cycles, cyclical layoffs and unemployment; now, in the 1980s, the forces of global trade were buffeting its traditional industrial base. Trade negotiations with the United States in the 1980s and 1990s began with the elimination of tariffs on primary and manufactured goods and gave way to an unrestricted continentalism symbolized by the North American Free Trade Agreement (NAFTA). At the same time, organized labour was following a path toward economic nationalism by seceding from the international UAW in 1984 and forming the Canadian Auto Workers (CAW). Intent on diversifying and expanding into a national leadership role, the CAW attracted a number of non-automotive unions and succeeded locally in organizing the Casino Windsor work force. Ironically, a leading economist argued for closer integration and claimed that Ontario was becoming the fifty-first state with its cross-border trade to the United States totaling 80 percent of its exports. An auto industry bolstered by "just in time" inventory techniques and "open trade" corridors seemed to rejuvenate the historic Michigan/Ontario claim to world auto dominance.

Given the new realities of trade, maintaining an open border crossing was more crucial than ever. The city took over ownership of its half of the Detroit-Windsor Auto Tunnel following the expiration of a sixty-year agreement with its builders. The tunnel not only generated significant revenues for the city, but also gave municipal leaders an opportunity to play a more significant role in the border-crossing debates that followed. The privately owned Ambassador Bridge was reaching capacity and there was discussion about the need for another bridge. Crossing an international boundary connecting two federally organized nations by tunnel or bridge would require consultation with at least half a dozen governments and numerous agencies, not to mention the citizenry on both sides. An agreement between the Canadian National and the Canadian Pacific Railways to share the rail tunnel beneath the Detroit River allowed significant consolidation of their trackage, resulting in surplus rail properties becoming available for municipal purposes. The uninterrupted riverfront dream would finally become a reality.[1]

In the new decade, Windsor Jews continued to be plagued by such problems as an aging population and a diminishing birth rate. Consequently, they really had to ask themselves, "Will there even be a Jewish community in the next century?" Joseph Eisenberg already had explored the subject in the late 1970s, when he told the annual meeting of Windsor's Jewish Community Council, "It was *hemshech* — survival and continuity — that brought you together. It is now time to consider the old Jewish dictum '*hashomer achi anochi*' — 'Am I my brother's keeper?'"[2]

Community Fundraising

Faced with a declining population, Windsor's Jewish community leaders had to find new ways of raising funds to pay for their ambitious social programs. For many years, Congregation Beth El did so by sponsoring raffles and its Monte Carlo nights. And Shaar Hashomayim had raised money through contributions to its Sigal Tree of Life that stood in the synagogue's Charles Zalev Social Hall and through donations to the memorial boards hanging on its sanctuary wall.[3]

Although these events had been successful in the past, by the 1980s they no longer attracted sufficient numbers of people to make them worthwhile. That was why both congregations welcomed bingo as a viable fundraising option,

that popular game of chance introduced to Windsor by Shaar Hashomayim member C. Herbert Pasikov. Starting in 1979, he acted as the liaison between the bingo owners and the various Jewish organizations, as well as between the different charities and the City of Windsor. When he had to resign for health reasons, Barbara Shanbaum carried on this important work for him.

Congregation Beth El sponsored its first bingo night in June 1980. Held at a local community bingo hall with Morton Kaplan handling every facet of the event, it attracted all the Jewish organizations in the Windsor area.[4] Shaar Hashomayim did not sponsor any bingo games on the Sabbath or during Jewish holidays, but its members actively supported them on the days that did not coincide with religious observances. Since they raised hundreds of thousands of dollars for Windsor's Jewish causes, it is fair to say that without the income derived from them, many communal projects could not have succeeded.

Thanks to the efforts of a devoted group of volunteers, the Jewish National Fund's Negev Dinners also brought in substantial amounts of money and, next to the United Jewish Appeal, became the second biggest fundraiser for Windsor's Jewish community. In 1980, the honoree was the Right Honourable Herb Gray, Windsor's own native son; in the following year, JNF paid tribute to Albert Weeks, mayor of the City of Windsor. In 1982, Molly Cohen, Helen Glaser, and Malka Yuzpe — three women who had each worked tirelessly for their community — shared the honours. On June 22, 1983, Joseph Eisenberg was rewarded for his many years of service, while Morris Brodsky's accomplishments in the field of education were acknowledged in 1984. As a past president of the Jewish National Fund of Windsor and an active member of its Jewish and non-Jewish communities, I had the privilege of being named the Negev Dinner's honoree in 1985. Melvin Sorffer, a past president of Windsor's JNF as well as a past president of its Jewish Community Council, followed in 1986. The next year, the honour went to Leona Schott, a past president of the Windsor Jewish Community Council, in recognition of her many years of Friendship Club leadership. Gerald Freed was the deserving JNF recipient in 1988 and, as the decade drew to a close, the honour went to Dr. Ronald Ianni, president of the University of Windsor. Tributes were also paid to Herbert Brudner, another past president of the Windsor Jewish Community Council, in 1990, to the dedicated community fundraiser C. Herbert Pasikov in 1991, and to former Windsor Mayor John Millson in 1992.

Chabad House Seeks a Windsor Presence

At the beginning of the 1980s, the prospect of opening another religious school in Windsor seemed dim, to say the least. However, representatives of the Lubavitch Movement were anxious to open a facility in Windsor. Members of this ultra-Orthodox Jewish sect go to various places to establish religious schools known as Chabad Houses — Chabad being an acronym of the Hebrew words for wisdom, intelligence, and knowledge. In January 1980, they succeeded in establishing a Chabad House kindergarten in Windsor and, as financial support was coming from the organization's Detroit branch, tuition fees were either minimal or children could attend free of charge. For a short time, it occupied the vacant I. L. Peretz Shule premises. But when they no longer were available, Rabbi Joseph Hecht, the school's principal, requested that the Jewish Community Centre's facilities be made available to him.[5]

At the beginning of 1981, Rabbi Hecht and his wife organized a community-wide Melaveh Malkah feast to further promote the school. Beth El's Arthur Barat acted as the chairman for this party that celebrates the end of Shabbat. It included an audio-visual presentation about the history and development of the Chabad–Lubavitch Movement, as well as a talk given by David Lieberman, the chief rabbi–designate of Antwerp in Belgium, who outlined the importance of its youth program for Windsor. In the following year, another program, chaired by Dr. Abraham Teich, featured Dr. Yitzchak (Irving) Block as the guest speaker. Addressing more than 150 people, this professor of philosophy at London's University of Western Ontario described in glowing terms the good works the Lubavitchers were doing.[6]

Plans for a musical program at Windsor's Cleary Auditorium, as well as other ambitious events had to be abandoned when Chabad House devotees were unable to attract a sufficient number of students to make their movement's presence in the city worthwhile.[7] The failure to successfully establish the Chabad House school after all of the efforts from outside money, support, key speakers, and events highlighted the reality of economic conditions at a time of declining birth rate and foreshadowed the looming fate of Jewish education at Shaar Hashomayim and Beth El.

A New Rabbi for Shaar Hashomayim

Following Rabbi Benjamin Z. Holczer's departure from Windsor in September 1980, Rabbi Ira Samuel Grussgott became Shaar Hashomayim's new spiritual leader.[8] Born and bred in Brooklyn, New York, he had received his basic Jewish education at Yeshiva Torah Voda'ath and at the Rabbinical Academy Mesivta Rabbi Chaim Berlin. After graduating from Brooklyn College and Yeshiva University in New York City, he attained his s'micha (ordination), a post-graduate degree in Jewish philosophy, and the university's Cantorial Arts Certificate that focuses on the professional skills and knowledge needed to lead Jewish prayer services.

Right from the start, Rabbi Grussgott established a good relationship with the members of Congregation Beth El. During the time their building was undergoing renovations, he went so far as to offer to them the Shaar Hashomayim sanctuary for the b'nai mitzvah of three young Beth El members — for Matthew Ordower, scheduled for September 5, 1981; for Adam Mock, scheduled for September 26, 1981; and for Marc Ordower, scheduled for December 19, 1981. These three celebrations were allowed to proceed following the synagogue's regular Shabbat morning services.[9] By sanctioning them, Shaar Hashomayim's board of directors had, for the first time, shown a willingness to promote better understanding between the two congregations.[10]

There is no doubt that Rabbi Grussgott had a more for-ward-looking Orthodox approach than his predecessor, as well as a genuine interest in bringing the community together. Yet, he was censured by his board of directors for not advising the synagogue's president or its executive before approving another bar mitzvah that was to take place, partly at Beth El and partly at Shaar Hashomayim with Beth El being in charge of the student's training.[11]

Here is Rabbi Grussgott's own assessment of his tenure at Shaar Hashomayim:

> I came to the Shaar with an agenda and an approach that was very different from that of my predecessor because I am more part of what I call "open Orthodoxy." That means maintaining the respect and rever-ence I have for tradition and Jewish law while, at the same time, being very open and sensitive to the world around me.
>
> The idea was for the Shaar not to be an entity unto itself but a unified and co-oper-ative community, notwithstanding the struggle it had to maintain its uniqueness. In other words, there was more to be gained from working together with others rather than zealously guarding turf and territory. I also felt appreciative of Rabbi Plaut's reach-ing out to me as a colleague and friend, as well as guiding and enlightening me on the dynamics of the community. I did not hide our association, even though there were people who felt that I was too open in my personal relationship with him and wanted me to be more reticent and on guard.
>
> The members of the Shaar were mavens who knew how to daven, they understood their traditions and respected the rabbi's role as preacher, teacher, pastor and coun-sellor. On a spiritual level, I connected to the European and Yiddish-speaking mem-bers of that community, as they provided me with a sense of my own childhood upbringing and background.[12]

In Alan Abram's book *Why Windsor?* Rabbi Grussgott expressed his thoughts about Windsor's Jewish community in general:

> I am an American — I was born in Brooklyn — [and I] am impressed with the fact that Canadian Jewry, in general, is a good twenty years behind the United States. And I mean that in a very positive sense.… I feel and I have been told this as well that the Canadian synagogue can offer the rabbi a congregation that is a bit more traditional or at least more loyal to tradi-tion than its American counterpart.
>
> You have a Jewish community that still respects its traditions, that is closer in a way to the immigrant experience.… The community, in general, still has a respect-ful attitude toward the rabbi and what his position is. And a rabbi can have great impact within the community.
>
> Another thing that has impressed me is that Windsor Jews still maintain that old pioneer spirit about making it on their own terms. It is a lesson even the Israelis can learn from Windsorites.
>
> This is a community proud of its her-itage, a little worried about its future, but trying to do what has to be done to see that it remains a viable part of the general community.[13]

Rabbi Grussgott's most cordial relationship with Congregation Beth El did compromise his relationship with his congregation, but it helped open the way for future co-operation between the two synagogues.

Congregation Beth El's Expansion Project

In the early 1980s, Congregation Beth El was a thriving institution that needed more space to accommodate and serve its growing membership. At that time, plans to expand were facing a number of obstacles, primarily the effects of exceedingly high interest rates and the possible bankruptcy of Chrysler Canada, one of the region's main employers.

Yet the campaign to raise funds for the expansion seemed to be moving along quite well, thanks to the generosity of some Beth El members and despite the fact that the land expropriation issue was still unresolved.[14] As early as February 1979, Leon Paroian, the lawyer retained to deal with the expropriation, had suggested that the best course of action was to hire experts to investigate the excessive noise levels the E. C. Row Expressway would create once it was built. He also had felt that the expropriation of the congregation's property would entitle its members to claim damages as high as $100,000.[15]

Two years later, a meeting was held in Beth El's social hall to further initiate negotiations. I was present to speak for the congregation, along with Leon Paroian, Arthur B. Weingarden, and Fred Katzman, while those representing the Province of Ontario included its adjudicator, Richard Walker, and a team of sound attenuation experts from Toronto. The following is my memory of what transpired at that meeting:

> We were seated around a long table with Mr. Walker at the head when the sound attenuation experts began their pitch trying to convince him that the noises expected to come from the new highway would not be an impediment to worship during synagogue services.
>
> Mr. Paroian, who sat next to Mr. Walker, then drew our attention to the rumbling sounds made by the trucks driving along the nearby Third Concession Road. He proceeded to make it clear to us,

with a great deal of passion in his voice, that the noise levels would be even higher once the expressway was built, especially, as the new road would run even closer to the synagogue building.

> After adjourning for a short break, the meeting reconvened, only this time Mr. Paroian sat down at the other end of the table, across from Mr. Walker and several feet away from him. Trucks kept rolling by, only now Mr. Paroian spoke in a barely audible voice. All of us, therefore, had to strain to hear what he was saying, especially, Mr. Walker who, visibly annoyed, criticized the lawyer for what he called "game playing."
>
> Ultimately, however, Mr. Walker had to admit that there was, indeed a severe noise problem in the room, one that likely could adversely affect the quality of synagogue worship.[16]

In view of the encumbrances Beth El's physical location might impose on any new structure, a Building Planning Committee was appointed to study various design options. Chaired by Paula Taub, it consisted of Nancy Barat, Betty Pazner, Dr. Michael Malowitz, Bernard Rosenblum, and Lawrence Greene, with Arthur B. Weingarden, Fred Katzman, and I also attending the committee meetings on a regular basis.

The members of the building planning committee travelled to various locations to obtain information about different synagogue designs. They visited Ann Arbor, Pontiac, and Saginaw in Michigan, as well as New York City, where they viewed numerous slides of houses of worship, sanctuaries, and Holy Ark areas at the office of the Union of American Hebrew Congregations. They brought back fifty slides for Architect John Hreno's perusal and he, in turn, produced a number of sketches for the sanctuary. The designs for the *bimah* and the Holy Ark area, however, were entrusted to the New York firm of Albert Wood and Five Sons.[17]

Negotiations with the Province of Ontario regarding the monetary settlement for the expropriated land dragged on until February 1981, when Leon Paroian, Arthur B. Weingarden, Fred Katzman, and Hilary Payne — the latter representing the City of Windsor — met in Toronto with the Ontario deputy minister of transportation and communications. This is how Fred Katzman remembered the meeting:

When the Minister made what he called "a first, last and non-negotiable offer of $53,000," having taken into account the $19,200 we already had received, my heart went quickly and directly down to my stomach as the continuation and completion of the project seemed in serious jeopardy. This was not the level of relief we had been looking for.

Fortunately, that offer was not the Minister's final one because, about two hours later, it had risen to $82,000. At that point in time, Leon Paroian said that he wanted to "caucus" with Arthur [Weingarden] and me. To allow us to do so we were provided with our own private meeting room down the hall — the men's room!

One hour after resuming our meeting with the Minister, he agreed to pay $146,000. Once again, the three of us asked for permission to retire to our "chambers" to consider his offer. We emerged half an hour later, having decided to reject it. Even after the Minister had upped the ante to $157,000 our answer was still no. But upon hearing $170,000, Leon indicated to us that we probably had gotten the Province to move as far as it was going to move and that we had all the financial relief we were going to get.[18]

These unusual proceedings had lasted more than three hours. Taking a cursory backward look at them, what stuck in Fred Katzman's memory more than anything else "was the incongruous picture of Arthur, Leon, and I deliberating the congregation's future while caucusing in the men's room, lined up at the three urinals."[19]

Beth El's board of directors accepted the Ministry's $170,000 offer on February 17, 1981.[20] About two weeks later, Arthur B. Weingarden advised the building planning committee that to complete the expansion project would cost $800,000, adding, much to the delight of the Beth El membership, "Coincidentally, we have that amount of money."[21] The building expansion finance committee approved John Hreno's drawings, authorizing him to proceed with the project's specifications[22] and the building contract, totalling $422,700, was awarded to Metro Century.[23] The Glenwood Avenue house, purchased in 1979, was sold and eventually moved off the property.[24]

The groundbreaking ceremony for the new Beth El building, organized by Betty Pazner and her sister Ann Cohen, with help from Shirley Shanbon, took place on June 14, 1981. It began at 4:30 in the afternoon and, as the first sod was being turned, all the invited dignitaries extended their good wishes to the congregation. Among them were Lottie Bernholtz, president of the Windsor Jewish Community Council, Congregation Shaar Hashomayim's Rabbi Ira Grussgott, Joseph Eisenberg, John Hreno, Leon Paroian, and David Glaser, president of Congregation Shaarey Zedek.[25] A cocktail party, a dinner, and a meeting concluded the day's events.

Elaborate plans were drawn up for the laying of the cornerstone on Sunday, September 20, 1981. According to Betty Pazner, the ceremony included removing from the old cornerstone a cylinder "containing an old picture of the 1st Temple and a parchment, written by Arthur Weingarden Sr., listing all the charter members."[26] Mr. Weingarden, who also had written the names of current Beth El members on parchment, then read that list as well as the earlier one. Both lists then were placed into the cylinder of the new cornerstone, together with the front

The laying of the cornerstone of Congregation Beth El on September 20, 1981. Left to right are William Tepperman, me, Paula Taub, Arthur B. Weingarden, Fred P. Katzman, and Scott Katzman.

page of the previous day's *Windsor Star* announcing the cornerstone laying.[27]

Congregation Beth El conducted its 1981 High Holiday services at the Jewish Community Centre, in anticipation of the dedication of its new building that was to take place on February 4, 1982, during a special Friday evening service. The special service began with the solemn act of carrying the Torahs into the new sanctuary and placing them in the Holy Ark. Participating in the ceremony were Beth El's past presidents; members of the building expansion committee; senior rabbi of Temple Beth El in Detroit, Dr. Richard C. Hertz; and senior rabbi of Holy Blossom Temple in Toronto, Dr. W. Gunther Plaut, who had attended Beth El's first dedication service in 1962. A gala dinner dance, featuring Rabbi Sherwin T. Wine as the guest speaker, was held in the synagogue's new social hall on the following evening.[28]

The Pillette Road Cemetery

The separation of the two congregations' cemeteries into individual units was complete once Shaar Hashomayim had met the Ontario government's perpetual-care requirements and the City of Windsor had approved the rezoning of Beth El's land.[29] The only matter still to be settled was an agreement between the two congregations on a unified pricing structure for their individual burial grounds.[30]

On October 4, 1981, after a fourteen-year struggle, Congregation Beth El finally dedicated its own cemetery in a ceremony attended by between forty-five and fifty people. Arthur Barat had already begun implementing his beautification plans, aided by Earl Burstyn, who had donated the shrubs and provided the services of a gardener to plant them.[31]

In the summer of 1983, Shaar Hashomayim received a gift from the estate of the late Abie Philipps to be used to construct at the "most northern part of the cemetery" a new building that was to have four functions — a chapel, living quarters for the caretaker, a storage place for equipment, and public washrooms.[32] While a building was never constructed, the bequest was used to pay for digging the foundation for a house to be moved onto the property.[33] It would be November 1989, nearly the end of the decade before the Abie and Millie Philipps Cemetery Chapel was completed and ready for occupancy.[34]

The I. L. Peretz House

After the I. L. Peretz Shule had closed and transferred its property to the new I. L. Peretz Property Development Corporation, planning began for a Jewish seniors' residence to be built next door to the Jewish Community Centre. Many years earlier, Michael Sumner had spoken about the need for such a facility, and Joseph Eisenberg had predicted that its presence in Windsor would establish the city as a leader in the field of gerontology.[35]

The I. L. Peretz property development committee set up a board that could submit decisions for approval to the Windsor Jewish Community Council.[36] As a result, "all systems were go" early in 1981 for a housing complex be known as the I. L. Peretz House.[37] In addition, plans were underway to connect the building with the Jewish Community Centre to provide an "organic flow of both people and programs between the two."[38]

How to finance this apartment house project created a serious dilemma for the Council's board of directors. Mortgaging "the entire properties of the Peretz Senior Citizens Corporation and the Windsor Jewish Communal Projects" would have been the obvious solution,[39] but having to pay the current high interest rates of almost 22 percent per annum would have resulted in a $1 million overrun. The alternative, cancelling the project altogether, would have meant losing the Province of Ontario's one-time offer of financial assistance.[40]

As everyone had agreed that the facility was needed and that the opportunity to build it must not be missed, it was Eli Goldin who broke the impasse at the Jewish Community Council's July 1981 meeting. He had been Council president during the planning stage of the Jewish Community Centre in 1957 and compared the current undertaking with that situation — in which the Centre's fate had similarly hung in the balance — and urged action. But it was Morris Tabachnick, the prominent and generous contributor to various community projects who ended the debate by proposing a campaign to raise the necessary funds to build the I. L. Peretz House. His motion received unanimous approval.[41]

In that context, Ted Hochberg drew attention to the Jewish Community Centre and the need to refurbish it to make it more attractive to young people. By suggesting that money be spent on enclosing its swimming pool and renovating its health club he had, in effect, moved "that consideration be given to the running of a combined campaign that would include alterations to the Community Centre building," as well as to the construction of the new residence for seniors.[42] Significantly, that motion also passed.

The Windsor Jewish Community Council's board of directors would have had difficulties financing the project had it not been able to obtain an acceptable mortgage from Central Mortgage and Housing Corporation. Under its terms, CMHC was willing to write down the 22 percent interest rate to 2 percent, offering a thirty-year mortgage renewable every five years. Under these conditions, the Council decided to build the maximum number of units CMHC was willing to underwrite, even though it knew that that number exceeded the Jewish community's requirements. As a result of that move, the I. L. Peretz House became a residence for both Jewish and non-Jewish seniors.

Since the CMHC mortgage only covered the cost of constructing the new building, the purpose of the fundraising campaign proposed by Mr. Tabachnick was to have enough money on hand to provide for kitchen and dining room facilities, as well as for other amenities that would enhance the structure's interior. Concerns about a shortfall were somewhat allayed in September 1981, when Gerald Freed, chairman of the I. L. Peretz building committee, announced that the proceeds from the 1979 sale of the Tifereth Israel property had yielded $15,000 and that nine other pledges, totalling $265,000, had been received.[43]

With economic conditions still uncertain during the early 1980s, even the United Jewish Appeal's campaigns were affected. Since no one was willing to accept the chairmanship — not wishing to be identified with failure — I was appointed chairman of both the 1982 and the 1983 UJA campaigns, a position no Windsor rabbi had ever held.[44]

The groundbreaking ceremony for the new seniors' residence took place on Sunday, November 8, 1981, with Morris Brodsky, co-chair of the I. L. Peretz Senior Citizens Corporation, presiding.[45] But to complete the project, Harold Taub, the newly appointed co-ordinator of the I. L. Peretz property development committee had to face many new challenges.[46] The first thing he did was to form several committees, among them the building committee, chaired by Harriet Whiteman and including Louis Bluestone, David Glanz, Melvin Sorffer, Paula Taub, and Milton Whiteman. Apart from setting operations guidelines that would take effect once the building was completed, the committee's task was to supervise construction and furnish the interior.[47] There also was a management committee headed by Peter Miller; a finance committee under Fred Katzman; a fundraising committee chaired by Jerry Alexis; and a public relations committee led by me. Gerald Freed was chairman of the I. L. Peretz building committee as well as chairman of the I. L. Peretz Senior Citizens Corporation, and Morris Brodsky was his co-chair.[48]

One problem that remained to be solved was to investigate the liens some of the subcontractors had placed on the building while it was under construction. It so happened that the I. L. Peretz House could not have been officially turned over to the Jewish community until these liens were removed.[49] There were concerns relating to achieving full occupancy of the apartments and fully financing the project.[50] Those eligible to reside at the I. L. Peretz House were single individuals and couples, provided that one of the partners was at least 60 years of age, or 50 if disabled.[51] To ensure adequate occupancy once the building was completed, deposits from these prospective tenants were being accepted during construction.[52]

The facility was designed to have thirty 2-bedroom units and two deluxe 2-bedroom suites, forty 1-bedroom units and one deluxe 1-bedroom suite. Each apartment was to have a living room with a dining area and a balcony. Both the 1- and 2-bedroom units would have ample closet space, one-and-a-half bathrooms, a kitchen, and a large storage room. All the apartments were equipped with emergency call buttons and provided space for the tenants' own air conditioners. To encourage social interaction, there were common lounge areas, a chapel with a Holy Ark and three Torah scrolls that had come from Tifereth Israel.[53] Since the Jewish Community Centre was easily accessible to all I. L. Peretz House residents, there was an opportunity for them to become involved in its activities and participate, together with their children and grandchildren, in such Jewish holiday celebrations as Purim, Passover, Sukkoth, and Chanukkah.[54]

The new Peretz House, a senior citizens facility and the Windsor Jewish Federation.

Even though the first tenants were able to move into the I. L. Peretz House in December 1982, the Open House was not held until January 23, 1983. Some two hundred people came to watch Morris Brodsky, Rabbi Samuel Stollman, Rabbi Ira Grussgott, and me affix *mezuzot* to the doorpost of each entrance. William Silver, president of the Windsor Jewish Community Council, acted as the master of ceremonies while Harold Taub, first vice president and co-ordinator of the I. L. Peretz House, delivered a progress report on the project.[55]

The dedication of the I. L. Peretz House took place on Sunday, December 4, 1983, with Morris Brodsky chairing the event that drew two hundred guests, including member of Parliament Herb Gray, other federal and provincial representatives, rabbis, and representatives from Canada Mortgage and Housing Corporation. Apart from hearing speeches and numerous congratulatory expressions, those present also witnessed the highlight of the ceremony — the placing of the Tifereth Israel Torah scrolls into the chapel's Holy Ark.[56]

To acknowledge the Tabachnick Foundation's generous contribution of an additional $150,000 that had been used to furnish the dining room and the kitchen, it was decided to officially name the new senior residence the Freda and Morris Tabachnick I. L. Peretz House.[57] Inside the building

there also is a plaque that lists the names of the original I. L. Peretz Shule founders alphabetically: Zundel Bogin, Louis Bookman, Morris Brodsky, Joseph F. Cohen, Harry Forman, Jane Freed, Sam Freed, Barash Glaser, Eli Glaser, Isaac Goldman, Chaim Gordner, Harry Gray, Sam Kaner, Ann Katzman, Hessie Katzman, Barney Madoff, Max Madoff, Rubin Madoff, Sarah Madoff, Max Parnes, Oscar Posen, Harry Rubin, Joe Soble, Morris Tabachnick, and Sam Winograd.

In September 1981, the Windsor Jewish Community Council hired Sandra Malowitz to conduct a survey to determine why Jewish seniors might want to live in a residence like I. L. Peretz House and to encourage potential residents to move there once the building was completed. With a Master's degree in social work, she was well qualified to supervise the team of volunteers who had been recruited to conduct the interviews. Ms. Malowitz has remained on staff at the Centre ever since the successful completion of the project and over a tenure of more than twenty-five years has been involved with setting new policies and practical guidelines for the I. L. Peretz House, along with assuming many other duties, especially during interim periods when there was no executive director.[58]

By June 1984, the Freda and Morris Tabachnick I. L. Peretz House was fully occupied. Two years later, it was reportedly "in the black" with a long waiting list for its apartments.[59]

Soviet Immigration

In the late 1970s, the tide temporarily had turned in favour of Soviet Jews wishing to immigrate to other countries. In response to an initiative by Sidney Katzman, more than fifty families came to Windsor. As the president of Zalev Brothers, Sid Katzman had sent someone to Soviet Russia to recruit engineers that he needed to make steel pellets for his scrap-metal operation. In 1982, he "learned of the Hebrew Immigrant Aid Society, which brought Russian Jews out of the former Soviet Union and moved them to temporary holding camps in Rome."[60] According to Herb Brudner, "not only could Katzman bring in these people but he also received funding from the Canadian government."[61] A *Bulletin* article written by Windsor Community Council President Bernard Putterman clearly shows how warmly Windsor's Jewish population had received them, as well as other Russian immigrants:

> We bid our new arrivals welcome to our community, each and everyone, individually and collectively. We rejoice with them in their newfound freedom to be what they want to be, to practice that which they want to practice and to live in dignity and equality in this free and great country.
>
> This community has always extended a helping hand whenever and wherever needed. We will continue to do so in the future. Let us take the opportunity to get to know each other, to work together, to make this, our community, a better place to live both for ourselves and our children.[62]

Although many of the Russian immigrants only stayed in Windsor briefly before moving to other parts of Canada, those who remained received assistance in finding employment and becoming acclimatized not only to life in Canada, but also to Jewish life.[63] One of the volunteers involved in this process was Jacob Rosenthal, who received the Jewish Immigrant Aid Society's (JIAS) Award in recognition of his efforts.[64]

To help educate the children of these new Russian immigrants, Morris Brodsky, as chairman of the Jewish education committee, proposed that $15,000 be set aside to allow them to attend a day school in Detroit.[65] Of course, it took some time to obtain the proper papers to permit them to enter the United States, just as raising the funds to pay for their transportation proved somewhat problematic. However, thanks to a letter-writing campaign to prospective donors, enough money was raised for nine Russian immigrant children to attend Detroit's Yeshiva Beth Yehuda,[66] with the stipulation that the transportation subvention for the 1981–82 school year not exceed $10,000.[67] When it ended, Shaar Hashomayim asked that the Windsor Jewish Community Council help defray the cost of the $3,425 needed to pay for the teacher. Having agreed to pay half that amount, the money ultimately came out of the JIAS Jewish Education Fund.[68]

On May 1, 1983, seven Jewish couples — all recent arrivals from the Soviet Union — were married at the Shaar Hashomayim Synagogue. Sid Katzman was instrumental in co-ordinating this wedding ceremony.[69] The wedding service was led by Rabbi Ira Samuel Grussgott with my participation, and the reception that followed attracted some 350 people.[70]

There is no doubt that coming together to rejoice with the seven couples had given Windsor's Jewish community a great deal of satisfaction. They had, after all, formally accepted Judaism as their faith and had been married in accordance with Jewish law. Stressing the emotional aspects of the event, the *Bulletin* reminded its readers that "the denial of spiritual freedom in the Soviet Union [that] prohibits religious education, discourages religious faith, and conducts massive anti-religious propaganda [had made] any religious practice impossible."[71]

To further assist Russian immigrants, Windsor's Jewish community had received a $5,000 federal grant from ISAP — the Immigration Settlement and Adaptation Program.[72] In 1991, Windsor's Jewish community approached the Honourable Barbara McDougall, then minister of employment and immigration, asking her to expedite the immigration to Canada of Jews from the Soviet Union and from other Eastern Bloc countries, "so that they may be reunited with family members already living in Canada."[73] Bringing these newcomers to Windsor would also augment a Jewish population that had drastically declined in recent years.

Whenever Jews are in peril, Jewish communities everywhere rally in support of their brethren. That was why Jewish federations from across the United States and Canada launched a campaign, known as Operation

Exodus, that would fund the rescue of Jews from the Soviet Union and their settlement in Israel. Some 860,000 Jews had immigrated there since the Soviet Union opened its gates in the early 1980s. And although Operation Exodus raised $1 billion between 1990 and 1997, additional UJA funds were still needed, especially during the 1991 Persian Gulf War when the threat of Iraqi Scud missiles severely crippled Israel's economy.

As in previous years, the Windsor Jewish Community Council, together with other Jewish communities across Canada, had borrowed money to be sent to Israel during times of crisis. In 1992, to protect the United Israel Appeal of Canada, the agency that guaranteed these loans, the Council signed a Loan Indemnification Agreement that stipulated that North American Jewish federations would reimburse Israeli banks for loan defaults beyond the $200 million reserve funded through Operation Exodus. It further stated "the outside exposure for the Windsor Federation, determined by a fair share formula, would be approximately $500,000 to be funded through the regular UJA Campaign."[74] In other words, if there were a default, the money would come from future United Jewish Appeal allocations. To help other Soviet Jews immigrate to Israel, Windsor's Jewish community again signed the loan agreement in 1994.[75]

Tributes, Honours, and Other Celebrations

To acknowledge Reverend Irwin Dubitsky's many years of service to Shaar Hashomayim and to Windsor's Jewish community, the synagogue paid tribute to him over the weekend of May 30–31, 1981.[76] The celebration began with a Shabbat morning service, featuring former Shaar Hashomayim Rabbi Benjamin Groner as guest speaker. It continued that same evening with a testimonial dinner at the synagogue attended by almost four hundred people.[77] The guest list included more than 110 "boys" whom Reverend Dubitsky had prepared for their bar mitzvahs in years gone by. A Sunday brunch concluded the festivities.[78]

Reverend Irwin Dubitsky was born in 1905 in Poland. He attended yeshivot in Eastern Europe, where he also received certificates qualifying him as a *shochet* — a ritual butcher. Arriving in Canada in 1930, he served Jewish communities in Smith Falls, Perth, and Belleville, Ontario before coming to Windsor to take on the task of being Shaar Hashomayim's *baal tefillah*, its leader of prayers. An Orthodox rabbi in his own right, Reverend Dubitsky not only taught the bar mitzvah students, but served briefly as the congregation's spiritual head before Rabbi Stollman's installation. For many decades, he also acted as the Jewish community's *shochet* as well as Shaar Hashomayim's *mashgiach* — supervisor of Jewish dietary laws — making sure that the many dinners served at the synagogue were strictly kosher.[79]

This very knowledgeable man, whose warm personality and devotion had endeared him to everyone in the community, died on March 7, 1983.[80]

On June 22, 1983, the Jewish National Fund paid tribute to Joseph Eisenberg when it named him as that year's Negev Dinner honoree. William Silver acted as the chairman of the event that featured Rabbi Jordan Pearlson of Temple Sinai in Toronto as the keynote speaker. In the course of the evening, Eli Goldin presented Mr. Eisenberg with a JNF citation and Judge Carl Zalev, president of the Jewish National Fund, commended him for his "expert guidance," under which "a sophisticated network of educational, social and recreational programs has been developed." After expressing his admiration for the way Mr. Eisenberg had applied his "vast store of knowledge, administrative skills and deep personal commitment to enhance the quality of life for all of us," he also thanked him for being "the strong catalyst for the yearly campaign to mobilize funds for vital humanitarian causes at home and overseas."[81]

Five months after JNF's tribute to Mr. Eisenberg, Windsor's entire Jewish community turned out to celebrate the twenty-five years of faithful service this man — affectionately known to many as the "King of the Jews" — had given to its members. This "Roast and Toast" took place on November 6, 1983, with Alan Orman acting as the master of ceremonies and Howard Eisenberg, Doris Bakst, Norma Slopen, Edmund Glinert, Harold Taub, William Silver, Martin Wunder, and Rabbi Ira Grussgott actively participating in the roasting. The evening's entertainment also included the Community Centre Theatre Workshop's performance of a medley of songs with special lyrics written by Mikie Freed and Beverley Alexis.[82]

Congregation Beth El celebrated its twenty-fifth anniversary during the weekend of November 9–10, 1984. The event began with a Friday evening service attended by Rabbi Richard C. Hertz and Rabbi W. Gunther Plaut, who both had provided guidance to the fledgling congregation twenty-five years earlier.[83] Another guest at the Saturday night gala dinner dance was Rabbi Sherwin Wine, Beth El's first spiritual leader, who once again delighted his audience with stories about the Temple's early days. In the course of the evening, members of the congregation also paid tribute to their founding president, Arthur B. Weingarden — affectionately known as "Mr. Temple" — thanking him for "his commitment, love and devotion."[84]

A notable UJA gala dinner took place on November 14, 1987, to honour Morris Tabachnick, Charles Zalev, and Eli Goldin — three pillars of Windsor's Jewish community who had not only defended the cause of Israel for many decades, but had also shown great leadership of other humanitarian causes.[85]

Windsor's first B'nai B'rith Recognition Dinner was held at the beginning of 1988 to pay tribute to Maurice J. Closs, president and CEO of Chrysler Canada, for the support he had given to the community.[86]

Windsor Jews in Sports

Almost since their first arrival, Windsor's Jewish youth have participated in sport. Attendance in public schools offered opportunities to participate in organized programs or collegiate sports, and sponsored church or club sports and other forms of amateur athletics existed for those outside of traditional school programs. Over the years, Windsor produced a number of outstanding local athletes — too many to mention here — in part because it was assumed that participation in sports would make the world a better place and that competition would encourage our youth to pursue excellence throughout their lives.

In the twentieth century, as is still true, the Olympics commanded the greatest attention and admiration for amateur athletes who competed as representatives of their nations. In the early 1980s the names of three Jewish athletes were enshrined in the Windsor–Essex County Sports Athletic Hall of Fame: William "Moose" Rogin in 1992, Julius "Goldie" Goldman in 1990, and Irving "Toots" Meretsky in 1996. Though they were honoured for their long, successful, and varied sports careers, it was their participation in the 1936 Berlin Olympics that is most relevant to our chronicle of Windsor's Jewish community. Each of the three had poignant memories about this seminal event in their young lives. The story deserves retelling.

The following is the personal story of William "Moose" Rogin, the six-foot-two-inch basketball star who played for Windsor's Assumption College in the 1930s.

[Assumption College] had nothing to do with present-day Assumption High School or Assumption University. It just happened that I went to Windsor Collegiate and Patterson Collegiate, which was the same school, and then the only post-secondary education place in Windsor was Assumption College, which was run by the Basilian Fathers.

In 1936, I was a student at Assumption College, playing basketball for Coach Reverend W. P. McGee. I was not a member of the team, the Ford V–8s, who had won the Canadian championship. They had defeated us in a five-game series. That was the famous playoff series when the Fords deliberately cut down the size of the Kennedy Collegiate court so that it was the same size as the little Assumption gym. Anyway, the Fords went on to win the Ontario, Eastern Canada, and Canadian championships.

The Windsor Ford V–8s were going to Berlin to represent Canada in basketball in the 1936 Summer Olympic Games. They were given permission to augment their team with five players for the trip to Germany. I could have made the trip if I could have come up with $500 to cover the costs….

Gordon Fuller, one of the three coaches of the team, asked me to go if I paid my own way. I was really honoured. But my father was just about to go bankrupt and lose his business, which he ultimately did that December. I had no way — or method — of raising the $500 for boat fare, hotels, meals, everything else. The Ford Motor Company of Canada, who sponsored the V–8s, said they had contributed enough money and could not support any additions. I went to the Jewish community and nothing was done. So I reluctantly had to drop out, and it was a big disappointment, the biggest of my life.[87]

Apart from playing basketball, William Rogin also competed in football and track and made "Canadian sports history as a referee in the famous disputed 1947 Grey Cup football classic" when the cup was almost destroyed by fire while on display at the Toronto Argonaut Rowing Club.[88]

In addition to being named to the Windsor–Essex County Sports Athletic Hall of Fame in 1982, Rogin was inducted into the Canadian Basketball Hall of Fame in 1999. According to its records, he scored thirty-five points in one game "in the early 1930s and 1940s, when basketball scores were in the 20s–30s, setting an American Collegiate (pre-NCAA) record." He also "scored 13 consecutive free throws in one game — a world record."[89]

Irving "Toots" Meretsky attended school with William Rogin, playing with the "Five Fighting Freshmen," a team that, according to Frank Wansbrough, mayor of the City of Windsor from 1970 to 1974, "was the best team that ever came out of Windsor."[90] In 1935, Meretsky was forced to drop out of college to go to work. But he did play with the Ford V–8s and, when they beat Rogin's Assumption College team, they were allowed to enter the Canadian basketball championship. Having won the Canadian basketball championship, Irving "Toots" Meretsky now was eligible to represent Canada at the 1936 Summer Olympic Games held in Berlin. In an article published in 1976 in the *Windsor Star*, Gord Aitchison, a member of the Olympic basketball team, described the events leading up to these games:

> In 1935, the team got by Assumption College after a bitter series and fought its way to the Canadian finals against Victoria, B.C. Packed houses at Kennedy Collegiate saw Windsor take the title and the right to represent Canada in Berlin.' Apparently, twenty-four people were making the trip, including "14 players, 5 wives and 5 officials," many of them having little if any money for it.[91]

Recalling his experiences in what then was Nazi Germany, Irving "Toots" Meretsky told the *Windsor Star* in 2002, "You didn't dare to drop so much as a candy bar wrapper on the street, and you also were told not to go out at night. But you could walk about freely during the day."[92]

Meretsky also remembered that the Ford V–8 team beat Latvia, Brazil, Uruguay, and Poland before bowing to the United States with a 19–8 loss. In that connection, he spoke of the US players' tremendous height advantage that could have been offset if William "Moose" Rogin with his big frame could have joined the Ford V–8 team in Berlin. Another disadvantage was the fact that the game had to be played during a steady rain on an outdoor court and could not be postponed because the team's return trip already had been booked.

All the members of the Ford V–8 team won silver medals, but "the games committee only had silver medals for eight players and lesser 'commemorative medals' for the others."[93] Irving "Toots" Meretsky finally received his Olympic Silver Medal in 1996, after his daughter, Dr. Lynn Meretsky, pressed the Canadian Olympic Committee to award the medals to all those who deserved them. That was sixty years after the event, in the same year as her father was inducted into the Windsor–Essex County Sports Athletic Hall of Fame. Three years later, he also became a member of the University of Windsor Alumni Sports Hall of Fame.[94]

Another member of the famous 1936 Ford V–8s Olympic basketball team was Julius "Goldie" Goldman. Although he was not eligible to play for Canada because he was born in the United States, he did, however, attend the Games as a coach.[95]

Not all athletes were able to experience the Olympic Games, but one particularly memorable champion season for local Jewish athletes was 1953. In 1953, the Shaar Hashomayim became the sponsor of the Shaar Blues, a basketball team that had taken its name to honour the Israeli blue-and-white flag. Its members included Gerald Freed, William Tepperman, Earl Cherniak, Earl Rosenbaum, Jerry Weingarden, Sid Borofsky, Jerry Alexis, Jack Polsky, Harold Glaser, and Ron Brown. When they first started to play, their coach, Saul Nosanchuk, asked William Rogin to assist him. Competing with other "community churches" in the Windsor area church league, the Shaar Blues eventually won the Canadian Juvenile A Championship.[96]

That same year, the Shaar Bantams, another Shaar Hashomayim–sponsored team won the Ontario Church Basketball Association bantam championship. Coached by Olympic basketball champion Irving "Toots" Meretsky, its leading scorers were Joel Glynn and Robert Weingarden, who were ably assisted by Bernard Lyons, Nels Katzman, and Carl Cohen.

Other sports activities exclusively for Jewish participants were the Maccabiah Games, sometimes referred to as the "Jewish Olympics." The Maccabiah Games were first held in Palestine in 1932, in the midst of the worldwide Depression. Three hundred and ninety athletes from fourteen nations competed in the event, a participation figure similar to that of the very first Olympic Games that had taken place thirty-six years earlier.[97] The second Maccabiah Games were held in 1935, again in Palestine, while the 1950 venue was the newly created State of Israel. Ever since then, athletes meet there every four years to compete four sports categories — Juniors, Open (all ages), Masters (over 40s), and the Disabled.

In 1966, two years after the 1964 Maccabiah Games, the first Pan-American Maccabiah Games took place in Sao Paulo, Brazil and since then they are mostly held in other South American cities. Over the years, several Windsorites, including Dan Katzman, Dr. Ron Polsky, Judge Steve Rogin, Dave Rose, David Shanbaum, and Joe Shanbaum, have represented Canada in these games as well in the Maccabiah.

The JCC North American Maccabiah Games, begun in 1982 in Memphis, Tennessee, are held at numerous locations in Canada and in the United States. About 450 athletes, ranging in age from 13 to 16, compete each year in a variety of events — although the number of athletes who participated in the 1984 Detroit Maccabiah Games jumped to about nine hundred. In 1986, Dr. Ron Polsky became the driving force behind the Jewish Community Centre Maccabiah Games when he started taking between ten and twenty Windsor athletes to these sporting festivals every two years. In August 1988, when they were held in Chicago, Illinois, thirteen young people from Windsor were among the more than 3,000 athletes in fifty delegations around the world.[98] Whether on local, national, or even international fields of sport, Windsor's Jewish athletes have established an enviable record of participation and achievement.

Rabbinical Comings and Goings

Starting in 1984, several changes occurred at Windsor's Jewish religious institutions. Shaar Hashomayim's Rabbi Grussgott left in the summer of that year to accept a position in Philadelphia, Pennsylvania; Rabbi Edward S. Feigelman succeeded him a few weeks later. Having served as cantor of Beth Israel Congregation in Côte St. Luc, Montreal, he had come to Windsor to be closer to his hometown of Detroit, the residence of his aging parents, as well as to teach on a part-time basis at that city's Yeshiva Beth Yehuda. When he was asked about the prevailing mood at Shaar Hashomayim at the beginning of his tenure, he felt that [the congregation] "wanted to become Conservative and more lenient," but that "there was a strong nucleus of congregants who strived to maintain the more traditional status quo."[99]

Rabbi Feigelman left Shaar Hashomayim in November 1985 and, even though he returned in 1986 to help out temporarily, the synagogue was without rabbinical leadership until the fall of 1986, when Martin J. Applebaum became the new spiritual leader of the congregation. Despite the fact that he was a very charismatic man who appealed to the congregation's younger members, others were less pleased with him.[100] Once again, after some unpleasant months of rancor he endured with various members of the congregation, he resigned.[101]

Windsor Jewish Community Council Activities

Economically depressed times often unleash words and deeds that may be offensive to Jews. That was the case in the early 1980s, when Windsor's Jewish Community Council set up a community relations committee to deal with what it considered to be overtly anti-Semitic attacks. Headed by Ted Hochberg, it was supposed to monitor "the condition of the Jewish people locally and overseas," with special emphasis on the ever-changing events in the Middle East.[102] In its attempt to educate the general public, the committee also tried to forge links with elected government officials, repre-sentatives in the print and electronic media, union leaders, and community agencies. For instance, it would intervene whenever a scurrilous reference appeared in the University of Windsor's student paper.[103] It also would respond to such exclusory remarks as the one made by a famous Detroit Pistons' basketball player in 1986, who told an audience at Windsor's Massey Secondary School that "anyone who was not a born-again Christian was doomed."[104] The committee would take action whenever the commencement date for University of Windsor classes coincided with a Jewish holiday, when an insensitive cartoon appeared in a local newspaper, and when the Jews for Jesus Ministry approached Jewish community members without their prior consent.[105] And whenever a politician made a derogatory remark about Israel, a committee member would pay him or her a visit.[106]

It was equally important for Windsor's Jewish Community Council to maintain good relationships with all the local synagogues. That was why its executive director, Joseph Eisenberg, liked my suggestion to establish a "summit committee" that could provide a liaison between the rabbis and presidents of the three congregations and the president and executive director of Windsor's Jewish Community Council.[107] To implement the proposal, Eisenberg soon began hosting monthly meetings at the Jewish Community Centre that touched on a variety of subjects. These meetings informed the different groups about developments, programs, and plans, but also helped resolve certain issues before they were made public. And whenever an emergency arose that affected the entire community, the Summit Committee could step in, disseminating information, even during religious services.

When Shaar Hashomayim member Joseph Ozad died in 1978, this Windsor industrialist and owner of the Electrozad Electrical Supply Company had bequeathed moneys to various charities. Six years later, Windsor Community Council President Harold Taub suggested to the summit committee that the portion earmarked for Jewish education be equally divided among Windsor's three Jewish learning institutions, instead of going to one organization. His proposal was accepted by Mr. Ozad's executors and ultimately benefited the Hebrew Collegiate Institute, Shaar Hashomayim Synagogue, and Congregation Beth El, who each received one-third of the amount. It is gratifying to note that Taub's action, apart from enhancing these schools' individual programs, also brought about greater unity within the Jewish community.[108]

Commenting on the success of the summit committee, Joseph Eisenberg stated in his 1987 *Annual Report*:

> I touched upon the problem of conflict between different ideologies. That brings me to my final area — Synagogue/Federation relationships. At the Council of Jewish Federations General Assembly this past November (1986), the Windsor Jewish Community Council was the recipient of the Charles Goodall Award for our Summit Committee, which directly addresses the Synagogue/Federation relationship.
>
> The Committee, which includes the Presidents and Rabbis of our synagogues and the President of the Windsor Jewish Community Council and its professional staff, meets monthly to discuss issues of common concern and to plan community programs. The theme of last year's General Assembly was *klal Yisrael*, the Federation's role in building community. The issue of unity was the central theme.
>
> Our Summit Committee is a model highly regarded by many communities because it assists in maintaining a strong link between our synagogues and our Federation, thus creating a united, disciplined Jewish community at the same time recognizing and appreciating the differences that exist among us.[109]

To further evaluate areas of concern facing Windsor's Jewish community, a retreat was held on September 1, 1987, at the home of Diana and Alan Orman. One of the items on the agenda was the Endowment Fund and its chances to reach its $1 million goal.[110] The fund had originally been established in September 1978 by Windsor's Jewish Community Council and still boasted substantial assets a decade later. Nonetheless, despite the fact that the Council of Jewish Federations had rewarded its founding president Herb Brudner for his efforts in perpetuating the financial strength of Windsor's Jewish community, these assets were insufficient to guarantee that community's future.[111]

Other matters discussed at the retreat centred on leadership development within a small community such as Windsor's and on the difficulties encountered in trying to attract young Jews to the Community Centre. In that connection, it was suggested that plans for its expansion should be brought to the attention of major donors wishing to invest in giving the place "a basic face lift" as a means of creating lasting legacies for future generations.

Joseph Eisenberg Retires

At the end of June 1982, when Jerry Solomon gave up his position as the program director of Windsor's Jewish Community Centre, Barry Swartz took over from him. This native of Toronto, who held a Master's degree in Jewish Communal Services from Brandeis University in Waltham, Massachusetts, subsequently became the Council's first assistant executive director.[112]

Mr. Swartz resigned three years later — in April 1985 — and Arlene Potashner became the Centre's new program supervisor, while Deborah Silver-Medler took on the program director's role.[113] When Ms. Silver-Medler left a few months later, Arlene Potashner became Joseph Eisenberg's assistant.[114] Two years, however, later the Community Council executive director "gave notice of his retirement," setting the date for his departure in June 1989.[115] The search to replace him began almost immediately, especially since Arlene Potashner wanted to leave at the end of that summer as well.[116]

Before long, Dr. Allan Juris was engaged as the Council's new executive director, having served previously as associate executive director of the Jewish Welfare Federation of Detroit. He started his new job on August 1, 1989.[117]

To celebrate Joseph Eisenberg's long and illustrious career, a farewell tribute was planned for August 20, 1989, together with the publication of a special commemorative booklet, documenting his many accomplishments during his thirty-one years as leader of Windsor's Jewish Community Council. The following remarks by Mr. Eisenberg were included in the booklet:

> During the presidency of Eli Goldin the Windsor Jewish Community Centre opened its doors on Sunday, April 19, 1959. If it were possible to close our eyes and hibernate for fifty years and be awakened like Rip Van Winkle, we would see that what we have done collectively has made Windsor, Canada and the world a better place in which to live.[118]

Apart from the success of the Jewish Community Centre itself, Joseph Eisenberg's legacy comprises the creation of its Theatre Workshop, of Camp Yomee, of the Friendship Club, and, thanks to his interest in education, the founding of the Hebrew Collegiate Institute. Although he also was involved in all the United Jewish Appeal campaigns and in promoting the Endowment Fund, his crowning achievement certainly was the establishment of the I. L. Peretz House.

After his retirement, Mr. Eisenberg scrupulously removed himself from all Windsor Jewish Community Council activities to give its new leadership a chance to develop its own plans. During his illustrious tenure, Eisenberg had witnessed many changes within the community. He was troubled by the sweeping assimilation that threatened the future of Windsor Jewry and the steady movement of the young to communities in other parts of Canada and the United States. But, he was instrumental in making the Windsor Jewish Community Council the central organization within the Jewish community and united all the various organizations and different factions under the Council's umbrella. Eisenberg was recognized in regional and national meetings for initiating new and unusual programs, which led to an improvement in the quality of Jewish communal life. Regrettably, he died on May 5, 1998.

In 1990, the two-hundred-year anniversary of Moses David's first appearance in the area passed unnoticed within the Jewish community. Over the years, the Jewish community had established a viable presence and adapted quite well to Jewish life in Canada. Many Jews held prominent positions within the general community and made significant contributions to the betterment of the Windsor community. Needless to say, however, as the twenty-first century approached, new challenges confronted the Jewish community.

Chapter 13
Toward the Twenty-first Century and Beyond

Windsor in the 1990s

Windsor's centennial celebration in 1992 was a boisterous affair, but beneath its air of confidence was a troubled community facing immense problems. The urban population had not grown much in the past thirty years; people continued moving to the suburbs and now businesses and workplaces were joining them. The malls and big-box stores with acres of parking threatened the viability of the downtown business core; investment was attracted from the city to its growing fringes. Bold steps had to be taken if the city were to revive its central business district and attract a residential population back into the inner city. City officials put their hopes on the waterfront, new cultural amenities and the promise of new sports facilities. Tourism was touted as the answer to Windsor's too-long reliance upon the auto industry. The announcement that Windsor had been selected as the site of Ontario's first casino had an electrifying effect upon the city. The promise of thousands of jobs and multitudes of visitors filling hotels and restaurants led to unrealistic expectations; the real work of reviving the city and moving into the future would be far less dramatic, but more productive in the long run. Rehabilitation of older neighbourhoods, a diverse array of urban housing in the core, environmental sensitivity, and an effective mass transportation system are just some of the projected solutions found in the myriad of plans commissioned over time by the city. The city continued to be a immigration destination for many nationalities seeking a better life.

Windsor's strengths remain what they have always been — its border location and its people.[1]

Looking Back

Until 1993, all Negev Dinners had been held at the Shaar Hashomayim Synagogue. However, when Alan Orman was honoured, the Giovanni Caboto Club became the new venue carrying on the tradition of serving only kosher meals. The 1994 recipients were Paula and Harold Taub and Alan Dershowitz, the eminent Harvard University law professor who was that year's guest speaker. Honorees for the next two years were the Survivors of the Holocaust and Frances Parnes, respectively.

Negev Dinners reached new attendance records in 1997, when almost 1,000 people packed Caboto Hall to honour G. Yves Landry, the president of Chrysler Canada. In 1998, Michael Hurst, the mayor of the City of Windsor, was chosen and the following year Anthony P. Toldo became the JNF recipient in recognition of his outstanding philanthropic work. In the year 2000, the honoree was Carl S. Cohen and B. Thomas Joy in 2001. He was followed in 2002 by five couples — Beverley and Jerry Alexis, Sharon and Ted Hochberg, Sharon and Morton Kaplan, Marcey and Fred Katzman, and Harriet and Milton Whiteman. In 2003, Premier Ernie Eves, was honoured; the following year the Honourable Carl Zalev and Vicky Zalev and Rochelle and William Tepperman in 2005 and Harvey Strosberg the following year. Since these dinners reached out to the wider community and honoured non-Jews as well as their own, these yearly dinners became the premier event of the year, not only in the Jewish community but also in the general community. Being the recipient for the year garnered the honouree great prestige and publicity. The large attendance at these carefully planned dinners with headline speakers helped make it a must-attend event each year.

On November 18, 2005, Gerald Freed was invested as a Member of the Order of Canada for his major contribution to the Windsor community over the past forty years. Freed was the first Jewish resident to be so honoured.

Rabbinical Comings and Goings

Shaar Hashomayim's new spiritual leader was Rabbi Yosil Rosenzweig. Having been asked to serve the congregation during the 1989 High Holiday season, he apparently "did such a fabulous job," that the synagogue's board of directors offered him the job on a full-time basis. He accepted it in November 1989, following a stint as camp director of Young Israel in Greater Cleveland, Ohio.[2]

I am pictured here (on the right) with Gerald Freed, the only native Jewish permanent resident of Windsor to become a member of the Order of Canada.

Rabbi Rosenzweig was born in Europe in a displaced persons camp and immigrated to Canada with his parents, Jacob and Helene Rosenzweig, settling in Windsor, which he considered his hometown. To welcome him, a dinner was held on May 6, 1990, during which Rabbi Irwin Witty, director of the Toronto Board of Jewish Education, performed the rites of installation.[3]

When he was asked about his new appointment by the *Windsor Star*, Rabbi Rosenzweig said, "I grew up here [in Windsor]. The question is can I be effective here? I see my main role and challenge in Windsor as being one of education and outreach and to raise the education level of both children and adults."[4]

Rabbi Rosenzweig resigned in 1996 to serve a congregation in Newport News, Virginia.[5] Taking over from him was Cantor David Neumark, whose job at Shaar

Hashomayim was to be its Torah reader and teacher, but not its spiritual leader, despite the fact that he had been ordained by Yeshiva University's famous Talmudic scholar Aaron Soloveitchik.

At the end of 1984, after almost fifteen years as Congregation Beth El's spiritual head, I resigned to accept a pulpit in California. My successor, Rabbi Howard M. Folb, started his new assignment in July 1985. Born on April 4, 1943, in Akron, Ohio, he first had attended the University of Cincinnati and then Hebrew Union College–Jewish Institute of Religion, the institution where he was ordained in 1970. Before coming to Windsor, Rabbi Folb had served a congregation in Florence, South Carolina, as well as acting as the Jewish Federation's "community rabbi" for three small congregations in Southern Illinois, Southeastern Missouri, and Western Kentucky.[6]

Rabbi Folb's installation at Congregation Beth El was attended by his mentor, Rabbi Herman Schaalman of Chicago's Emanuel Congregation, and took place during a Friday evening service on September 20, 1985. It was followed by a community-wide reception the next evening.[7]

Rabbi Howard Folb considered himself a classical Reform rabbi; this contrasted with my approach during my tenure at Beth El, which was to move toward the more traditional side of Reform Judaism — a move that incidentally had helped to augment our membership. Rabbi Folb encountered some resistance from those members of his congregation who cherished these religious practices and wanted to continue worshipping in a manner they considered traditional but not Orthodox. Rabbi Folb established an adult b'nai mitzvah class and was very involved in ecumenical dialogues and in projects designed to educate Christian clergymen about Judaism.

When she was asked to describe Rabbi Folb's special characteristics, Beth El member Esther Goldstein said, "He came from the American South and was very impressed by its gentility and the civility that existed among individuals. He was polite and wanted people to speak with respect, believing that you may disagree with someone, but you don't attack that person personally or publicly."[8]

Rabbi Folb remained Congregation Beth El's spiritual leader until 1993. He died tragically in Akron, Ohio on March 3, 1998, while sitting shiva for his father — a Jewish custom observed following the burial of a close relative. Succeeding him was Rabbi Jeffrey Ableser who arrived in Windsor in August 1993, after serving congregations on the West Coast of the United States. When he was asked why he had accepted a rabbinical position in Canada, he said, "What attracted me to Windsor was the sense of community that was readily evident on my initial visits to the congregation."[9]

Rabbi Ableser was the Jewish community's only full-time rabbi between 1996 and 2002, when Rabbi Mitchell Kornspan came to Shaar Hashomayim. During that time, Rabbi Ableser performed funerals and other religious functions when asked to do so. On issues relating to traditional Orthodox law, the community consulted Rabbi Joseph Krupnik, the part-time spiritual leader of Windsor's Shaarey Zedek, who worked during the week as Kashrut director of the Council of Orthodox Rabbis of Greater Detroit, although he continued to live in Windsor. Soon, the Shaar Hashomayim could no longer retain a full-time spiritual leader because of financial constraints. A guest rabbi led High Holiday services, but the absence of rabbinic leadership at the Shaar Hashomayim did not augur well for its long-term viability.

When he was asked to comment on the fact that the Jewish Community Council and other organizations had always deferred to Shaar Hashomayim's Orthodox rabbis as Windsor's only religious authority, Rabbi Ableser stated, "By the 1990s, the power struggle between the Shaar Hashomayim and Beth El was largely a thing of the past."[10]

Miriam Jerris, the daughter of Marilyn Matthews-Muroff and Hy Muroff, is the second person born and raised in Windsor to receive rabbinical ordination. After graduating from Detroit's Wayne State University, she obtained her PhD, in Jewish Studies, with a specialization in pastoral counselling, from the Union Institute and University in Cincinnati, Ohio. She attended the International Institute for Secular Humanistic Judaism in Farmington Hills, Michigan, where she was ordained on October 9, 2001. She occasionally returns to Windsor to officiate at friends' life-cycle functions.

The Renaissance Project

The very fact that the Jewish population was dwindling made consideration of any renovation to the Jewish Community Centre impractical. Of course, there had been talk of expanding of the Jewish Community Centre in the past, such as building an enclosure for the swimming pool, a new jogging track, and racquetball courts, as well as renovating the health club. However, no action was taken until shortly after the Diana and Alan Orman retreat in 1989, when the Community Council's executive committee recommended that "$5,000 in seed money be approved for the purpose of retaining an architect and to conduct a needs study to determine what form the expansion should take."[11] Many thought that if renovation did not occur, the Jewish community was sealing its future fate. Should monies be expended for a project when the population was dwindling and there were so many other financial needs? The Jewish community leadership was divided on the future course of action. But, moving forward seemed to win the day.

Another impetus for what became known as the Renaissance Project was a discussion between Jewish Community Council President Jerry Alexis and his vice president, Harriet Whiteman. When he had asked her "most urgently" to purchase "if nothing else but new curtains for the Centre's board room," as he could not stand the present ones, she simply replied, "I absolutely will not do so. We are either going to renovate the Centre completely or just leave it for someone else to stumble over after we have gone."[12]

Heeding Harriet Whiteman's strong words, Alexis appointed her as head of the Renaissance Project's building and planning committee that included Milton Whiteman, Lou Bluestone, Alan Zekelman, and Dr. Allan Juris, executive director of the Windsor Community Council. And, following the receipt of two grants large enough to pay for the services of an architect, Gregory McLean had been hired.[13] Explaining why McLean had been selected for the job, Whiteman stated, "He had a very upbeat and contemporary approach toward the renovation project and it showed in his design."[14]

In the course of the building committee's regular meetings that were held over an eighteen-month period, many suggestions were considered — "improvements to the stage, including curtains and a sound system, better chairs, renovations to the library, the kitchen, the adult and youth lounges, the health club and the gym."[15] When it transpired that these improvements would cost around $750,000, some people felt that even more money should be spent on them, while others wanted that figure scaled down, claiming that Russian immigrant assistance had put too great a financial strain on the community.[16]

Although there was consensus that the project must come in on budget and that the needs of the handicapped should be addressed in the final plans, by December 1991 the Windsor Jewish Community Council was asked to approve "an application to the Ministry of Tourism and Recreation for a capital conservation grant based on construction costs of $660,000." Plans for Phase One of the project included "a curtain-wall front of the building, landscaping, a library, an adult lounge, lobby areas, as well as renovations to the east rooms in the basement of the Centre."[17] By 1994, $300,000 had been set aside, having been raised principally through bingo games, capital donations, endowments, the Freed/Orman families' $100,000 lead gift, as well as $250,000 from an anonymous donor.[18] A few key leaders wanted the project to move forward, feeling that without renovation, the Centre would never meet the future needs of the Jewish community in the new millennium.

As these donations warranted an increase in the amount spent on the project, Harriet Whiteman asked the Council's board of directors to move up total expenditure to $2.2 million, "since government funds are provided on a one-third/two-third match."[19] A subsequent assessment study also showed that there was a need for "a modernized open, welcoming, functional facility" involving "all generations participating together and separately with a continuing emphasis on the Jewish in Jewish Community Centre. People want a community focal point, a central social home, a place where they feel they belong."[20]

By the spring of 1995, after the Province of Ontario had approved $676,000 for the building's renovations, Council President Ted Hochberg, had become chairman of the Renaissance Project with Gary Katz serving as co-chair. Heading the various committees were Harriet Whiteman, building and planning committee; Gerald Freed and Alan Orman, fundraising committee; Paula and Harold Taub, publicity and marketing committee; and Fred Katzman, finance committee; with Jerry Alexis, Marcey Katzman, and Milton Whiteman serving as advisors to the "Renaissance Cabinet."[21] Following the government's approval of the project's general concept, Trillium Corporation was awarded the construction contract in the amount of $3,005,794.[22] The groundbreaking ceremony, chaired by Harold and Paula Taub, took place on February 4, 1996 and the newly renovated building was dedicated during the November 23–24, 1996, weekend. A dance was held on Saturday night and a ribbon-cutting ceremony on Sunday.[23]

The doors of the remodelled Jewish Community Centre were finally opened before the end of the 1990s, albeit after a great deal of soul searching as to its likely usefulness in the next millennium. At that point in time, a new issue arose, never before raised, namely, to open the premises to the public on Sabbath afternoons. Past generations

The Windsor Jewish Community Centre after completion of the Renaissance Project Renovation.

never would have entertained such a move. However, in the 1990s, the idea had few detractors.[24] In fact, during those years, it was more important to keep the building open on the Sabbath so that Jewish teenagers could get together there rather than in a non-Jewish environment. Had this same consideration occurred a decades earlier, the younger generation might have remained in the city.

Community Centre Leadership

Joseph Eisenberg had dominated the Jewish community for thirty-one years, but after his retirement in 1989, many changes occurred in the professional staffing. Many came initially to gain experience and realized that their future must be elsewhere. In January 1991, Elaine Kamienny became the Windsor Jewish Community Council's new program director, remaining in that position to the end of 1994.[25] Succeeding Elaine Kamienny in March 1995 as assistant executive director was Garson Herzfeld, a Reform rabbi who had served as director of the Southern Florida University Hillel and as director of Israel Services for the North Shore Jewish Centre and Federation.[26] He remained in Windsor until the early part of 1998.[27]

Allan Juris resigned as executive director of the Windsor Jewish Community Council on April 30, 1995 — in the midst of the Renaissance Project. Stephen Brownstein assumed the position a few months later.[28] In August 1998, Sandy Malowitz was promoted to program co-ordinator for adult services and Tamara Cirino became director of youth and family services.[29] Stephen Brownstein left Windsor in January 2000 to become executive director of the JCC in Clearwater, Florida.

Five months later, Harvey Kessler took over as executive director of Windsor's Jewish Community Council.[30] Born and raised in Windsor and holding a Master's degree in social work from Wilfrid Laurier University in Waterloo, Ontario, he first had worked with the United Nations development program overseas and as the Canadian Hearing Society's director for Southwestern Ontario for the next ten years. Before assuming his position with the Jewish

Community Council, Kessler had spent seven years as director of planning and research with the United Way of Windsor–Essex County.

Looking Forward

To non-Jews in the Windsor community the Jewish presence always has appeared greater than the actual numbers, mainly because of its many high-profile leaders. Joseph Eisenberg, well known for keeping accurate statistics on the city's Jewish population, revealed in 1984 that Windsor had 1,915 Jewish residents — 489 couples, 152 widows, 28 widowers, 79 divorced or unmarried men, 43 divorced or unmarried women, 44 single men, and 39 single women. Almost ten years later, in 1993, another demographic profile showed only 724 Jewish households — 266 with single occupants, 273 with two or more, and 185 with children. Although Jewish residents numbered 1,505, there was an assumption that there was "an unidentified Jewish population" of 10 percent, which would have brought the actual total to 1,700 — 29 percent that were 65 years of age or older and 18 percent that were high school age or younger.[31] Another study, completed in 2001, reported 1,530 Jews living in Windsor — a mere 0.5 percent of its total population. These statistics show that the number of Jewish residents had declined by 255 or 14.3 percent between 1991 and 2001.

Also of interest is the fact that the 1981 census listed 325 persons in the 15 to 24 year age group, that their numbers had dropped to 215 ten years later, and to 130 in 2001 — a clear indication that during that period many young people had left Windsor for other communities. Remarkably, the 45 to 65+ age group remained the same, with the median age of Windsor's Jews being 45.9 years — ten years older (35.8) than the city's total population — compared to the average age of Canada's Jewish population (40.2 years).[32] However, the percentage of Jewish seniors in Windsor is significantly greater — 24.8 percent — compared to the 12 percent of the city's total population and 16.7 percent nationwide.[33] Other signs of population decline became evident in 1997, when

the Balfour Branch of the Royal Canadian Legion reported that it only had 31 members.[34]

School enrolment had also dropped, which prompted the Windsor Community Council's summit committee to discuss the feasibility of having just one religious school, despite the great ideological differences between Congregation Shaar Hashomayim and Congregation Beth El.[35] In 1997, the former even went so far as to suggest amalgamation. As a result, a venture known as the Windsor Jewish Community Religious School came into being in the fall of 1998. Although it offered joint classes from kindergarten through Grade 2, each congregation continued to provide separate instruction for students in Grades 3 through 8.[36]

Sharing has continued in a variety of ways. Although the Windsor Jewish Centre had always rejected holding any religious services on their premises for fear of interfering with the other congregations, soon it became expedient to hold daily services at the Peretz House instead of the Shaar Hashomayim to more easily guarantee a *minyan*. The congregations send not only their bulletin to their own membership, but also include in their mailing the bulletin from the other congregation. Shared services once a month were also implemented to the surprise of many. Future consolidation of the existing religious institutions would be inevitable for both financial and demographic reasons.

The Future

How do these demographics affect the future of a firmly established community whose population had drastically declined? The following are the predictions of three Jewish leaders:

Joseph Eisenberg had this to say in 1990:

I don't see major growth in Windsor's Jewish population. I do, however, see that a kind of plateau has been reached even though I still see the flight of our young people. So what we are left with is an aging community, which will have to shift its emphasis in services from youth to the senior citizens. That's coming as sure as God made green apples. I don't see any new institutions starting. I do see, and this is my own observation, that there will be a movement towards the middle by the Shaar Hashomayim. It will not maintain its steadfast Orthodoxy. Interestingly, it's an Orthodox synagogue but it has no Orthodox members; maybe two.[37]

In 2003, Harvey Kessler, executive director of the Windsor Jewish Federation, offered the following prognosis:

Even though we are hoping that our pop-ulation will stabilize, the demographics are significantly changing. So what will the impact be on the Jewish community as it ages? We likely shall lose about 25 percent over the next twenty years or so, including some of our significant leaders and philanthropists and a lot of the younger Jewish professionals. That will have an impact on our infrastructure and I wonder whether we shall have the base to support three synagogues, a Federation, a Community Centre, and a senior apartment building.

Synagogue survival will depend on the Jewish community alone. We — the Community Centre — can rely on other sources for funding, such as memberships, tenants, and donors. We can expand our base because we are a United Way Agency that is open to the general public, even though we always shall be a Jewish Community Centre with the emphasis on

Jewish. In other words, our future is very different from that of the synagogue world.[38]

There is no doubt that for Windsor's synagogues to survive in the twenty-first century their character will have to change. The first attempt to persuade Shaar Hashomayim to become a Conservative congregation was made in 1959. It resulted in the establishment of Congregation Beth El. The second attempt was made in 1974 during the presidency of Kiva Dodick, when Shaar Hashomayim's board of directors half-heartedly approved Marten Brodsky's proposal to allow women to become offi-cers of the congregation, as well as directors at large. However, they still were excluded from such positions as presidents, executive and religious vice presidents, as well as gabbai.[39] At that time, the congregation even had amended its constitution to entrench "in a substantially permanent manner the supremacy of Halacha." It also had stipulated that "any change from this is to require the agree-ment of two-thirds of the entire regular membership of the Congregation," and that a large number of directors and congregants had to vote for these changes.[40] In 2002, how-ever, when sufficient signatures were collected to require a vote by the entire membership, the lines were drawn between those in favour of becoming a Conservative syna-gogue and those committed to maintaining the Orthodox traditions. Although the latter won the day by a narrow margin, that outcome signalled discontent among a large faction of the congregation. One way to rectify the situa-tion would be for Beth El to move from its more traditional Reform stance to a more Conservative identity and for Shaar Hashomayim to move from its Orthodoxy to the middle ground of Conservative Judaism. At the time, nei-ther wanted to accept moving closer to the other religious philosophy, but in the ensuing years, shared services once a month and even more modern Orthodox High Holiday services transpired, which created much discussion on the Shaar Hashomayim's future direction

With regard to the availability of certain social serv-ices, Harvey Kessler expressed some doubt in 2003 whether kosher "meals-on-wheels" and a place for people to enjoy kosher dining would still be needed in the future and whether Windsor's Jewish community would be able to afford them. "Strangely enough," he said, "the demand is decreasing at a time when the number of Jewish seniors is increasing. We shall have to begin exploring why that is happening. Is it the kosher nature of the program, its location, or the menu selection? Overall, we shall have to look at how we can continue our current infrastructure or whether we shall have to downsize it over the next few years to support what we have."[41]

Kessler also discussed the major changes that had taken place in the area of fundraising:

> Surprisingly enough, we have fewer people giving more and I think that's a trend, not just locally but nationwide. We have actually increased our donor base over the last three years because we did a lot more work. But you know the equation: you need to have more people giving in order to stabilize your revenue base. Today's donors really are giving less than the previous generation and the generation before them. Whereas my grandparents, my parents, and some of my peers gave to Jewish charities first, the younger generation's concept of philanthropy is quite different. Particularly, professionals in their 20s, 30s, and going into their 40s, are giving to the general community as well as to the Jewish community, having to respond to both because they are engaged in both. The competition for the dollar is much stronger, the increase in intermarriage has lessened the younger generation's commitment to Jewish causes, and finding leaders to serve the various organizations has become more difficult. In other words, patterns and trends have significantly changed.[42]

Based on Windsor's campaign totals from 1993 to 2003, the money raised annually through UJA campaigns had decreased by more than 30 percent during that period. To safeguard the community's future in the next millennium, the Windsor Jewish Community Council, in conjunction with the Federations of London and Hamilton, Ontario, hired Frank Simkevitz, an endowment professional, to raise money for each of the respective communities' endowment programs. After assuming the role of director of planned giving for Hamilton, London, and Windsor on September 2, 1997, he stated, "Windsor already has demonstrated its capacity to generate the funds needed to maintain its strong Jewish presence. It will be my task to ensure that it continues to do so."[43]

With regard to the decreasing 2003 financial base from annual campaigns, Harvey Kessler felt that " there will be a real crunch to make up for it, unless we do a very good job today and the next day to raise the levels of planned giving in the whole area of endowments. It will be in our future's interest to encourage our older adults to leave money to the Jewish community, in addition to what they bequeath to their families. Right now we are in the range of $1.5 million in terms of the endowment promises as well as in actual dollars. We are going to have to double that over the next ten years if we want to perpetuate the resources we need." [44]

Beth El's Rabbi Jeffrey Ableser offered this prediction on the future of Windsor's Jewish community:

> While the numbers continue to fall — Jewish Windsor has been "dying" for close to a century — refugees have revitalized the city after each World War and through waves of Jews leaving the inhospitality of life in Montreal or in the former Soviet Union. We also may benefit from the economic meltdowns in Argentina and Brazil or simply from the lack of affordable housing in Toronto. Windsor still is a great place to raise one's kids and it has the

advantages of being "a stone's throw" away from Metro Detroit.[45]

It is true that to offset the decline in Windsor 's Jewish population, there has been great interest in transplanting Jews from other lands. In the fall of 1997, the Windsor Jewish Community Council formed a recruitment committee, chaired by Sharon Hochberg, that was trying to attract prospective newcomers from Argentina and the former Soviet Union.[46] Indeed, as families from these countries were beginning to arrive in Canada, the Recruitment Committee did manage to persuade some of them to move to Windsor. In addition, a web site to provide information about the city had been developed and arrangements had been made for Dr. Michael Briks, national director of the Jewish Immigrant Aid Society (JIAS), Dr. Sharon Horlick, and William Botton to go to Sao Paulo and Rio de Janeiro in Brazil and to Buenos Aires in Argentina to inform individuals considering a move to Canada about "our great community."[47]

Windsor's Lasting Legacy

Windsor always will provide a spiritual home for Jews because the roots their forebears planted there almost two hundred years ago truly run deep. The following are testimonials given by several people who grew up in Windsor but now live and work in other Jewish communities.

Dr. Marilyn (Miller) Kronmal received her Jewish training at Windsor's I. L. Peretz Shule. She now is the regional director of the Southwest Region of B'nai Brith in Los Angeles, California:

> Growing up in the Windsor Jewish community in the 1940s and 1950s shaped my life. The seeds planted by the I. L. Peretz School rooted me in a tradition of Yiddish culture that challenged my mind, opening up and nurturing my Jewish spirit. Its curriculum of philosophy, history, Yiddish, Hebrew, Jewish literature, drama and song brought me an understanding and a closeness to my Eastern–European Jewish heritage and provided me with an education in Jewish values and Jewish life. For me, the Peretz School was a very special place to be.

> The B'nai B'rith Youth Organization's Maurice Strosberg Girls No.99 Program led me to develop my path into adulthood and started me along the road to becoming a Jewish community professional. The organizational and leadership skills I acquired, the friendships I formed, and the community responsibilities in which I took part provided me with positive experiences, identifying for me the common aspirations of the Jewish people, enhancing my knowledge of religion and culture, and fostering in me the idea of "learning by doing."

> I have often been grateful to this small Jewish community. The sense of familial duty and responsibility I acquired in Windsor afforded me to use the scope of Jewish expression as the foundation for building my life.[48]

Pam (Weingarden) Albert's religious training began at Congregation Beth El. She is the Canadian director for Toronto's One Family, an Israel-based organization.

> There was a sense of community in Windsor. I learned from my parents how you pull together and make things happen, from baking cakes for Shabbat, helping people who needed support, welcoming strangers by inviting them for dinner, to donating land to build a Reform Synagogue. I learned that you follow your heart and make what you believe in become reality."

Now living in Toronto and belonging to Holy Blossom Temple, a 2,000-family congregation, I miss the intimacy of a small congregation. I miss the feeling of belonging to a small community. But I have made it my mission to help others find their small community within Holy Blossom's large community on many levels.[49]

Amy (Whiteman) Shafron was a Shaar Hashomayim student. She was working in Seattle when she originally gave this interview. Currently, she is the director of leadership development at Davis Academy in Atlanta, Georgia.

I look back on my childhood in Windsor with warmth and appreciation. The Jewish community was small and safe, nurturing and caring. At the same time, it offered everything a child could need "Jewishly" — education, camps, youth groups and an Israel experience. It gave me a true sense of community alongside the necessary components to build one's knowledge and a foundation for adulthood.

A community like Windsor also enabled my parents to be leaders and role models in meaningful Jewish activities, which instilled in me the importance of providing for those in need, of giving something back to the community, and of building for the future — all values that now form the foundation of my life.

Upon reflection, my Jewish education at the Shaar Hashomayim was both broad and deep, leaving me with a strong sense of identity and a knowledge of our history, our prayers, our Hebrew language and our traditions. I also gained the ability to make educated choices. I am invigorated by what I know.

Having been part of Windsor's Jewish community is who I am. That sense of belonging made me feel at home in the various places where I have lived. Camp Yomee, BBYO, and the activities at the Jewish Community Centre instilled in me a sense of "Jewish joy" that still follows me. It is because I attended this camp and participated in community service projects, holiday celebrations, the "Walks for Israel," and in the other activities I remember from my childhood, that my husband, my children, and I find our friendships and a sense of community in Seattle that now is our home. By working professionally for its Jewish community, I try to strengthen the ties that bind Jews together to ensure that the next generation is educated, involved, and committed to Judaism and the Jewish people.

Some may believe that growing up in a larger city offers more opportunity and that may be true. But I believe that the strong sense of family, the closeness of community, the depth of Jewish education, and the emphasis on commitment I gained from my upbringing in Windsor, gave me the essence of my identity as an adult. It was a unique gift that only a few were lucky enough to receive.[50]

Despite concerns about the survival of their community in the twenty-first century, the Jews of Windsor can be justly proud of their accomplishments and of the place they hold in what has become a multicultural society. Almost two hundred years ago, they may have been an insignificant religious minority in what then was a frontier town. Today, they are a small but influential group of citizens, actively involved in various pursuits and ready to tackle the new challenges of the future.

Endnotes

Chapter 1: Moses David Windsor's First Jewish Settler

1. Sheldon J. and Judith C. Godfrey, *Search Out the Land: The Jews and the Growth of Equality in British Colonial America, 1740–1867* (Montreal and Kingston: McGill-Queen's University Press, 1995), xiii.

2. Gerald Tulchinsky, *Taking Root: The Origins of the Canadian Jewish Community* (Toronto: Stoddard Publishing Company, 1997), 31.

3. Records of Harline David Ruben, great-granddaughter of Lazarus David, files of Evelyn Miller, Montreal; Clarence I. de Sola, *150th Anniversary of Spanish and Portuguese Jews of Montreal* (Montreal, 1918), files of Evelyn Miller, Montreal.

4. Records of Harline David Ruben, 11; "David" by Clarence I. de Sola. *The Jewish Encyclopedia*, 1901 ed.; Irving I. Katz, *The First Jew of Windsor (Canada) and His Family*, Historic File, American Jewish Archives, 3; Irving I. Katz, "The First Jew in Windsor" *Detroit Jewish News*, January 27, 1961, 20.

5. Records of Harline David Ruben question whether Phoebe Samuel was born in 1736 or 1737, while de Sola, 459, accepts 1736 as her birth date.

6. Records of Harline David Ruben; Malcolm H. Stern, *Americans of Jewish Descent: A Compendium of Genealogy* (Cincinnati: American Jewish Archives, 1960), 37; Katz, 30. These references mention year of birth as 1768; de Sola, 458, cited 1767 but month and day are not given. The Records of Harline David Ruben would appear to be the most accurate source.

7. Minutes of Spanish and Portuguese Synagogue, Solomon Frank, *Two Centuries in the Life of a Synagogue* (Montreal: Spanish and Portuguese Congregation, 1968), 28; Benjamin Sack, *History of the Jews in Canada* (Montreal: Harvest House, 1965), 53; de Sola, 13.

8. Records of Harline David Ruben; Esther I. Blaustein, Rachel A. Esar, and Evelyn Miller, *Spanish and Portuguese Synagogue (Shearith Israel) Montreal, 1768–1968*, The Jewish Historical Society of England, Vol. 33, (London: University College, 1971), 114–15; Benjamin Sack, 109–12, 134–36; Notary: John Gerbrand Beek, Jean Baptiste Dodlain, files of Moses David, ex. Pour Deux Annex, March 12, 1805, no. 1828, Archives Nationales de Quebec, Montreal. The apprenticeship of David Hayes to Moses David confirms that Abigail and Andrew Hayes had another son. The document indicates that Abigail and Andrew apprenticed their son David Hayes; *Samuel David Diary*, Public Archives of Canada. The death of Abigail David Hayes has been recorded erroneously in several places. Katz, *The First Jew of Windsor*, 5; Katz, "The First Jew in Windsor," 30; Records of Harline David Ruben. The 1801 date appears from the notations in the *Diary* to be correct.

9. de Sola, 13.
10. Records of Harline David Ruben.
11. Sack, 96.
12. Godfrey, 185.
13. Sack, 96; de Sola, 34.
14. Sack, 96; de Sola, 34.
15. The other synagogues established before Shearith Israel in 1768 were: Spanish Portuguese of New York, 1675; Mikveh Israel, Savannah, Georgia, 1734; Mikveh Israel, Philadelphia, 1745; Beth Elohim, Charleston, South Carolina, 1749, Jeshvat Israel, Newport, Rhode Island, 1760.
16. De Sola, 13.
17. Sack, 50, n 1; Louis Rosenberg, *Some Aspects of the Historical Development of the Canadian Jewish Community*, Jewish Population Studies, Population Characteristic, series no. 4, (Montreal: Bureau of Social and Economic Research, Canadian Jewish Congress, 1960).
18. Frank, 29.
19. de Sola, 13–15.
20. James H. Lambert, "David David," *Dictionary of Canadian Biography*, Vol. VI, 179–81.
21. Blaustein, 113–14.
22. Claus Papers, M.G. 19, f. 1, Vol. 6, 20–30, Public Archives of Canada. In this reference, Moses David's name appears as Moses Davis; *Michigan Pioneer and Historical Collection*, Vol. 12 (1887), 85–86. This reference is a copy of the original document cited above; however, Moses David appears as Moses Dare; Simcoe Papers, Vol. 5, 76; Hiram Walker Historical Museum, Windsor, Ontario, cites the original source.
23. This letter mentioned Mr. Selby, Mr. Smith, and Mr. Pattison. In other correspondence Moses David had business dealings with them or a connection was made in a letter indicating a business relationship.
24. Claus Papers, MG 19, f. 1, Vol. 6, 20–30, Public Archives of Canada. From this document it is possible to infer that Moses David was already in the Detroit-Windsor area in 1790.
25. E. J. Lajeunesse, *The Windsor Border Region: Canada's Southernmost Frontier: A Collection of Documents* (Toronto: The Champlain Society, University of Toronto Press, 1960.
26. Ibid., cxvii–xix.
27. Ibid., cxvii.
28. Godfrey, 165.
29. Ibid., 191–92.
30. Ibid., cxvii–xxi.
31. Ibid., 193-95.
32. Ibid., cxx.
33. Ibid., 193.
34. Ibid., 165.
35. Ibid., 158.
36. Ibid, 159.
37. Lajeunesse, 196–98.
38. Ibid, 199.
39. Ibid, 203–04.
40. See Essex County Registry Office for old Sandwich map; Moses David and wife to Augustine Roy, January 10, 1814, Essex County Registry Office, Town of Sandwich, Abstract Index east side Lot 3; Old Book A, 62.
41. John Askin to Moses David, September 8, 1801, LMS John Askin Papers, Burton Historical Collection.
42. Ibid., November 23, 1801.
43. J. B. Barthe and wife to Moses David, February 3, 1803, Essex County Registry Office, Town of Sandwich, Abstract Index, east side Bedford Street, Lot 3, Old Book A 134, 62.
44. Godfrey, 165–66.
45. Ibid., 167.
46. Essex County Registry Office, Town of Sandwich, Abstract Index, park lots north side of Centre road, Old Book A, 366; Patent Book, nos. 476–580, February 20, 1804, no. 572; Patent Index, 266.
47. Godfrey, 167.
48. Ibid.
49. Ibid., 168–69.
50. Labadie Family Papers, April 24, 1794, Burton Historical Collection.
51. David David to Gabriel Godfroy, October 4, 1805, Godfroy Papers, Burton Historical Collection.
52. M. S. Hands Papers, L4, 1791–1811, 134–35, Burton Historical Collection.
53. Ibid.
54. Ibid.
55. John Clarke, *Land, Power and Economics on the Frontier of Upper Canada* (Montreal: McGill Queen's University Press, 2001), 565; letter of Moses David to Jacob Franks, Vol. 19, 293–94, Wisconsin Historical Collections.
56. Letter of Moses David to Jacob Franks, Vol. 19, 293–94, Wisconsin Historical Collections.
57. Wayne County, North West Territory Papers C 835/C7, December 1802, Burton Historical Collection.

58. Peltier vs. Lavelle, C835/C7, December 1803, Court of Common Pleas, Wayne County, Indiana Territorial Papers, Burton Historical Collection.

59. Francis Badgley to Solomon Sibley, April 28, 1804, Solomon Sibley Papers, ALS 20:134, 2 p, Burton Historical Collection.

60. Ibid.

61. Solomon Sibley Papers, August 25, 1804, ALS 20:246 2

62. Ibid.

63. Ibid.

64. James May to Moses David, August 9, 1806, Solomon Sibley Papers, ALS 15:23, 3 , Burton Historical Collection.

65. Solomon Sibley Papers, January 30, 1809, ALS 15:232, 2 , Burton Historical Collection.

66. Solomon Sibley Papers, June 25, 1812, ALS, 33:202, 1, Burton Historical Collection.

67. "Return of the Officers Belonging to the Northeast Regiment of Essex Militia, Specifying their names, rank, dates of commission now held, July 6, 1808," John Askin Papers, 1807–1808, Burton Historical Collection.

68. Among these officers listed along with Captain Moses David, were Colonel John Askin, Lieutenant Colonel Baptiste Baby, Major Thomas McKee, Captain Alexis Maisonnville, Captain Richard Pattinsons, Captain Alexis LaBukesor, Captain Francois Drouillards, Captain Jean Batiste Barthe, Captain Vila Demouchellis, Captain Pierre LaBukes, and Captain John Askin.

69. Clarke, 565. Note 276 draws on information provided by Shelton and Judy Godfrey.

70. Ibid., 413.

71. Ibid., 363.

72. George Ermatinger and wife to Moses David, September 27, 1805, Essex County Registry Office, Town of Amherstburg, Abstract Index, Lot 5 or 17 Ramsey street, west side and S. Murray, Old Book B 378, 78; George Ermatinger to Moses David, September 27, 1805, Lot 17 or 1 Bathurst street, east side, Old Book B. 378, 96; George Ermatinger to Moses David, September 27, 1805, Lot 2 or 17 Apsley Street, west side, Old Book B 278, 188; George Ermatinger to Moses David, September 27, 1805, Lot 31 or 17 Segnour Street, east side, Old Book B 378, 237; George Ermatinger to Moses David, September 27, 1805, Lot 31 or 17 King street, east side, Old Book B., 279; Thomas Smith to Moses David, September 11, 1806, Lot 41 of 1st Concession, Doc. B. 275, Old Book A, 155.

73. Thomas Smith to Moses David, September 11, 1806, Essex County Registry Office, Township of Sandwich East, Abstract Index, Lot 141, of 1st. Concession, Doc. B.275, Old Book A, 155.

74. Ibid.

75. Moses David to Joseph Mayoux, January 16, 1808, Essex County Registry Office, Township of Sandwich East, Abstract Index, Lot 141 of 1st. Concession, Doc. B. 367, Old Book A, 155.

76. Essex County Registry Office, Township of Sandwich, Abstract Index, Old Book B 378, September 27, 1805.

77. George Ermatinger to Moses David, September 27, 1805, Essex County Registry Office, Township of Colchester, Abstract Index, south Lot 46, in the 4th Concession, Old Book A, 226; Old Book B 378.

78. Alexander McKenzie to David David, September 6, 1820, Essex County Registry Office, Township of Colchester, Abstract Index, south Lot 46 in 4th Concession, Old Book D, No. 198, 226.

79. Executor of Last Will of David David to Henry Huffman, October 9, 1832, Essex County Registry Office, Township of Colchester, Abstract Index, south Lot 46, in the 4th Concession, old Book A, 226.

80. David David to Gabriel Godfroy, October 4, 1805, Godfroy Papers, Burton Historical Collection.

81. Godfroy Papers, Burton Historical Collection, August 28, 1806.

82. Notary: John Gerbrand Beck, Jean Baptiste Dodlain files of Moses David, ex. Pour Deux Annex, March 12, 1805, no. 1828, Archives Nationales de Quebec, Montreal.

83. David Hayes to Moses David of Sandwich Upper Canada, apprenticeship for four years, May 6, 1805, Jean Baptiste Dodlain files of Moses David, ex. Pour Deux Annex, Archives Nationales de Quebec, Montreal.

84. John Pare to Moses David, June 21, 1806, Essex County Registry Office, Township of Sandwich East, Abstract Index, Old Copy Book B, no. 266; Thomas Smith to Moses David, September 11, 1806, Old Copy Book B, no. 275; George Ermatinger to Moses David, September 27, 1805, Town of Amherstburg and Town of Colchester, Old Copy Book B., no. 378. In all these references, David Hayes' name appeared as a witness to the transactions of Moses David.

85. Jean Baptiste Pare to Moses David, June 21, 1806, Essex County Registry Office, Township of Sandwich East, Abstract Index, Lot 135 of 1st Concession, Old Book A, 129; Old Copy Book B, OBB 266.

86. Essex County Registry Office, Township of Colchester, Abstract Index, South Gore between 11 and 12 in the 2nd Concession, January 31, 1811, Old Book A., 436, South Gore in 3rd Concession, 472; Old Copy Book C, no. 98.

87. John Bell to Moses David, April 6, 1807, Essex County Registry Office, Township of Gosfield, Lot 24, 1st Concession, Book B., 341, Old Records, Essex County.

88. Robert Livingston to Moses David, September 12, 1809, Essex County Registry Office, Elizabethtown, Lot 27, Book C, 32, Old Records, Essex County.

89. James Heward to Moses David, September 23, 1808, Essex County Registry Office, Town of Colchester, Abstract Index, South Gore between 11 and 12 in 2nd Concession, Old Copy Book B, no. 404, 436, 472.

90. Joseph Drouillard to Moses David, July 2, 1807, Essex County Registry Office, Town of Sandwich West, Abstract Index, Old Book A, 306; John Drouillard to Moses David, July 2, 1807, Old Copy Book B, no. B. 350.

91. Francis Badgley to Moses David, August 25, 1804, Solomon Sibley Papers, ALS 15: 227, 1 p; James May to Moses David, March 12, 1805, Burton Historical Collection, ALS 15:228, 2, Burton Historical Collection.

92. Prayer Books of Moses David, film of Mrs. Evelyn Miller.

93. St. John's Church, 1807–1857, March 23, 1807, Burton Historical Collection, 24522283, 3.

94. Registry Book of Marriages, Christenings and Burials, Vol. 1, 1802–1812, St. John's Church, Windsor, Ontario, July 24, 1810.

95. Fannie Anderson, *Doctors Under Three Flags* (Detroit: Wayne State University Press, 1951), 84–86.

96. George F. Macdonald, "Richard Pollard and St. John's Church, Sandwich, Ontario, 1804–1812," Abstract Book, Hiram Walker Historical Museum, 20–135, 101.

97. *Samuel David Diary*, July 26, 1804, Public Archives of Canada.

98. Francis Badgley to Solomon Sibley, August 25, 1804, Solomon Sibley Papers, ALS 20: 246, 2 p, Burton Historical Collection.

99. Robert M. Fuller, *Windsor Heritage* (Windsor: Herald Press, 1972), 60, cites "Grave of Moses David: Originally a stone mausoleum" and "He (Moses David) had come from Montreal with his wife who was a Gentile." With reference to "stone mausoleum," see *Amherstburg Echo*, June 25, 1880, Malden National Historical Park, which refers to the grave marking as "an old relic in the shape of a tombstone which was erected to the memory of Moses David by his wife Charlotte David." As for "his wife who was a Gentile," see marriage contract between Moses David and Charlotte Hart, quote footnotes 101, 102, and 132. Fuller also writes, "Rumour says he accepted some responsible function aiding Pollard." Reverend Pollard served as a registrar of land records and was an ordained priest later in life. What responsible function Moses David assumed other than the possible pew seat he had or witnessing a marriage, is unclear from Fuller's writings. Mr. Fuller bases his sources on conversations with George F. Macdonald (November 23, 1877–August 1959) a prominent Windsor merchant who was interested in Windsor history. There are no references to any of Mr. Macdonald's work, nor in the writings of Mr. Fuller.

100. Notes of Lewis Hart, files of Miss Alma Hart; Minutes of Spanish and Portuguese Synagogue.

101. N. B. Docet, Notary, October 6, 1804, no. 226, Archives Nationales de Quebec, Montreal.

102. J. A. Grey, Notary, September 29, 1811, vol. 4, 929.3, Q 3, Archives Nationales de Quebec, Montreal.

103. Ibid.

104. Ibid.

105. Records of Harline David Ruben.

106. The map is the lot plan of Sandwich in 1800 and has no date. See Essex County Registry Office for old Sandwich map.

107. Moses David and wife to Augustine Roy, January 10, 1814, Essex County Registry Office, Town of Sandwich, Abstract Index, east side Lot 3. Old Book A, 62.

108. L'Hon. Judge Favre Surveyoer et Franets – J. Audet, Des Députés des Trois Rivières (1792–1808) Les Trois Rivières, 1933, no. 9, ser. A, 80 Archives Department, Montreal Jewish Public Library.

109. Records of Harline David Ruben.

110. Ibid.

111. Ibid.

112. Ibid.

113. Obituary, Moses Eleazar David, from either *Witness*, *Herald*, *Gazette*, or *Star*, Montreal, October 1, 1892.

114. Records of Harline David Ruben.

115. Ibid.

116. Ibid.

117. de Sola, 35; *Montreal Daily Star*, December 30, 1893, 6; Blaustein, 115.

118. Notebook of Fanny Joseph in Files of Miss Annette Wolff, Montreal.

119. Obituary, Moses Eleazar David, See n. 181.

120. Hart, 504.

121. Records of Harline David Ruben; Isaac Leeser, ed., *The Occident*, Vol. 1, no. 11, February 1844, 564.

122. Essex County Registry Office, Township of Sandwich, Abstract Index, Oct. 14, 1891, Old Book A, 366.

123. George Meldrum and William Park to Moses David, January 14, 1811, Essex County Registry Office, Township of Sandwich, Abstract Index, east side Bedford street, Lot 4, Old Book A 106, 64.

124. See also Jane Phyllis McKee to Adolphe Gignac, October 22, 1913, Essex County Registry Office, Town of Sandwich, Abstract Index, east side Bedford Street, Lot 3, Book N. 7117. Remark recorded on Abstract Index is "excepting therefrom the Jewish Cemetery at the east corner thereof." J. B. Barthe and wife to Moses David, February 3, 1803, Essex County Registry Office, Town of Sandwich, Abstract Index, east side Bedford Street, Lot 3, Old Book A 134, 62.

125. Ibid.

126. John R. Williams Papers, 2M3, November 18, 1805–April 24, 1812, Burton Historical Collection; Solomon Sibley Papers, ALS, August 23, 1819.

127. Thomas Bedorin, Notary, July 15, 1825, no. 2401, Archives Nationales de Quebec.

128. J. M. Cadieux, Notary, November 29, 1825, no. 562, Archives Nationales de Quebec.

129. J. M. Cadieux, Notary, December 27, 1825, no. 587, Archives Nationales de Quebec.

130. G. D. Arnolds, Notary, July 24, 1829, no. 501, Archives Nationales de Quebec.

131. Records of Harline David Ruben.

132. Registry Book of Births, Funerals and Marriages, kept by Rev. Abraham de Sola, January 1847–1854, Spanish and Portuguese Synagogue, verified death of Charlotte Hart David, widow of Moses David, in Montreal, January 5, 1844, buried by David Piza, Minister, January 12, 1844.

133. Moses Eleazar David's tombstone states "to the memory of Moses Eleazer David born in Sandwich Ontario, March 10, 1813 died in Montreal October 1, 1892, erected by his sorrowing widow and son."

134. Registry Book of Births, Funerals and Marriages kept by Rev. Aaron David Meldola de Sola, February 2, 1885 to October 6, 1892, Spanish and Portuguese Synagogue.

135. *Amherstburg Echo*, June 25, 1880.

136. Jane Phyllis McKee to Adolphe Gignac, October 22, 1913, Essex County Registry Office, Town of Sandwich, Abstract Index, east side Bedford Street, Lot 3, Book N. 7117. Remark recorded on Abstract Index is "excepting therefrom the Jewish Cemetery at the east corner thereof."

137. Essex County Registry Office, Plan 40, no. 11856.

138. Essex County Registry Office, Plan 40, no. 30590, January 31, 1936.

139. Essex County Registry Office, Plan 40, no. 697476, May 12, 1977.

140. Kroon, Leonard, *Final Report Submitted to the Windsor Jewish Community*, in private collection of Jonathan V. Plaut.

141. Moses David rests at the entrance of the Shaar Hashomayim Synagogue. The original tombstone has been placed over his grave and has a protective Plexiglas covering.

Chapter 2: The Earliest Jews Who Chose Windsor

1. Introduction drawn from Neil Morrison, *Garden Gateway to Canada* (Windsor: Herald Press, 1954); and T. Price and L. Kulisek, *Windsor 1892–1992: A Centennial Celebration* (Windsor: Chamber Publications, 1992).

2. The area newspapers of this period were the *Canadian Immigrant and Western District Advertiser,* 1831–1836; the *Western District Advertiser,* 1838–1843; the *Voice of the Fugitive,* 1851–1853; the *Windsor Herald,* 1855–1856; the *Essex Record,* 1871–1892; the *Windsor Review,* 1895–1896. I have also examined the Census Records of 1851, 1861, and 1871; Charles Berczy of Amherstburg, attorney for Moses Judah Hayes and Isaac Valentine, executors for David David, February 24, 1834, Essex County Registry Office, County of Essex, Book 4, 326, Old Records, Essex County.

3. See note 1; all available Windsor and area newspapers have been read as listed in note 1, as well as the *Evening Record,* 1893–December 31, 1917; the *Windsor Record,* January 2, 1918–August 30, 1918; the *Border Cities Star,* September 3, 1918–June 29, 1935; the *Windsor Daily Star,* July 2, 1935–December 31,1939.

4. *Border Cities Star,* April 8, 1926, 3; *Evening Record*, February 11, 1914, 1; interview with I. M. Meretsky, July 1, 1974.

5. *Evening Record*, February 11, 1914, 1; interview with I. M. Meretsky, July 1, 1974 confirms that Mr. Englander spoke many languages fluently and served as an interpreter for the city. Other interviews also confirmed his

linguistic abilities, including interview with Joshua Gitlin, April 26, 1972.

6. *Evening Record*, February 11, 1914, 1; interview with I. M. Meretsky, July 1,1974.

7. *Windsor City Directory* including Sandwich and Walkerville (Ingersoll: Union Publishing Co.) for the years 1891, 25; 1894, 36; 1891, 25; 1897–98, 33. interview with I. M. Meretsky, July 1, 1974.

8. *Evening Record*, February 22, 1895, 4; interview with Joshua Gitlin, April 26, 1972.

9. *Evening Record*, December 19, 1898, 1.

10. *Evening Record*, January 13, 1899, 1.

11. *Evening Record*, January 23, 1899, 243.

12. Interview with I. M. Meretsky, July 1, 1974; *Border Cities Star*, April 8, 1926, 3.

13. Windsor Council Minutes, (January 1885–June 1890), March 8, 1886. Due to the poor condition of the Council Minutes some pages are not legible.

14. Windsor Council Minutes, May 3, 1886.

15. Windsor Council Minutes, June 26, 1899.

16. *Evening Record*, January 29, 1900, 8.

17. Ibid.

18. *Evening Record*, April 17, 1900, 8.

19. *Evening Record*, August 1, 1900, 1

20. Ibid.

21. Council Minutes, October 15, 1900, 381.

22. Council Minutes, November 26, 1900, 351; February 11, 1901, 393; *Evening Record*, December 31, 1900, 1.

23. *Evening Record*, February 11, 1914, 1.

24. Interview with I. M. Meretsky, July 1, 1974.

25. Ibid.; *Border Cities Star*, June 29, 1921, 3; April 1, 1926, 5; April 8, 1926, 3; September 3, 1925, 9.

26. Records of Shaar Hashomayim Cemetery, Windsor, Ontario; interview with Mrs. Tibe Burnstine, June 13, 1974; interview with I. M. Meretsky, July 1, 1974.

27. I. M. Meretsky interview, July 1, 1974.

28. Mrs. Tibe Burnstine interview, June 13, 1974; I. M. Meretsky interview, July 1, 1974.

29. If Simon Meretsky was born in 1880, then his mother, Katherine, came to Windsor in 1887 and Aaron, her husband, arrived in 1880. Since Tibe Meretsky Burnstine was born in Canada in 1894, it is possible that her mother did not come until 1890–1893. This makes it possible for Aaron to have arrived sometime from 1883 to 1886, and Simon would have been over seven years of age when he arrived in Windsor. The presumption remains that Aaron Meretsky came in 1880 and his wife, Katherine, came in 1887 or 1888 when Simon was seven. Interviews with I. M. Meretsky, July 1, 1974; Mrs. Tibe Burnstine, June 12, 1974; Milton Meretsky, June 11, 1974; *Evening Record*, May 27, 1898, 8, relates Simon Meretsky's testimony in court when he mentions he has "been in country six years." This would place Aaron Meretsky in Windsor no earlier than 1885.

30. I. M. Meretsky is unclear as to what amount of money his mother brought over, but she had money when she came. He recalls that it was a considerable sum at that time.

31. Interviews with I. M. Meretsky, July 1, 1974; Mrs. Tibe Burnstine, June 13, 1974; Milton Meretsky, June 11, 1974.

32. *Windsor City Directory*, 1894, 82 lists Aaron Meretsky as a poultry dealer at 35 Mercer Street and in 1899 at the same address as a peddler; in 1900 he is listed as a junk dealer.

33. *Evening Record*, December 8, 1910, 1.

34. *Evening Record*, January 7, 1911, 1; Council Minutes (September 19, 1910–December 31, 1913) January 10, 1911; January 11, 1911.

35. *Evening Record*, January 17, 1911, 1.

36. *Evening Record*, May 21, 1912, 1; May 7, 1912, 1.

37. *Evening Record*, June 20, 1911, 1.

38. *Evening Record*, August 29, 1911, 1.

39. Council Minutes, September 27, 1911; *Evening Record*, December 11, 1911, 3; December 22, 1911, 1.

40. *Evening Record*, December 23, 1911, 3; December 26, 1911, 3; December 27, 1911, 3; December 28, 1911, 5; December 29, 1911, 3.

41. *Evening Record*, December 22, 1911, 1.

42. *Evening Record*, August 31, 1911, 2; January 2, 1912, 1; Council Minutes, January 8, 1912, 172.

43. *Evening Record*, July 20, 1912, 1.

44. *Evening Record*, October 11, 1912, 7; October 12, 1912, 7; November 18, 1912, 7; Council Minutes, October 21, 1912, 288.

45. *Evening Record*, September 1, 1912, 1; Council Minutes, August 26,1912, 266.

46. *Evening Record*, January 7, 1913, 2.

47. *Evening Record*, January 12, 1914, 1; Council Minutes (January 12, 1914–December 31, 1915), January 12, 1914, 1.

48. *Evening Record*, January 27, 1914, 9; February 17, 1914, 1; February 25, 1914, 5.

49. *Evening Record*, January 5, 1915, 2.

50. *Border Cities Star*, December 15, 1925, 3. The obituary of

Jacob Meretsky, 78, states that he came from Russia-Poland to Windsor fifty years ago. This would place him in Windsor in 1875. However, this time period could be exaggerated slightly. In another article in the *Evening Record* (August 16, 1911, 1), Jacob Meretsky is quoted as saying, "I have lived in Windsor for thirty-two years," and this would date his arrival at 1879. This conflicts with an earlier reference to Aaron being in Windsor no earlier than 1885.

51. Interview with Mrs. Goldie Meretsky and Mrs. Dora Bloom, June 24, 1974.

52. Records of Shaar Hashomayim Cemetery; *Evening Record,* May 26, 1896, 8; Gitlin interview, August 14, 1973.

53. The store was Meretsky and Gitlin, *Windsor City Directory,* 1911, 465.

54. "The marriage of David Meretsky and Goldie Bernstein (Max Bernstein's daughter) took place at Curry Hall with 250 invited guests. Rabbi Levine of Detroit performed the rites." *Evening Record,* April 2, 1906, 1.

55. Interview with Abe Katzman, I. Bert Meretsky, and I.M. Meretsky, June 26, 1974. Harry Meretsky, brother of I. Bert Meretsky, has two married daughters, Barbara (Dr. Morton) Bernstein, Windsor, and Marilyn Woot, New York; I. Bert Meretsky has two sons, Harvey and Ronald.

56. Max Bernstein and Eli Herman Benstein were first cousins. Max Bernstein added an "r" to his name because merchandise sent to Eli and Max in Windsor was being confused; their name originally was Benstein. Interview with Mrs. Vivian Berry, June 23, 1974.

57. The first Jewish child born in Windsor was Moses Eleazar David, the son of Moses David, who was born in Sandwich in 1813. Interviews with Mrs. Goldie Meretsky, June 28, 1973, and Jacob Geller, June 11,1974.

58. Records of Beth Olam Cemetery, Detroit, Michigan; Mrs. Goldie Meretsky interview, June 28, 1973.

59. Mrs. Goldie Meretsky interview, June 28, 1973.

60. Mrs. Vivian Berry interview, June 23, 1974; letter from Mrs. Vivian Berry, August 20, 1973; letter from Mrs. Ida Benstein, July 29, 1973.

61. Mrs. Ida Benstein interview, February 25, 1974.

62. Ibid.; see also records of Beth Olam Cemetery, Detroit; *Evening Record,* August 19, 1898, 8; and interview with Mrs. Vivian Berry, June 23, 1974.

63. Interview with Mrs. Ida Benstein, February 25, 1974.

64. *Windsor City Directory,* 1905–06, 108.

65. Interview with Max Weingarden, October 20, 1973; telephone conversations with Abner Weingarden, June 11, 1976; and Arthur Weingarden, June 11, 1976.

66. Interview with Mrs. Betty Kovinsky, Mrs. Betty Passman, and Mrs. Sarah Lewin, August 21, 1974. Their recollection is Dr. Kovan's first marriage was to Charlotte Lebster, a second to "Marge" (no surname known), and a third marriage to Lillian Connelly, who bore him two daughters, Marilyn and Cathy; Benjamin is known to have married Sadie, whose surname is also unknown at this time.

67. *Windsor City Directory,* 1893, 48; Julius Kovensky, Samuel Kovensky; 1894, 63, Charles Kovansky, Frank Kovensky, Julius Kovensky, Samuel Kovensky; 1896, 62, Abram Kovensky, Morice Kovensky, Samuel Kovensky, Charles Kowinsky, Frank Kowinsky, John Kowinsky, Julius Kowinsky, 1897–98, 58; Abram Kovensky, Charles Kovensky, Herman Kovensky, Morice Kovensky ,Samuel Kovensky, Julius Kowinsky.

68. Ibid.

69. I. M. Meretsky interview, August 15, 1973; *Border Cities Star,* March 7, 1925, 2.

70. Miss Frances Geller and Jacob Geller interview, February 15, 1972.

71. *Windsor City Directory,* 1895, 71; I. Bert Meretsky interview, June 10, 1974; Mrs. Tibe Burnstine interview with, June 12, 1974.

72. Eli Gottesman, compiler, *Canadian Jewish Reference Book and Directory* (Ottawa: Mortimer Ltd., 1963) 356; *Evening Record,* May 14, 1894, 2; Jacob Geller interview, June 11, 1974.

73. I. Bert Meretsky interview, June 10, 1974; Mrs. Tibe Burnstine interview, June 12, 1974.

74. *Windsor City Directory,* 1896, 84.

75. Records of Shaar Hashomayim Cemetery.

76. Letter from Mrs. Julia Rabin, June 21, 1974; *Windsor City Directory,* 1891.

77. Mrs. Vivian Berry interview, June 23, 1974; letter from Mrs. Julia Rabin, June 27, 1974.

78. *Evening Record,* April 20, 1895, 8; April 22, 1895, 4; April 27, 1895, 8; April 30, 1895, 4; January 26, 1898, 4; *Windsor City Directory,* 1895.

79. Records of Shaar Hashomayim Cemetery, Nathan Kaplan, d. June 3, 1943, at age 84; Michael Sumner interview, June 4, 1974; Jacob Geller interview, June 11, 1974; Mrs. Goldie Meretsky interview, June 28, 1973; I. M. Meretsky interview, August 15, 1973, in which he notes that there were two Kaplans in the city.

80. I. Bert Meretsky interview, June 10, 1974. Louis and Joseph Stone are listed as residing at 55 Assumption Street, *Windsor City Directory*, 1897–98, 1899; *Evening Record*, July 6, 1901, 5; July 8, 1901, 5. *Windsor City Directory*, 1905–06; 1906–07; 1911, 436.

81. *General Directory* of Windsor, Sandwich and Amherstburg, 1875–76 (London: Charlton & Co.), 25; I. M. Meretsky interview, August 15, 1973; *Windsor City Directory*, 1897–98, 14; I. M. Meretsky, I. Bert Meretsky, and Abe Katzman interviews, June 26, 1974.

82. *Windsor City Directory*, 1900, 161; *Evening Record*, September 2, 1893, 8; March 1, 1895, 4; *Windsor City Directory*, 1894, 57; 1895, 49; 1896, 56.

83. Mrs. Dora Bloom and Mrs. Goldie Meretsky interview, June 24, 1974; *Windsor City Directory*, 1900, 111.

Chapter 3: A Community Puts Down Roots

1. Introduction drawn from Neil Morrison, *Garden Gateway to Canada* (Windsor: Herald Press, 1954); and T. Price and L. Kulisek, *Windsor 1892–1992: A Centennial Celebration* (Windsor: Chamber Publications, 1992).

2. *Evening Record*, July 12, 1913, 1, states that services were held in private homes; Eli Gottesman, compiler, *Canadian Jewish Reference Book and Directory* (Ottawa: Mortimer Ltd., 1963), 356, maintains that services were held in homes on Mercer Street. Since most Jews lived in the area of Mercer Street, it is likely that both are correct.

3. Interview with I. M. Meretsky, August 15, 1973; interview with Jacob Geller, June 11, 1974; both mention services were held in the warehouse of Baum and Brody, Sandwich Street East.

4. If one looks at the building adjacent to the fire hall and the building adjacent to the Meretsky store, one can visualize what the first synagogue looked like in 1893.

5. *Evening Record*, July 12, 1913, 1; Gottesman, 356. The interviews also confirm this was the location of the first synagogue.

6. Interview with Mrs. Tibe Burnstine, June 13, 1974; interview with Mrs. Goldie Meretsky and Mrs. Dora Bloom, June 24, 1974. There is some difference as to whether David Meretsky owned the building and the synagogue or whether Herman Benstein owned it. Herman Benstein may have sold it to David Meretsky later on. Possibly

William Englander owned it; *Evening Record*, June 7, 1895, 4, he (Englander) "is said to own the synagogue."

7. Mrs. Tibe Burnstine interview, June 13, 1974; Mrs. Goldie Meretsky and Mrs. Dora Bloom interview, June 24, 1974; Gottesman.

8. *Evening Record*, July 16, 1895, 4.

9. *Windsor City Directory* (Ingersoll: Union Publishing Co.), 1895, 168.

10. *Evening Record*, March 21, 1899, 8; William R. Gross, "The Redevelopment Area of Windsor to 1900," (master's thesis, University of Windsor, 1961), 155–56, indicates that the synagogue opened in 1899 and David Meretsky was the first president. This appears to be incorrect.

11. *Evening Record*, April 4, 1901, 4; April 23, 1902, 1.

12. *Evening Record*, March 11, 1897.

13. *Evening Record*, September 24, 1900, 4; *Windsor City Directory*, 1900, Rev. Louis Hirsch, Rabbi.

14. *Evening Record*, September 30, 1902, 5.

15. *Evening Record*, September 1, 1904, 5.

16. *Evening Record*, July 30, 1904, 1.

17. *Evening Record*, March 21, 1903, 5.

18. *Evening Record*, September 6, 1904, 5; September 9, 1904, 5; February 23, 1904, 5.

19. Interview with Arthur Gitlin, August 14, 1973.

20. Ibid.

21. *Evening Record*, April 4, 1901, 4; October 2, 1902, 5.

22. *Evening Record*, March 14, 1903, 5.

23. *Evening Record*,, March 21, 1903, 5; March 23, 1903, 5; March 28, 1903, 5; April 4, 1903, 5.

24. *Evening Record*, February 16, 1903, 5; February 23, 1904, 5.

25. *Evening Record*, November 14, 1905, 1.

26. *Evening Record*, November 17, 1905, 1.

27. *Evening Record*, November 18, 1905, 1.

28. *Evening Record*, November 8, 1911, 3; October 28, 1912, 3; September 11, 1913, 8; July 13, 1917, 9; *Border Cities Star*, December 19, 1919, 3; December 20, 1919, 5; *Windsor City Directory*, 1913–1914, 301; 1914, 382.

29. *Evening Record*, April 3, 1908, 7; April 8, 1908, 7; April 9, 1908, 7; April 11, 1908, 7.

30. *Windsor City Directory*, 1897–98, 33; interview with I. M. Meretsky, July 1, 1974.

31. *Evening Record*, October 25, 1912, 2; October 22, 1917, 5.

32. *Evening Record*, October 23, 1903, 5.

33. Interview with Harry Cherniak, undated.

34. Ibid; *Windsor City Directory*, 1906–07.

35. Interview with Gerald Glanz, January 27, 1972.
36. Cherniak interview.
37. Interview with Abe Katzman, I. M. Meretsky, and I. Bert Meretsky, June 26, 1974.
38. Ibid.
39. Records of Shaar Hashomayim Cemetery.
40. Interview with Mary, Edsel, and Mrs. Rose Williams, June 11, 1974.
41. Ibid.
42. Mrs. Dora Bloom and Mrs. Goldie Meretsky interview, June 24, 1974.
43. *Windsor City Directory*, 1919–20, 73–74; 1920–21, 80.
44. *Evening Record*, June 30, 1904, 1.
45. *Evening Record*, October 1, 1904, 5.
46. *Evening Record*, May 2, 1905, 5.
47. *Evening Record*, November 28, 1905, 1; December 2, 1905, 5; The Indenture names the sellers, Albert and wife, Mary Park, Essex County Registry Office, Book Q, plan 122, Lot 88, November 28, 1905.
48. *Evening Record*, November 17, 1905, 5.
49. *Evening Record*, May 21, 1905, 7; June 29, 1906, 7; October 11, 1906, 7; December 29, 1906, 1.
50. *Evening Record*, July 5, 1906, 7.
51. *Evening Record*, February 13, 1907, 7.
52. Trustees of Congregation Shaarey Zedek to Mike Meretsky, Agreement for sale of seat, September 23, 1906, signed by S. Meretsky, pres. And Mike Meretsky; I. Weingarden, Sec'y. in 1906, 1907; N. Cohn signed as Treas. In 1909–13, the seat was designated as trustee seat no. 11 on the ground floor and seat no. 11 in the gallery, for the sum of $50.
53. *Evening Record*, October 12, 1908, 1; October 31, 1908, 7.
54. *Evening Record*, October 23, 1908, 7.
55. *Evening Record*, March 7, 1908, 1.
56. *Evening Record*, November 7, 1910, 7.
57. *Evening Record*, October 10, 1911, 3.
58. *Evening Record*, January 4, 1916, 4.
59. *Evening Record*, October 7, 1911, 7.
60. Gitlin interview.
61. Samuel Abrahamson's name is spelled "Abrahamson" and "Abramson. It is unclear which is the proper spelling.
62. *Evening Record*, July 4, 1912, 1.
63. *Evening Record*, July 3, 1912, 7; July 4, 1912, 1.
64. *Evening Record*, October 4, 1912, 7; October 14, 1912, 7; October 21, 1912, 2.
65. *Evening Record*, July 4, 1912, 1.
66. *Evening Record*, October 18, 1912, 3.
67. *Evening Record*, November 16, 1912, 12
68. *Evening Record*, June 26, 1912, 1; July 3, 1912, 7; September 19, 1912, 1; September 25, 1912, 7.
69. Geller interview.
70. *Evening Record*, July 31, 1917, 3; September 25, 1912, 7.
71. *Evening Record*, May 5, 1915, 3; September 27, 1915, 5.
72. *Evening Record*, September 27, 1915, 5.
73. Interview with Milton Meretsky, June 11, 1974.
74. Glanz interview, January 27, 1972.
75. Interview with Michael Sumner, June 4, 1974.
76. Records of Shaar Hashomayim Cemetery.
77. *Evening Record*, April 23, 1917, 3.
78. *Evening Record*, January 18, 1917, 4.
79. *Evening Record*, June 26, 1912, 1; July 3, 1912, 7; September 19, 1912, 1; September 25, 1912, 7.
80. Interview with Mary, Edsel, and Mrs. Rose Williams, June 11, 1974.
81. *Evening Record*, December 8, 1914, 5.
82. *Evening Record*, December 8, 1914, 5; March 11, 1916, 2. Tifereth Israel, 62 Mercer Street, was also referred to as the Katzman schul. The Ford City synagogue, which started in 1917, chose the name Tifereth Israel in 1926 when their synagogue was built. This was approximately two years after the Mercer Street Tifereth Israel ceased holding services.
83. *Windsor City Directory*, 1919, 73.
84. *Evening Record*, January 18, 1917, 4.
85. Abe Katzman, I. M. Meretsky, and I. Bert Meretsky interview, June 26, 1974.
86. Ibid.
87. Ibid.
88. Ibid.
89. *Evening Record*, October 7, 1901, 6.
90. Louis Rosenberg, *Some Aspects of the Historical Development of the Canadian Jewish Community*, Jewish Population Studies, Population Characteristic, series no. 4, (Montreal: Bureau of Social and Economic Research, Canadian Jewish Congress, 1960), Kroon, Leonard, *Final Report Submitted to the Windsor Jewish Community*, in private collection of Jonathan V. Plaut, 2.
91. *Windsor City Directory*, 1899, 1900.
92. *Windsor City Directory*, 1906, 1907.
93. *Windsor City Directory*, 1906, 1907, I. M. Meretsky interview, August 15, 1973.
94. *Windsor City Directory*, 1906, 1907.

95. *Windsor City Directory*, 1904.
96. *Windsor City Directory*, 1900, 1901, 174; 1903; 1904; 1905–06; 1906–07, 152; 1911, 462; *Evening Record,* October 18, 1912, 7.
97. *Evening Record*, January 15, 1902, 5.
98. *Windsor City Directory*, 1905–06, 108.
99. *Windsor City Directory*, 1900, 161.
100. *Windsor City Directory*, 1894.
101. Ibid.
102. *Windsor City Director*, 1911, 455.
103. *Evening Record*, April 14, 1906, 7.
104. *Evening Record*, August 2, 1909, 7.
105. *Evening Record*, March 23, 1912, 7.
106. *Evening Record*, April 12, 1906, 3; April 16, 1906, 6.
107. *Windsor City Directory*, 1910, 410–11.
108. Ibid., 417–18, 425.
109. Ibid.
110. Ibid., 413.
111. Ibid., 430.
112. Ibid., 539.
113. *Evening Record,* January 23, 1897, 8; March 7, 1896, 8; April 26, 1893, 2; October 6, 1893, 4; November 6, 1893, 4; July 5, 1895, 4; September 27, 1898, 8; September 28, 1898, 4.
114. I. M. Meretsky interview, July 1, 1974.
115. *Evening Record*, December 17, 1898, 4; October 29, 1900, 8; November 9, 1895, 8; February 18, 1896, 8; February 14, 1896, 8; February 29, 1896, 8; March 3, 1896, 8; May 13, 1897, 8; February 22, 1895, 4; June 14, 1897, 8; February 18, 1895, 8; January 8, 1895, 4; February 11, 1898, 8; June 5, 1896, 8; October 18, 1897, 8; October 19, 1897, 8; August 20, 1898, 8; March 21, 1899, 8; April 16, 1896, 8; April 17, 1896 8; April 16, 1894, 4; September 12, 1898, 5.
116. *Evening Record*, February 6, 1900, 8; April 19, 1900, 8; February 20, 1902, 8; March 17, 1902, 8; December 4, 1903, 1; June 19, 1906, 7; June 21, 1906, 1; August 19, 1906, 7; October 25, 1907, 1; October 29, 1907, 7; April 11, 1908, 1; May 15, 1908, 1; March 9, 1909, 1; April 17, 1909, 7; June 11, 1909, 7; June 14, 1909, 7; July 9, 1909, 7; March 17, 1911, 3; March 27, 1911, 3; November 11, 1911, 9; November 18, 1911, 1; November 24, 1911, 1; December 1, 1911, 7; January 5, 1912, 11; October 12, 1912, 2; October 26, 1912, 5; November 2, 1912, 6; November 12, 1912, 2.
117. *Evening Record*, September 23, 1896, 8; February 22, 1895, 4.
118. *Evening Record*, March 21, 1900, 1; April 9, 1900, 4; June 8, 1900, 8; August 25, 1900, 8; September 18, 1900, 8; September 22, 1900, 8; October 29, 1900, 8; January 25, 1901, 4; January 28, 1901, 4; February 1, 1901, 4; January 28, 1901, 4; February 1, 1901, 4; February 4, 1901, 4; February 8, 1901, 5; March 25, 1901, 1; March 26, 1901, 5; April 3, 1901, 4; April 24, 1901, 5; May 1, 1901, 5, 4; May 23, 1901, 5; June 10, 1901, 5; November 11, 1901, 5; November 22, 1901, 5; November 26, 1901, 1; December 2, 1901, 5; December 4, 1901, 8; December 5, 1901, 8; January 19, 1906, 5; February 6, 1906, 5; June 1, 1906, 1; June 4, 1906, 7; June 6, 1906, 7; July 13, 1906, 1; November 7, 1906, 7; November 10, 1906, 7; January 28, 1907, 7; October 21, 1907, 7; October 29, 108, 7; January 13, 1901, 1; March 8, 1909, 1; April 20, 1909, 7; May 6, 1909, 7; January 29, 1910, 1; June 9, 1910, 7; June 20, 1910, 7; February 13, 1911, 7; September 15, 1911, 7; October 14, 1911, 1; October 17, 1911, 7; November 4, 1911, 7; November 6, 1911, 2; November 8, 1911, 2; November 11, 1911, 9; November 13, 1911, 7; November 17, 1911, 3; December 27, 1911, 7; May 2, 1912, 7; May 18, 1912, 7; June 14, 1912, 5; June 21, 1912, 1; November 8, 1912, 2; November 15, 1912, 7; November 16, 1912, 2; February 28, 1913, 2; March 4, 1913, 2; June 7, 1913, 2; June 25, 1913, 9; November 18, 1913, 8; March 5, 1913, 2; April 15, 1913, 5; June 9, 1913, 2; August 25, 1914, 2; October 7, 1914, 3; April 10, 1916, 3; April 11, 1916, 2; April 22, 1916, 3; March 16, 1917, 8; March 23, 19197, 10; March 30, 1917, 1; May 12, 1917, 2; July 13, 1917, 9; *Windsor Record,* April 5, 1918, 10; May 13, 1918, 7; June 15, 1918, 2; August 7, 1918, 3; August 14, 1918, 3; August 27, 1918, 2; *Border Cities Star,* October 7, 1918, 3; October 29, 1918, 5; February 12, 1919, 3; February 15, 1919, 3; June 19, 1919, 6; December 10, 1919, 3.
119. *Evening Record*, January 12, 1900, 8; December 8, 1900, 8; November 13, 1905, 5; February 10, 1906, 5; March 13, 1906, 5; March 26, 1906, 5; May 7, 1906, 8; August 31, 1906, 7; September 19 1906, 1; January 2, 1907, 7; December 11, 1907, 7; November 21, 1908, 7; December 21, 1908, 1; October 29, 1909, 7; March 28, 1910, 7; October 11, 1910, 1; October 14, 1910, 7; January 24, 1911, 7; November 18, 1911, 3; December 16, 1911, 3; January 10, 1912, 7; September 22, 1914, 3; September 23, 1914, 3; February 16, 1915, 6; June 1, 1915, 1; November 25, 1916, 2; January 8, 1917, 6; November 6, 1917, 2; *Windsor Record,* January 25, 1918, 9; *Border Cities Star,* December 23, 1918, 11; December 27, 1918, 3; January 23, 1919, 3; April 14, 1919, 3; May 29, 1919, 3; December 22,

1919, 3; December 27, 1919, 3.

120. *Evening Record*, February 26, 1900, 8; April 19, 1900, 8; February 20, 1902, 8; March 17, 1902, 8; December 4, 1903, 1; June 19, 1906, 7; June 21, 1906, 1; August 19, 1906, 7; October 25, 1907, 1; October 29, 1907, 7; April 11, 1908, 1; May 15, 1908, 1; March 9, 1909, 1; April 17, 1909, 7; June 11, 1909, 7; June 14, 1909, 7; July 9, 1909, 7; March 17, 1911, 3; March 27, 1911, 3; November 11, 1911, 9; November 18, 1911, 1; November 24, 1911, 1; December 1, 1911, 7; January 5, 1912, 11; October 12, 1912, 2; October 26, 1912, 5; November 2, 1912, 6; November 12, 1912, 2.

121. See references in note 120.

122. *Evening Record*, August 24, 1914, 2; August 25, 1914, 2.

123. *Evening Record*, April 9, 1900, 4; August 25, 1900, 8; November 26, 1901, 8.

124. *Evening Record*, February 28, 1912, 3; December 13, 1910, 1.

125. *Windsor City Directory*, 1919–1920, 211.

126. Ibid., 547.

127. Ibid., 539.

128. Ibid., 530

129. Ibid.

130. Ibid., 536–38.

131. Ibid., 547.

132. Ibid., 529.

133. *Evening Record*, April 25, 1919, 8.

134. *Evening Record*, April 17, 1900, 8; May 1, 1907, 7.

135. *Evening Record*, April 20, 1912, 9.

136. *Evening Record*, July 26, 1912, 7; December 23, 1912, 1; October 27, 1913, 1; October 28, 1913, 1; November 21, 1913, 14; June 13, 1917, 3; *Windsor Record,* January 3, 1918, 3; *Border Cities Star,* September 28, 1918, 3; September 5, 1919, 3; September 6, 1919, 3; November 8, 1919, 3.

137. *Evening Record*, February 5, 1905, 5; February 16, 1907, 7; February 27, 1907, 7; November 17, 1908, 7; April 9, 1912, 7; October 24, 1913, 2; May 12, 1914, 3; May 26, 1914, 7; August 18, 1914, 3; July 15, 1915, 7; August 11, 1916, 3; June 4, 1917, 2; April 28, 1919, 1; July 28, 1919, 1; July 18, 1919, 3; November 8, 1919. 7;

138. *Evening Record*, December 22, 1900, 2; June 8, 1901, 4; June 25, 1910, 1.

139. *Evening Record*, June 6, 1907, 1; May 15, 1909, 3; July 9, 1912, 8.

140. *Evening Record*, June 16, 1914, 1.

141. *Evening Record*, June 5, 1915, 1.

142. *Evening Record*, May 29, 1917, 3, 10; June 1, 1917, 10; June 4, 1917, 1; September 25, 1917, 12; *Border Cities Star,* June 12, 1918, 6; March 20, 1919, 9.

Chapter 4: Widening the Horizon

1. Introduction drawn from Neil Morrison, *Garden Gateway to Canada* (Windsor: Herald Press, 1954); and T. Price and L. Kulisek, *Windsor 1892–1992: A Centennial Celebration* (Windsor: Chamber Publications, 1992).

2. *Evening Record*, September 14, 1907, 5.

3. *Evening Record*, December 8, 1914, 5; March 11, 1916, 2. Tifereth Israel, 62 Mercer Street, was also referred to as the Katzman shul. The Ford City synagogue, which started in 1917, chose the name Tifereth Israel in 1926 when their synagogue was built. This was approximately two years after the Mercer Street Tifereth Israel ceased holding services.

4. Records of the Board of Education Entrance Exam, 1900–19, Board of Education, Windsor, Ontario; *Evening Record,* March 27, 1914, 2.

5. Morrison, 200; *Evening Record,* September 28, 1909, 1.

6. *Evening Record,* September 20, 1900, 8; September 22, 1900, 8; March 6, 1906, 4.

7. Morrison, 201; *Evening Record,* March 24, 1906, 6; September 10, 1910, 1; April 9, 1913, 1.

8. Records of the Board of Education Entrance Exam, 1900–19, Board of Education, Windsor, Ontario; *Evening Record,* March 27, 1914, 2.

9. *Evening Record,* July 12, 1901, 4; April 13, 1906, 1; July 3, 1908, 1; July 6, 1908, 1, 7; December 21, 1910, 1; August 15, 1911, 1; October 5, 1911, 3; July 19, 1912, 1; August 10, 1914, 10; December 23, 1914, 3; March 10, 1915, 1; June 24, 1919, 3; May 23, 1919, 3; May 31, 1917, 2; July 17, 1917, 3; *Windsor Record,* March 26, 1918, 2; *Border Cities Star,* June 17, 1919, 5; July 7, 1919, 5; July 8, 1919, 8; December 18, 1919, 3, 7; December 20, 1919, 3.

10. Interview with Milton Meretsky, June 11, 1974.

11. *Evening Record,* July 12, 1901, 4; April 13, 1906, 1; July 3, 1908, 1; July 6, 1908, 1, 7; December 21, 1910, 1; August 15, 1911, 1; October 5, 1911, 3; July 19, 1912, 1; August 10, 1914, 10; December 23, 1914, 3; March 10, 1915, 1; June 24, 1915, 3; May 23, 1916, 3; May 31, 1917, 2; July 17, 1917, 3; *Windsor Record,* March 26, 1918, 2; *Border Cities Star,*

June 17, 1919, 5; July 7, 1919, 5; July 8, 1919, 8; December 18, 1919, 3, 7; December 20, 1919, 3.

12. *Evening Record,* June 7, 1911, 4.
13. Milton Meretsky interview.
14. Interview with Edsel Meretsky, Harry Cherniak, Michael Sumner, and Harry Meretsky. April 16, 1971.
15. Sumner interview, June 4, 1974.
16. Interview with Abe Katzman, I. M. Meretsky, and I. Bert Meretsky, June 26, 1974.
17. Michael Sumner interview, June 4, 1974.
18. Milton Meretsky interview.
19. Katzman, I. M. Meretsky, and I. Bert Meretsky interview, June 26, 1974; Sumner interview; *Evening Record,* February 25, 1916, 9.
20. *Evening Record,* November 12, 1915, 2.
21. *Evening Record,* December 2, 1915, 2.
22. *Evening Record,* January 24, 1916, 3.
23. *Evening Record,* December 2, 1915, 2.
24. *Evening Record,* September 28, 1912, 1.
25. *Evening Record,* October 11, 1917, 10
26. *Evening Record,* October 13, 1918, 11.
27. *Evening Record,* November 10, 1916, 14; September 27, 1917, 8.
28. *Border Cities Star,* September 12, 1918, 10; September 27, 1918, 11; November 30, 1918, 14; December 4, 1918, 14; December 19, 1919, 11.
29. *Evening Record,* January 11, 1918, 14; February 2, 1918, 5; April 17, 1918; 9; *Border Cities Star,* April 22, 1919, 11.
30. *Border Cities Star,* June 9, 1919, 10.
31. *Evening Record,* December 6, 1913, 8; December 20, 1913, 6; July 2, 1915, 14; September 22, 1917, 16; *Border Cities Star,* June 20, 1918, 12; June 20, 1919, 8; June 25, 1919, 5; June 28, 1919, 10; July 26, 1919, 3.
32. *Evening Record,* May 3, 1902, 5; February 7, 1911, 8; March 4, 1912, 8; June 8, 1912, 8; June 13, 1912, 8; August 9, 1915, 10; March 2, 1916, 12; March 10, 1916, 16; August 11, 1916, 7; August15, 1916, 10; March 23, 1917, 11.
33. *Evening Record,* December 23, 1911, 3; June 25, 1912, 8; August 13, 1912, 8; November 18, 1912, 8; January 3, 1913, 6; May 26, 1913, 12; August 25, 1914, 10; September 15, 1914, 12; April 21, 1915, 12; April 22, 1915, 3; June 15, 1915, 10; July 23, 1915, 9; August 6, 1915, 14; March 18, 1916, 2; May 17, 1916, 10; September 6, 1916, 10; September 9, 1916, 10; September 12, 1916, 10; August 24, 1917, 10; *Windsor Record,* August 2, 1918, 2; *Border Cities Star,* July 28, 1919, 9; August 5, 1919, 8; August 14, 1919, 6; July 12, 1919, 8; June 30, 1919, 13.
34. *Evening Record,* September 14, 1901, 8.
35. *Windsor Record,* January 17, 1918; April 15, 1919, 2; April 26, 1918, 4; May 10, 1918, 2; September 11, 1918, 5; October 22, 1918, 3; July 9, 1918, 2; March 15, 1919, 8; August 31, 1914, 2.
36. *Evening Record,* June 29, 1905, 1; *Border Cities Star,* June 17, 1919, 5.
37. *Ibid.,* February 13, 1917, 2; March 30, 1917, 11; July 9, 1917, 6; July 11, 1917, 10; July 17, 19197, 2; July 18, 1917, 2.
38. *Evening Record,* July 16, 1917, 1.
39. *Evening Record,* August 25, 1917, 12; *Windsor Record,* January 26, 1918, 10; February 26, 1918, 10; April 5, 1918, 13; April 24, 1918, 10; May 1, 1918, 12; May 7, 1918, 7; May 8, 1918, 12; May 16, 1918, 12; June 5, 1918, 6; July 6, 1918, 5; *Border Cities Star,* November 9, 1918, 9.
40. *Evening Record,* June 10, 1916, 12.
41. *Border Cities Star,* July 12, 1917, 4.
42. *Border Cities Star,* March 12, 1919, 5.
43. *Border Cities Star,* March 1, 1919, 12
44. *Border Cities Star,* April 6, 1920, 3; February 14, 1920, 3.
45. *Border Cities Star,* April 13, 1920, 5.
46. *Border Cities Star,* November 16, 1920, 3; December 30, 1920, 3; December 27, 1920, 3; December 22, 1920, 3.
47. *Border Cities Star,* September 24, 1921, 3; September 27, 1921, 17; March 28, 1922, 12.
48. *Border Cities Star,* June 12, 1925, 12; June 13, 1925, 5; June 16, 1925, 8; June 17, 1925, 3, 5; September 2, 1925, 1; November 10, 1926, 7; November 25, 1926, 3; December 2, 1926, 5; July 5, 1928, 3; August 26, 1929, 1; September 1, 1929, 7.
49. *Evening Record,* April 1, 1911, 1; April 4, 1911, 1; April 5, 1911, 2; April 6, 1911, 1; April 6, 1911, 5; August 12, 1911, 1; July 10, 1913, 7.
50. *Border Cities Star,* April 27, 1928, 7.
51. *Evening Record,* July 6, 1915, 1.
52. Much of the story was never told for fear that non-Jews may be hurt. Letters and many records pertaining to the work are in the private collection of David Glanz.
53. *Evening Record,* December 1, 1914, 2; December 10, 1914, 4; December 14, 1914, 3,
54. Interview with Ben Baum, August 13, 1973.
55. Ibid.
56. Council Minutes (January 12, 1914–December 31, 1915), June 14, 1915, 286; *Evening Record,* June 11, 1915, 6.

57. Council Minutes, June 21, 1915, 295.
58. Council Minutes, April 26, 1915, 268; *Evening Record*, April 27, 1915, 1; April 28, 1915, 1.
59. Council Minutes, June 14, 1915, 289; August 16, 1915, 321.
60. *Evening Record*, January 4, 1916, 1.
61. Council Minutes (1916–19), January 10, 1916.
62. Council Minutes, January 31, 1916, 11; February 4, 1916, 13; March 13, 1916, 28; May 22, 19196, 62; July 17, 1916, 99.
63. *Evening Record*, November 25, 1916, 2; November 27, 1916, 2.
64. Council Minutes, January 8, 1917; *Evening Record*, January 8, 1917, 1.
65. Council Minutes, May 11, 1917, 224.
66. Council Minutes, February 27, 1917, 178.
67. *Evening Record*, December 6, 1917, 3.
68. *Windsor Record*, January 2, 1918, 1, 8; January 3, 1918, 3.
69. *Windsor Record*, January 8, 1918, 1.
70. Council Minutes, February 18, 1918, 326.
71. *Windsor Record*, April 6, 1918, 3.
72. *Windsor Record*, April 19, 1918, 9.
73. *Border Cities Star*, January 2, 1919, 3.
74. Edsel Meretsky, Harry Cherniak, Michael Sumner, and Harry Meretsky, interview, April 16, 1971; interview with Senator David A. Croll, March 22, 1974; interview with Jacob Geller, June 11, 1974.
75. Interview with Norman Hurwitz, June 12, 1974; letter from William Hurwitz, July 12, 1972.
76. Norman Hurwitz interview.
77. Ibid.
78. Ibid.
79. Nicholas Palahnuk, Ford City, to Abram Adler, March 23, 1925, Essex County Registry Office, Town of Ford City, Lot 111, East side of Hickory, Plan 120, Book H, no. 7895.
80. *Border Cities Star*, August 14, 1925, 5.
81. Ibid.
82. Ibid.
83. Ibid.
84. *Border Cities Star*, December 1, 1925, 3.
85. Abram Adler to Abam Adler, Barney Hurwitz, Samuel Samberg, Sam Katzman, and Fanny Adler, Essex County Registry Office, Town of Ford City, No. 7896.
86. Abram Adler, Barney Hurwitz, Samuel Samberg, Sam Katzman and Fanny Adler to themselves as trustees, March 27, 1926, Essex County Registry Office, Town of Ford City, Book I, No. 9146. See also No. 9165, March 31, 1926, Book I.
87. *Windsor City Directory* 1925–26 (Ingersoll: Union Publishing Co.), 398; Kamenkowitz died December 1, 1926.
88. *Border Cities Star*, August 14, 1925, 5.
89. Ibid.
90. *Border Cities Star*, July 14, 1927, 8.
91. *Border Cities Star*, January 22, 1927, 7.
92. Interview with Mr. and Mrs. Harry Luborsky, August 13, 1973.
93. *Border Cities Star*, March 15, 1928, 10.
94. *Evening Record*, June 17, 1904, 1.
95. Ibid.
96. *Windsor Record*, May 17, 1918, 10; *Border Cities Star*, March 3, 1919, 3; May 15, 1919, 5; July 10, 1919, 10; October 3, 1919, 9; October 6, 1919, 3.
97. *Windsor Record*, January 17, 1918; April 15, 1919, 2; April 26, 1918, 4; May 10, 1918, 2; September 11, 1918, 5; October 22, 1918, 3; July 9, 1918, 2; March 15, 1919, 8; August 31, 1914, 2.
98. *Windsor Record*, May 15, 1918, 1.
99. *Border Cities Star*, March 11, 1919, 6; May 28, 1919, 5.
100. *Evening Record*, August 25, 1917, 12; *Windsor Record*, January 26, 1918, 10; February 26, 1918, 10; April 5, 1918, 13; April 24, 1918, 10; May 1, 1918, 12; May 7, 1918, 7; May 8, 1918, 12; May 16, 1918, 12; June 5, 1918, 6; July 6, 1918, 5; *Border Cities Star*, November 9, 1918, 9.
101. *Border Cities Star*, October 18, 1919, 8; October 30, 1919, 8.
102. *Border Cities Star*, February 7, 1921, 10.
103. *Border Cities Star*, May 5, 1921, 19.
104. *Border Cities Star*, May 30, 1921, 13.
105. *Border Cities Star*, November 28, 1927, 5; April 18, 1928, 5; April 23, 1928, 5.
106. *Border Cities Star*, May 3, 1921, 12.
107. *Border Cities Star*, May 21, 1921, 19; May 26, 1921, 3; May 27, 1921, 113.
108. *Border Cities Star*, March 27, 1926, 14.
109. *Border Cities Star*, April 19, 1926, 3; April 20, 1926, 3; April 28, 1926, 3.
110. *Border Cities Star*, May 8, 1926, 3.
111. *Border Cities Star*, October 13, 1926, 5.
112. *Border Cities Star*, May 20, 1927, 5.
113. *Border Cities Star*, September 5, 1929, 5.
114. *Border Cities Star*, June 12, 1925, 12; June 13, 1925, 5; June 16, 1925, 8; June 17, 1925, 3, 5; September 2, 1925, 1; November 10, 1926, 7; November 15, 1926, 3; December 2, 1926, 5; July 5, 1928, 3; August 26, 1929, 1, September 1, 1929, 7.

115. *Evening Record*, December 18, 1919, 3; March 5, 1917, 5.
116. *Evening Record*, August 20, 1918, 5.
117. *Border Cities Star*, November 2, 1918, 5.
118. *Border Cities Star*, May 17, 1919, 3.
119. *Border Cities Star*, September 17, 1918, 5.
120. *Border Cities Star*, August 18, 1919, 3.
121. Mortgage for $15,000 contracted between Agudas B'nai Zion Society of Windsor and Robert C. Struthers, mortgagee, December 1, 1919, Essex County Registry Office, City of Windsor, no. 141, Plan 126, Block 25, part of Lot 1 and Lot 2, Old Book C, Windsor.
122. *Border Cities Star*, December 20, 1919, 3.
123. Sumner interview.
124. *Border Cities Star*, April 13, 1920, 3.
125. *Border Cities Star*, May 7, 1920, 3.
126. Talmud Torah *Golden Book*, in the private collection of David Glanz, Windsor.
127. *Border Cities Star*, November 14, 1922, 3.
128. *Border Cities Star*, December 17, 1920, 16; March 15, 1933, 3; January 29, 1923, 11; February 10, 1934, 5; October 4, 1934, 23.
129. *Border Cities Star*, April 14, 1925, 16; April 21, 1925, 3.
130. *Border Cities Star*, November 4, 1927, 9; November 8, 1927, 3.
131. *Border Cities Star*, April 13, 1928, 3.
132. *Border Cities Star*, January 19, 1929, 3; January 21, 1929, 5.
133. *Border Cities Star*, January 21, 1929, 5.
134. *Border Cities Star*, January 30, 1928, 3.
135. *Border Cities Star*, January 17, 1930, 3; January 23, 1930, 5.
136. *Windsor City Directory*, 1924–25, 690.
137. *Golden Book*.
138. Sumner interview.
139. *Border Cities Star*, March 11, 1931, 9.
140. *Border Cities Star*, June 25, 1928, 11.
141. *Border Cities Star*, February 16, 1931, 3.
142. Interview with Bernard Madoff, June 11, 1974.
143. Ibid.
144. Ibid.
145. Essex County Registry Office, County of Essex, Lot 34, east side of Parent Avenue, Plan 143, March 5,1930.
146. *Windsor City Directory*, 1937, 412.
147. *Wikipedia, the free Encyclopedia*, online source, http://en.wikipedia.org/wiki/Isaac_Leib_Peretz
148. Minutes of Peretz Shule, Windsor, November 19, 1934–1937, written in Yiddish.
149. *Border Cities Star*, May 31, 1935, 25.
150. *Border Cities Star*, November 22, 1933, 3.
151. *Border Cities Star*, October 22, 1924, 3.
152. Interview with Mrs. Ida Benstein, February 25, 1976. The list of B'nai B'rith presidents was taken from the original records of Edsel Benstein, now in possession of his widow, Mrs. Ida Benstein.
153. *Windsor Daily Star*, January 14, 1928, 14.
154. *Border Cities Star*, January 25, 1929, 3; February 14, 1921, 11.
155. *Border Cities Star*, April 13, 1928, 3.
156. *Border Cities Star*, January 17, 1930, 3; January 23, 1920, 5.
157. Interview with Sockley Kamin, June 25, 1974.
158. Records of Shaar Hashomayim Cemetery.
159. *Border Cities Star*, May 30, 3.
160. Kamin interview.
161. *Border Cities Star*, May 30, 1927, 3.
162. Kamin interview.
163. *Border Cities Star*, May 30, 1927, 3.
164. Sumner interview.
165. *Border Cities Star*, January 14, 1927, 3. The article on Rabbi Ashinsky was written for the *Border Cities Star* by David A. Croll.

Chapter 5: Good Times, Bad Times

1. Introduction drawn from Neil Morrison, *Garden Gateway to Canada* (Windsor: Herald Press, 1954) and T. Price and L. Kulisek, *Windsor 1892–1992: A Centennial Celebration* (Windsor: Chamber Publications, 1992).
2. *Border Cities Star*, March 6, 1920, 1; September 1, 1920, 3; December 2, 1920, 3; February 4, 1922, 7; April 3, 1922, 5; June 2, 1922, 3; July 4, 1922, 16; November 1, 1922, 7; November 25, 1922, 3; January 3, 1923, 3; April 4, 1923, 3; May 2, 1923, 11; May 16, 1923, 3; May 28, 1923, 1; June 23, 14; September 6, 1923, 8; October 4, 1923, 32; October 23, 1923, 7; October 30, 1923, 10; February 16, 1924, 1; February 22, 1924, 1; April 17, 1925, 3; September 11, 1925, 3; June 28, 1926, 3; February 22, 1927, 1; April 26, 1927, 1; June 10, 1927, 1; June 21, 1927, 5; July 7, 1927, 3; August 3, 1927, 1.
3. *Border Cities Star*, February 2, 1920, 5; March 1,1920, 6; March 6, 1920, 3; March 19, 1920, 3; April 3, 1920, 6; April 7,1920, 3; April 8,1920, 3; April 13, 1920, 3; April 21, 1920, 3; June 11, 1920, 3; August 325, 1920, 6; September 30, 1920,

12; October 13, 1920, 3; December 10, 1920, 3; December 29, 1920, 3; January 31, 1922, 3; February 8, 1922, 3; August 10, 1921, 1; October 24, 1921, 3; December 16, 1921, 9; December 16, 1921, 3; December 17, 1921, 3; April 4, 1922, 7; July 20, 1922, 3; August 1922, 3; November 9, 1922, 3; November 22, 1922, 7; November 29, 1922, 7; December 9, 1922, 3; March 28, 1922, 3; February 23, 1923, 3; March 28, 1923, 3; July 16, 1923, 3; May 21, 1923, 10; September 14, 1923, 3; September 21, 1923, 3; June 30, 1924, 3; September 30, 1925, 3; November 30, 1925, 3; December 2, 1925, 5; July 27, 1926, 3; July 28, 1926, 3; August 18, 1926, 3; March 27, 1928, 3; April 4, 1928, 3; May 3, 1927, 3; October 26, 1927, 3; December 20, 1927, 6; January6 5, 1928, 3; June 13, 1928, 3; July 11, 1928, 1; October 8, 1928, 5; February 5, 1929, 3; February 5, 1920, 3; November 18, 1930, 5; December 8, 1930, 6; November 23, 1932, 3; December 11, 1933, 3; December 20, 1933, 3; January 8, 1934, 3; *Windsor Daily Star,* November 18, 1926, 3.

4. *Border Cities Star,* February 12, 1920, 3,4; July 12, 1920, 4; April 19, 1921, 1, 3; May 15, 1922, 3; June 15, 1922, 3; June 16, 1922, 4; November 17, 1924, 1; May 20, 1925, 1; March 13, 1926, 1; December 2, 1926, 1; January 18, 1927, 3; March 10, 1927, 1; April 10, 1927, 1,2; May 16, 1927, 3; May 17, 1927, 3; September 15, 1927, 1; February 7, 19028, 1; July 23, 1928, 1; August 10, 1928, 1; August 17, 1928, 1.

5. *Border Cities Star,* June 1, 1927, 3.

6. *Border Cities Star,* January 9, 1930, 3.

7. *Border Cities Star,* September 15, 1920, 3; September 18, 1920, 12.

8. *Border Cities Star,* November 5, 1921, 14; December 27, 1921, 9; February 6, 1922, 3; July 27, 1922, 3; November 29, 1922, 3; December 5, 1922, 2; December 7, 1922, 11; October 5, 1923, 7; May 9, 1925, 5; June 17, 1926, 5; July 28, 1926, 6; September 12, 1928, 8; October 2, 1928, 5; January 23, 1929, 3; August 7, 1929, 3; August 8, 1929, 10; April 1, 1935, 3; *Windsor Daily Star,* July 17, 1935, 5.

9. *Windsor Star,* March 24, 1980, 1–10.

10. Ibid.

11. *Windsor Star,* November 22, 1922, 6; October 21, 1923, 12; February 6, 1924, 10; January 17, 1928, 12.

12. *Windsor Star,* January 28, 1920, 6.

13. *Border Cities Star,* October 4, 1922, 8, 9; October 6, 1922, 11; April 17, 1925, 9; May 7, 1925, 11.

14. *Border Cities Star,* April 27, 1932, 8.

15. Records of Shaar Hashomayim Cemetery.

16. *Border Cities Star,* December 30, 1919, 7.

17. *Border Cities Star,* December 28, 1921, 7.

18. *Border Cities Star,* December 1, 1923, 3; December 3, 1923, 10.

19. *Border Cities Star,* November 27, 1923, 3.

20. Council Minutes (1926–1929) January 3, 1928, 293–95; *Border Cities Star,* December 29, 1927, 3.

21. *Border Cities Star,* November 27, 1922, 3; November 26, 1923, 3.

22. *Border Cities Star,* November 30, 1925, 3; December 4, 1925, 10; December 5, 1925, 8; December 8, 1925, 1.

23. Interview with Arthur Gitlin, August 14, 1973; interview with Joshua Gitlin, April 26, 1972; Records of the Shaar Hashomayim Cemetery.

24. See references for note 23.

25. *Border Cities Star,* December 6, 1927, 3; December 31, 1927, 3.

26. Council Minutes, January 3, 1928, 288.

27. Ibid., 308.

28. Council Minutes, July 9, 1928, 369.

29. *Border Cities Star,* March 6, 1928, 3; April 3, 1928, 7.

30. *Border Cities Star,* May 1, 1928, 9.

31. *Border Cities Star,* February 15, 1928, 3.

32. *Border Cities Star,* February 20, 1928, 3.

33. *Border Cities Star,* February 25, 1929, 3.

34. *Border Cities Star,* December 3, 1929, 1.

35. *Border Cities Star,* January 31, 1924, 9; February 28, 1924, 9; April 21, 1924, 9; June 7, 1924, 6; June 9, 1924, 9; October 22, 1926, 9; April 28, 1927, 11; May 5, 1927, 9; May 11, 1927, 5; May 19, 1927, 7; November 28, 1927, 9; June 8, 1928, 9; December 18, 1928, 11; September 19, 1929, 13; July 31, 1930, 9; January 13, 1931, 5; February 7, 1931, 11; February 16, 1931, 7; December 19, 1931, 9; January 22, 1932, 7; April 25, 1932, 9; October 14, 1932, 19; February 23, 1933, 21; September 29, 1933, 21; February 26 1935, 13.

36. *Border Cities Star,* July 12, 1923, 9; January 3, 1925, 8; June 14, 1923, 3; March 11, 1926, 5; June 10, 1926, 6; September 2, 1926, 9; October 27, 1926 3; January 8, 1927, 9; January 21, 1927, 9; February 8, 1927, 9; February 16, 1927, 5; February 25, 1927, 9; April 20, 1927, 8; April 20, 1927, 6; June 22, 1927, 5; June 25, 1927, 7; January 6, 1928, 7; February 15, 1928, 5; February 17, 1928, 7; April 12, 1928, 13; June 28, 1928, 1, 13; July 6, 1928, 9; March 7, 1929, 11; March 19, 1929, 11; March 27, 1929, 5; March 29, 1929, 11; April 5, 1929, 9; April 30, 1929, 8; June 17, 1929, 11; June 18,

1929, 11; August 14, 1929, 1; September 6, 1929, 7; September 21, 1929, 9; September 21, 1929, 9; September 25, 1929, 5; January 8, 1920, 5; January 18, 1930, 9; February 27, 1930, 1; February 28, 1930, 11; May 10, 1930, 7; May 21, 1930, 11; February 28, 1930, 11; May 10, 1930, 7; May 21, 1930, 5; June 26, 1930, 9; July 15, 1930, 9; February 23, 1931, 11; March 21, 1931, 13; July 23, 1931, 9; September 24, 1931, 11; October 19, 1931, 9; October 27, 1931, 9; December 26, 1931, 9; March 31, 1932, 13; May 26, 1932, 9; June 2, 1932, 11; June 16, 1932, 13; August 16, 1932, 9; November 29, 1932, 15; January 4, 1933, 13; May 23, 1933, 15; October 14 1933, 11; November 3, 1933, 13; December 13, 1933, 5; March 19, 1923, 15; September 28, 1934, 21; October 4, 1934, 21; November 22, 1934, 21; February 20, 1935, 17; June 22, 1935, 12; July 10, 1935, 13; December 4, 1935, 21.

37. *Border Cities Star*, July 15, 1922, 3; December 13, 1923, 6; December 15, 1923, 9; January 10, 1924, 3; December 9, 1925, 2; July 16, 1926, 7; July 22, 1926, 7; September 4, 1926 3; November 27, 1926 11; March 5, 1927, 9; December 13, 1930, 9.

38. *Border Cities Star*, September 17, 1922, 11; December 4, 1926, 9; December 6, 1926, 11; October 22, 1928, 5; July 17, 1930, 5; November 10, 1933, 16; November 16, 1934, 22; December 23, 1934, 11; February 6, 1935, 20; February 8, 1935, 20.

39. *Border Cities Star*, July 28, 1924, 6; August 18, 1925, 9; April 11, 1930, 9; June 6, 1931, 11; June 24, 1931, 8; August 22, 1931, 9; February 12, 1932, 3; April 25, 1932, 11.

40. Interview with Michael Sumner, June 4, 1974.

41. *Border Cities Star,* December 7, 1928, 3.

42. Letter from Mrs. I. Lebendiger, June 30, 1976.

43. *Border Cities Star*, December 14, 1928, 7.

44. *Border Cities Star*, December 19, 1928, 3.

45. *Border Cities Star*, January 18, 1929, 5.

46. *Border Cities Star*, January 31, 1929, 5.

47. *Border Cities Star*, February 2, 1929, 11.

48. *Border Cities Star*, January 31, 1929, 5.

49. *Border Cities Star*, March 7, 1929, 3; February 1, 1929, 5; February 4, 1929, 3; February 5, 1929, 3.

50. *Border Cities Star*, March 1, 1929, 5.

51. *Border Cities Star*, March 26, 1929, 5.

52. *Border Cities Star*, June 20, 1929, 3; April 19, 1929, 5.

53. *Border Cities Star*, June 20, 1929, 3; June 21, 1929, 3.

54. *Border Cities Star*, April 24, 1929, 7; October 18, 1929, 13; September 30, 1929, 7; October 7, 1929, 5; September 23, 1929, 7.

55. *Border Cities Star*, September 10, 1928, 3; September 12, 1928, 5; September 21, 1928, 5; September 22, 1930, 14.

56. $65,000 at 6½%, signed by Louis Kaplan, Maurice Nathanson, Simon Meretsky, Joseph Kovinsky, Robert G. Cohen, Joseph Becker, David Meretsky, Joel Gelber, Benjamin Brody, Maxwell Schott, Moise Silver, Jerry A. Glanz, David A. Croll and David B. Caplan, January 11, 1930, Essex County Registry Office, City of Windsor, no. 39072.

57. *Border Cities Star*, February 10, 1930, 3.

58. *Border Cities Star*, February 25, 1930, 3.

59. *Border Cities Star*, February 4, 1930, 3; February 5, 1920, 4; February 8, 1930, 3.

60. *Border Cities Star*, February 17, 1930, 3; February 18, 1930, 3.

61. *Border Cities Star*, March 28, 1930, 3.

62. *Border Cities Star*, April 10, 1930, 3; April 14, 1930, 7.

63. *Border Cities Star*, April 26, 1930, 3.

64. *Border Cities Star*, May 24, 1930, 7.

65. *Border Cities Star*, May 26, 1930, 5, 7.

66. *Border Cities Star*, August 29, 1930, 3; September 12, 1930, 5; September 18, 1930, 3; September 30, 1930, 3; September 22, 1930, 5; September 23, 1930, 5; September 25, 1930, 3.

67. Morrison; Price and Kulisek.

68. *Border Cities Star*, January 7, 1931, 5; October 21, 1931, 8; October 29, 1931, 12; May 11, 1931, 9.

69. *Border Cities Star*, December 15, 1931, 5; December 17, 1931, 9; December 14, 1931, 10.

70. *Border Cities Star*, June 9 1931, 9.

71. *Border Cities Star*, February 26, 1932, 15.

72. *Border Cities Star*, November 23, 1931, 9.

73. *Border Cities Star*, February 9, 1937, 5; February 13, 1934, 14; April 19, 1935, 20; January 23, 1924, 13; February 10, 1934, 8; February 3, 1934, 5; February 3, 1934, 6; February 6, 1935, 2; *Windsor Daily Star,* November 30, 1935, 6; May 22, 1933, 15; October 17, 1935, 5; *Evening Record,* May 18, 1943, 7; May 16, 1932, 11; May 14, 1932, 9; May 11, 1932, 11; May 6, 1932, 7; April 28, 1932, 9; March 28, 1932, 9; May 19, 1932, 20.

74. *Border Cities Star*, January 14, 1928, 14; March 2, 1935, 8; March 7, 1935, 9; March 25, 1935, 9; *Windsor Daily Star,* August 30, 1935, 3; October 5, 1935, 11; October 26, 1935, 7; October 28, 1935, 13; November 7, 1935, 15; November 28, 1935, 21; December 13, 1935, 25; December 19, 1935, 21; January 21, 1936, 10; February 14, 1936, 23; April 6, 1936, 9; April 14, 1936, 10; May 6, 1936, 23.

75. *Border Cities Star*, October 1, 1923, 5; June 4, 1932, 5; November 4, 1932, 3; September 30, 1932, 9; September 24, 1932, 5; February 14, 1934, 15.

76. *Border Cities Star*, September 21, 1933, 17; September 29, 1933, 3; September 15, 1933, 5.

77. *Windsor Daily Star*, October 30, 1934, 10.

78. Interview with Rabbi Nahum Schulman, March 28, 1976.

79. *Border Cities Star*, January 3, 1934, 5; January 4, 1934, 5; January 4, 1934, 17.

80. *Border Cities Star*, February 1, 1933, 3; March 29, 1933, 5; March 31, 1933, 3; November 6, 1933, 3; December 11, 1934, 7; December 14, 1934, 7.

81. *Windsor Daily Star*, March 20, 1936, 3.

82. *Border Cities Star,* April 20, 1933, 3; April 22, 1933, 10; October 20, 1933, 5.

83. *Border Cities Star*, March 28, 1933, 5; April 1, 1933, 2.

84. *Border Cities Star*, March 21, 1935, 6; June 4, 1935, 2; *Windsor Daily Star,* September 15, 1936 3; September 30, 1935, 16; October 4, 1935, 20; October 11, 1935, 23; January 3, 1936, 12; December 13, 1936, 5.

85. *Border Cities Star*, March 1, 1921, 3; June 15, 1921, 6; May 24, 1932, 10.

86. Much of the story could not be told for fear that Jews may be hurt. Letters and many records pertaining to the work are in the private collection of David Glanz.

87. *Book of Dedication,* commemorating the opening of the Louis and Rachel Kaplan Shaar Hashomayim Religious School and the 36th Anniversary of Congregation Shaar Hashomayim (1929–1965) January 31, 1965; *Windsor Daily Star,* May 29, 1936, 16.

88. Minutes of Peretz Shule, Windsor, November 19, 1934–1937, written in Yiddish.

89. Ibid.

Chapter 6: Senator David A. Croll

1. Alan Abrams, *Why Windsor? An Anecdotal History of the Town of Windsor and Essex County* (Windsor: Black Moss Press, 1981), 17.

2. Ibid.

3. *Border Cities Star*, March 2, 1929, 13; December 2, 1930, 3–16; December 9, 1930, 9; December 10, 1930, 5; (Sandra was born in 1936).

4. Abrams, 23.

5. *Border Cities Star*, November 5, 1930, 3; November 7, 1930, 3; November 14, 1930, 5; November 7, 1930, 3; November 29, 1930, 16; November 29, 1930, 9.

6. *Border Cities Star*, December 2, 1930, 1, 15.

7. *Border Cities Star*, December 2, 1930, 4.

8. *Border Cities Star*, December 15, 1930, 3.

9. Windsor City Council Minutes (1930–33) December 29, 1930, 122; *Border Cities Star*, December 8, 1930, 3; December 23, 1930, 3.

10. *Border Cities Star*, October 29, 1930, 3; November 29, 1930, 15; November 29, 1930, 8; October 30, 1930, 15.

11. *Border Cities Star*, December 22, 1930, 3.

12. Council Minutes, January 5, 1931, 126; *Border Cities Star*, January 5, 1931, 126; *Border Cities Star*, January 5, 1931, 3.

13. *Border Cities Star*, January 9, 1931, 3; January 10, 1931, 1; January 21, 1931, 3; January 22, 1931, 3; January 23, 1931, 3; February 24, 1931, 1; Council Minutes, January 9, 1931.

14. Abrams, 23.

15. *Border Cities Star*, January 6, 1931, 5; January 8, 1931, 3; January 9, 1931, 3; January 12, 1931, 8; January 14, 1931, 5.

16. *Border Cities Star*, January 9, 1931, 3; January 13, 1931, 3; Council Minutes, January 12, 1931, 134.

17. *Border Cities Star*, March 25, 1931, 3.

18. *Border Cities Star*, May 3, 1931, 3.

19. *Border Cities Star*, October 8, 1931, 5; October 9, 1931, 3; November 10, 1931, 3.

20. *Border Cities Star*, October 28, 1931, 3; October 29, 1931, 3; November 13, 1931, 5.

21. *Border Cities Star*, June 6, 1931, 3.

22. *Border Cities Star*, December 6, 1932, 4.

23. *Border Cities Star*, December 31, 1932, 5.

24. City Council Minutes, January 4, 1932, 261.

25. *Border Cities Star*, January 16, 1933, 3; January 20, 1933, 5; January 23, 1933, 5; February 1, 1933, 3; February 4, 1933, 3 February 20, 1933, 3; February 21, 1933, 5; March 2, 1933, 3.

26. *Border Cities Star*, April 24, 1933, 5; May 24, 1933, 3; May 27, 1933, 3; June 2, 1933, 3; June 5, 1933, 3, 5; June 11, 1933, 3; June 13, 1933, 5; July 14, 1933, 5; June 17, 1933, 3; June 30, 1933, 3; December 8, 1933, 3.

27. *Border Cities Star*, February 21, 1934, 3; February 26, 1934, 3; January 16, 1934, 3; February 6, 1934, 1; February 8, 1934, 5; February 17, 1934, 3; February 19, 1934, 1; February 20, 1934, 3; August 28, 1934, 3; October 10, 1934, 3; August 29, 1934, 3; August 30, 1934, 3; August 31, 1934, 5; October 15, 1934, 3; October 25, 1934, 3; October 29, 1934, 3; October 3, 1934, 3.

28. *Border Cities Star*, August 24, 1934, 5; August 26, 1934, 3; September 13, 1934, 3.
29. Abrams, 23–24.
30. *Windsor Daily Star*, December 10, 1934, 5; December 31, 1934, 3; December 19, 1934, 5; December 21, 1934, 3.
31. Abrams, 25.
32. *Windsor Daily Star*, January 8, 1935, 3; January 26, 1935, 3; February 4, 1935, 5; February 22, 1935, 3; March 1, 1935, 18; March 12, 1935, 3; March 1, 1935, 18; March 12, 1935, 3; March 13, 1935, 7; March 21, 1935, 3; April 5, 1935, 3; April 6, 1935, 4; June 20, 1935, 5; July 29, 1935, 3; August 17, 1935, 3; August 23, 1935, 3; August 26, 1935, 3; August 29, 1935, 3; August 30, 1935, 3; December 10, 1935, 1; December 13, 1935, 5; February 4, 1936, 5; February 5, 1935, 10; February 5, 1936, 3; February 12, 1936, 5; March 2, 1936, 3; March 9, 1936, 3; June 15, 1936, 3; October 1, 1936, 6; January 14, 1937, 3; January 15, 1937, 3; January 7, 1937, 3.
33. *Windsor Daily Star*, February 13, 1935, 3; March 7, 1935, 3; April 11, 1935, 5; April 12, 1935, 7; June 11, 1935, 5; July 15, 1935, 11; December 20, 1935, 4; February 13, 1936, 3; February 17, 1936, 3; February 27, 1936, 5; April 3, 1936, 5; April 6, 19365, 3; May 4, 1936, 5; April 3, 1936, 5; April 6, 1936, 3; May 4, 1936, 15; December 10, 1936, 21; December 17, 1936, 3; December 31, 1936, 3; January 11, 1937, 3; January 27, 1937, 3; March 9, 1937, 11; March 16, 1937, 7; March 26, 1937, 3.
34. *Windsor Daily Star*, April 13, 1937, 1; April 14, 1937, 1.
35. Abrams, 25.
36. Abrams, 25–29
37. *Windsor Daily Star*, November 25, 1939, 12; November 26, 1938, 3; November 25, 1938, 12; November 30, 1938, 3; December 1, 1938, 3; December 3, 1938, 3; December 3, 1938, 5, 11.
38. *Windsor Daily Star*, January 12, 1939, 3.
39. Abrams, 29–31.
40. Senator David A. Croll, biographical information published by the Canadian Senate, 3.
41. Ibid.
42. Abrams, 36.
43. "Aged giant honored at last," *Windsor Star*, July 25, 1990.
44. "Senator Croll: His remarkable career," *Windsor Star*, June 12, 1991.

Chapter 7: War and Peace

1. Introduction drawn from Neil Morrison, *Garden Gateway to Canada* (Windsor: Herald Press, 1954) and T. Price and L. Kulisek, *Windsor 1892–1992: A Centennial Celebration* (Windsor: Chamber Publications, 1992).
2. "Canadian Jewry and the war effort," *Windsor's Jewish Community Bulletin* 3(2), February 16, 1944.
3. *Bulletin Shaar Hashomayim* 1(3), November 25, 1942.
4. Ibid.
5. *Bulletin Shaar Hashomayim* 1(6), December 16, 1942.
6. Comment by Nancy Klein Helm, January 13, 2004.
7. Ibid.
8. Lee Shai Weissbach, *Jewish Life in Small Town America: A History* (New Haven: Yale University Press, 2005), 155.
9. Interview with Rabbi Nahum Schulman, March 28, 1976.
10. Interview with Rabbi Benjamin Groner, November 12, 1979.
11. Interview with Rabbi Benjamin Groner, 1990.
12. "Friday evening services," *Bulletin Shaar Hashomayim* 1(2), November 18, 1942.
13. "Shaar Hashomayim starts Oneg Shabbos Friday," *Jewish Community Bulletin* 4(4) March 8, 1945.
14. Groner interview, 1979.
15. "A word about Friday nights," *Jewish Community Bulletin* 2(26), January 19, 1944.
16. Groner interview, 1979.
17. Ibid.
18. "Editorial," *Jewish Community Bulletin* 2(1) January 27, 1943.
19. *Jewish Community Bulletin* 2(1), January 27, 1943.
20. "Another job for our community," *Jewish Community Bulletin* 2(5), March 24, 1943.
21. "Communal co-ordination," *Jewish Community Bulletin* 2(6), April 7, 1943.
22. "The Va'ad Hakashruth," *Jewish Community Bulletin* 3(4), March 15, 1943.
23. "Joint action planned by Windsor's synagogue," *Jewish Community Bulletin* 2(11), June 16, 1943.
24. "Va'ad Hakashruth bringing new shochet to city," *Jewish Community Bulletin* 3(12), July 20, 1943.
25. Groner interview, 1990.
26. "Broaden the Welfare Council," *Jewish Community Bulletin* 3(5), March 30, 1944.
27. "United Jewish Welfare Council set up at last meeting," *Jewish Community Bulletin* 2(13), July 16, 1943.

28. "Welfare Council to hold first meeting October 18th," *Jewish Community Bulletin* 2(18), October 6, 1943.
29. "Welfare drive opens with over $20,000 subscribed," *Jewish Community Bulletin* 2(22), December 1, 1943.
30. Jewish Community Council, Executive Committee Minutes, October 15, 1944.
31. Jewish Community Council, United Jewish Welfare Council Minutes, November 3, 1943.
32. "Broaden the Welfare Council," *Jewish Community Bulletin* 3(5), March 30, 1944.
33. "Male Autocrats," *Jewish Community Bulletin* 2(20), November 10, 1943.
34. "Welfare Council meets Thursday, May 18th at Shaar," *Jewish Community Bulletin* 3(8), May 10, 1944.
35. United Jewish Welfare Council Minutes, January 10, 1944.
36. Ibid.
37. "All amendments carry — now Community Council," *Jewish Community Bulletin* 3(9), May 25, 1944.
38. I. L. Peretz Schule, Executive Meeting Minutes, March 5, 1945.
39. Windsor Jewish Community Council Minutes, September 26, 1945.
40. Jewish Community Council Minutes, November 21, 1945.
41. "Dr. Lefkowitz arrives in Windsor," *Jewish Community Bulletin* 4(21), January 10, 1946.
42. Jewish Community Council Minutes, January 6, 1946.
43. "Youth organizations form youth council," *Jewish Community Bulletin* 2(26), January 19, 1944.
44. "Long-felt need filled," *Jewish Community Bulletin* 2(18), November 17, 1944.
45. "Skepticism and indifference overcome — Progress at last," *Jewish Community Bulletin* 2(20), December 21, 1944.
46. "Shaar Sisterhood to function as Talmud Torah auxiliary," *Jewish Community Bulletin* 4(1), January 12, 1945.
47. "Shaar Hashomayim to open nursery school shortly," *Jewish Community Bulletin* 4(13), September 26, 1945.
48. "Rabbi Adler to speak at Shaar's dinner and annual meeting," *Jewish Community Bulletin* 2(5), March 24, 1943.
49. I. L. Peretz Schule, *Program Booklet*, Tenth Annual Concert of the I. L. Peretz School of Windsor, Ontario, June 18, 1944. See also "10th Annual Peretz School concert takes place Sunday," *Jewish Community Bulletin* 3(10), June 15, 1945.
50. "Welfare Fund Campaign report," *Jewish Community Bulletin* 2(26), January 19, 1944.
51. "Shaar to conduct open house on May 21," *Jewish Community Bulletin* 3(7), April 26, 1944.
52. Groner interview, 1979.
53. "Many Christians here visit and learn about synagogue," *Windsor Daily Star*, May 22, 1944.
54. "Your Jewish neighbor," *Jewish Community Bulletin* 3(10), June 15, 1944.
55. "A letter to the rabbi," *Jewish Community Bulletin* 3(13), August 17, 1944. The additional information on Rabbi Mossman was supplied in a telephone interview with Sara Kirzner.
56. Letter from Michael Sumner; "Report on Open House," held at the Shaar Hashomayim Synagogue, Windsor Ontario, Sunday, May 21, 1944.
57. "3,000 attend Shaar Hashomayim open house," *Windsor Daily Star*, June 9, 1947.
58. "Legion presents plaque," *Jewish Community Council Bulletin*, September 21, 1949.
59. *Jewish Standard*, Cover Picture, February 15, 1990.
60. Helm comment, 2004.
61. "V-Day observance," *Jewish Community Bulletin* 4(5), March 21, 1945.
62. "Canadian Palestine Committee issues brief," *Jewish Community Bulletin* 4(6) April 5, 1945.
63. "Thanks," *Jewish Community Bulletin* 4(13), August 23, 1945.
64. "Jewish world shocked by impending blow! British to maintain vicious white paper! World wide protest!" *Jewish Community Bulletin* 4(16), October 2, 1945.
65. "News briefs," *Jewish Community Bulletin* 4(17), October 24, 1945, and 4(19), December 27, 1945.
66. *Jewish Community Bulletin* 4(17), October 24, 1945.
67. "If ye will not have faith surely ye shall not be established," *Jewish Community Bulletin* 4(17), October 24, 1945.
68. Rabbi Benjamin Groner, "5706 — A Review," *Shaar Hashomayim Year Book, 1946–5707*, 59.
69. Interviews with Joseph Eisenberg and others, undated.
70. "What future for Windsor's Jewish community," *Jewish Community Bulletin* 4(13), August 23, 1945.
71. "Shaar Hashomayim and the future," *Jewish Community Bulletin* 4(8), November 21, 1945.
72. "The Shaar elections return J. A. Glanz to presidency," *Jewish Community Bulletin* 4(19), December 27, 1945.
73. "Mortgage campaign of Shaar Hashomayim under way," *Jewish Community Bulletin* 2(9), May 19, 1943.

74. "Memorial service for late Joel Gelber to feature concluding phase of successful mortgage campaign drive," *Jewish Community Bulletin* 2(15), August 18, 1943.

75. "Honorable menschen," *Jewish Community Bulletin* 4(6), April 5, 1945.

76. "The Shaar elections return J. A. Glanz to presidency," *Jewish Community Bulletin* 4(19), December 27, 1945.

77. *Shaar Hashomayim Year Book*, 1946, 7.

78. "Mortgage burning outstanding event," *Jewish Community Bulletin* 5(9), June 20, 1946.

79. "B'nai B'rith and the community," *Jewish Community Bulletin* 4(19), December 27, 1945.

80. "Vets have new name," *Jewish Community Bulletin* 5(21), January 10, 1947.

81. "Bulletin financial report — 1945," *Jewish Community Bulletin* 5(3), March 28, 1946.

82. Jewish Community Council, Bulletin Editorial Committee Minutes, July 5, 1946.

83. "Community Council obtains new executive director," *Jewish Community Bulletin* 3(2), March 13, 1946.

84. Interview with Louis Lieblich, April 19, 1991.

85. "Where do we go from here?" *Jewish Community Bulletin* 5(8), June 5, 1946.

86. "Community Council plans day camp," *Jewish Community Bulletin* 5(5), April 25, 1946.

87. "Institute of Jewish Studies Planned," *Jewish Community Bulletin* 5(8), June 5, 1946.

88. "Talmud Torah classes begin September 4th," *Jewish Community Bulletin* 5(12), August 22, 1946.

89. Joshua Gitlin, "The president's new year's message," *Shaar Hashomayim Yearbook*, 13.

90. Groner, *Shaar Hashomayim Yearbook*, 1945, 590.

91. "Citizenship week," *Jewish Community Council Bulletin* 5(21), January 10, 1947.

92. Interview with Joseph Eisenberg, November 12, 1990.

93. Windsor Jewish Community Council, Executive Minutes, October 9, 1947.

94. "Group of men interested in support of yeshivot," Windsor Jewish Community Council Minutes, October 29, 1947.

95. "Community gives homes to 16 orphans," *Community Council Bulletin*, 7(2), February 26, 1948.

96. Interview with Michael Sumner, March 8, 1988.

97. "Pledges to orphans' fund," *Jewish Community Council Bulletin* 7(2), February 26, 1948.

98. "Wanted — more homes," *Jewish Community Bulletin* 7(3), March 18, 1948.

99. "A DP camp or a Canadian home?" *Jewish Community Council Bulletin* 7(4), April 22, 1948.

100. Ibid.

101. Ibid.

102. Peretz Schule Minutes, September 13, 1948.

103. Peretz Schule Minutes, January 24, 1949.

104. Peretz Schule Minutes, June 13, 1949.

105. "Welcome," *Jewish Community Council Bulletin* 8(8), July 18, 1949.

106. Ibid.

107. *Jewish Community Council Bulletin* 9(3), "We need your help," March 31, 1950. See also "Jobs wanted," *Jewish Community Bulletin* 8(2), March 3, 1949.

108. "Harry Rosenthal elected president of Ontario Zionist Region," *Jewish Community Council Bulletin* 5(14), September 20, 1946, and "Rosenthal to be given testimonial dinner," *Jewish Community Bulletin* 5(15), October 3, 1946.

109. "Windsor prominent in CJC conference," *Jewish Community Council Bulletin* 5(21), January 10, 1947.

110. "Madoff to represent Windsor at CJFWF assembly," *Jewish Community Council Bulletin* 5(21), January 10, 1947.

111. "JDC Toronto conference," *Jewish Community Council Bulletin* 5(26), March 11, 1947.

112. "Windsor host to 19th regional conference, Central Region ZOC," *Jewish Community Council Bulletin* 8(8), July 18, 1949.

113. "Schott elected again," *Jewish Community Council Bulletin* 5(23), March 24, 1947.

114. "Eli Goldin honoured," *Jewish Community Council Bulletin* 7(9), August 22, 1948.

115. "Archie Cherniak Wins," *Jewish Community Council Bulletin* 8(6), May 13, 1949.

116. "Windsor Jewish community protests Palestine attack," *Jewish Community Council Bulletin* 5(10), July 11, 1946.

117. "Read this Bulletin," *Jewish Community Council Bulletin* 5(10), July 11, 1946.

118. Interview with Michael and Lyle Sumner, 1988.

119. Ibid.

120. "Jewish state reborn," *Jewish Community Council Bulletin* 6(8), December 11, 1947.

121. Jewish Community Council Minutes, May 12, 1948.

122. "Drive for aid to Israel launched," *Jewish Community Council Bulletin* 7(6), June 11, 1948.

123. "Borrow $50,000 for UPA," *Jewish Community Council Bulletin* 7(8), August 13, 1948.

124. "Bank loan paid in full," *Jewish Community Council Bulletin* 8(1), January 27, 1949.

125. "A tribute," *Jewish Community Council Bulletin* 7(10), October 29, 1948.

126. Lyle and Michael Sumner interview, 1988.

127. "$60,000 loan For Israel," *Jewish Community Council Bulletin* 8(4), April 1, 1949.

128. "Crisis in Israel," *Jewish Community Council Bulletin* 8(4), April 1, 1949.

129. Groner interview, 1979.

130. "Rev. Dubitsky acting rabbi," *Jewish Community Bulletin* 8(4), April 1, 1949.

Chapter 8: The Stollman Era

1. Introduction drawn from Neil Morrison, *Garden Gateway to Canada* (Windsor: Herald Press, 1954) and T. Price and L. Kulisek, *Windsor 1892–1992: A Centennial Celebration* (Windsor: Chamber Publications, 1992).

2. Interview with Rabbi Samuel S. Stollman, August 14, 1989.

3. E-mail from Rabbi S. Stollman, December 2003.

4. Ibid.

5. Interview with Michael Sumner, 1988.

6. "Rabbi Stollman to be installed," *Windsor Jewish Community Council Bulletin* 8(12), November 11, 1949.

7. Sidney Bolkolsky, *Harmony and Dissonance: Voices of Jewish Identity in Detroit, 1914–1967* (Detroit: Wayne State University Press, 1991), 388–89.

8. "New Shaar Hashomayim Religious School to open September 7," *Jewish Community Council Bulletin* 8(8), July 18, 1949.

9. Ibid.

10. "From our rabbi's desk," *Jewish Community Council Bulletin* 8(1), January 17, 1950.

11. "From our rabbi's desk," *Jewish Community Council Bulletin* 9(2), February 16, 1950.

12. "Adult Institute," *Jewish Community Council Bulletin*, December 1951.

13. "Tefillin Club," *Jewish Community Council Bulletin*, December 1951.

14. I. L. Peretz Shule Minutes, March 1934.

15. "Graduation ceremonies at the Peretz School," *Jewish Community Council Bulletin* 9(1), January 17, 1950.

16. "Shaar Zedek establishes school," *Jewish Community Council Bulletin* 9(6), August 9, 1950.

17. "Bible study class organized," *Jewish Community Council Bulletin* 9(1), January 17, 1950.

18. "Our rabbi's desk," Windsor Jewish Community Council, Executive Meeting Minutes, January 24, 1950. See also *Jewish Community Council Bulletin* 9(3), March 31, 1950.

19. Jewish Community Council, Board of Governors Minutes, February 28, 1950. See also "From our rabbi's desk," *Jewish Community Council Bulletin* 9(3), March 31, 1950.

20. Jewish Community Council, Jewish Education Committee Minutes, February 14, 1950.

21. Ibid.

22. Jewish Community Council, Jewish Education Committee Minutes, May 9, 1950.

23. Jewish Community Council, Jewish Education Committee Minutes, May 25, 1950.

24. Jewish Community Council, Board of Governors Minutes, June 22, 1950.

25. Jewish Community Council, Board of Governors Minutes, September 28, 1950.

26. Interview with Joseph Eisenberg, November 12, 1990.

27. Jewish Community Council, Education Committee Minutes, April 1, 1950.

28. Jewish Community Council, Board of Governors Minutes, April 2, 1950.

29. Windsor Jewish Community Council, Va'ad Hayeshivot Committee Minutes, February 2, 1950.

30. Jewish Community Council, Va'ad Hayeshivot Committee Minutes, March 22, 1950.

31. Jewish Community Council, Va'ad Hayeshivot Committee Minutes, July 6, 1950.

32. Jewish Community Council, Executive Committee Minutes, October 14, 1954.

33. Jewish Community Council, Report of the School Allocation Committee Minutes, January 20, 1957.

34. "We're growing," *Jewish Community Council Bulletin* 5(25), March 24, 1947. See also "Campaign to open May 15," *Jewish Community Council Bulletin* 5(27), April 25, 1947.

35. "9 sub-committees appointed," *Jewish Community Council Bulletin* 5(25), March 24, 1947.

36. "Campaign to open May 15," *Jewish Community Council Bulletin* 5(27), April 25, 1947.

37. "Contributors guarantee centre gifts not to affect welfare fund donations," *Jewish Community Council Bulletin* 5(28), May 9, 1947.
38. "Community centre movement growing in Canada," *Jewish Community Council Bulletin* 8(2), March 3, 1949.
39. Eisenberg interview, 1990.
40. Ibid.
41. "From our rabbi's desk," *Jewish Community Council Bulletin* 9(5), June 9, 1950.
42. Jewish Community Council, Minutes of the meeting of the larger contributors and members of the Council's Executive Committee, March 29, 1950.
43. Jewish Community Council, Executive Committee Minutes, April 18, 1950.
44. Jewish Community Council, Executive Committee Minutes, June 15, 1950.
45. "Community centre — now!" *Jewish Community Council Bulletin* 11(2), February 1951.
46. Jewish Community Council, Executive Committee Minutes, November 27, 1950.
47. Jewish Community Council, Executive Committee Minutes, February 20, 1951.
48. "Annex," *Jewish Community Council Bulletin* 11(4), April 1951.
49. Eisenberg interview, 1990.
50. "Shaar Hashomayim men's club organized; launches first program," *Jewish Community Council Bulletin* 11(7), June 1951.
51. "Shaar Hashomayim news," *Jewish Community Council Bulletin* 11(2), February 1951.
52. "From our rabbi's desk," *Jewish Community Council Bulletin* 11(4), April 1951.
53. Jewish Community Council, Executive Committee Minutes, April 12, 1951.
54. Jewish Community Council, Executive Committee Minutes, May 15, 1951.
55. Jewish Community Council, Executive Committee Minutes, October 25, 1951.
56. Jewish Community Council, Board of Governors' Minutes, January 22, 1952.
57. "National conference For Israel March 25–26," *Jewish Community Council Bulletin* 11(3), March 1951.
58. "National conference asks Windsor to accept quota of $125,000," *Jewish Community Council Bulletin* 11(4), April 1951.
59. "President's report," *Jewish Community Council Bulletin* 11(7), June 1951.
60. "The Martyrs' Forest," *Jewish Community Council Bulletin* 11(9), September 1951.
61. "Shaarey Zedek to build apartment in Israel," *Jewish Community Council Bulletin* 8(11), October 18, 1949.
62. "Windsor Celebrates 100th Anniversary of I. L. Peretz, Wednesday February 6th 1952," *Jewish Community Council Bulletin*, February 1952.
63. Dr. Louis Perlman in the "President's Message," *Shaar Hashomayim Year Book, 1949—5710*, 5–7.
64. Interview with Michael Sumner and Lyle Sumner, 1988.
65. *Jewish Community Council Bulletin* 9(4), May 8, 1950.
66. Jewish Community Council, Board of Governors Minutes, April 19, 1950.
67. Ibid.
68. "Chesed Shel Emes Minutes," *Jewish Community Council Bulletin,* February, 1952,
69. Jewish Community Council, Chesed Shel Emes Committee Meeting, October 17, 1950.
70. Jewish Community Council, Chesed Shel Emes Committee Meeting, April 28, 1953.
71. Jewish Community Council, Executive Committee Minutes, May 29, 1952.
72. Jewish Community Council, Board of Directors Minutes, March 27, 1968.
73. Jewish Community Council, Executive Committee Minutes, January 30, 1953.
74. Jewish Community Council, Minutes of the Joint Meeting of the Executive and Board of Governors, September 15, 1953.
75. Jewish Community Council Minutes, October 20, 1953.
76. Jewish Community Council Minutes, November 18, 1953.
77. Jewish Community Council Minutes, January 7, 1954.
78. Jewish Community Council Minutes, February 3, 1954.
79. Jewish Community Council Minutes, March 31, 1954.
80. Jewish Community Council, Minutes of the Meeting of the Community Centre Planning and Site Committee, April 4, 1954.
81. Jewish Community Council, Minutes of the Joint Meeting of the Executive and Board of Governors, April 12, 1954.
82. Jewish Community Council, Minutes of the Meeting of the Community Centre Planning and Site Committee, August 17, 1954.
83. Jewish Community Council Minutes, September 20, 1954.

84. Jewish Community Council Minutes, September 23, 1954.
85. Ibid.
86. Ibid.
87. Ibid.
88. Ibid.
89. Ibid.
90. Ibid.
91. Jewish Community Council, Constitutional Committee Minutes, October 27, 1954.
92. Jewish Community Council, Board of Governors, Minutes, October 28, 1954.
93. Jewish Community Council, School Sub-Committee Minutes, October 27, 1954.
94. Executive Director's Report to the Annual Meeting ,Jewish Community Council, March 31, 1955.
95. Jewish Community Council, Minutes of the Meeting of the Contributors to the Community Centre Project, November 12, 1954.
96. Jewish Community Council, Executive Committee Minutes, May 10, 1955.
97. Jewish Community Council, May 31, 1955.
98. Jewish Community Council, Minutes of the Meeting of Contributors of the Community Centre Campaign, July 19, 1955.
99. "Community purchases centre site," *Jewish Community Council Bulletin,* January 1956.
100. Jewish Community Council, Executive Meeting Minutes, September 25, 1956.
101. Jewish Community Council, Architects and Executive Committee Minutes, December 19, 1956. See also Jewish Community Council, Builders Committee Minutes, March 14, 1957.
102. Jewish Community Council, Board of Directors Minutes, June 18, 1953.
103. Jewish Community Council, Annual Meeting Minutes, March 31, 1955.
104. "Day camping is here," *Jewish Community Council Bulletin,* May 1956.
105. Ibid.
106. Jewish Community Council, Board of Governors Minutes, April 11, 1955.
107. "Program director takes up duties," *Jewish Community Council Bulletin,* September 1955.
108. Adapted from the Jewish National Fund web site, http://www.jnf-canada.org.

109. Jewish Community Council, Board of Governors Minutes, November 19, 1952.
110. Ibid.
111. Jewish Community Council, Board of Governors Minutes, October 27, 1955.
112. "Negev Dinner to honour Reuben Madoff," *Jewish Community Council Bulletin,* November 1955.
113. Jewish Community Council, Executive Minutes, January 31, 1956.
114. "Bronfman visits Windsor — April 23," *Jewish Community Council Bulletin,* April 1956.
115. Jewish Community Council, Executive Committee Minutes August 9, 1956.
116. "Leaders return from Israel describe urgent need for cash," *Jewish Community Council Bulletin,* December 1958.
117. "How Israel lost the world's sympathy," *Jewish Community Council Bulletin,* January 1957.
118. "State of Israel historical survey," *Encyclopedia Judaica* 9 (Jerusalem: Keter Publishing House, 1971), 383–97.
119. "Immigrants are a boon to Canada's growth," *Jewish Community Council Bulletin,* August 1957.
120. "Rosh Hashonah — 5718," *Jewish Community Council Bulletin,* September 1957.
121. "An open letter," *Jewish Community Council Bulletin,* September 1957.
122. Jewish Community Council, letter from L. Gordner, President of Shaarey Zedek, June 4, 1957.
123. Jewish Community Council, Executive Committee Minutes, June 4, 1957.
124. *Jewish Community Council Bulletin,* September 1957.
125. "Shaarey Zedek Synagogue resumes building activities" *Jewish Community Council Bulletin,* December 1957.
126. "Shaarey Zedek Synagogue news," *Jewish Community Council Bulletin,* December, 1958.
127. "B'nai B'rith turns over gift to centre," *Jewish Community Council Bulletin,* December 1956.
128. "Al Goldberg displays capable leadership," *Jewish Community Council Bulletin,* June-July, 1958.
129. "Young Leadership guides community centre completion campaign," *Jewish Community Council Bulletin,* February 1957.
130. Jewish Community Council, Board of Governors Minutes, August 27, 1957
131. "Ground breaking for community centre building — date

set for Monday, Oct. 14, at 11 a.m." *Jewish Community Council Bulletin*, August 1957.

132. Jewish Community Council, Executive Committee Minutes, September 10, 1957.
133. Jewish Community Council, Board of Governors Minutes, May 6, 1958.
134. Jewish Community Council, Executive Committee Minutes, June 10, 1958.
135. "Community centre contract awarded — construction begins May 27," *Jewish Community Council Bulletin*, May 1958.
136. Jewish Community Council, Executive Committee Minutes, October 14, 1958.
137. Jewish Community Council, Executive Committee Minutes, September 10, 1957.
138. Interview with Montague Pomm, November 4, 2003.
139. Letter from K. Z. Paltiel to Eli Goldin, Jewish Community Council, June 25, 1958.
140. Jewish Community Council, Executive Committee Minutes, August 12, 1957.
141. Interview with Joseph Eisenberg, November 12, 1990.
142. "Canadian Jewish Congress meets first time in Windsor, January 17, 18, 19," *Jewish Community Council Bulletin*, January 1958.
143. "Meyer Dorn heads Israel's 10th anniversary celebration — four community-wide events planned," *Jewish Community Council Bulletin*, March 1958.
144. "Hon. Paul Martin and George Jessel to appear at Shaar on November 9," *Jewish Community Council Bulletin*, November 1958.
145. Paul Martin, *A Very Public Life*, Volume I, (Toronto: Deneau Publishers, 1985), 335.
146. "The dream a reality," *Jewish Community Council Bulletin*, January 1959.
147. "Operation centre begins — programs under way — committees formed," *Jewish Community Council Bulletin*, February 1959.
148. "Philip Bernstein makes outstanding gift — Jewish centre building to bear his name," *Jewish Community Council Bulletin*, May 1959.
149. *Jewish Community Council Bulletin*, November 1959.
150. "Building Plans," *Jewish Community Council Bulletin*, April 1959.
151. "Shaar Hashomayim Synagogue expansion fund," *Jewish Community Council Bulletin*, November 1959.
152. I. L. Peretz Schule Minutes, November 10, 1959.
153. "Rabbi Samuel Stollman," *Jewish Community Council Bulletin*, May 1959.
154. "1759 bicentennial briefs 1959," *Jewish Community Council Bulletin*, December 1959.

Chapter 9: Reform Judaism Arrives in Windsor

1. Introduction drawn from Neil Morrison, *Garden Gateway to Canada* (Windsor: Herald Press, 1954); and T. Price and L. Kulisek, *Windsor 1892–1992: A Centennial Celebration* (Windsor: Chamber Publications, 1992).
2. Interview with Michael Sumner, 1988.
3. Michael Sumner, chairman, *Congregation Shaar Hashomayim Golden Jubilee Book* (Windsor: Sumner Press, 1980), 37.
4. Interview with Rabbi Samuel S. Stollman, August 14, 1989.
5. Interview with Robert Cohen, January 28, 1979.
6. Ibid.
7. Letter from Arthur B. Weingarden, June 27, 2002.
8. E-mail from Larry Greene, June 9, 2002.
9. Stollman interview, 1989.
10. Ibid.
11. Interview with Joseph Eisenberg, November 12, 1990.
12. Windsor Jewish Community Council, Executive Committee Special Meeting Minutes, January 26, 1960.
13. Joint Statement, Jewish Community Council, Board of Governors, January 27, 1960.
14. "Expansion fund campaign in high gear," *Windsor Jewish Community Council Bulletin*, January 1960.
15. "Expansion project progress — additional lot purchased," *Jewish Community Council Bulletin*, November 1960.
16. "Mr. & Mrs. Louis Kaplan announce $36,000 gift," *Jewish Community Council Bulletin*, October 1964.
17. "Dedication weekend," *Jewish Community Council Bulletin*, January 1965.
18. "Shaar Hashomayim news," *Jewish Community Council Bulletin*, April 1966.
19. Executive Director's Report, Jewish Community Council Annual Meeting Minutes, June 28, 1965.
20. "Shaar rebuilds auditorium and kitchen facilities," *Jewish Community Council Bulletin*, January 1969.
21. "Dedication of the Charles Zalev Social Hall crowns Shaar Hashomayim 40th anniversary celebration," *Jewish*

Community Council Bulletin, December 1969.

22. "Shaarey Zedek news," *Jewish Community Council Bulletin*, January 1960.

23. "A layman's viewpoint," *Jewish Community Council Bulletin*, March 1962.

24. "Shaarey Zedek," *Jewish Community Council Bulletin*, September 1962.

25. "Tifereth Israel Synagogue," *Jewish Community Council Bulletin*, November 1963, April 1964, and March 1969.

26. Arthur B. Weingarden letter, 2002.

27. Congregation Beth El Minutes, December 22, 1959.

28. Ibid.

29. Ibid.

30. Congregation Beth El Minutes, December 27, 1959.

31. Ibid.

32. Congregation Beth El Minutes, January 28, 1960.

33. Congregation Beth El Minutes, February 7 and March 8, 1960.

34. Congregation Beth El Minutes, March 11, 1960.

35. Ibid.

36. Congregation Beth El Minutes, April 28, 1960.

37. Congregation Beth El Minutes, April 28 and June 28, 1960.

38. E-mail from Rabbi Sherwin Wine, May 14, 2002.

39. Congregation Beth El Minutes, June 28, 1960.

40. Congregation Beth El Minutes, July 7, 1960.

41. Congregation Beth El Minutes, July 28, 1960

42. Milton C. Meretsky and Lawrence Kert, Congregation Beth El house lease, August 16, 1960.

43. Congregation Beth El Minutes, September 25, 1960.

44. Congregation Beth El Minutes, November 3, 1960.

45. Letter from Paul Taylor to Gignac, Sutts Henriksen & Zalev, Congregation Shaar Hashomayim, Board of Directors Minutes, February 2, 1967.

46. Comment from Herb Brudner, December 2, 2003

47. Congregation Beth El Minutes, Cemetery Report, April 26, 1961, April and May 1961.

48. Congregation Beth El Minutes, "Main Points reached and agreed upon at First Meeting of Shaar Cemetery Committee and Representatives of Temple Beth El," April 29, 1968.

49. Comment from Arthur Barat, December 2, 2003, and January 30, 2004.

50. Comment from Arthur Barat, December 2, 2003.

51. Arthur B. Weingarden letter, 2002.

52. Congregation Beth El Minutes, December 15, 1960.

53. Ibid.

54. Congregation Beth El Minutes, June 6, 1961.

55. Congregation Beth El Minutes, July 13, 1961.

56. "Ground-breaking ceremony," *Jewish Community Council Bulletin*, November 1961.

57. Congregation Beth El, Board of Directors Minutes, May 14, 1962.

58. "Temple dedication service," *Jewish Community Council Bulletin*, November 1962.

59. Eisenberg interview, 1990.

60. "L'Shanah Tovah Tikosevu," *Jewish Community Council Bulletin*, September 1961.

61. Jewish Community Council, Board of Governors Minutes, November 27, 1963.

62. Jewish Community Council, Officers Meeting Minutes, February 13, 1966.

63. Jewish Community Council, Special Allocations Committee Minutes, February 5, 1967.

64. "Executive director's report at Council's annual meeting," *Jewish Community Council Bulletin*, September 1961.

65. Ibid.

66. Jewish Community Council Minutes, December 1961.

67. "Morris Tabachnick honoured in Israel," *Jewish Community Council Bulletin*, March 1962.

68. "A federation is born in Windsor," *Jewish Community Council Bulletin*, September 1965.

69. President's report, Jewish Community Council, Annual Meeting Minutes, June 28, 1965. See also Jewish Community Council, Executive Committee Minutes, September 14, 1965.

70. Jewish Community Council, Executive Committee Minutes, September 14, 1965.

71. "Hadassah bazaar news," *Jewish Community Council Bulletin*, March 1967.

72. Jewish Community Council, "Hadassah council," November and December 1967.

73. Executive Director's Report, Jewish Community Council, Annual Meeting Minutes, June 1967.

74. Jewish Community Council, Annual Meeting Minutes, June 20, 1963.

75. Jewish Community Council, Executive Committee Minutes, August 13, 1963.

76. "Your president reports," *Jewish Community Council Bulletin*, October 1964.

77. Letter from Arthur B. Weingarden, Jewish Community

Council, Board of Directors Minutes, October 27, 1966.

78. Jewish Community Council, Board of Directors Minutes, November 29, 1967.

79. Jewish Community Council, Executive Committee Minutes, March 8, 1966; See also Executive Director's Report, Jewish Community Council, Annual Meeting Minutes, June 1966.

80. Jewish Community Council, Board of Directors Minutes, February 1, 1967.

81. "Preliminary report on the housing needs of the aged Jewish population of Windsor," Jewish Community Council, November 29, 1967.

82. "Windsor's Chesed Shel Emes," *Jewish Community Council Bulletin*, September 1967.

83. Executive Director's Report, Jewish Community Council, Annual Meeting Minutes, June 20, 1963.

84. "A message," *Jewish Community Council Bulletin*, January 1963.

85. "Spotlight — problems of adolescence and Jewish education," *Jewish Community Council Bulletin*, December 1962.

86. "Important issues of Jewish life — Jewish education — a matter of will," *Jewish Community Council Bulletin*, March 1963.

87. "Important issues of Jewish life — the Jewish adolescent," *Jewish Community Council Bulletin*, February 1963.

88. "An invitation to learning," *Jewish Community Council Bulletin*, January 1963.

89. "Achieving Jewish objectives — community centre chosen as research agency," *Jewish Community Council Bulletin*, June 1963.

90. "Blue Haven Foundation disburses funds to communal institutions," *Jewish Community Council Bulletin*, November 1964.

91. President's Annual Report, Jewish Community Council, Annual Meeting Minutes, June 28, 1965.

92. Executive Committee Digest, Jewish Community Council, December 1965.

93. Congregation Beth El Minutes, November 7, 1962.

94. Arthur B. Weingarden letter, 2002.

95. "Testimonial dinner," *Jewish Community Council Bulletin*, June 1964.

96. Congregation Beth El Minutes, August 19, 1964.

97. "A word from the rabbi," *Jewish Community Council Bulletin*, September 1964.

98. I. L. Peretz Schule Minutes, March 7, 1960.

99. I. L. Peretz Schule Minutes, April 25, 1960.

100. I. L. Peretz Schule Minutes, May 9, 1960.

101. I. L. Peretz Schule Minutes, June 20, July 11. See also Minutes for September 26,1960.

102. "Our new principal," *Jewish Community Council Bulletin*, October 1963.

103. Jewish Community Council, Executive Committee Minutes, February 11, 1964.

104. Ibid.

105. Jewish Community Council, Special Jewish Education Committee Minutes, March 18, 1964.

106. "New quarters for the Shule," *Jewish Community Council Bulletin*, June 1964.

107. "I. L. Peretz Study Club," *Jewish Community Council Bulletin*, October 1965.

108. Jewish Community Council, Board of Directors Minutes, December 29, 1968.

109. Jewish Community Council, Board of Directors Minutes, March 6, 1969.

110. Ibid.

111. Congregation Beth El Minutes, March 13, 1969.

112. Eisenberg interview, 1990.

113. Israel Defence Forces web site.

114. Jewish Community Council, Board of Directors, Minutes, May 31, 1967.

115. Jewish Community Council, Annual Meeting Minutes, June 28, 1967.

116. Ibid., Executive Director's Report.

117. "JNF council organized," *Jewish Community Council Bulletin*, October 1968.

118. Jewish Community Council, Board of Directors Minutes, November 1968.

119. "JNF news," *Jewish Community Council Bulletin*, November 1968.

120. Ibid.

121. Chris Edwards and Elaine Weeks, "Black Day in July," *Detroit News* Rearview Mirror Archives (*Walkerville Times*, November 25, 2003).

122. Executive Director's Report, Jewish Community Council, Annual Meeting Minutes, June 1968.

123. Stollman interview, October 31, 1988.

124. Jewish Community Council, Board of Governors Minutes, April 18, 1965.

125. Jewish Community Council, Board of Directors Minutes, September 27, 1967.

126. President's Report and Executive Director's Report, Jewish

Community Council, Annual Meeting Minutes, June 1965.

127. Jewish Community Council, Board of Directors Minutes, January 1968.

128. Jewish Community Council, Board of Directors Minutes, October 30, 1968, October 28, 1969.

129. Congregation Beth El Minutes, October 12, 1967.

130. Congregation Beth El Minutes, January 7, 1968.

131. "Involvement drives rabbi away," *Windsor Star*, in Congregation Beth El Minutes, May 3, 1970.

132. Congregation Beth El Minutes, May 3, 1970.

133. Letter from Rabbi Robert Benjamin to Arthur Barat, Congregation Beth El Minutes, May 3, 1970.

134. Congregation Beth El Minutes, April 11, 1968.

135. Congregation Beth El Minutes, October 23, 1969.

136. Congregation Beth El Minutes, Joint Meeting of Windsor Va'ad Hakashruth and Representatives of Windsor Congregations, April 22, 1968.

137. Jewish Community Council, Board of Directors Minutes, June 24, 1970; "Patronize the Shaffer kosher meat market," *Jewish Community Council Bulletin*, September 1970.

138. Congregation Shaar Hashomayim, Board of Directors Minutes, November 13, 1974.

139. Congregation Shaar Hashomayim, Board of Directors Minutes, January 15, 1975.

Chapter 10: Consolidation and Realignment

1. Introduction drawn from Neil Morrison, *Garden Gateway to Canada* (Windsor: Herald Press, 1954); and T. Price and L. Kulisek, *Windsor 1892–1992: A Centennial Celebration* (Windsor: Chamber Publications, 1992).

2. Windsor Jewish Community Council, Board of Directors Minutes, February 25, 1970, Letter to Joseph Eisenberg from Dr. Joseph Klinghofer, CJC Educational Director," February 13, 1970.

3. Ibid.

4. Jewish Community Council, Minutes, May 27, 1970.

5. Ibid.

6. "I. L Peretz School," *Windsor Jewish Community Council Bulletin*, September 1970.

7. Congregation Beth El, Board of Directors Minutes, January 21, 1971.

8. Congregation Beth El, Board of Directors Minutes, February 18, 1971.

9. Jewish Community Council, Jewish Education Committee Minutes, February 10, 1971.

10. Congregation Beth El Minutes, February 18, 1971. See also "An historic document," *Jewish Community Council Bulletin*, March 1971.

11. Congregation Beth El Minutes, May 4, 1971.

12. Jewish Community Council, Jewish Education Committee Minutes, June 21, 1971.

13. "Amalgamation," *Jewish Community Council Bulletin*, June 1971.

14. Congregation Beth El Minutes, "The Hebrew Academy & I. L. Peretz School," October 1971.

15. Jewish Community Council, Board of Directors Minutes, May 30, 1973.

16. "Hebrew Academy of Windsor," *Jewish Community Council Bulletin*, September 1972.

17. Jewish Community Council, Board of Directors Minutes, June 29, 1977.

18. Jewish Community Council, Jewish Education Committee Emergency Meeting Minutes, June 27, 1977. See also Jewish Community Council, Board of Directors Minutes, September 29, 1977.

19. "Crumbling time capsule," *Windsor Star*, February 15, 1973.

20. "Tifereth Israel," *Jewish Community Council Bulletin*, September 1970.

21. "Congregation Tifereth Israel," *Jewish Community Council Bulletin*, November 1971.

22. Essex County Land Registry Office, County of Essex #12. Lot 111, Registered Plan 620, No. 788467, September 17, 1979, and "East End Synagogue Sold," *Windsor Star*, October 2, 1979.

23. "Installation," *Jewish Community Council Bulletin*, September 1970.

24. Congregation Beth El, Board of Directors Minutes, August 17, 1972.

25. Congregation Beth El, Board of Directors Minutes, October 19, 1972.

26. Congregation Beth El, Board of Directors Minutes, March 29, 1973.

27. Jewish Community Council, Budget and Finance Committee Minutes, March 20, 1973.

28. Congregation Shaar Hashomayim, Board of Directors Minutes, January 16, 1974.

29. "In farewell," *Jewish Community Council Bulletin*, June 1972.

30. Congregation Shaar Hashomayim, Board of Directors Minutes, May 16, 1974. See also "Shaar Hashomayim Religious School welcomes new principal," *Jewish Community Council Bulletin*, June 1974.

31. Congregation Shaar Hashomayim, Board of Directors Minutes, November 30, 1975.

32. "Rabbi Gartenhaus," *Jewish Community Council Bulletin*, September 1976. See also Congregation Shaar Hashomayim, Board of Directors Minutes, September 15, 1976.

33. "Ira Zaidman," *Jewish Community Council Bulletin*, September 1978. See also Congregation Shaar Hashomayim, Board of Directors Minutes, April 8, 1981.

34. Congregation Shaar Hashomayim, Board of Directors Minutes, February 16, 1977.

35. Congregation Shaar Hashomayim, Board of Directors Minutes, February 6, 1978.

36. Jewish Community Council, Budget and Finance Committee Minutes, January 18, 1972.

37. Jewish Community Council, Budget and Finance Committee Minutes, March 20, 1973.

38. Jewish Community Council, Special Committee on School Allocations Minutes, March 5, 1974.

39. Congregation Beth El Minutes, Minority Report to the Executive and Board of Directors, Windsor Jewish Community Council, March 26, 1974.

40. Jewish Community Council, Special Committee on School Allocations Minutes, March 5, 1974.

41. Jewish Community Council, Board of Directors Minutes, April 30, 1975.

42. Jewish Community Council, Board of Directors Minutes, September 24, 1975. See also Report of the Executive Director, Jewish Community Council, Annual Meeting Minutes, June 29, 1977.

43. Jewish Community Council, Board of Directors Minutes, May 25, 1977.

44. Jewish Community Council, Board of Directors Minutes, March 30, 1978.

45. "Soviet Jewry," *Jewish Community Council Bulletin*, January 1971.

46. Jewish Community Council, Board of Directors Minutes , September 29, 1970, October 28, 1970, and November 25, 1970.

47. Jewish Community Council, Special Board of Directors Meeting Minutes, January 14, 1971. See also Jewish Community Council, Board of Directors Minutes, January 14, 1971, and *Jewish Community Council Bulletin*, February 1971.

48. Jewish Community Council, Board of Directors Minutes, April 28, 1971.

49. "Kosygin's visit to Canada," *Jewish Community Council Bulletin*, October 1971.

50. Jewish Community Council, Board of Directors Minutes, November 24, 1971.

51. Jewish Community Council, Board of Directors Minutes, March 9, 1972.

52. Ibid.

53. Jewish Community Council, Board of Directors Minutes, March 22, 1972. See also Jewish Community Council, Annual Meeting Minutes, June 28, 1972.

54. Jewish Community Council, Board of Directors Minutes, September 27, 1972, and October 24, 1972.

55. Jewish Community Council, Board of Directors Minutes, November 29, 1972.

56. Ibid.

57. "Dr. Henry Shanfield chosen to head biggest campaign in Windsor for economic aid to Israel," *Jewish Community Council Bulletin*, September 1973.

58. "Israel mission," *Jewish Community Council Bulletin*, June 1979.

59. Plaut, W. Gunther, *Unfinished Business* (Toronto: Lester & Orpen Dennys, 1981), 287.

60. Ibid., 289.

61. Ibid.

62. Jewish Community Council, Board of Directors Minutes, March 9, 1972.

63. Jewish Community Council, Board of Directors Minutes, November 29, 1972.

64. Jewish Community Council, Board of Directors Minutes, letter attached, May 30, 1973.

65. "Veteran judge calls it a career," *Windsor Star*, September 12, 2003.

66. Price and Kulisek, 79.

67. *Windsor Star*, June 23, 2003. See also City of Windsor Parks and Recreation web site, http://www.citywindsor.ca/000522.asp.

68. Jewish Community Council, Board of Directors Minutes, March 28, 1979.

69. "Temple Beth El gallery wall," *Jewish Community Council Bulletin*, September 1970.

70. "Academy of Jewish studies," *Jewish Community Council*

Bulletin, September 1971.

71. "New program director joins JCC staff," *Jewish Community Council Bulletin*, June 1973.

72. Jewish Community Council, Board of Directors Minutes, May 28, 1975.

73. Jewish Community Council, Board of Directors Minutes, March 30, 1978.

74. Jewish Community Council, Board of Directors Minutes, November 24, 1971.

75. "Senator Paul Martin to address Windsor Negev Dinner," *Jewish Community Council Bulletin*, May 1972.

76. Letter from Kurt Weinberg, undated.

77. Jewish Community Council, Board of Directors Minutes, September 27, 1972.

78. "Eli C. Goldin to receive Jewish communal tribute," *Jewish Community Council Bulletin*, June 1978.

79. "Windsor Negev Dinner to honour Charles Zalev," *Jewish Community Council Bulletin*, June 1979.

80. "Israel Record," Anti-Defamation League web site, http://www.adl.org/Israel/Record/index.asp.

81. Jewish Community Council, Board of Directors Minutes, January 31, 1973.

82. "Israel Record," Anti-Defamation League web site.

83. Jewish Community Council, Board of Directors Minutes, December 5, 1973.

84. "Letter to the community by Joseph Eisenberg," *Jewish Community Council Bulletin*, May 1970.

85. Jewish Community Council, Board of Directors Minutes, March 23, 1975.

86. "High holiday effort by Windsor synagogues will focus on meeting heightened economic needs of Israel through Israel bonds," *Jewish Community Council Bulletin*, September 1974.

87. Congregation Shaar Hashomayim, Board of Directors Minutes, May 16, 1974.

88. Congregation Shaar Hashomayim, Board of Directors Minutes, June 19, 1974.

89. Congregation Shaar Hashomayim, Board of Directors Minutes, January 27, 1975.

90. Congregation Shaar Hashomayim, Board of Directors Minutes, February 5, 1975.

91. Report of the Executive Director, Jewish Community Council, Annual Meeting Minutes, June 30, 1976.

92. Louis Rosenberg, "A gazetteer of Jewish communities in Canada showing the Jewish population in each of the cities, towns & villages in Canada in the census years 1851–1951." *Canadian Jewish Population Studies* 7. (Montreal: Canadian Jewish Congress Bureau of Social and Economic Research, 1957), 14.

93. Report of the Executive Director, Jewish Community Council, Annual Meeting Minutes, June 29, 1977.

94. Jewish Community Council, Board of Directors Minutes, May 30, 1973.

95. Report of the Executive Director, Jewish Community Council, Annual Meeting Minutes, June 29, 1977.

96. Jewish Community Council, Special Executive Committee Meeting Minutes, August 18, 1977.

97. Jewish Community Council, Board of Directors Minutes, September 29, 1977.

98. Jewish Community Council, Board of Directors Minutes, February 22, 1978.

99. Congregation Shaar Hashomayim, Board of Directors Minutes, March 16, 1977.

100. Congregation Shaar Hashomayim, Board of Directors Minutes, May 18, 1977.

101. "A special evening," *Jewish Community Council Bulletin*, October 1977.

102. "Rabbi remembers 28 years," *Windsor Star*, October 22, 1977.

103. Interview with Rabbi Samuel S. Stollman, August 14, 1989.

104. Interview with Joseph Eisenberg, November 12, 1990.

105. "Rachel Kaplan Hebrew cornerstone dedicated by Minnie Slobasky," *Jewish Community Council Bulletin*, January 1978.

106. "The New Shaarey Zedek Synagogue," *Jewish Community Council Bulletin*, January 1978.

107. Congregation Shaar Hashomayim, Board of Directors Minutes, May 5, 1978.

108. Congregation Shaar Hashomayim, Board of Directors Minutes, June 29, 1978. See also "Rachel Kaplan Hebrew Memorial Chapel," *Jewish Community Council Bulletin*, June 1978.

109. "Congregation Shaar Hashomayim invites you to the dedication ceremonies of the Rachel Kaplan Hebrew Memorial Chapel," *Jewish Community Council Bulletin*, September 1979.

110. Congregation Shaar Hashomayim, Special Board of Directors Meeting Minutes, August 23, 1978.

111. "Rabbi Benjamin Z. Holczer," *Jewish Community Council Bulletin*, September 1978.

112. Congregation Shaar Hashomayim, Special Executive and Chevra Kadisha Meeting Minutes, May 24, 1979.

113. Eisenberg interview, 1990.

114. Congregation Shaar Hashomayim, Special Board of Directors Meeting Minutes, July 4, 1979. See also Letter from Rabbi Benjamin Z. Holczer, Congregation Shaar Hashomayim, Board of Directors Minutes, July 14, 1979; and Employment Agreement between Congregation Shaar Hashomayim and Rabbi Benjamin Z. Holczer, Congregation Shaar Hashomayim, Board of Directors Minutes, July 14, 1979.

115. "Golden Jubilee celebration program," *Jewish Community Council Bulletin*, October 1979.

116. Michael Sumner, chairman, *Congregation Shaar Hashomayim Golden Jubilee Book* (Windsor: Sumner Press, 1980), 25.

117. Ibid., 27.

118. Letter from Rabbi Benjamin Holczer, to David Glanz, Congregation Shaar Hashomayim, January 24, 1980.

119. Letter from Ted J. Hochberg and Philip Strosberg to B'nai B'rith Lodge 1011, Congregation Beth El Minutes, July 27, 1971; Congregation Beth El Minutes, August 19, 1971.

120. Congregation Beth El Minutes, December 19, 1974.

121. Congregation Beth El Minutes, May 20, 1976. See also Congregation Shaar Hashomayim, Board of Directors Minutes, December 15, 1976; Congregation Beth El Board of Directors Minutes, December 15, 1976.

122. Congregation Beth El Minutes, December 15, 1976.

123. Congregation Shaar Hashomayim, Board of Directors Minutes, January 19, 1977.

124. Congregation Beth El Minutes, March 28, 1977.

125. Jewish Community Council Minutes, March 30, 1978.

126. Congregation Shaar Hashomayim, Board of Directors Minutes, May 5, 1978.

127. Congregation Beth El Minutes, May 18, 1978; June 4,1978.

128. Congregation Beth El Minutes, November 16, 1978; December 21, 1978.

129. Congregation Beth El Minutes, January 25, 1979.

130. Letter from H. C. Fletcher to Arthur Barat, Congregation Beth El Minutes, December 20, 1979.

131. Congregation Beth El Minutes, January 20, 1972.

132. Congregation Beth El Minutes, February 20, 1975.

133. Congregation Beth El Minutes, March 18, 1976 and July 15, 1976.

134. Congregation Beth El Minutes, August 25, 1976.

135. Ibid.

136. Congregation Beth El Minutes, September 15, 1977.

137. Congregation Beth El Minutes, March 15, 1979; April 26, 1979.

138. Congregation Beth El Minutes, June 10, 1979.

139. Congregation Beth El Minutes, September 15, 1979.

140. Letter from Rabbi Jonathan V. Plaut to Arthur B. Weingarden, September 19, 1979.

141. Stephen Mandel and R. H. Wagenberg, *The Governance of the Jewish Community of Windsor* (Philadelphia: Center for Jewish Community Studies, 1974), 18.

142. Ibid., 23.

143. Ibid., 22.

144. Ibid., 20.

Chapter 11: The Right Honourable Herb Gray

1. Alan Abrams, *Why Windsor? An Anecdotal History of the Town of Windsor and Essex County* (Windsor: Black Moss Press, 1981), 67–68. The Right Honourable Herb Gray read the manuscript, adding personal comments to the text for the purposes of clarifications or corrections of a factual nature; the assessment of Herb Gray's career are those of the author. He stated that the marriage of Fannie Lifitz and Harry Gray took place in Detroit.

2. Abrams, 67–68.

3. Ibid.

4. Comments from the Rt. Hon. Herb Gray, micro-cassette 1, May 2003.

5. "Workaholic Herb Gray (yes, the one from Windsor) rocks on," *Toronto Star*, December 21, 1993.

6. "Windsor cops oratory title," *Windsor Star*, March 26, 1949.

7. Ibid.

8. Abrams, 74.

9. Comments from the Rt. Hon. Herb Gray, micro-cassette 3, August 2003.

10. "Hard work opens cabinet door for Herb," *Windsor Star*, October 16, 1969.

11. Abrams, 75.

12. Comments from the Rt. Hon. Herb Gray, micro-cassette 3, August 2003.

13. *Canadian Parliamentary Guide*, House of Commons, 1995, 263.

14. "Former oratory champ speechless in victory," *Windsor Star*, June 19, 1962.

15. Abrams, 69.
16. Ibid.
17. "History of the Federal Electoral Ridings since 1867," Library of Parliament, Information and Documentation Branch B, Government of Canada, Ottawa, 2001.
18. "Herb wins big edge over Tory," *Windsor Daily Star*, April 9, 1962.
19. Abrams, 78.
20. "Gray sworn in bilingual ceremony," *Windsor Daily Star*, September 27, 1962.
21. "Gray slams decline in jobs," *Windsor Daily Star*, October 30, 1962.
22. Ibid.
23. "W. O. hurt by unfair rail rates," *Windsor Daily Star*, December 4, 1962.
24. "Plan youth legislation," *Windsor Daily Star*, March 27, 1963.
25. "Backs jobs for youth," *Windsor Daily Star*, February 12, 1963.
26. "History of the Federal Electoral Ridings since 1867."
27. Ibid.
28. "Promotion in order for Herb," *Windsor Daily Star*, April 17, 1963.
29. Ibid.
30. "Herb Gray on mission to Columbia," *Windsor Daily Star*, May 2, 1963.
31. "Essex West MP lauds new flag," *Windsor Daily Star*, July 4, 1964.
32. "Gray urges expanded immigration," *Windsor Daily Star*, August 15, 1964.
33. "Grit Gray grins," *Windsor Daily Star*, November 9, 1965.
34. "Gray and Whelan head major committees," *Windsor Daily Star*, February 18, 1966.
35. "First Jewish federal minister wins reputation as hard worker," *Windsor Star*, October 16, 1969.
36. Abrams, 84.
37. "Interest in politics leads to law and romance," *Windsor Daily Star*, April 17, 1967.
38. "Gray plans to enter Windsor West race," *Windsor Star*, April 27, 1968.
39. Abrams, 84–85.
40. "Gray remains calm in fourth straight win," *Windsor Star*, June 25, 1968.
41. "Herb, Gene given posts," *Windsor Daily Star*, August 30, 1968.
42. "Herb Gray's star rises," *Windsor Daily Star*, September 11, 1968.
43. "Now it's official," *Windsor Daily Star*, October 21, 1969.
44. "It was Herb's day on Parliament Hill," *Windsor Daily Star*, January 30, 1970.
45. "Gray cites emerging consensus on foreign ownership policies," *Globe and Mail*, April 9, 1970.
46. "Gray's credentials are known and all of them will be needed," *Globe and Mail*, October 1, 1970.
47. Comments from the Rt. Hon. Herb Gray, micro-cassette 1, May 2003.
48. Robert Bothwell, Ian Drummond, and John English, *Canada since 1945 — Power, Politics and Provincialism* (Toronto: University of Toronto Press, 1981), 416.
49. "An MP for all seasons," *Maclean's* 105(25), June 22, 1992.
50. "After two polls it was like old times for Gray's Grits," *Windsor Star*, October 31, 1972.
51. "Revision to reflect consideration of public interest," *Windsor Daily Star*, undated.
52. "Herb Gray...calm cool and effective," *Windsor Daily Star*, March 2, 1974.
53. "History of the Federal Electoral Ridings since 1867."
54. "Gray all the way," *Windsor Star*, July 9, 1974.
55. "Horatio Alger in reverse," *London Free Press, Canadian magazine*, August 30, 1975.
56. Ibid.
57. Ibid.
58. Ibid.
59. Ibid.
60. "Gray considering Nixon bid to join Ontario Liberals," *Windsor Star*, February 8, 1975.
61. "Gray says he'll stay in Ottawa," *Windsor Star*, August 13, 1975.
62. "Herb Gray riding high again," *Windsor Star*, November 16, 1979.
63. "Political obituary for Herb Gray was written too soon," *Globe and Mail*, 1975.
64. "What's Gray going to do?" *Windsor Star*, March 20, 1975.
65. "Gray's stock up as critic," *Windsor Star*, February 2, 1976.
66. "Gray to meet with official over Smith's," *Windsor Star*, August 12, 1976.
67. "Gray questions effectiveness of foreign investment agency," *Windsor Star*, November 26, 1977.
68. "Gray urges tighter controls for freight cars," *Windsor Star*, March 15, 1978.

69. "Gray criticizes approval of proposed Simpsons deal," *Windsor Star*, December 16, 1978.

70. "Gray demands results from 5-year oil industry probe," *Windsor Star*, January 5, 1979.

71. "Review of Bell contract urged," *Windsor Star*, January 11, 1979.

72. "Gray claims Autopact violated," *Windsor Star*, April 19, 1978.

73. "MP Gray protests airline takeover," *Windsor Star*, August 30, 1978.

74. "Gray aims and blasts," *Windsor Star*, March 5, 1979.

75. "Herb Gray riding high again," *Windsor Star*, November 16, 1979.

76. "Herb Gray: Right man running" *Windsor Star*, May 23, 1979.

77. "Watchdog Gray: Ensuring PCs do 'the least possible damage,'" *Windsor Star*, November 3, 1979.

78. "Heere's Gray...& Grit homilies," *Windsor Star*, January 18, 1980.

79. "History of the Federal Electoral Ridings since 1867."

80. "Herb Gray gets one more plum," *Windsor Star*, March 20, 1980.

81. "Gray is excited by Cabinet job to spur industry," *Globe and Mail*, March 4, 1980.

82. "Gray to move on Autopact," *Globe and Mail*, March 4, 1980.

83. Ibid.

84. "Bid to change Autopact backed by parts makers," *Windsor Star*, March 22, 1980.

85. "Iacocca, Gray huddle in Toronto," *Windsor Star*, May 10, 1980.

86. "Gray on the gallop," *Windsor Star*, May 12, 1980.

87. "UAW asks Gray to be tough with Chrysler," *Windsor Star*, March 19, 1980.

88. "Gray will meet Ford brass on closing," *Globe and Mail*, April 17, 1980.

89. "Gray cancels Ford meeting—Ford wonders why," *Windsor Star*, April 25, 1980.

90. "Gray issues import threat," *Windsor Star*, June 5, 1980.

91. "Gray's car pitch striking out with Japanese," *Windsor Star*, August 5, 1980.

92. "Gray's always the true Grit," *Windsor Star*, November 16, 1983.

93. "Gray's post may include added clout," *Windsor Star*, June 30, 1984.

94. "Gray in 6th campaign," *Windsor Star*, July 10, 1984.

95. "Gray accepts challenge to begin rebuilding party," *Windsor Star*, September 5, 1984.

96. "He makes transition with ease," *Windsor Star*, October 6, 1984.

97. "Gray riding Turner fortunes," *Windsor Star*, May 5, 1988.

98. "'Solomon' gearing up for battle," *Windsor Star*, June 14, 1988.

99. "NDP, Tories in search for a giant slayer," *Windsor Star*, October 15, 1988.

100. "Kishkon won't run against Gray," *Windsor Star*, August 24, 1988.

101. "Forder seeking Gray's job," *Windsor Star*, September 13, 1988.

102. "Windsor West Tories pick Silcox," *Windsor Star*, October 13, 1988.

103. James Bickerton, Alain G. Gagnon, and Patrick J. Smith, *The Almanac of Canadian Politics* (Peterborough, ON: Broadview Press, 1991).

104. "Forder and Co., patiently await Gray's quitting," *Windsor Star*, November 22, 1988.

105. "Gray reappointed, ends leadership rumour," *Windsor Star*, November 26, 1988.

106. "Gray appointment fuels speculation Turner may retire," *Windsor Star*, January 11, 1989.

107. "Grits still liberal, Herb Gray insists," *Windsor Star*, March 22, 1989.

108. "Herb Gray playing it coy as all eyes turn to Turner," *Windsor Star*, February 7, 1990.

109. "Liberal leadership race: Gray likely to fill in as leader after Turner goes," *Windsor Star*, June 20, 1989.

110. "Liberal Leadership: Grits grappling over support for a new boss," *Windsor Star*, November 2, 1989.

111. "Local MPs show no favouritism," *Windsor Star*, January 25, 1990.

112. "Gray to get more than status in job," *Windsor Star*, February 8, 1990.

113. "Herb Gray: A matter of trust," *Windsor Star*, February 9, 1990.

114. "Gray asks for tolerance on divisive language issue," *Windsor Star*, February 16, 1990.

115. "Minister denies promises of GST-related price cuts," *Windsor Star*, April 28, 1990.

116. "Meech Lake Accord," *The Columbia Encyclopedia*, Sixth Edition (New York: Columbia University Press, 2001).

117. "Workaholic Herb Gray (yes, the one from Windsor) rocks on," *Toronto Star*, December 21, 1993.

118. "And now, heeere's Herbie," *Windsor Star*, May 1, 1990.

119. "A Liberal gathering: Gray whips up troops," *Windsor Star*, June 22, 1990.

120. Ibid.

121. "Gray will keep job," *Windsor Star*, June 25, 1990.

122. Comment from the Rt. Hon. Herb Gray, micro-cassette 2, June 2003.

123. "Tough times: opposition MPs arm Wilson with recession-fighting tips," *Windsor Star*, February 23, 1991.

124. "MP's dad, founder of Gray's Department Store, dead at 96," *Windsor Star*, December 30, 1991.

125. "Take our PM, please," editorial, *Windsor Star*, March 4, 1992.

126. Ibid., "Gray says study shows free trade deal a loser" April 7, 1992.

127. "Parliament Hill pays tribute to 'rock' of ages: Party marks Gray's 30th year in House," *Windsor Star*, June 18, 1992.

128. Ibid.

129. "A touch of Gray," *Windsor Star*, June 18, 1992.

130. "An MP for all seasons," *Maclean's*, June 22, 1992.

131. "Herb Gray area's best bet for Cabinet post," *Windsor Star*, October 26, 1993.

132. "Gray gets double duty in cabinet," *Windsor Star*, November 4, 1993.

133. "Gray wants anti-crime panel to seek justice, safety," *Windsor Star*, November 16, 1993.

134. Ibid.

135. "Workaholic Herb Gray (yes the one from Windsor) rocks on," *Toronto Star*, December 21, 1993.

136. Ibid.

137. "Gray's office flooded with calls of support," *Windsor Star*, April 23, 1996.

138. "Herb Gray wishes for a quick recovery," *Windsor Star*, April 24, 1996.

139. "Gray on the mend after cancer surgery," *Windsor Star*, August 30, 1990.

140. "Oh, lucky man," *Windsor Star*, November 16, 1996.

141. "Herb Gray, well done," *Windsor Star*, February 21, 1997.

142. "Gray offers insight into cancer," *Windsor Star*, April 4, 1998.

143. Chief Electoral Officer of Canada, "1997 Official Electoral Results," Thirty-Sixth General Election, 1997.

144. "Gray first full-time deputy PM," *Windsor Star*, June 12, 1997.

145. "Man of record: honourable to the end," *Windsor Star*, January 16, 2002.

146. "The Gray millennium," *Maclean's*, February 16, 1998.

147. "Gray wins 13th consecutive election; Comartin defeats Limoges," *Windsor Star*, November 28, 2000.

148. "Gray facing open-heart surgery," *Windsor Star*, August 30, 2001.

149. Comments from the Rt. Hon. Herb Gray, micro-cassette 2, June 2003.

150. Ibid.

151. "Deputy PM quits at behest of Chrétien," *National Post*, January 16, 2002.

152. "ERCA: A foundation for the future," *Windsor Star*, July 29, 1998.

153. "Unlucky 13? Grays find it isn't true," *Windsor Star*, July 24, 1980.

154. "Whole lotta shakin' going on in Commons," *Globe and Mail*, November 10, 2001.

155. "National honour for Gray" *Windsor Star*, December 3, 1998.

156. Ibid.

157. McGill University, list of Distinctions, Degrees and Recognition, prepared for Award of Honorary Doctorate of Laws, June 13, 2002, to the Rt. Honourable Herb Gray, C, QC, and includes the following:
    PC — Privy Councilor
    QC — Queen's Counsel
    Designation as "The Right Honourable"
    B. Comm (McGill)
    LLB — Osgoode Hall, York University
    LLD (Hon) — University of Windsor
    LLD (Hon) — Assumption University of Windsor
    Doctor (Hon) — Catholic University of Lublin, Poland
    Honourary Graduate — St. Claire College, Windsor
    Centennial Medal
    Queen's Silver Jubilee Medal
    Canada's 125 Medal
    (the first) John Fraser Award for Environmental Achievement presented by the Sierra Club of Canada
    Ordre de la Francophonie Pleiade — Officier
    Negev Dinner Honouree
    B'nai Brith Award of Merit

158. Comments from the Rt. Hon. Herb Gray, micro-cassette 2, June 2003.

Chapter 12: The Bicentennial of Windsor Jewish Life

1. Introduction drawn from T. Price and L. Kulisek, *Windsor 1892–1992: A Centennial Celebration* (Windsor: Chamber Publications, 1992).
2. Windsor Jewish Community Council, Annual Meeting Minutes, June 27, 1979.
3. Congregation Shaar Hashomayim, Board of Directors Minutes, March 18, 1981.
4. Congregation Beth El, Board of Directors Minutes, July 24, 1980.
5. Jewish Community Council, Board of Directors Minutes, January 30, 1980.
6. "Chabad House News," *Jewish Community Council Bulletin*, February 1981.
7. Ibid.
8. Letter from David Glanz, Congregation Shaar Hashomayim, committee to select a rabbi, May 7, 1980.
9. Congregation Shaar Hashomayim, Board of Directors Minutes, May 20, 1981.
10. Congregation Beth El, Board of Directors Minutes, March 26, 1981.
11. Congregation Shaar Hashomayim, Board of Directors Minutes, February 15, 1983.
12. Telephone interview with Rabbi Grussgott, April 4, 2004.
13. Alan Abrams, *Why Windsor? An Anecdotal History of the Town of Windsor and Essex County* (Windsor: Black Moss Press, 1981), 106, 107, 109.
14. Fred Katzman, presentation comments, Congregation Beth El, Double Chai Weekend, November 17, 1995.
15. Congregation Beth El, Executive Committee Minutes, February 6, 1979.
16. Rabbi Jonathan V. Plaut, personal recollections; Congregation Beth El, Board of Directors Minutes, January 8, 1981.
17. Congregation Beth El, Board of Directors Minutes, January 17, 1980, and July 24, 1980.
18. Fred Katzman, presentation comments.
19. Ibid.
20. Congregation Beth El Special Meeting Minutes, February 17, 1981.
21. Congregation Beth El Minutes, March 4, 1981.
22. Ibid.
23. Congregation Beth El Minutes, May 20, 1981.
24. Congregation Beth El Minutes, September 17, 1981.
25. Congregation Beth El Minutes, May 28, 1981.
26. "Laying the cornerstone of our new building," *Windsor Jewish Community Council Bulletin*, September, 1981; Congregation Beth El, Board of Directors Minutes, September 17, 1981.
27. Congregation Beth El, Board of Directors Minutes, September 17, 1981.
28. Congregation Beth El, *25th Anniversary Rededication Booklet*, November 10, 1984.
29. Congregation Beth El Minutes, April 28, 1981; Congregation Shaar Hashomayim, Board of Directors Minutes, August 19, 1981.
30. Congregation Shaar Hashomayim, Board of Directors Minutes, March 24, 1982.
31. Congregation Beth El, Special Meeting Minutes, March 4, 1981.
32. Congregation Shaar Hashomayim, Board of Directors Minutes, August 24, 1983.
33. Congregation Shaar Hashomayim, Board of Directors Minutes, December 17, 1985.
34. Congregation Shaar Hashomayim, Board of Directors Minutes, July 23, 1986. See also Congregation Shaar Hashomayim, Annual Meeting Minutes, November 23, 1989.
35. Jewish Community Council, Annual Meeting Minutes, June 28, 1980.
36. Jewish Community Council, Board of Directors Minutes, May 30, 1979.
37. Jewish Community Council, Board of Directors Minutes, January 28, 1981. See also Board of Directors Minutes, March 25, 1981.
38. Jewish Community Council, Board of Directors Minutes, April 29, 1981.
39. Jewish Community Council, Board of Directors Minutes, May 28, 1981.
40. Ibid.
41. Jewish Community Council, Board of Directors Minutes, July 6, 1981.
42. Jewish Community Council, Special Board of Directors Minutes, July 6, 1981.
43. Jewish Community Council, Board of Directors Minutes, September 23, 1981.
44. Jewish Community Council, Board of Directors Minutes, October 28, 1981.
45. "A dream becomes a reality," *Jewish Community Council Bulletin*, January 1982.

46. Jewish Community Council, Board of Directors Minutes, April 28, 1982. See also "Newsletter of the I. L. Peretz House," *Windsor Jewish Community Council Bulletin*, June 1982.

47. "Newsletter of the I .L. Peretz House."

48. "A dream becomes a reality," *Jewish Community Council Bulletin*.

49. Jewish Community Council, Board of Directors Minutes, December 9, 1982.

50. Jewish Community Council, Board of Directors Minutes, September 29, 1982.

51. "The I. L. Peretz House," *Jewish Community Council Bulletin*, Special Issue, January 1983.

52. Jewish Community Council, Board of Directors Minutes, September 29, 1982.

53. "The I. L .Peretz House," *Jewish Community Council Bulletin*.

54. "Peretz highlights," *Jewish Community Council Bulletin*, May 1983.

55. "Peretz highlights," *Jewish Community Council Bulletin*, February 1983.

56. "I. L. Peretz House highlights," *Jewish Community Council Bulletin*, March 1984.

57. Jewish Community Council, Board of Directors Minutes, January 30, 1985.

58. E-mail from Sandra Malowitz, July 31, 2003.

59. Jewish Community Council, Board of Directors Minutes, January 29, 1986.

60. "Obituary — Sidney Katzman," *Detroit Jewish News*, May 14, 2004.

61. Comments by Herb Brudner, Chapter Review Meeting Minutes, May 18, 2004.

62. "Jews from Soviet Russia," *Jewish Community Council Bulletin*, February 1980.

63. Jewish Community Council, Board of Directors Minutes, September 26, 1979.

64. Jewish Community Council, Board of Directors Minutes, April 30, 1980.

65. Jewish Community Council, Board of Directors Minutes, August 28, 1980.

66. Jewish Community Council, Board of Directors Minutes, January 28, 1981; "Hemschech!!! Windsor does it again," *Jewish Community Council Bulletin*, February 1981.

67. Jewish Community Council, Board of Directors Minutes, May 28, 1981.

68. Jewish Community Council, Administration and Finance Committee Minutes, December 14, 1983.

69. "Obituary—Sidney Katzman," *Detroit Jewish News*, May 14, 2004.

70. "Russian Weddings," *Jewish Community Council Bulletin*, May 1983.

71. Ibid.

72. Jewish Community Council, Board of Directors Minutes, May 25, 1983.

73. Letter from Jerry Alexis to Barbara McDougall, Jewish Community Council, Board of Directors Minutes, April 7, 1991.

74. Jewish Community Council, Board of Directors Minutes, February 20, 1992.

75. Agreement between United Israel Appeal of Canada and Windsor Jewish Federation, Jewish Community Council, Board of Directors Minutes, May 20, 1994.

76. Jewish Community Council, Board of Directors Minutes, May 28, 1981.

77. "Reverend Irwin Dubitsky," *Jewish Community Council Bulletin*, April 1981.

78. Congregation Shaar Hashomayim, Board of Directors Minutes, May 6, 1981, and June 17, 1981.

79. "In Memoriam Reverend Irwin Dubitsky," *Jewish Community Council Bulletin*, May 1983.

80. Ibid.

81. "Windsor Negev Dinner Honours Joe Eisenberg," *Jewish Community Council Bulletin*, May, 1983; "1983 Negev Dinner," *Jewish Community Council Bulletin*, August, 1983.

82. "Tribute to Joseph Eisenberg," *Jewish Community Council Bulletin*, December, 1983.

83. Congregation Beth El section, *Jewish Community Council Bulletin*, December 1984.

84. Beth El, *25th Anniversary Rededication Booklet*; Congregation Beth El section, *Jewish Community Council Bulletin*, December 1984.

85. *Jewish Community Council Bulletin*, December 1987.

86. Jewish Community Council, Board of Directors Minutes, January 13, 1988.

87. Abrams, 95–99.

88. Ibid., 103.

89. "Comment on William 'Moose' Rogin," Canadian Basketball Hall of Fame.

90. Abrams, 95.

91. "Down Memory Lane to 1936 Games," *Windsor Star*, February 16, 1976.

92. "Hall of Famer Recalls Berlin Trip," *Windsor Star*, October 21, 2002.
93. Ibid.
94. Ibid.
95. Abrams, 99.
96. Interview with the Honourable Mr. Justice Sal Nosanchuk, March 19, 2004; "Shaar brings Dominion juvenile title," *Windsor Daily Star*, April 15, 1953.
97. International Olympic Games web site, http://www.olympic.org.
98. "Maccabiah Games," *Jewish Community Council Bulletin*, March 1988; "North American Youth Maccabiah Games," *Jewish Community Council Bulletin*, September 1988.
99. E-mail from Rabbi Edward S. Feigelman, July 24, 2003.
100. Congregation Shaar Hashomayim, Board of Directors Minutes, February 15, 1989.
101. Congregation Shaar Hashomayim, Board of Directors Minutes, March 15, 1989, and April 12, 1989.
102. Community Relations Committee Report in the Report of Standing Committees, Jewish Community Council, Annual Meeting Minutes, June 29, 1983.
103. Ibid.
104. Jewish Community Council, Board of Directors Minutes, January 29, 1986.
105. Jewish Community Council, Board of Directors Minutes, January 13, 1988, and February 25, 1988; Ibid., February 25, 1988.
106. Jewish Community Council, Board of Directors Minutes, January 25, 1984.
107. Jewish Community Council, Summit Committee Minutes, December 6, 1984.
108. Jewish Community Council, Officers Meeting Minutes, June 18,1987.
109. Report of Joseph Eisenberg, Jewish Community Council Minutes, June 18, 1987.
110. "Retreat at Diana and Alan Orman's home," Jewish Community Council Minutes, September 1, 1987.
111. Jewish Community Council Minutes, June 18, 1987.
112. Jewish Community Council, Annual Meeting Minutes, June 30, 1982. See also "Barry Swartz," *Jewish Community Council Bulletin*, September 1982.
113. Jewish Community Council, Board of Directors Minutes, October 2, 1985.
114. Jewish Community Council, Board of Directors Minutes, April 15, 1986, and October 29, 1986.
115. Jewish Community Council, Board of Directors Minutes, October 20, 1988.
116. Jewish Community Council, Annual Meeting Minutes, June 21, 1989.
117. Jewish Community Council, Executive Board of Directors Minutes, May 18, 1989, and June 21, 1989.
118. "The Eisenberg Era 1958-1989," *Jewish Community Council Bulletin*, Special Edition, August 1989.

Chapter 13: Toward the Twenty-First Century and Beyond

1. Introduction drawn from T. Price and L. Kulisek, *Windsor 1892–1992: A Centennial Celebration* (Windsor: Chamber Publications, 1992).
2. Congregation Shaar Hashomayim, Board of Directors Minutes, November 29, 1989.
3. "His induction a homecoming for rabbi," *Windsor Star*, May 19, 1990.
4. Ibid.
5. Windsor Jewish Community Council, Board of Directors Minutes, October 28, 1996.
6. Irwin S. Ehrlich and Howard Michael Folk, "Rabbi Howard M. Folb — a tribute," in *Yearbook of the Central Conference of American Rabbis*, Vol. 108, edited by Elliot L. Stevens and Camilla Relucio, 120–21; "Rabbi Howard M. Folb," *Windsor Jewish Community Council Bulletin*, May 1985.
7. "Congregation Beth El welcome to Rabbi Howard M. Folb," *Jewish Community Council Bulletin*, September 1985.
8. Conversation with Esther Goldstein, August 5, 2003.
9. E-mail from Rabbi Jeffrey Ableser, November 5, 2003.
10. Ibid.
11. "Retreat at Diana and Alan Orman's home," Jewish Community Council, Board of Directors Minutes, September 30, 1987.
12. Interview with Harriet Whiteman, May 19, 2004.
13. Jewish Community Council, Executive Board of Directors Minutes, March 22, 1989.
14. Whiteman interview.
15. Jewish Community Council, Executive Board of Directors Minutes, February 16, 1989.
16. Jewish Community Council, Executive Board of Directors Minutes, May 18, 1989.

17. Jewish Community Council, Special Board of Directors Meeting Minutes, December 19, 1991.

18. Jewish Community Council, Board of Directors Minutes, January 20, 1994.

19. Ibid.

20. "Message from the president," *Jewish Community Centre Bulletin,* April 1994.

21. Jewish Community Council, Board of Directors Minutes, March 27, 1995, and May 23, 1995.

22. Jewish Community Council, Board of Directors Minutes, January 29, 1996.

23. Jewish Community Council, Board of Directors Minutes, January 29, 1996, and July 22, 1996.

24. Jewish Community Council, Board of Directors Minutes, February 26, 1996.

25. Jewish Community Council, Board of Directors Minutes, January 29, 1991. See also Minutes of September 1, 1994.

26. Jewish Community Council, Board of Directors Minutes, February 28, 1998.

27. Jewish Community Council, Board of Directors Minutes, January 26, 1998.

28. Jewish Community Council, Board of Directors Minutes, June 19, 1995.

29. Jewish Community Council, Board of Directors Minutes, August 24, 1998.

30. Jewish Community Council, Board of Directors Minutes, October 25, 1999.

31. "Demographic Profile of the Windsor Jewish Community," Jewish Community Council, Board of Directors Minutes, February 11, 1993.

32. Charles Shahar, "The Jewish Community of Windsor, Part 1, Basic Demographics," *2001 Census Analysis Series*, 2.

33. Ibid., 7.

34. Jewish Community Council, Board of Directors Minutes, September 22, 1997.

35. Jewish Community Council, Board of Directors Minutes, October 27, 1997.

36. "Community religious school news," *Jewish Community Centre Bulletin*, Autumn 1998.

37. Interview with Joseph Eisenberg, November 12, 1990.

38. Interview with Harvey Kessler, November 4, 2003.

39. Congregation Shaar Hashomayim, Board of Directors Minutes, January 27, 1975.

40. Congregation Shaar Hashomayim, Board of Directors Minutes, June 19, 1974 and January 27, 1975.

41. Kessler interview.

42. Ibid.

43. "Endowment professional hired," *Jewish Community Centre Bulletin*, Winter 1997.

44. E-mail from Rabbi Jeffrey Ableser, November 5, 2003.

45. Jewish Community Centre, Board of Directors Minutes, September 22, 1997.

46. Jewish Community Centre, Board of Directors Minutes, October 27, 1997.

47. "Windsor delegation to South America," *Jewish Community Centre Bulletin*, Autumn 1998.

48. E-mail from Dr. Marilyn (Miller) Kronmal, April 1, 2004.

49. E-mail from Pam (Weingarden) Albert, March 29, 2004.

50. E-mail from Amy (Whiteman) Shafton, March 26, 2004.

Bibliography

Books

Abella, Irving. *A Coat of Many Colours: Two Centuries of Jewish Life*. Toronto: Lester Orpen Dennys, 1990.

Abrams, Alan, *Why Windsor: An Anecdotal History of the Town of Windsor and Essex County*. Windsor: Black Moss Press, 1981.

Albrecht-Carrie, Rene. *A Diplomatic History of Europe Since the Congress of Vienna*. New York: Harper and Row, 1958.

Anderson, Fannie. *Doctor's Under Three Flags*. Wayne State University Press, 1951.

Armour, David A., ed. *Attack at Michilimackinac 1763 — Alexander Henry's Travel & Adventures in Canada & the Indian Territories Between 1760 & 1764*. Mackinac Island, MI: Mackinac State Historic Parks, 1995.

Baker, Max and Paul Masserman. *The Jews Come to America*. New York: Block Publishing Co., 1932.

Barrie, James, *Old Forts of the Great Lakes: Sentinels in the Wilderness*. Lansing, Michigan: Thunder Bay Press, 1994.

Belkin, Simon. *Through Narrow Gates: A Review of Jewish Immigration, Colonization and Immigration Aid Work in Canada, 1840–1940*. Montreal: The Eagle Publishing Co. Ltd., 1966.

Biano, Anthony. *The Reichmanns: Family, Faith, Fortune, and the Empire of Olympia & York*. New York: Random House, 1997.

Bickerton, James, Alain G. Gagnon, Patrick J. Smith. *The Almanac of Canadian Politics*. Peterborough, ON: Broadview Press, 1991.

Bolkosky, Sidney. *Harmony and Dissonance: Voices of Jewish Identity in Detroit, 1914–1967*. Detroit: Wayne State University Press, 1991.

Borthwick, J. Douglas. *Montreal, History and Biographical Gazetteer to the Year 1892*. Montreal: John Lovell & Son, 1892.

Bothwell, Robert, Ian Drummond, and John English. *Canada Since 1945 — Power, Politics and Provincialism*. Toronto: University of Toronto Press, 1981.

Bulchinsky Gerald. *Taking Root: The Origins of the Canadian Jewish Community*. Toronto: Stoddard Publishing Co., 1992.

Canada: Indian Treaties and Surrenders. Volume 1. Brown Chamberlin, Printer to the Queen's Most Excellent Majesty, 1891.

The Canada Year Book, 1927–1928. Ottawa, 1928.

Chauvin, Francis X. *Men of Achievement*. Essex County, Ontario. Volume 1, 1927 edition; Volume 2, 1929 edition.

Clarke, John, *Land, Power, and Economics on the Frontier of Upper Canada*. Montreal: McGill-Queen's University Press, 2001.

Conrad, Margaret and Alvin Finkel. *History of the Canadian Peoples: Beginnings to 1867*. Volume 1. 3rd ed. Toronto: Addison Wesley Longman, 2002.

Current, Richard N., Frank Freidel, and T. Harry Williams. *A History of the United States*. New York: Alfred A. Knopf, 1959.

de Sola, Clarence I. *150th Anniversary of Spanish and Portuguese Jews of Montreal*. Montreal, 1918.

Doyle, William. *The Oxford History of the French Revolution*. 2nd ed. New York: Oxford University Press, 2002.

Frank, Solomon. *Two Centuries in the Life of a Synagogue*. Montreal: Spanish and Portuguese Congregation, 1968.

Fuller, Robert M. *Windsor Heritage*. Windsor: Herald Press, 1972.

Gaxotte, Pierre. *Frederick the Great*. Trans. by R. A. Bell. London: G. Bell and Sons Ltd., 1941.

Geller, Jacob J. *It's Jake with Me*. Markham, ON: PaperJacks, 1983.

Godfrey, Sheldon and Judy Godfrey. *Search Out the Land: The Jews and the Growth of Equality in British Colonial America, 1740–1867*. Montreal: McGill-Queen's University Press, 1995.

Goodkind, S. B. *Eminent Jews of America: A Collection of Biographical Sketches of Jews Who Have Distinguished Themselves in Commercial, Professional and Religious Endeavor*. Toledo, Ohio: The American Hebrew Biographical Company, Inc., 1818.

Gottesman, Eli, ed. *Canadian Jewish Reference Book and Directory*. Montreal: Mortimer Ltd., 1963.

Graff, George. *The People of Michigan*. Lansing, MI: Department of Education State Library Services, 1974.

Hart, A. D. *The Jews in Canada*. Montreal: Jewish Publication Ltd., 1926.

Heineman, David E. *Jewish Beginnings in Michigan Before 1850*. Reprinted from Publications of the American Jewish Historical Society No. 13., 1905.

Hennepin, Jean Louis. *Description de la Louisane nouvelement découverte*. Paris, 1683.

Hershkowitz, Leo and Isidore S. Meyer. *The Lee Max Friedman Collection of American Jewish Colonial Correspondence, Letters of the Frank Family, 1733–1748*. Waltham, MA: American Jewish Historical Society, 1968.

Howe, Irving. *World of Our Fathers*. New York: Harcourt Brace Jovanovich, 1976.

Kage, Joseph. *With Faith and Thanksgiving: The Story of Two Hundred Years of Jewish Immigration and Immigration Aid Effort in Canada (1760–1960)*. Montreal: The Eagle Publishing Co. Ltd., 1962.

Katz, Irving I. *The Beth El Story*. Detroit: Wayne State University Press, 1955.

Kurelek, William. *Jewish Life in Canada*. Edmonton: Hurtig Publishers, 1976.

Lajeunesse, Ernest J. *The Windsor Border Region*. Toronto: University of Toronto Press, 1960.

Lescarbot, Marc. *Histoire de la Nouvelle-France, suive des moies de la Nouvelle-France*. 3 vols. Paris: Edwin Tross, 1866.

Marcus, Jacob Rader. *Early American Jewry*. Vol. 1. Philadelphia: Jewish Publication Society of America, 1953.

_____. *Early American Jewry: The Jews of New York, New England and Canada, 1649–1794*. New York: KTVA Publishing House Inc., 1975.

Martin, Paul. *A Very Public Life*. Volume I. Toronto: Deneau Publishers,1985.

Masserman, Paul and Max Baker. *The Jews Come to America*. New York: Block Publishing Co., 1932.

Michigan Department of Education. "Family Trails: Michigan Jewish Family History, State of Michigan." *State Library Services* 4(3), Spring 1974.

Microsoft Encarta Encyclopedia 99. Microsoft Corporation, 1998. http://store.viosoftware.biz/.

Morawska, Ewa. *Insecure Prosperity: Small-Town Jews in Industrial America, 1890–1940*. New Haven: Princeton University Press, 1996.

Morgan, Carl. *Birth of a City*. Windsor: Border Press, 1991.

Morrison, Neal F. *Garden Gateway to Canada*. Toronto: Ryerson Press, 1954.

O'Callaghan, E. B., ed. *Documents Relating to the Colonial History of the State of New York*. Vol. 4. Baltimore : Genealogical Publishing Co., 1979.

Peckham, Howard H. *Pontiac and the Indian Uprising*. Detroit: Wayne State University Press, 1994.

Plaut, W. Gunther. *Unfinished Business*. Toronto: Lester & Orpen Dennys, 1981.

Price, Trevor and Larry Kulisek. *Windsor 1892–1992: A Centennial Celebration*. Windsor: Chamber Publications, 1992.

Rockaway, Robert. *The Jews of Detroit: From the Beginning, 1762–1914*. Detroit: Wayne State University Press, 1986.

Rome, David. *A Selected Bibliography of Jewish Canadiana*. Montreal: Canadian Jewish Congress, 1959.

Rosenberg, Louis. *Canada's Jews: A Social and Economic Study of the Jews in Canada*. Montreal: Bureau of Social and Economic Research, 1939.

_____. *Chronology of Canadian-Jewish History*. Montreal: National Bicentenary Committee of the Canadian Jewish Congress, 1959.

_____. *A Population Study of Windsor Jewish Community*. Montreal: Bureau of Social and Economic Research, 1951.

_____. *Programming Kit*. Canadian Jewish Congress, 1959.

_____. *Some Aspects of the Historical Development of the Canadian Jewish Community*. Canadian Jewish Population Studies, ser. no. 4. Montreal: Bureau of Social and Economic Research, Canadian Jewish Congress, 1960.

Rosenberg, Stuart E. *The Jewish Community in Canada, A History*. Vol. 2. Toronto: McClelland & Stewart, 1971.

Rosenbloom, Joseph R. *A Biographical Dictionary of Early American Jews*. Lexington: University of Kentucky Press, 1960.

Rudausky, David. *Emancipation and Adjustment*. New York: Diplomatic Press, 1967.

Sack, Benjamin. *History of the Jews in Canada*. Montreal: Harvest House, 1965.

Scharf, J. and J. Westcott. *History of Philadelphia 1609–1844*. Vol. 2. Philadelphia: Everets & Co., 1884.

Seaman, L. C. B. *From Vienna to Versailles*. New York: Harper Colophon, 1963.

Stern, Malcolm H. *Americans of Jewish Descent: A Compendium of Genealogy*. Cincinnati: American Jewish Archives, 1960.

Sumner, Michael, ed. *The Golden Jubilee Book Celebrating the Fiftieth Anniversary Of the Building of Shaar Hashomayim Synagogue in Windsor, Ontario, Canada*. Windsor: Sumner Press, 1980.

Sutherland, D. M. G. *France, 1789–1815: Revolution and Counter Revolution*. 4th ed. New York: Fontana History of Modern France, 1985.

Taylor, Alastair M. and T. Walter Wallbank. Vol. 2. 4th ed. *Civilization Past and Present*. Chicago: Scott, Foresman and Company, 1961.

Thwaites, R.G., ed. 1896-1901. *The Jesuit Relations and Allied Documents: Travels and Explorations of the Jesuit Missionaries in New France, 1610–1791*. Vol. 21. Cleveland: Burrows Bros. Co.

Tulchinsky, Gerald. *Taking Root: The Origins of the Canadian Jewish Community*. Toronto: Stoddart Publishing Co., 1992.

Vaugeois, Denis. *Les Juifs et la Nouvelle-France*. Trois Rivières: Editions Boreal Express, 1968.

Wallace, Stewart W. *Dictionary of Canadian Biography*. Toronto: Macmillan Co., 1926.

Wallbank, Walter and Alastair M. Taylor. *Civilization Past and Present*. Vol. 2. 4th ed. Chicago: Scott, Foresman and Co., 1961.

Weepers, Bob. *We Are the Champions: Canadian Championship Sports Teams, Windsor, Ontario, 20th Century*. Windsor: Windsor/Essex County Sports Hall of Fame, 2000.

Weissbach, Lee Shai. *Jewish Life in Small Town America: A History*. New Haven: Yale University Press, 2005.

Who's Who in Canadian Jewry. Jerusalem: Hebrew University of Jerusalem, 1969.

Articles

"An MP for all seasons." *Maclean's* 105(25) (June 22, 1992).

Armour, David A. "Alexander Henry." In *Dictionary of Canadian Biography*, edited by Francess G. Halpenny and Jean Hamelin. Volume VI, 1821–1835. Toronto: University of Toronto Press, 1987.

Arnold, A. J. "Encyclopedia marred by contradictions." *Canadian Jewish News*, April 12, 1974.

Blaustein, Esther I., Rachel A. Esar, and Evelyn Miller. "Spanish and Portuguese Synagogue (Shearith Israel) Montreal, 1768–1968." *The Jewish Historical Society of England* 33 (1971).

"British Museum." *European Magazine* 39 (March 1801).

Brown, Jennifer. "George Sutherland." In *Dictionary of Canadian Biography*, edited by Francess G. Halpenny and Jean Hamelin. Volume IV, 1771–1800. Toronto: University of Toronto Press, 1979.

Burgess, Joanne. "William Grant." In *Dictionary of Canadian Biography*, edited by Francess G. Halpenny and Jean Hamelin. Volume V, 1801–1820. Toronto: University of Toronto Press, 1983.

Canadian Basketball Hall of Fame. "William 'Moose' Rogin."

Canadian Senate. Senator David A. Croll, biographical information.

Chevrette, Louis. "Pontiac." In *Dictionary of Canadian Biography*, edited by Francess G. Halpenny and Jean Hamelin. Volume III, 1741–1770. Toronto: University of Toronto Press, 1974.

Chief Electoral Officer of Canada. "1997 Official Electoral Results." Thirty-Sixth General Election, 1997.

Davis, Moshe. "Centres of Jewry in the western hemisphere: a comparative approach." *Jewish Journal of Sociology* 5 (June 1963).

de Sola, Clarence I. "David." In *The Jewish Encyclopedia*. 1901 ed. New York: Funk and Wagnalls.

"Dedication May 25th 1930 Shaar Hashomayim Synagogue." *Border Cities Star*, 1930.

"Deputy PM quits at behest of Chrétien." *National Post*, January 16, 2002.

Dublin, Frances. "Jewish colonial enterprise in the light of the Amherst papers (1758–1763)." *American Jewish Historical Society*, no. 35.

Dunn, Walter S. "Lucius Levy Solomons." In *Dictionary of Canadian Biography*, edited by Francess G. Halpenny and Jean Hamelin. Volume IV, 1771–1800. Toronto: University of Toronto Press, 1979.

Edwards, Chris and Elaine Weeks. "Black day in July." *Detroit News*. Rearview Mirror Archives, published in *Walkerville Times*, November 25, 2003.

Ehrlich, Irwin S. "Howard Michael Folb — a tribute." In *Central Conference of American Rabbis Yearbook* 108 (1999), edited by Elliot L. Stevens and Camilla Relucio.

Eisen, Dr. David. "Jewish settlers of old Toronto." *Jewish Standard* (December 15, 1965).

Gildea, Robert. "Recent discussion of complex issues of occupation, neutrality, responsibility." In *Marianne in Chains: In Search of the German Occupation of France*, 1940–1945. New York: Metropolitan Books, 2003.

Government of Canada. "History of the federal electoral ridings since 1867." Library of Parliament, Information and Documentation Branch B, Ottawa, 2001.

"Gray cites emerging consensus on foreign ownership policies." *Globe and Mail*, April 9, 1970.

Gross, William R. "The redevelopment area of Windsor to 1900." Master's thesis, University of Windsor, 1961.

Heldman, Donald. "Michigan's first Jewish settlers: a view from the Solomons-Levy Trading House at Fort Michilimackinac, 1765–1781." *Journal of New World Archaeology* VI(4) (June 1986).

Henry, Alexander. "Travels in the Indiana Territories 1760–1809." *Canadian Magazine and Literary Repository* 2(10) (April 1824).

"Horatio Alger in reverse." *Canadian Magazine*. London Free Press, August 30, 1975.

"Israel Record." Anti-Defamation League web site. http://www.adl.org/Israel/Record/index.asp.

"Journal of Schomberg." In *The Jewish Encyclopedia*. 1901 ed. New York: Funk and Wagnalls.

Katz, Irving I. "Chapman Abraham: an early Jewish settler in Detroit." *American Jewish Historical Society* 40 (I) (September 1950).

_____. "Ezekiel Solomons: the first Jew in Michigan." *Michigan History* 32 (September 1948).

_____. "The first Jew in Windsor." *Detroit Jewish News* (January 27, 1961).

_____. "The first Jew of Windsor (Canada) and his family." Historic File, American Jewish Archives: Cincinnati, Ohio.

_____. "Jewish traders captured during 1763 Indian uprising." *Detroit Historical Society Bulletin* 20(5) (February 1964).

_____. "Jews in Detroit prior to and including 1850." *Detroit Historical Society Bulletin* 6(5) (February 1950).

Kyte, Elinor, Sr., in collaboration with James H. Lambert. "David David." In *Dictionary of Canadian Biography*, edited by Francess G. Halpenny and Jean Hamelin. Volume VI, 1821–1835. Toronto: University of Toronto Press, 1987.

L'Heureux, Jacques. "George Sucking." In *Dictionary of Canadian Biography*, edited by Francess G. Halpenny and Jean Hamelin. Volume IV, 1771–1800. Toronto: University of Toronto Press, 1979.

Le Canadien (March 2, 1808).

Leeser, Isaac, ed. *The Occident* 1(11) (February 1844).

"Meech Lake Accord," In *The Columbia Encyclopedia*, 6th ed. New York: Columbia University Press, 2001.

Plaut, Rabbi Jonathan V. "Reforming and conforming: a history of the Jew of Windsor,1790–1940." Unpublished doctoral dissertation, Hebrew Union College–Jewish Institute of Religion, 1976.

Rivkin, Dr. Ellis. "A decisive pattern in American Jewish history." In *Essays in American Jewish History*. Cincinnati, Ohio: Hebrew Union College Press, 1958.

Rome, David. "Jacob Raphael Cohen." In *Dictionary of Canadian Biography*, edited by Francess G. Halpenny and Jean Hamelin. Volume V, 1801–1820. Toronto: University of Toronto Press, 1983.

Sarna, Jonathan D. "Jewish immigration to North America: the Canadian experience 1870–1900." *Jewish Journal of Sociology* 18 (June 1976).

Scott, Elizabeth May. "'Such diet as benefitted his station as clerk': the archaeology of subsistence and cultural diversity at Fort Michilimackinac, 1761–1781." Unpublished doctoral dissertation, University of Minnesota, 1991.

Skaggs, David Curtis. "The Sixty Years' War for the Great Lakes, 1754–1814: an overview." In *The Sixty Years' War for the Great Lakes, 1754-1814*, edited by David Curtis Skaggs and Larry L. Nelson. Detroit: Wayne State University Press, 2001.

"State of Israel — Historical Survey." In *Encyclopedia Judaica*. Jerusalem: Keter Publishing House Ltd, 1971.

Thorman, George, "Germain Maugenest." In *Dictionary of Canadian Biography*, edited by Francess G. Halpenny and Jean Hamelin. Volume IV, 1771–1800. Toronto: University of Toronto Press, 1979.

Winryb, Bernard D. "Jewish immigration and accommodation to America." In *The Jews*, edited by Marshall Sklare. Glencoe, IL: The Free Press, 1958.

Widder, Keith R. "The French connection: the interior French and their role in French-British relations in the western Great Lakes region, 1760–1755." In *The Sixty Years' War for the Great Lakes, 1754-1814*, edited by David Curtis Skaggs and Larry L. Nelson. Detroit: Wayne State University Press, 2001.

"Workaholic Herb Gray (yes, the one from Windsor) rocks on." *Toronto Star*, December 21, 1993.

Young, James E. "Bad times for the Jews." Review of *A People Apart: The Jews of Europe, 1789–1939*, by David Vital. *New York Times*, November 7, 1999.

Burton Historical Collection, Detroit Public Library

Cadillac papers. Vol. 33.

Catlin papers. "Detroit's earliest cemeteries."

Cicotte book.

Daniel Morrison Mackinac journal. 1769–1772.

Gladwin manuscripts. Vol. 27. 1897.

Godfroy papers. October 4, 1805; December 18, 1805; August 12, 1815.

Haldimand papers, Michigan Pioneer and Historical Collection. Vol. 10 (Lansing, 1888).

Herschel Whitaker papers. January 17, 1824.

James Sterling letter book. 1761–1765.

John Askin papers. John Askin ledgers, 1780–1782; John Askin account book, 1780-1782.

John R. Williams papers. November 18, 1805–April 24, 1812.

Labadie family papers. April 24, 1794.

Lewis Bond papers. Vol. 10 (1888); Vol. 37 (1909).

Michigan Pioneer and Historical Collection. Vol. 1; vol. 10 (Lansing 1908, 2nd ed); Vol. 12 (1887); Vol. 15 (1890); vol. 19.

Quaife, Milo M., ed. John Askin papers. 1796–1820. Detroit Library Commission, 1931.

Solomon Sibley papers.

St. John's Church records.1807–1857.

Thomas Smith papers. May 18, 1800.

Thomas Williams papers. May 18, 1800.

William Hands papers. 1791–1811.

Interviews and Telephone Conversations

Baum, Ben. Interview, August 13, 1973.

Benstein, Ida. Interview, February 25, 1974.

Berry, Vivian. Interviews, June 23, 1974; August 20, 1973.

Bloom, Dora and Goldie Meretsky. Interview, June 24, 1974.

Brodsky, Morris, David Glanz, and others. Interview, October 30, 1988.

Brody, Louis. Interview, August 13, 1973.

Burnstein, Tibe. Interview, June 13, 1974.

Cherniak, Harry. Interview, undated.

Cherniak, Harry, Edsel Meretsky, Harry Meretsky, and Michael Sumner. Interview, April 16, 1971.

Cohen, Abe and Harry Burstyn. Interview, May 8, 1975.

Cohen, Robert and Bess Cohen. Interview, January 28, 1975.

Croll, Senator David A. Interviews, March 22, 1974; August 12, 1988.

Eisenberg, Joseph. Interview, November 12, 1990.

Eisenberg, Joseph and others. Interview, undated.

Geller, Frances and Jacob Geller. Interview, February 15, 1972.

Geller, Jacob. Interview, June 11, 1974.

Gitlin, Arthur. Interview, August 14, 1973.

Gitlin, Joshua. Interview, April 26, 1972.

Gitlin, Mrs. Joshua. Interview, August 22, 1974.

Glanz, Gerald. Interview, January 27, 1972.

Glazer, Bernard. Interview, January 28, 1975.

Goldstein, Esther. Conversation, August 5, 2003.

Groner, Rabbi Benjamin. Interviews, November 12, 1979; undated.

Grussgott, Rabbi Ira Samuel. Telephone interview, April 4, 2004.

Hurwitz, Norman. Interview, June 12, 1974.

Kamin, Sockley. Interview, June 25, 1974.

Katzman, Abe. Interview, June 26, 1974.

Katzman, Mrs. Abe. Conversation, undated.

Katzman, Abe, I. Bert Meretsky, and I. M. Meretsky. Interview, June 26, 1974.

Kellerman, Al. Telephone interview, October 2, 2003.

Kessler, Harvey. Interview, November 4, 2003.

Kirzner, Mrs. Irving. Interview, June 26, 1974; telephone interview, undated.

Kovinsky, Betty, Sarah Levin, and Betty Passman. Interview, August 21, 1974.

Lieblich, Louis. Interview, April 19, 1991.

Luborsky, Mr. and Mrs. Harry. Interviews, August 13, 1973; June 3, 1974.

Madoff, Bernard. Interview, June 11, 1974.

Meretsky, I. Bert. Interview, June 10, 1974.

Meretsky, Irving (Toots). Telephone interview, January 5, 2004.

Meretsky, Israel (Slaw). Interviews, August 15, 1973; July 1, 1974.

Meretsky, Milton. Interview, June 11, 1974.

Meretsky, Mrs. David, and Dr. Peter Bernstein. Interview, June 28, 1973.

Meyers, Dr. Charles. Conversations, undated.

Nosanchuk, The Honourable Mr. Justice Saul. Interview, March 19, 2004.

Polsky, Dr. Ronald. Telephone interview, October 1, 2003.

Pomm, Montague. Telephone interview, November 4, 2003.

Schott, Maxwell. Interview, June 11, 1974.

Schulman, Rabbi Nahum. Interviews, March 28, 1976; June 11, 1974; November 12, 1979.

Stollman, Rabbi Samuel. Interview, August 14, 1989.

Stollman, Rabbi Samuel, and others. Interview, October 31, 1988.

Strosberg, Sylvia. Conversation, June 11, 1976.

Sumner, Michael. Interviews, June 4, 1974; March 8, 1988; November 11, 1990; and November 12, 1990.

Sumner, Lyle and Michael. Interview, 1988.

Sumner, Sarah. Interview, February 16, 1972.

Weingarden, Abner and Arthur. Conversations, June 11, 1976.

Weingarden, Maxwell. Interview, October 20, 1972.

Whiteman, Harriett. Interview, May 19, 2003.

Winograd, Mrs. Ralph (Ann). Interview, January 12, 2004.

Williams, Edsel, Mary, and Rose. Interview, June 11, 1974.

Yuffy, Ben. Interview, June 25, 1974.

Zimmerman, Shalamas. Interview, October 10, 2003.

Newspapers and Directories

Amherstburg Echo. June 25, 1880.

Border Cities Star (Windsor). September 3, 1918–June 29, 1935.

Burton, C. M. *City Directory from 1837 — Detroit.*

_____. Papers, Historical Memorandum, Detroit.

Canada Directory. Montreal: John Lovell, 1851.

Canadian Immigrant and Western District Advertiser (Sandwich). 1831–1836.

Canadian Parliamentary Guide, House of Commons, 1995.

County of Essex Gazeteer and General and Business Directory for 1866–1867. Sutherland & Co: Woodstock, 1866.

Daily Star (Montreal). December 30, 1893.

Detroit City Directory. 1855–1914.

Detroit Jewish News. 2004.

Directory for the Town of Windsor and City of Essex. 1887.

Essex Record (Windsor). 1871–1892 (except 1879).

Evening Record. 1893–December 31, 1917.

Gazette (Montreal). April 17, 1935.

Vernon's City of Windsor, Sandwich, Walkerville and Ford City, Alphabetical Business and Miscellaneous Directory for the Year 1919–1920.

Voice of the Fugitive (Sandwich). 1851–1853.

Western District Advertiser. 1838–1843.

Western Herald (Sandwich). 1838–1843.

Windsor City Directory: Including Sandwich and Walkerville. 1891, 1893, 1894, 1895, 1896,1897–98, 1899, 1900, 1901, 1903, 1904, 1905–06, 1906–07, 1911, 1913–14, 1914, 1916, 1919–20, 1920–21, 1921–22, 1922–23, 1923–24, 1924–25, 1926–27, 1927–28, 1928–29, 1931, 1933, 1934, 1935, 1937.

Windsor Daily Star. July 2, 1935–December 31, 1939.

Windsor Herald. 1855–1856.

Windsor Record. January 2, 1918–August 30, 1918.

Windsor Review. 1895–1896.

Windsor Sports News.

Windsor Star. 1959-.

Miscellaneous Sources

A tribute to Joseph Eisenberg. Special edition. *The Eisenberg Era 1958–1989.* Windsor Jewish Community Council, 1989.

Archives Nationales du Quebec, Files of Moses David, no. 1828.

Archives Nationales du Quebec, Montreal. Notarial records.

Bibliography

Archives Nationales, Archives des Colonies, Ottawa. Claus Papers M. G. 19, F. 1. vol. 6.

Archives Nationales, Archives des Colonies, Ottawa. Ser./vol. B–68–1, B–71, A–15, B–217, C–2, F–70, F–71, Q–2, Q–33–1, Q–322.

Beaver Club Minute Book. McCord Museum, Montreal.

Beth Olam cemetery records, Detroit, Michigan.

Bishop College papers. McCord Museum, Montreal.

Cahier des dix. Malchelosse and Gerard, 1939.

Canadian Archives. Vol. 1. 1955–1959; Vol. 1(2) (June 1956); Vol. 2 1769–1790.

Census records. 1851; 1861; 1871.

Congregation Beth El. 25th anniversary rededication. Windsor. November 10, 1984.

Congregation Beth El. Cemetery records. Detroit. 1871–1913.

Congregation Beth El. Constitution. Detroit. 1851.

Congregation Beth El. Minutes. Detroit.

Congregation Beth El. Minutes. Windsor.

Congregation Beth El. Windsor. *Bulletins.*

Congregation Shaar Hashomayim. *Book of Dedication, commemorating the opening of the Louis and Rachel Kaplan Shaar Hashomayim Religious School and the 36th Anniversary of Congregation Shaar Hashomayim.* 1929–1965.

Congregation Shaar Hashomayim. *Bulletins.* Windsor.

Congregation Shaar Hashomayim. Cemetery records. Windsor.

Congregation Shaar Hashomayim. Minutes. Windsor.

Congregation Shaar Hashomayim. *Year Book.* Windsor: Sumner Printing 1939, 1943, 1945–1949.

Ezekiel Hart file. Archives Department, Montreal Jewish Public Library.

Fraser, Alexander. *Third Report of the Bureau of Archives for the Province of Ontario.* Toronto, 1905.

General orders. Vol. Militia (1). McCord Museum, Montreal.

Gray, Hon. Herbert. Speech delivered before Rotary, Three Rivers, November 18, 1969.

Harline David Ruben records, Archives Department, Montreal Public Library.

Hart, Aaron. Family Tree. Canadian Jewish Congress, Montreal.

Hart, Alma. Personal files.

Hayman, Julius. *Jewish Standard*. June 15–30, 1983; August 15–25, 1989; September 29, 1989; October 1–15, 1989; January 15–31, 1991; February 15–28, 1990; January 30–February 15, 1994.

Holy Blossom Temple. Minutes. Toronto.

I. L. Peretz Shule. Minutes. Windsor.

Jewish Community Council. Board minutes. 1941–2000.

Jewish Community Council. *Bulletin.* 1941–2004.

Joseph, Fanny. Notebook. Files of Annette Wolff, Montreal.

Journal of Schomberg. 1759–1776. Army and Navy. London: April, 1898. Public Archives of Canada.

Journals of the House of Assembly of Lower Canada, January 29, to April 17, 1808. Archives Department, Montreal Jewish Public Library.

Journals of the House of Assembly of Lower Canada. 1834. Archives Department, Montreal Jewish Public Library.

Julius Magnus collections. Hebrew Union College, Los Angeles, California.

Katzman, Fred. Congregation Beth El Double Chai Weekend presentation. November 17, 1995.

Kroon, Leonard, Final report submitted to the Windsor Jewish community.

Macdonald, George F. "Richard Pollard and St. John's Church, Sandwich, Ontario." Abstract Book, Hiram Walker Historical Museum.

Mackinac Register. 19:101–128. Madison, Wisconsin. 1910. Wisconsin Historical Collection.

Mandel, Stephen and R. H. Wagenberg, "The governance of the Jewish community of Windsor." Center for Jewish Community Studies, Study of Jewish Community Organizations: Canada Project. 1974

Marmette, Joseph. Report on Canadian Archives. 1886, 1894.

Marriage Register of Holy Blossom Temple, Toronto.

McGregor Waste Book, Fort Malden National Historical Park, Amherstburg, Ontario.

Memorial of Levi Solomons et al., Lower Canada, S. 13, 1768. Public Archives of Canada.

Miller, Evelyn. Personal files. Montreal.

Moses David's prayer books. Files of Evelyn Miller. Montreal.

Papers of the Continental Congress 35(a, b, c).

Peltier vs. Lavelle, C 835/C7, Court of Common Pleas, Wayne County, Indiana Territorial Papers, December 1803.

Potier Gazette. Archives of St. Mary's College, Montreal.

Provincial Statutes of Lower Canada, 1832. Archives Department, Montreal Jewish Public Library.

Quebec Chancery Archives, Archives de L'Archeveche de Quebec. ser. E, V. Vol. 5.

Records of the Board of Education entrance exam. 1900–1910. Windsor Board of Education.

Report of the Public Archives of Canada for 1923.

Resolution in the House of Assembly, February 17, 1808. Ezekiel Hart File, Archives Department, Montreal Jewish Public Library.

Rosenberg, Louis. *A Gazetteer of Jewish Communities in Canada Showing The Jewish Population in Each of the Cities, Towns & Villages in Canada in the Census Years 1851–1951.* Canadian Jewish Populations Studies 7. 1957. Canadian Jewish Congress, Bureau of Social and Economic Research.

Roy, D. G. Rapport de l'archiviste de la Province de Quebec. 1927–28.

Samuel David diary. Public Archives of Canada.

Shahar, Charles. 2001 Census Analysis Series: the Jewish community of Windsor, Part 1, Basic Demographics. UIA Federation Canada, November 2003.

Simcoe papers. Vol. 5. Hiram Walker Historical Museum, Windsor.

Solomons, Ezekiel. Certificates showing Ezekiel Solomons to deal with the Indian Natives, May, 1770 and license to travel isolated from Montreal to Michilimackinac, April, 1770. Documents file, American Jewish Archives.

Spanish and Portuguese Synagogue. Minutes. Montreal.

Spanish and Portuguese Synagogue. Registry books. 1847-1854, 1885-1892. Montreal.

St. John's Church register. 1807–1857. Sandwich, Ontario.

St. John's registry of marriages, christenings, and burials. 1802–1812.

Tenth annual concert of the I. L. Peretz School of Windsor Ontario. Program booklet, June 18, 1944.

Wayne County, Michigan land records. Vols. B; C.1703–1796.

Wikipedia, the Free Encyclopedia, http:/en.wikipedia.org/wiki/Isaac_Leib_Peretz.

Windsor Jewish Community Council. *Bulletins*. 1941–1990.

Windsor Jewish Community Council. Minutes.

Correspondence

Ableser, Rabbi Jeffrey. E-mail to Rabbi Jonathan V. Plaut, November 5, 2003.

Albert, Pam (Weingarden). E-mail to Rabbi Jonathan V. Plaut, March 29, 2004.

Benstein, Mrs. Ida. Letter to Rabbi Jonathan V. Plaut. July 29,1973.

Berry, Mrs. Vivian. Letter to Rabbi Jonathan V. Plaut. August 20, 1973.

Bonhomme, Christine. E-mail to Rabbi Jonathan V. Plaut. October 21, 2003.

Brant, Mrs. Curt J. Letter to Rabbi Jonathan V. Plaut. July 14, 1974.

Chief Justice of Province of Quebec. Letter to Ezekiel Hart. April 20, 1807. Ezekiel Hart file. Archives Department, Montreal Jewish Public Library.

Croll, Senator David. Letter to Rabbi Jonathan V. Plaut. August 23,1988.

David, Moses. Letter to Jacob Franks. May 29, 1800.Wisconsin Historical Collection. Vol. 19.

Dodick (first name unreadable). Letter to Mr. and Mrs. Benheim. January 1, 1989.

Ellis, Rhonda. Fax to Rabbi Jonathan V. Plaut. January 19, 2004.

Epstein, Hetty J. Letter to Izzy Sigal. June 19, 1989.

Feigelman, Rabbi Edward. E-mails to Rabbi Jonathan V. Plaut. April 2, 2003; July 24, 2003; July 27, 2003.

Freed, Gerald. Fax to Rabbi Jonathan V. Plaut. December 10, 2003.

Giunta, Diana. E-mail to Rabbi Jonathan V. Plaut. July 27, 2003.

Goldberg, A. F. Letter to Burt Pazner. October 20, 1965.

Gray, The Right Honourable Herb. Letter to Rabbi Jonathan V. Plaut. November 6, 1990.

Greene, Larry. E-mail to Rabbi Jonathan V. Plaut. June 9, 2002.

Hurwitz, William. Letter to Rabbi Jonathan V. Plaut. July 12, 1972

Jerris, Rabbi Miriam. E-mails to Rabbi Jonathan V. Plaut. March 3, 2004; March 4, 2004.

Judah, Uriah. Letter to Aaron Hart. March 27, 1799. Hart microfilm reel 1, JC 3. Public Archives of Canada.

Kronmal, Dr. Marilyn (Miller). E-mail to Rabbi Jonathan V. Plaut, April 1, 2004.

Lasker, Rabbi Y. Mayer. Letter to Izzy Sigal. September 14, 1988.

Lasker, Rabbi Y. Mayer. Letter to Sidney Lazarus. August 4, 1988.

Lazarus, Sid. Letter to Dr. Norman Lamm. July 23, 1988.

Lebendiger, Mrs. Israel (Carrie). Letters to Rabbi Jonathan V. Plaut. June 30, 1976; July 6, 1976; August 29, 1976.

Malowitz, Sandi. E-mail to Rabbi Jonathan V. Plaut. July 31, 2003.

Marshall, Hattie. Letter to Temple Beth El. November 9, 1965.

Nerenberg, Rabbi David. Letter to Rabbi Martin Appelbaum. May 4, 1988.

Nosanchuk, Saul. Letter to Burt Pazner. September 22, 1965.

Plaut, Rabbi Jonathan V. Letter to Arthur B. Weingarden. September 19, 1979.

Polsky, Dr. Ronald. E-mails to Rabbi Jonathan V. Plaut. February 3, 2004; February 4, 2004.

Rabin, Mrs. Julia. Letters to Rabbi Jonathan V. Plaut. June 21, 1974; July 21, 1974.

Rosenthal, Richard. E-mails to Rabbi Jonathan V. Plaut. March 19, 2004; March 21, 2004.

Saposhnik, Dr. Tamar Lubin. Letter to Sidney Lazarus. August 1, 1988.

Schulman, Rabbi Nahum. Letter to Rabbi Jonathan V. Plaut. October 30, 1974.

Shafron, Amy (Whiteman). E-mails to Rabbi Jonathan V. Plaut. March 23, 2004; March 26, 2004.

Sigal, Izzy. Bulletin letter No. 1. February 21, 1989.

Bulletin letter No. 2. April 6, 1989.

Letter to Congregation Shaar Hashomayim Board of Directors. February 13, 1989.

Letter to Long Island University. August 23, 1988.

Letter to Mrs Claire Drattell. December 30, 1988.

Letter to Rabbi Joseph R. Radinsky. December 14, 1988.

Letters to Rabbi Y. Alster. September 6, 1988; November 28, 1988

Letter to Rabbi Y. Mayer Lasker. December 5, 1988.

Sir Machinac letter. 1777. Vol. 8. American Jewish Archives, Cincinnati, Ohio.

Stollman, Rabbi Samuel. E-mails to Rabbi Jonathan V. Plaut. October 12, 2003; October 13, 2003; October 16, 2003; January 29, 2004; February 8, 2004; February 9, 2004.

Sumner, Michael. Letter to Rabbi Jonathan V. Plaut. January 23, 1974.

Weinberg, Kurt. Letters to Rabbi Jonathan V. Plaut. July 8, 2002; undated.

Weingarden, Arthur B. Letter to Rabbi Jonathan V. Plaut. June 27, 2002.

Weiss, Rabbi Stewart M. Letter to Sidney Lazarus. August 8 1988.

Wine, Rabbi Sherwin. E-mail to Rabbi Jonathan V. Plaut. May 14, 2002.

Winograd, Anne. E-mails to Rabbi Jonathan V. Plaut. February 4, 2004; February 5, 2004.

Zucker, Rabbi Max. Letter to Sidney Lazarus. August 26, 1988.

Property Records

Essex County Registry Office.
City of Windsor, Abstract Index.
Elizabethtown, Abstract Index.
Patent Book and Patent Index.
Town of Amherstburg and Town of Colchester, Abstract Index.
Town of Amherstburg, Abstract Index.
Town of Ford City Register.
Town of Sandwich East, Abstract Index.
Town of Sandwich West, Abstract Index.
Town of Sandwich, Abstract Index.
Township of Colchester, Abstract Index.
Township of Gosfield, Abstract Index.

Windsor City Council Minutes

City of Windsor Bylaws 480–529. January 1886–September 1887.
City of Windsor Bylaws 950–1029. December 1897–July 1901.
Minute Book. August 1892–June 1896. City of Windsor.
Minute Book. Council Minutes. July 1896–December 31, 1901. City of Windsor.
Minute Book. Council Minutes. September 29, 1910–December 31, 1913. City of Windsor.
Minute Book. January 1885–June 1890. Town of Windsor.
Minute Book. June 1890–July 1892. Windsor.
Minute. 1926–1929. City of Windsor.
Minutes. 1916–1919. City of Windsor.
Minutes. 1930–1933. City of Windsor.
Windsor Amalgamated Council Minutes. July 2, 1935–June 30, 1937.
Windsor Council Minutes. July 1937–June 1938.
Windsor Council Minutes. July 1938–June 1939.
Windsor Council Minutes. July 1939–June 1940.

Index

Page references in italics refer to photographs

86–87, 94–96, 99–108, 133, 191, 201, 215, 217–35
Politzeon, 81
Polsky, Jack, 252
Polsky, Ron, 252
Pomm, Montague "Monty," 158, *159*, 180
Posen, Oscar, 205, 247
Potashner, Arlene, 254
Pregerson, Mary (Wine), 51
Primrose Club, 82
Proclamation of Faith and Thanksgiving, 161–62
Progressive Aid Society, 131
Project Renewal, 199–200
Putterman, Bernard, 198, 200, 248

R. Bernstein and Sons, 62
Rabin, Julia (Wine), 51
Rachel Kaplan Hebrew memorial Chapel, 208–209
Rackow, W., 93
Ramm, Norman, 117, 133
Rappaport, Max, 71, 72, 81
Rash, Jacob, 136, 144
Reaume, Mayor Arthur J., 123–24, 128, 139, 163
Reform Judaism, 17, 18, 151, 162, 164–66, 196, 258, 262
Regional Shopping Centres Limited, *139*
religious life and institutions, 20–21, 31, 54–62, 74–75, 82–83, 87–94, 113–17, 119–22, 137, 141–43, 164–66, 169–75, 189–90, 192, 194–96, 206, 208–214, 240–45, 253, 257–58, 261, 273n2. *See also* individual institutions.
Renaissance Project, 259–60
Resnick, Sidney, 196
Rezek, Dr. Joseph, 185
Richardson, Mr., 69, 74
Rivelis, Irwin "Butch," 211
Rogin, Charles, 57, 64, 65, 81, 86
Rogin, Sophie (Katzman), 58
Rogin, Steven, 201, 252
Rogin, William "Moose," 250–51, 252
Rosa, Mrs. L., 77
Rose, Archie, 133
Rose, Dave, 252
Rosen, H., 89
Rosen, Lena (Kahn), 51, 55
Rosen, Marty, 157
Rosen, Maurice, 64
Rosen, Michael, 50, 51–52, 55, 62
Rosen, Monte, 51, 75
Rosen, Sadie, 51
Rosen, Samuel, 51
Rosenbaum, Earl, 252
Rosenbaum, Hymie, 181
Rosenberg, Carl, *112*, 123
Rosenberg, I., 70, 77
Rosenberg, Max, 64, 70, 71

Rosenberg, Nate, 136
Rosenblum, Bernard, 242
Rosenfeld, Cantor A. A., 114
Rosenthal, Harry, 114, 117, 118, 124, 133, 133–34
Rosenthal, Jacob, 248
Rosenthal, Rabbi Harold, 97
Rosenthal, Richard, 197, 201, 211, 213
Rosenzweig, Jackson, *147*
Rosenzweig, Jacob, 181
Rosenzweig, Rabbi Yosil, 257
Rotenberg, N., 82, 89
Rotenberg, Saul, 82
Rotman, Mr., 116
Rubelsky, Dr. D., 78
Rubin, Barrie, 211
Rubin, Elliot, 180
Rubin, Gail, *143*
Rubin, Harry, 154, *154*, *183*, 184, 212, 247
Rubin, Mrs., 71
Rudover, Lonny, *177*
Rumscheidt, Rev. Martin, 200

Sachs, Rabbi Samuel, 88
Sacks, Rabbi Melvin, 196
Samberg, Samuel, 64, 74, 75
Samberg, Solomon, 64
Samrick, Marc, *158*
Samuels, H. H., 64
Sandwich, 16, 21, 22–25, 29–30, 32, 38, 39, 104–105, 191
Sarasohn, Berman, 51
Schaalman, Rabbi Herman, 258
Schenker, Cantor Saul. *See* Nadvan, Cantor Saul (Schenker).
Schloss, Rabbi Chaim, 196
Schott, Leona, 160, *164*, 176
Schott, M., 93
Schott, Maxwell, 82, *82*, 88, 89, 92, 93, 97, 114, 129, 133
Schulman, Rabbi Israel, 80, 81, 90
Schulman, Rabbi Nahum, 97, 98, 113, 114, 210
Schumann, Rabbi S., 58
Schwartz and Cherniak, 62
Schwartz and Kaplan, 63, 86
Schwartz, David (Cherniak), 57
Schwartz, E., 64
Schwartz, Fanny (Fisher), 48
Schwartz, Harry, 70, 81, 144
Schwartz, Jacob (Cherniak), 57, 63, 64, *76*, 77
Schwartz, Mel, *178*
Schwartz, Meyer, *112*, 123
Schwartz, Oscar, 81
Schwartz, Samuel (Cherniak) , 48, 57, 58, 63, 64, 65, 71, 77, 86
Seidelman, Morris B., 129–30, 143, 153
senior services, 153, 176, 180, 202, 207, 214, 245–47

Shaar Bantams, 252
Shaar Blues, 252
Shaar Hashomayim cemetery, 36, 60–61, 97, 126, 130, 172, 190, 192, 210–11, 245
Shaar Hashomayim Daughterhood, 96
Shaar Hashomayim Golden Jubilee, 209–10
Shaar Hashomayim Junior League, 96
Shaar Hashomayim Men's Club, 96, 146, 185, 202
Shaar Hashomayim Sisterhood, 89, 91, 96, 111–13, 114, 119, 131, 143, 176, 202, 213
Shaar Hashomayim, 18, 35, 87–94, *90*, *91*, 96, 97, 98, 111–15, 116, 119–22, *120*, *121*, 125–28, *128*, 130, 131, 134, 135, *135*, 137, 141–47, *147*, 149, 150–51, 154, *156*, 160–62, 164–69, 171, 172–73, 174, 176, 181, 190, 192–93, 196–98, 202, 206, 208–11, 213, 215, 239, 240–41, 245, 248, 249, 252, 253–54, 256, 257–58, 261, 262, 265
Shaarey Zedek cemetery, 97
Shaarey Zedek Ladies' Auxiliary, 176
Shaarey Zedek, 17, 18, 58–60, *59*, 68, 71, 72, 74, 78, 81, 87, 88, *88*, 90, 96, 97, 98, 113-14, 116, 131, 143–45, 149, 151, 155–57, *156*, 162, 169, 176, 192, 194, 202, 209, 213, 258
Shaffer's Kosher Meat Market, 190
Shafron, Amy (Whiteman), 265
Shalom Chapter, Hadassah, 176
Shanbaum, Barbara, 239
Shanbaum, David, 252
Shanbaum, Joe, 252
Shanbon, Shirley, 243
Shanfield, Henry, 199, 201, 213
Shapiro, Phyllis, *168*
Shapiro, S., 75
Shearith Israel (Montreal), 19, 20, 32–33
Shkolnik, Cantor David, 97
Shonberg, Edward, 47
Shonberg, Freda (Meretsky), 47
Shore, Harold, *177*
Shore, Harry, 74
Shore, Hymen, 64
Shuster, Ruth (Lebendiger), 88
Shuster, Ted, 88
Sibley, Solomon, 27
Sigal, Harry, 193
Sigal, Solomon, 193
Silver, M., 82, 92
Silver, Mrs. Barash, *202*
Silver, Mrs. M., 82, 96
Silver, William "Bill," 170, 171, 173, 212, 213, 247, 249, 250
Silverman, Cantor, 91
Silverman, David, *186*
Silver-Medler, Deborah, 254
Silverstein, Jacob, *112*, 123
Simkevitz, Frank, 263

Index